THE COMPLETE GUIDE TO BOWLING STRIKES

(The Encyclopedia of Strikes)

George Allen, Doctor of Business Administration

Dick Ritger, Professional Bowler

Tempe Publishers, Inc.
Tempe, Arizona

ACKNOWLEDGEMENTS: OUR SPECIAL THANKS TO . . .

the American Bowling Congress (ABC) for permission to use several statistics and oddities in Appendix B.

Bob Haux, Fair Lanes Corporation, for his encouragement and support of Volume 3, ***The Complete Guide to Bowling Spares*** (The Encyclopedia of Spares).

members of the PBA and WPBA who shared ideas and information with me.

the AMF Bowling Products Group, especially Al Spanjer, for support of the artwork and line drawings in this book.

the Brunswick Corporation, especially Art Serbo and Jim Bakula, for support of the artwork and line drawings in this book.

Heidi Hauch, for making a book out of a manuscript.

Chuck Pezzano, for his encouragement, support and good ideas.

Frank Ellenburg, for assistance in reviewing the manuscript.

my wife, Joanne, for editorial assistance.

Josef Wiener, Swedish National Bowling Coach, for sharing his knowledge with us.

my *Rags For Men* team in Kitchener/ Waterloo, Ontario, Canada.

Judy, Scott, Danny, Shari and Cindy.

Richard, Karen and Barbara.

Helen and Howell Babbitt.

Published in the United States of America by TEMPE PUBLISHERS, INC.

Library of Congress Card Number: 80-53200

ISBN: Series: 0-933554-14-1 Hard Cover: 0-933554-02-8 Soft Cover: 0-933554-03-6

Illustrated by Ed Choate.

Printed in the United States of America
by Imperial Litho/Graphics, Phoenix, AZ

CONTENTS

LIST OF EXHIBITS

PURPOSE OF THE BOOK

"The goal in every frame is to strike. Learning how to read the lanes and adjust to lane conditions—in order to make more strikes—is the purpose of this book."

The purpose of this book is to present a complete and comprehensive discussion of the principles of making strikes, so that you can increase your percentage of strikes. This requires (1) an ability to determine how the lane and ball are interacting, and (2) the capability to make *angle, equipment* or *delivery* adjustments to get the ball and lane working together for you. The objective is to make a strike on each delivery. Although this is impossible to achieve, it must remain your goal in every frame.

It is possible to make twelve strikes in a single game, and this degree of perfection is reached hundreds of times each year. Back-to-back 300 games have been achieved on many occasions. A doubles score of 300 + 300 = 600 has been reported. And there have even been reported cases of three perfect games rolled in one series—a perfect 900 series. However, the highest ABC sanctioned series is an 886 rolled by Allie Brandt in 1939. Appendix B gives the frame-by-frame score of that series, as well as other record high scores that have been recognized by the appropriate accrediting organizations.

It takes only a few minutes to learn how to roll a ball down a lane. *But, complete mastery of the game of bowling cannot be achieved in a lifetime.* Yet that remains the objective of every serious student of the game, and is the primary focus of this book.

All material in this book is addressed from both right handed and left handed bowlers' points of view. Five major topics are covered for left and right handers: principles of strikes; reading the lanes; angle adjustments; equipment adjustments; and delivery adjustments. These topics are directly related to making strikes. You must understand certain *principles* related to making strikes, be able to *read the lanes,* and then make *angle, equipment* or *delivery* adjustments. The result is a presentation of the best way to adjust to any lane condition that you might face in your bowling career. In short, we have tried to develop an encyclopedia of strikes so that any bowler can greatly improve his or her percentage of strikes.

This is a reference book. It is designed so you can locate any material related to strikes with a minimum of difficulty. *The side of each page contains an indexing system* which allows you to locate any topic with relative ease. The major topic of the section is indicated by bold type on the inside portion of the index box. Minor or sub-sections are indicated in the outside portion of the box.

At the beginning of each major section you will find a list of the contents of the section, with page numbers for quick reference. *To locate any topic,* simply *fan the pages* to locate the beginning of the appropriate section. Then, either check the page number reference, or continue fanning the pages until you locate the title of the material you are looking for.

The initials RHB on the inside portion of the index box stands for Right Handed Bowler. LHB stands for Left Handed Bowler. All pages with RHB on the index box are for right handed bowlers only, and those with LHB are for left handers.

SECTIONS 1 and 2 were written from *both left and right* handed points of view. They can be read by either one with *no translation* difficulties.

SECTIONS 3, 4 and 5 were written from the *right* handed bowler's point of view. Each page in these three sections contains the initials RHB inside the indexing box.

SECTIONS 6, 7 and 8 were written from the *left* handed bowler's point of view. Each page in these three sections contains the initials LHB inside the indexing box.

The three Appendices (A, B, and C) were written for *both left and right* handers.

Since there is a great deal of similarity in the material for the left and right handers, *please check the index box to be sure that you are reading the material written from your point of view.*

SECTION 1, PRINCIPLES OF STRIKES, discusses the major principles of making strikes. This section contains a great deal of material appearing in print for the first time, and also summarizes some of the available knowledge on shooting for strikes. Pictures of the ball hitting the pockets (1-3 for the RHB and 1-2 for the LHB) are provided on most pages to focus attention upon your goal in each frame — a perfect pocket hit. This hit must occur from the ideal pocket angle, at the correct speed, and with the right amount of action on the ball. The central focus of SECTION 1 is a discussion of the methods used to get the ball either *up to the pocket,* or *back to the pocket.* These are the two types of corrections or adjustments which all bowlers face when they are not hitting the pocket.

While this section only summarizes the major principles for making strikes, later sections expand these principles into complete details which you can use to improve your percentage of strikes. By learning how to hit the pocket consistently, you will not only increase the number of strikes you get, but you will also increase your *first ball count* (the number of pins you knock down on the first ball). This will improve your counts, and will make your spares easier ones to convert. So, even when you are not striking, you will be scoring better when you hit the pocket on a regular basis.

SECTION 2, READING THE LANES, provides an extensive discussion of lanes, how they are inspected for certification and how they should be conditioned for protection and proper scoring potential. Improper methods of lane conditioning are also discussed. The purpose of this section is to help you determine how the ball and the lane are going to interact. With this knowledge you can decide upon the adjustment technique(s) needed to allow you to play the lane to your advantage — to hit the pocket at the correct speed, angle and action to get strikes.

For purposes of analysis we have separated the lane into four portions: (1) the approach; (2) the headers (from the foul line to the arrows); (3) the mid-lane (from the arrows to the pin deck); and (4) the pin deck. The key elements within each of these lane portions are reviewed in order to determine the best method for getting the lane and ball working together for you. This section provides the most extensive and unusually detailed discussion of lane reading principles that has appeared in print, and which relates lane conditions to the appropriate adjustments for making strikes.

SECTION 3, ANGLE ADJUSTMENTS—*Right Handed Bowlers,* begins the first of three sections covering the major types of adjustments for right handed bowlers: *angle* (or line) adjustments; *equipment* adjustments; and *delivery* adjustments. Almost all adjustments made by high average bowlers can be classified into one of these three categories. Also, each adjustment can be related to an effort to get the ball either *up to* or *back to* the pocket. This section addresses the first of these adjustment techniques, and the one most frequently used by all bowlers, angle adjustments. In addition, *this section contains a very important personal formula that should enable you to find the correct angle to the pocket within two deliveries, or at most, three.*

All five strike lines are illustrated, as well as all angles within these lines. The discussion of each strike line highlights other adjustments that you might have to make to play each line, including aiming, stance and alignment considerations, walk pattern and drift, etc. If you wish to increase your ability to play all types of lane conditions, then you must develop the ability to use all five strike lines.

SECTION 4, EQUIPMENT ADJUSTMENTS—*Right Handed Bowlers,* covers the second category of adjustments for right handed bowlers, equipment adjustments. This section provides a coverage of *ball tracks, weight blocks* and the *three major types of equipment changes* made by top bowlers: *surface* changes (changing from one ball surface to another); *balance* changes (the use of positive and negative weights); and *fit* changes (altering spans and pitches). Both *label* and *axis weight* methods of altering ball balance are shown in detail and illustrated. This section also includes a discussion of the three most common types of ball fit; *conventional, semi-fingertip,* and *fingertip.* The advantages and disadvantages of each type of ball fit are presented.

SECTION 5, DELIVERY ADJUSTMENTS—*Right Handed Bowlers,* concludes the discussion of adjustments for *right* handed bowlers with a look at *delivery* adjustment techniques for making more strikes. Three major types of delivery changes are presented: *speed* changes, *loft* changes and *lift* changes. Also included is a section on the *four patterns of ball* roll descriptive of almost all bowlers: the *curve ball, hook, backup* and *straight* ball. For each type of delivery, we present techniques for making the ball more effective for making strikes. Ball *revolutions,* elements of an *effective delivery, wrist positions,* and other topics are also included in this section on delivery adjustments.

SECTIONS 3, 4 and 5 present a complete ADJUSTMENT ARSENAL for the RIGHT HANDED BOWLER. They provide a full range of alternatives for adjusting to various types of lane conditions and for playing all five strike lines. We have also attempted to rank or PRIORITIZE these adjustments, indicating which type of adjustment you might try first, and which ones you might try in case the first technique did not work, and so on down the line of possible adjustments.

SECTION 6, ANGLE ADJUSTMENTS—*Left Handed Bowlers,* begins the first of three sections covering the major types of adjustments for left handed bowlers: *angle* (or line) adjustments; *equipment* adjustments; and *delivery* adjustments. This section and the two which follow contain *translations* of all material previously covered for the right handed bowler. We have tried to eliminate all right handed bias, and present all material from both points of view. As such, the book should be equally beneficial for left and right handed bowlers.

This section addresses the first of the three adjustment techniques, *angle* (or strike line) adjustments. All *five strike lines* are presented and illustrated, including all angles within each of the five lines. Included in the discussion of each strike line and angle is a coverage of other adjustments that you might have to make to play the line or angle well: aiming, stance and alignment considerations, walk pattern and drift, etc. If you wish to increase your ability to play all types of lane conditions that you will find, then you must develop the capability of using all five of these strike lines and angles.

Also presented in this section is *a very important personal formula that should enable you to locate the correct angle to the pocket within two or three deliveries*. Using the formula, you can play any angle within any strike line. Through the discussion of various strike lines and angles, we relate adjustments to getting the ball either *up to* or *back to* the pocket. Angle adjustments are the most frequently used techniques for making these two corrections.

SECTION 7, EQUIPMENT ADJUSTMENTS—*Left Handed Bowlers,* covers the second category of adjustments for left handed bowlers, *equipment* adjustments. This section provides a coverage of *ball tracks, weight blocks,* and the three major types of equipment changes made by top bowlers: *surface* changes (changing from one ball surface to another); *weight and balance* changes in equipment; and *fit* changes (changes in spans or pitches). Both *axis* and *top (label) weight* methods of altering ball balance are shown. This section also includes a discussion of the three most common types of ball fit for the left hander: the *conventional, semi-fingertip* and *fingertip* grips. Advantages and disadvantages of each type of ball fit are explored.

SECTION 8, DELIVERY ADJUSTMENTS—*Left Handed Bowlers,* concludes the discussion of adjustment techniques for *left* handed bowlers by looking at *delivery* adjustment methods for making more strikes. Three major classes of delivery changes are covered: *speed, loft* and *lift.* Also included in this section is a discussion of the *four patterns of ball roll* descriptive of almost all bowlers: the *curve ball, hook, backup* and *straight* ball. For each type of delivery, we present techniques for making the ball more effective for strikes. Ball *revolutions,* elements of an *effective delivery, wrist positions,* and other related topics are also included in this discussion of delivery adjustments for left handers.

SECTIONS 6, 7 and 8 present a complete ADJUSTMENT ARSENAL for the LEFT HANDED BOWLER. They provide a full range of alternatives for adjusting to various types of lane conditions and for playing all five strike lines.

Appendix A (*Dictionary of Strike-Related Terms*) contains an extensive list of terms which are directly related to strikes. This appendix will assist you in learning many terms in a short period of time. It is also a useful *reference* to clarify some of the terms which might not be clear when you first read them in the text.

Appendix B (*Interesting Facts About Strikes*) gives you a look at some of the records in various categories, such as singles, teams, doubles and the subject of "300" games. You should find this *interesting and enjoyable* reading, and it may answer some of the questions you might have about strikes and record scores.

Appendix C (*Books for Additional Reading)* lists several books which will supplement the material in this book. We have included a brief overview of each book, and cited relevant portions that will give you a better understanding of the material covered in this book.

IMPORTANT NOTE TO BOWLERS WHO ROLL A BACKUP BALL: If you roll a backup ball, please read the following note. If you do NOT roll a backup ball, you may skip this note entirely.

THOSE OF YOU WHO ROLL A BACKUP BALL, AND WHO DO NOT WISH TO CONVERT TO A CURVE OR HOOK BALL, CAN BENEFIT FROM THE MATERIAL IN THIS BOOK. We suggest that you use the opposite pocket for your strikes (the Left Hander using the 1-3 pocket and the Right Hander using the 1-2 pocket). In addition, we also suggest that: RIGHT HANDED BOWLERS who roll a backup ball should read about this type of delivery in SECTION 5, and then follow the suggestions for making angle, equipment and delivery adjustments outlined there. LEFT HANDED BOWLERS who roll a backup ball should read about that type of delivery in SECTION 8 and then follow the suggestions for making angle, equipment and delivery adjustments outlined there.

AUTOGRAPH PAGE

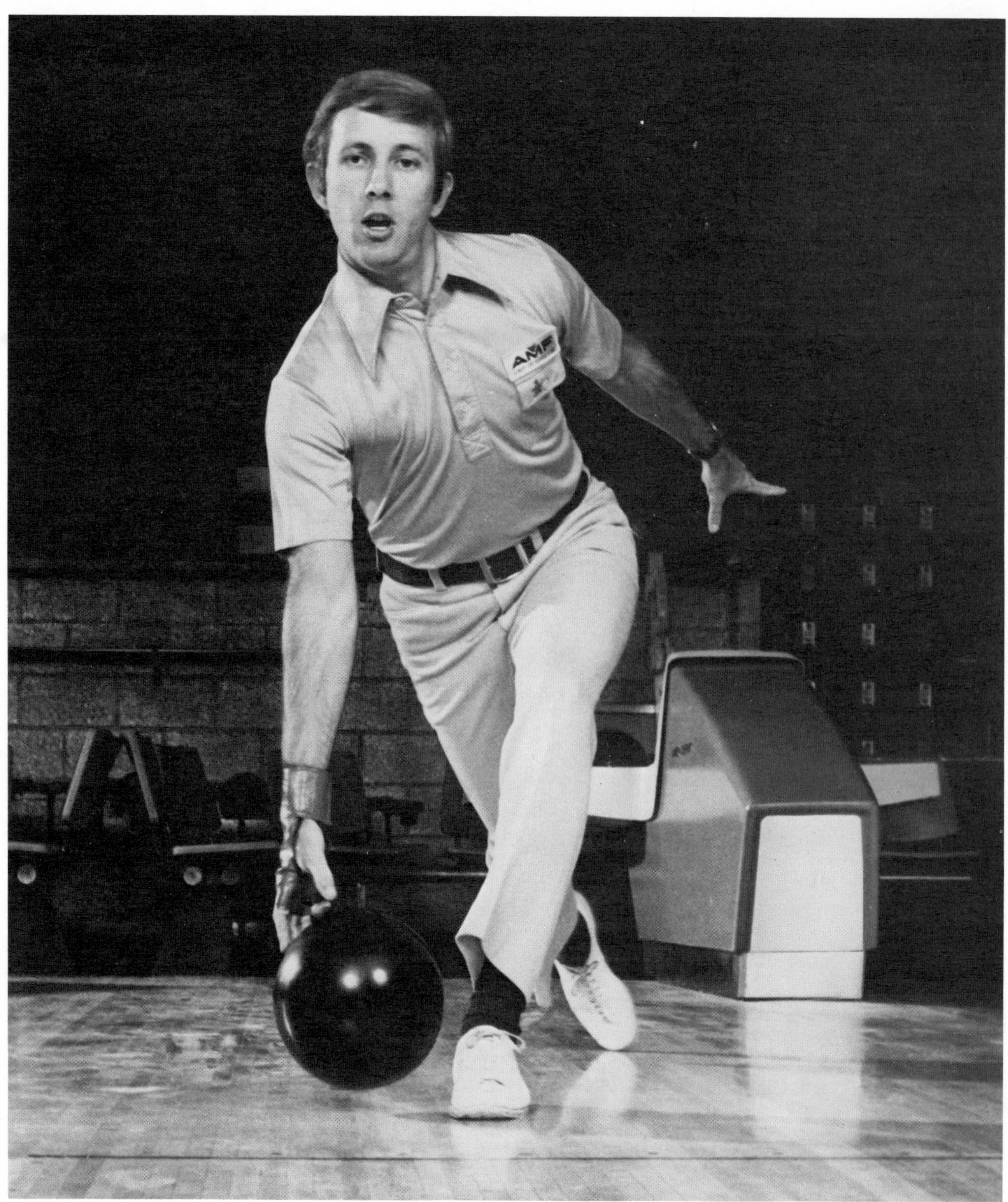

Dick Ritger, Professional Bowler

President, Professional Bowlers Association, 1977 and 1978.
Member, P.B.A. Hall of Fame.
Winner of 20 P.B.A. Titles.
Highest Average, 10 years (1970–1979), ABC Tournament.
Steve Nagy Sportsmanship Award, 1970 and 1973.

SECTION 1 PRINCIPLES OF STRIKE SHOOTING

"There are certain principles of bowling you must *understand* and *master* before you can become a consistent strike shooter."

CONTENTS PAGE

OVERVIEW

This section summarizes the major principles related to making strikes. Each principle is outlined briefly and then discussed in more depth. In the sections that follow these principles will be related to reading the lanes, and to making angle, equipment and delivery adjustments to increase your percentage of strikes.

There are no secrets to successful strike shooting; anyone can become extremely effective and consistent at making strikes. What is needed is a knowledge of the principles of bowling related to making strikes, and the desire to practice sufficiently to incorporate these principles into *your game. You must know your game and bowl within it.* This section presents a summary of those factors which will enable you to become a consistent strike shooter.

THE PERFECT STRIKE: There is general and widespread agreement upon what constitutes a perfect strike hit; the 1-3 pocket for the right handed bowler (RHB) and the 1-2 pocket for the left handed bowler (LHB). Pin and ball deflection follow a predictable pattern on the perfect strike hit. The ball takes out four pins and pin deflection takes out the other six. The perfect strike hit will be described, as well as those hits which produce a high percentage of strikes even though they are not perfect pocket hits. The key elements in making perfect strikes are to get the ball into the *pocket* from the proper *angle* with the correct *speed* and with the right amount of *action* on the ball.

THE POCKET ANGLE: The ball should enter the pocket from such an angle that it can maintain a particular path of deflection through the pins. This angle will be created when the ball begins its break toward the pocket, ideally within 10 to 15 feet in front of the pin setup. The correct pocket angle will allow both pin and ball deflection to produce the perfect strike hit.

PROPER SPEED: Too much speed is just as bad as not enough speed. You must decide what amount of speed is needed to keep the ball *on* its path *to the pins* and *in* its path of deflection *through the pins* after contacting the pocket. Speed can work for or against you, since it has an effect upon pin and ball deflection, upon the working action of the ball. The speed of your ball should be consistent, but on some lanes you will want to increase or reduce ball speed to improve your chances for strikes. Altering ball speed is one of the delivery adjustments you should practice and incorporate into your game.

CORRECT ACTION: The word *action* is sometimes referred to as *lift, turn, spin, hook,* and other similar terms. We refer to action as the *result* of these forces or factors and others, such as ball speed, condition of the lanes, timing of the hook, the break point, etc. A ball with the proper amount of action will cause both pin and ball deflection to maximize your chances for strikes. With proper action, the ball will maintain its path of deflection through the pins, as described in the section on *the perfect strike* hit. With proper action on the ball, the pins will be given the correct velocity to take out the pins they are supposed to take out on a strike hit. Means of changing the action on the ball will be discussed in this section, since there will be times when lane conditions suggest the need for more or less action on the ball.

AIMING: SPOT AND LINE BOWLING: Accuracy requires aiming. The two most common methods for aiming are *spot* bowling and *line* bowling. Each method has advantages and disadvantages. Both are related, since the objective is to place the ball into the proper path to the pocket. Only you can decide which method of aiming or some combination of both will be best for you. We will discuss both methods, so you can decide which one you will incorporate into your strike game.

GETTING UP TO THE POCKET: In the language of bowling, you have failed to get up to the pocket when you have missed the pocket toward the outside portion of the lane. An adjustment is needed to get *up to* the pocket. For the RHB, failure to get up to the pocket means hitting the pin setup on the right side. But for the LHB, the miss is to the left side. Several methods are available to get the ball up to the pocket after such misses. These adjustments, as do all adjustments, relate to changes in *angle, equipment, or delivery,* or some combination of these adjustment techniques.

GETTING BACK TO THE POCKET: When the ball hits the pocket too fully (too much of the head pin) or crosses over in front of it, an adjustment is necessary to get *back to* the pocket. For the RHB all such pocket misses are to the left side of the 1-3 pocket. For the LHB, the misses are to the right side of the 1-2 pocket. High pocket hits or *brooklyn hits* by either left or right handed bowlers are examples of incorrect strike hits that require an adjustment to get the ball back to the pocket. Obviously, adjustments to get the ball *back to* the pocket are just the *opposite* of adjustments to get the ball *up to* the pocket. *These two extremes represent the two categories into which all angle, equipment and delivery adjustments fall.*

READING THE LANES: The ball and the lane are going to interact. There is nothing you can do to prevent this interaction. Your objective is to get this interaction of the ball surface and the lane surface to work for and not against you. Reading lanes is both an art and a science. You must know the characteristics and markings on the lanes, and how they are conditioned for play. When you read a lane well, you know how the ball is going to react on the lane surface. This reading of the lane will tell you what adjustments are needed to get the ball into the pocket at the correct angle, speed, and action to get strikes. Correctly *reading lanes* is one of the two most important aspects of making strikes. *Adjusting to lane conditions* is the second item.

ADJUSTING TO LANE CONDITIONS: Once you have read the lane correctly, you must determine what adjustments will get the ball into the pocket. All of the usual methods of adjusting can be classified as one of three types: *line or angle* adjustments; *equipment* adjustments; or *delivery* adjustments. These three categories of adjustments are totally analyzed for you, indicating what type of lane condition suggests a particular adjustment, and what other changes in your game you may have to make to get the suggested adjustment to work well for you. To increase your percentage of strikes, you must know what adjustments will get the ball *up to* or *back to* the pocket, and you must be able to make these adjustments when necessary.

CHECKPOINTS ON ALL STRIKES: Concentration on each shot requires you to take into consideration all key elements in the strike delivery. We have developed a checklist of 10 items that are important to proper planning in each frame. Three of these items should be decided before you step onto the approach. The other 7 items occur on the approach. All 10 checkpoints should be practiced on every delivery you make until they become an automatic part of your game. (The 10 checkpoints are detailed on page 27).

Now we will discuss each of these principles for making strikes. In doing this we will use terms that may be new to you. It might be helpful for you to scan the list of strike-related terms in Appendix A before you begin reading this section on principles. A review of these terms may make it easier to understand the material which follows. You should also re-read this SECTION 1 from time to time so that these principles come into mind each time you bowl. Then you should become a very consistent strike shooter, as your percentage of strikes increases significantly.

THE PERFECT STRIKE

"When you hit the pocket from the correct angle, with the right action on the ball, and with the proper speed, you have the greatest chance to make a strike."

There is an ideal way to hit the pin setup to get a strike. It is called *the perfect strike* hit, and is one that will cause pin and ball deflection to take out the 10 pins in a particular pattern. This pattern of pin fall is illustrated on Exhibit 1-1. Study that exhibit carefully, since you should be familiar with *the path of the ball through the pins* and *the correct pattern of pin deflection* to take out the six pins not hit by the ball.

On *a perfect right handed bowler's 1-3 pocket strike hit,* the ball will only contact four pins: the 1-3-5-9 pins. The other six pins are taken out by pin deflection. The 1-pin takes out the 2-pin which causes a chain reaction. The 2-pin takes out the 4-pin and sends it into the 7-pin. The 3-pin takes out the 6-pin and sends it into the 10-pin. This pattern of pin and ball deflection is considered perfect to make a strike. In fact, however, two other patterns of pin fall could also be considered perfect.

On occasion the 3-pin will hit the 6-pin on the left side and take out the 9-pin just before the ball would have taken it out. Other times, the 6-pin will hit the kickback and take out the 10-pin by deflecting back into it. Both of these patterns of pin deflection could be considered perfect hits. However, whenever we refer to a perfect right handed bowler's (RHB) strike hit, we will be referring to the pattern of pin fall illustrated at the top of Exhibit 1-1.

On *a perfect left handed bowler's 1-2 pocket strike hit,* the ball will still only take out four pins, and pin deflection takes out the other six. The pattern of pin fall is similar to that for the right handed bowler. The ball takes out the 1-2-5-8 pins. The 1-pin sends the 3-pin into the 6-pin which should take out the 10-pin. The 2-pin sends the 4-pin into the 7-pin. This pattern of pin and ball deflection is considered perfect for the left handed bowler. However, two other patterns could also be considered perfect.

Often the 2-pin will hit the 4-pin on the right side and deflect into the 8-pin just before the ball would have taken it out. At other times the 4-pin will not take out the 7-pin directly, but will bounce back from the kickback and knock it over. Considering the shape of the pins and the opportunities for various types of bounces off other pins, it is little wonder that several patterns of deflection are possible, even on what we might call a perfect pocket hit. Whenever we refer to a perfect strike hit for the LHB we will be referring to the pattern of pin and ball deflection illustrated on the bottom portion of Exhibit 1-1.

Hitting either the 1-2 pocket (LHB) or the 1-3 pocket (RHB) does not guarantee you will get a strike. Faulty pin action, pins off spot, hitting the pocket at the wrong angle, not enough action or speed on the ball, and many other reasons may account for failure to strike on what looks like a perfect hit. On some hits, pins will fly over other pins they are supposed to take out, or will appear to wrap around a pin without knocking it over. The two most common occurrences or leaves resulting from pocket hits are the *tap* and the *pocket split.*

When the ball enters the pocket and everything *appears* to be correct (angle, action and speed) and a pin is still left standing, then a *tap* may have occurred. For the RHB a common tap is the 10-pin. For the LHB it is the 7-pin. They are often called *solid-7* or *solid-10* leaves. The implication is that the hit was perfect but deflection did not disturb the 7 or 10 pin. Such leaves may be caused by excessive speed, faulty pin action, or any of a number of reasons.

Many bowlers think there are only two real *taps* in bowling, the 9-pin for the LHB and the 8-pin for the RHB. Such results occur when the 5-pin is driven straight back into the pit by the ball. In effect, the 5-pin is chopped off the 9-pin (LHB) or the 8-pin (RHB).

There appears to be no way you can insure against taps. They are here to stay as part of the game. Changing the angle, speed, or action on the ball may reduce your chances for tapping one pin, but it will probably increase your chances for tap-

EXHIBIT 1-1
Ball and Pin Deflection on a Perfect Strike

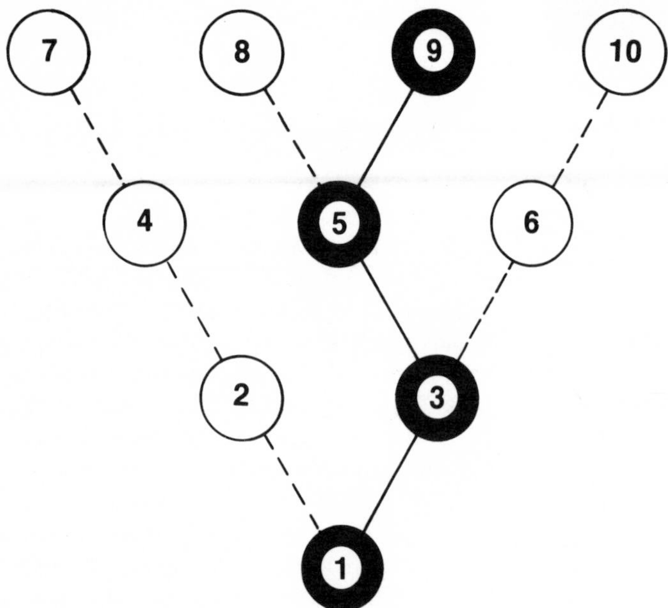

The *Right* Handed Bowler Covers the 1-3-5 and 9-pins with the Ball. The other six pins must be taken out by pin deflection. The 1-pin sends the 2 into the 4 and into the 7-pin. The 5-pin takes out the 8-pin. The 3-pin sends the 6-pin into the 10-pin.

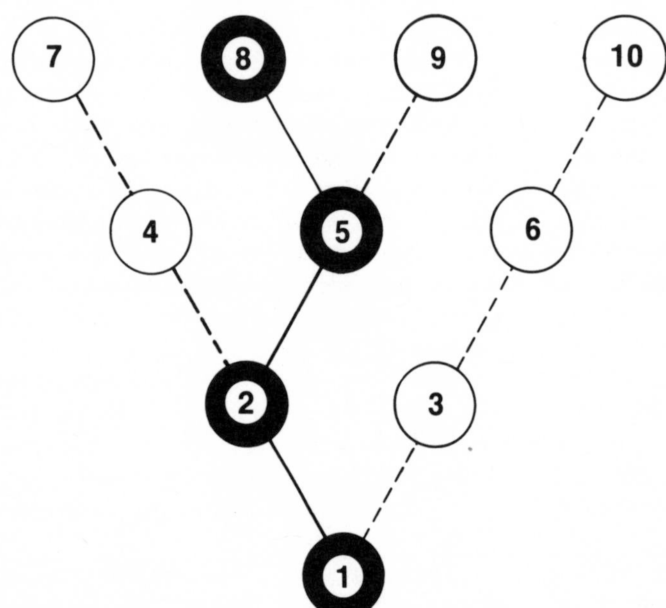

The *Left* Handed Bowler Covers the 1-2-5 and 8-pins with the Ball. The other six pins must be taken out by pin deflection. The 1-pin sends the 3 into the 6 and into the 10-pin. The 5-pin takes out the 9-pin. The 2-pin sends the 4-pin into the 7-pin.

ping another one. So, concentrate on hitting the pocket solidly, with the correct speed, angle and action, and forget about the taps you might get on occasion. If, however, you are getting several taps, you should consider making some adjustment in angle, equipment or delivery.

Pocket splits are another matter, and causes for such leaves can generally be attributed to faulty ball roll, incorrect angle, or too much ball deflection, etc. The latter term is perhaps the most important reason for pocket splits — ball deflection. When the ball is deflected out of its intended path through the four pins it is supposed to take out, a pocket split is a real possibility.

If the ball is deflected away from the 5-pin, the 5-7, 5-10 and 8-10 splits are real possibilities for the RHB, and the 5-10, 5-7 and 7-9 are split possibilities for the left handed bowler. When the ball drives through and hits too much of the 5-pin, the 4-9 split (RHB) or 6-8 split (LHB) will often be left.

Unlike the taps mentioned previously, there is more you can do to avoid pocket splits. One of the three critical strike elements—speed, angle, or action—must be adjusted to prevent the pocket split. Try to determine which of these three factors caused the split, and then make an angle, equipment or delivery adjustment to correct the situation. *Watching the pattern of pin fall and the location at which the ball went off the end of the pin deck will give you insights into what adjustment is necessary.* As with all strike hits, you should watch the path of the ball on its way *through the pins* to learn as much as you can about the pin and ball deflection taking place. These items tell you much about what adjustments might be needed.

Now let's return to our discussion of pocket hits that *do* result in strikes. Such hits are the goal of every bowler on the first ball delivered in each frame. Notice the four elements in the perfect strike hit: (1) the ball hits the 1-3 pocket for the RHB and the 1-2 pocket for the LHB; (2) the ball enters the pocket from the correct pocket angle (more on this later); (3) the ball enters the pocket with the correct amount of action (revolutions, spin, lift, etc.) on it; and (4) the ball arrives at the pin deck at a speed that will keep it in its intended path of deflection through the pins. When you are not striking on your pocket hits, one or more of these elements will not be correct. When you are striking (perfectly) all four will be correct. That *perfect strike hit should be your objective in each frame, with this one very important exception.*

On some occasions you will be hitting the pocket a little less than perfectly, perhaps slightly high or slightly light. Yet you will be getting strikes consistently. *Don't* make any adjustment to try for those perfect strikes. It may be that the weight of the pins, the resiliency of the kickbacks, the condition of the lane, or some other factor unknown to you is causing the fortunate situation. By trying to be *too perfect* you may create other problems for yourself. If you are striking consistently, for whatever reasons, *on fairly accurate pocket hits,* then there is nothing *more perfect* you can do. Accept your good luck and continue to hit the pocket as you are and continue to take your strikes on less-than-perfect hits. (Exhibit 1-2 illustrates many ways in which the pins fall for strikes.)

Despite these less-than-perfect strikes, all of the material we present in the following sections will be devoted toward improving your percentage of getting the ball into the pocket perfectly, from the correct angle, with the proper speed and action on the ball. When you are able to reach that goal with a high degree of consistency, you will have come as close to mastery of the strike ball as anyone has ever come.

EXHIBIT 1-2
Other-Than-Perfect Strikes

The perfect strike hit is only one way to knock down all ten pins. Here is a list of common ways the pins fall for a strike.

Brooklyn: An all-too-familiar hit for most bowlers. A 1-2 pocket hit for the right handed bowler and a 1-3 pocket hit for the left hander. This is sometimes called a *crossover* strike.

Blow the 5: A light pocket hit in which the ball has enough force or power on it to send the 5-pin directly across into the 4-7 pins (RHB) or the 6-10 pins (LHB). The ball literally *blows* the 5-pin across the pin deck.

Heavy pocket strike: (RHB) the 4 and 7 pins appear to fall straight back as the last two pins to go down. The 2-pin probably hit the 4-pin on the way to the pit. (LHB) the 6 and 10 pins appear to fall straight back as the last two pins to go down. The 3-pin probably hit the 6-pin on the way to the pit.

High hit: A direct hit on the head pin in which all pins appear to simply spread apart or to cave in. This strike is also called a *cave-in* or *nose-dive.*

Late-roll strike: Any time a pin rolls across the lane to take out the remaining pin or pins, we have an example of the late-roll strike. Usually the 7 or 10 pin is standing, and a pin begins to roll across the lane to knock it over in a delayed action. The pin falls just before the machine comes down to pick it up.

Late 10-pin: This strike results from a solid hit that appears to be a perfect strike, but the 10-pin is still standing. All other pins are in the pit and the 10-pin slowly topples. It was probably hit by the 6-pin as it *wrapped itself* around the 10-pin on the way to the pit.

Late 7-pin: Again, we have a solid hit that appears to be a perfect strike, but the 7-pin is standing. All other pins are in the pit, and the 7-pin slowly topples. It was probably hit by the 4-pin as it left the pin deck.

Light pocket strike: The 8 and 10 pins are still standing as the ball goes into the pit for the RHB, and the 7 and 9 pins for the LHB. Then both pins fall simultaneously. This type of strike is also called a *late 8-10* or *late 7-9* for obvious reasons.

Missed head pin: The ball completely misses the head pin and leaves either the 1-2-4 or 1-3-6 pins standing. Then these pins fall forward in domino fashion. Often a pin comes out of the pit to topple the 4 or 6 pin forward into the other pins.

Off-the-wall shot: A light hit in which the 5-7 or the 5-10 pins are standing. By delayed action, a pin comes off the kickback (wall) and takes out both pins.

Out of the pit: One or more pins are standing after the ball goes into the pit. A pin comes flying out of the pit and knocks down the remaining pins. (Pins have deflected back as far as the foul line, the approach, and even off the back end of the approach!)

Slap 10-pin strike: (A RHB strike) A light pocket hit leaves the 10-pin standing. The 6-pin is in the gutter and lays over to tap the 10-pin gently enough to knock it over. Often the top of the 6-pin will barely slap the 10-pin to take it out. (Sometimes called Cat's-Paw-10.)

Slap 7-pin strike: (A LHB strike) A light pocket hit leaves the 7-pin standing. The 4-pin is in the gutter and lays over to tap the 7-pin gently enough to knock it over. Often the top of the 4-pin will barely slap the 7-pin to topple it. (A Cat's Paw-7.)

Swisher: A high pocket hit in which the 1 and 5-pins go toward the kickbacks and come back onto the pin deck. The pins appear to swish around, going back and forth across the pin deck.

Trip four: (a RHB strike) A high 1-3 pocket hit in which the last pin to fall is the 4-pin, and it often falls forward as though tripped from behind.

Trip six: (a LHB strike) A high 1-2 pocket hit in which the last pin to fall is the 6-pin, and it often falls forward as though it were tripped from behind.

THE POCKET ANGLE

"There is one best angle into the pocket for any combination of lane conditions, equipment and pin weights."

If there is any aspect of bowling upon which there is almost complete agreement, it is upon the proper use of angles. Successful strike bowling requires the correct use of angles. On a full pin setup, the greater the angle at which the ball comes into the pocket, the greater the power on the ball in terms of carrying the pins for a strike.

For any combination of lane conditions, equipment (ball surface, weights and balances, etc.) and pin weights there is a best angle into the pocket that will maximize your chances for a strike. Your goal is to find that pocket angle, *the angle at which the ball enters the pocket.* If you can find it quickly enough you will score well. At times you will want to use a wide angle and at other times you will want to cut down on the pocket angle.

The value of finding the ideal pocket angle as quickly as possible is obvious. If it takes you three frames to find the best angle into the pocket, then 30% of the game has already passed. Unless you have filled those frames with marks, your maximum possible score has dropped considerably. During your practice, you should be able to find the best available pocket angle, instead of wasting valuable frames of the game. (Later, we will present a personal formula to help you find the best angle to the pocket within two or three deliveries.)

There is another way to locate the best pocket angle, for a particular lane at a given point in time. It is what we refer to as *pre-reading the lane.* Briefly, pre-reading the lane to locate the best pocket angle is essentially watching how others who bowl in a manner similar to the way you bowl are playing that lane. Pre-reading includes all those actions you take to find out what the lane is doing before you roll your first ball down that lane.

If you could watch someone who bowls exactly like you do, who is using the same type of equipment you plan to use, then it is possible to locate the best pocket angle and how to play the lane before you roll your first ball. But, you need to know what to look for and how to interpret what is happening on the lane. (SECTION 2 will provide additional material on the concept of pre-reading the lane.)

And now back to the pocket angle. On your strike delivery there are actually two angles with which you must concern yourself. One is the *foul line angle* (sometimes called the header angle), and the other is the subject under discussion here, the *pocket angle.* The foul line angle is covered extensively in SECTION 2, but we will outline it here, since it directly affects the pocket angle. (In fact, if you roll a straight ball the two angles are identical!) First we will define each angle.

The foul line angle is the direction taken by the ball as it begins its path down the lane. It is the angle created by the path of the ball from the foul line to the arrows. Since two lines are required to create an angle, what are the two lines? The *path of the ball* is one line, and *the foul line* is the other.

Essentially, the ball can be rolled straight down one particular board or it can be rolled on a path to the left or right. Each foul line angle can be described by giving two numbers: the number of the board that the center of the ball crosses at the foul line, and the number of the board that the ball rolls over at the arrows. The 10-to-10 foul line angle is one in which the ball rolls over the 10th board at the foul line (the first number) and the 10th board at the arrows (the second number). This is a straight angle (90 degrees) created by the path of the ball and the foul line. The 11-to-9 foul line angle describes a ball rolling across the 11th board at the foul line and the 9th board at the arrows. For the RHB this is an angle to the right, but for the LHB it is an angle to the left. (References to board numbers are always from the right side of the lane for right handers and from the left side for left handers. We will go into more detail about foul line angles a little later, in SECTION 2.)

The pocket angle is the path the ball takes once it is heading in the direction of the pocket. The perfect pocket angle, if extended back toward the bowler, would leave the lane approximately 20 to 25 feet in front of the pin deck. To roll a straight ball at the ideal pocket angle would require that you stand two approaches to the right (RHB) or to the left (LHB)! (For more details on this ideal pocket angle, we refer you to *The Perfect Game,* referenced in the bibliography. Chapter six in that book presents some of the best pictures of the perfect strike that you will ever see.)

To get the ball into this ideal or perfect pocket angle from the approach of the lane you are using, you must use either a curve or hook ball delivery. The hook (or angle) into the pocket must be delayed until the ball is well down the lane, perhaps to within 10-15 feet of the pin deck. This single piece of information explains why virtually every high average bowler uses a curve or hook. It also explains why those of you who roll a backup ball should use the opposite pocket for your strike hits (the RHB using the 1-2 pocket and the LHB using the 1-3 pocket). The perfect pocket angle has the ball entering the pocket in such a manner that it will *maintain its path of deflection through the pins* as described in THE PERFECT STRIKE section.

It should be clear that there is a direct relationship between the two major angles we have been discussing, the foul line and pocket angles. *The foul line angle starts the ball on its path to the pins,* but *the pocket angle is the one at which the ball contacts the pin setup at the pocket.*

The line created or described as the path of the ball from the foul line to the pin deck (pocket) has a third factor that should be familiar to everyone who is serious about improving his or her percentage of strikes. Let's look at all three factors, or locations along the strike line.

The first factor is the number of the board that the ball passes over at the foul line. The *second* is the board that the ball passes over at the arrows (your target board or area). And the *third* location on the path of the ball to the pins is the point down the lane where the ball *begins* its break or turn toward the pocket. These three locations on the path of the ball are the ones with which you should be most concerned. The first two items define the foul line angle. The third location begins the definition of the pocket angle. On every strike delivery you should have determined in advance what you want these three numbers to be.

If you roll a straight ball, the pocket angle begins at the foul line. If you roll either a hook, curve or backup ball then the angle to the pocket begins when the ball starts its turn to the pocket. In any case, every adjustment you make to try to get strikes can be described as an attempt to change the pocket angle, that is, to find the pocket angle that will consistently produce strikes. You will be trying to get either more of an angle, or less of an angle. If the

ball hits high in the pocket or passes by in front of the pocket, you have too much of an angle and have to reduce it. If the ball is light in the pocket or fails to get up to the pocket, you need to increase the angle. Using other terms, you will either be trying to get *up to* the pocket or *back to* it. (More on these two concepts later in this PRINCIPLES section.)

Changing the pocket angle, either increasing or reducing it, can be achieved in several ways. Such adjustments fall into one of the three categories of adjustments: angle, equipment or delivery. For the moment, we will only illustrate three ways to change the pocket angle, one from each of the three categories.

The pocket angle can be changed by increasing or decreasing the *speed of the ball.* Increasing the speed of the ball will straighten out the shot, reducing the pocket angle. Reducing the speed of the ball will have just the opposite effect, allowing the ball to get more of a pocket angle. These speed changes are, of course, related to curve, hook, and backup ball deliveries, and not the straight ball delivery.

The pocket angle can also be altered by changing the *foul line angle.* Moving to the right on the approach will normally increase the pocket angle for the right handed bowler, and to the left reduces the pocket angle. For the left handed bowler, the pocket angle is reduced by movements to the right on the approach, and moving to the left increases the pocket angle.

The type of ball roll has an influence on approach shifts and *pocket* angles. The relationship is as follows:

Type of Ball Roll	**To Increase Pocket Angle:**	**To Reduce Pocket Angle:**
RHB: Hook, Curve, Straight Ball	Move Right	Move Left
RHB: Backup Ball, Using 1-2 Pocket,	Move Left	Move Right
LHB: Hook, Curve, Straight Ball	Move Left	Move Right
LHB: Backup Ball, Using 1-3 Pocket	Move Right	Move Left

Ball weights and balances can be used to change the pocket angle. The use of positive weights will increase the pocket angle, and negative weights will reduce it. (Both positive and negative weight imbalances will be covered extensively in later sections.)

Still another method to change the pocket angle is to alter the amount of lift imparted on the ball. More lift will increase the angle, and less lift will reduce it. You could, of course combine any of these adjustment methods. But as a general rule, you should only make one adjustment at a time.

In summary, locating and using the ideal pocket angle is a very important factor in making strikes, and is even considered by some high average bowlers as *the* most important element in making strikes. Knowing how to make angle, equipment and delivery changes to find and use the correct pocket angle will put you well along the way toward making more strikes.

PROPER SPEED

"Improper ball speed is a common error in the strike ball delivery."

Too much ball speed is just as bad as not enough ball speed. It is impressive to hear the sound of a fast ball crashing into the pins, but not very effective in terms of making strikes. And, making strikes should be your goal, not trying to impress other bowlers with your ability to throw the ball down the lane instead of rolling it properly. Bowling is rolling; not throwing.

A ball is supposed to skid, roll and then hook as it heads toward the pocket (unless you are rolling a straight ball). Too much speed will increase the amount of skid and may prevent the ball from getting the correct number of turns (revolutions) on it before it hits the pocket. The result is an ineffective ball, one that does not work for you. There is very little mixing of the pins after contact with the ball. The pins fly almost in an upright position back into the pit and do not take out as many pins as they would if they were heading toward the pit in a horizontal position. With increased speed your strike ball has to be far more perfectly placed in the pocket than one rolled at the proper speed.

What is the proper speed for you? This will vary somewhat, but the average speed used by high average bowlers takes the ball down the lane in 2.2 seconds, plus or minus .2 of a second. Your speed will probably be within this range of 2.0 to 2.4 seconds, depending upon your personal style. *Find your ideal speed by having someone time you.* Develop a consistent and well-timed delivery, one that will allow you to keep a constant speed on the ball. Later, we will suggest ways to increase or reduce ball speed to play various lane conditions.

What is considered a fast speed for one bowler might not be considered the same for another. A difference in body build, height of the backswing, weight of the ball, personal strength, etc. might create a naturally fast delivery for one person. But there is an ideal speed for you, for your style, and you should determine what ball speed is best for your game.

Whether you normally roll the ball fast or slow is neither an advantage nor a disadvantage. If you are striking consistently, if the ball maintains its path of deflection through the pins, if pin and ball deflection are both as described in the perfect strike hit, then your speed must be correct.

We talked about the impact of too much speed. What about not enough speed on the ball? Too little speed on the ball creates special problems of deflection. A slowly rolled ball may literally bounce off the pins after making contact with the pocket. In extreme cases, very young or very old bowlers, the ball has actually stopped after making contact with the pins, not having sufficient speed to make it through the pins and into the pit! (The authors timed a 4-year old, whose ball took 19.3 seconds to make it to the pins. Now that's slow!)

A ball taking longer than 2.6 seconds to get from the foul line to the pin deck will probably not have enough strength to keep in its path of deflection through the 1-3-5-9 pins for the RHB, or the 1-2-5-8 pins for the LHB. Use of an outside angle might compensate for the slower speed, since the additional angle into the pocket may keep the ball in its path through the pins. And, that is the test of the adequacy of ball speed. Can it maintain its path of deflection through the pins?

Once you have determined the proper ball speed for you, you must learn how to adjust that speed to meet varying lane conditions. It is difficult to adjust ball speed without affecting your timing in the approach. (We will discuss this situation in later sections under delivery adjustments.) This ability to alter ball speed will normally require many hours of practice. You would, of course, want to develop this ability so this adjustment technique becomes a part of your *adjustment arsenal.*

Initially, consistency in your ball speed is far more important than the actual rate of speed. To achieve a very high average, you have to be able to change ball speed.

Develop a ball speed appropriate for your particular style of bowling. If the ball is always rolled the same way, with the same speed, you are in a position to control its path to the pocket, and to pre-

dict the amount of ball deflection you will have. You are also able to read the lanes more accurately when your speed control is good. Once you can read the lanes properly, you can adjust to any lane condition to raise your percentage of pocket hits and strikes.

CORRECT ACTION

"Action is important on strikes. Accuracy is important on spares."

The term *action* as used throughout this book refers to the ability of the ball to maintain its path of deflection through the pins, and to create the pattern of pin and ball deflection indicated in the discussion about THE PERFECT STRIKE hit. The ball will impart the correct velocity to the pins to get maximum pin deflection for making strikes when action is correct. Keep in mind that the ball only takes out four pins on a strike.

Action is sometimes called *lift, turn, fingers, spin, revolutions,* etc. Most references to action on the ball call attention to the position of the thumb and fingers at the moment the ball is released. In addition, the comment is frequently made that action is *placed* or *put* on the ball by the type of release used. Although we agree in principle that action in the general sense is put on the ball at the release point, *we have expanded the term* to include other factors that determine what action is on the ball *when it hits the pocket.*

Action is the result of many factors and forces on the ball. Lane conditions, speed, ball weights and imbalances, weight and center of gravity of the pins, foul line and pocket angles, etc., all have some influence on the action of the ball when it arrives at the pocket, and as it continues in its path of deflection through the pins.

If there is *too much action* on the ball when it hits the pocket, it will drive through the pocket and not maintain the ideal path of deflection off the 1-3-5-9 pins (RHB) or 1-2-5-8 pins (LHB). Spare leaves on the opposite side of the pin deck often indicate that the ball had too much action on it (leaves on the left side for RHB and the right side for LHB).

If there is *not enough action* on the ball when it hits the pocket, the ball will be deflected away from the pocket, will hit too much of the 3-pin (RHB) or too much of the 2-pin (LHB) and not enough of the 5-pin by either one. Spare leaves on the same side of the pin deck (and 5-7, 5-10, 8-10, and 7-9 leaves) often indicate that action was not sufficient.

With *the correct amount of ball action,* the ball keeps its proper path of deflection, drives into the pin setup to the 18½ board and creates pin and ball deflection as described in the perfect strike hit. *The key signal to indicate that ball action is correct is ball deflection.* What happens to the ball after it hits the pocket? Where does it leave the end of the pin deck?

The relationship of the many factors influencing or creating ball action might be more clear with a couple of examples. A small amount of lift or turn imparted to the ball at the release point, combined with the use of the deep outside angle (from the outside portion of the approach) may create enough action to result in perfect strikes. Use of the deep inside line and more lift on the ball may also be enough to hit the pocket with enough action to strike. Thus, the strike line and the amount of lift or turn imparted to the ball at the moment of release are directly related to the action on the ball *when it arrives at the pocket.* Similarly, increased loft reduces the amount of turn on the ball and thereby reduces the action on the ball. Less loft often results in a stronger ball, more action on it, than a ball that is lofted too far out on the lanes.

To illustrate further, *ball revolutions* and *the pins* influence ball action. A ball that is rolling well, is revolving strongly at the moment it makes contact with the pocket, will have more action on it than one that has either started its roll too soon or too late. An early roll often results in a weak hitting ball, one that is *rolled out* by the time it hits the pocket. A late roll does not give the ball sufficient time to get the revolutions up to maximum strength by the time the ball hits the pins. Ball revolutions are directly related to the amount of drive on the ball, which determines in some measure how the ball reacts when it hits the pocket. (More on ball revolutions in SECTIONS 5 and 8 under DELIVERY ADJUSTMENTS.)

Although the weight and center of gravity *of the pins* do not alter the amount of action *on the ball,* such factors do determine whether a given amount of action is enough or too much. In other words, heavy pins require a ball with more action on it than light pins would need. (More on the influence of pins

on the path and action of the ball in SECTION 2, under THE PIN DECK.)

We have attempted to consider all the factors or forces working on the ball in our term *action: the ability of the ball to maintain its path of deflection through the pins and to create ideal pin and ball deflection.* In this way it is clear that action on the ball can be altered in a number of ways, including (but not limited to) what happens as the ball is released. If we limited the term action simply to that which is put on the ball by the method of release, then the assumption would be that any change in action would need some change in the release. This would limit the range of adjustment techniques you might consider if there was a requirement for changing the action on the ball. It might also suggest that you make a delivery change, when an angle or equipment change might be easier to do and more effective.

Any adjustment you make, in angle, equipment or delivery, will have some impact upon the action of the ball at the moment it hits the pins. When the action is correct, ball and pin deflection will be as described in THE PERFECT STRIKE section. That action, however you are able to create it, is your goal on each strike ball delivery.

AIMING: SPOT AND LINE BOWLING

"Accuracy requires aiming. Select your target and hit it consistently."

Bowling for strikes requires a high degree of accuracy in hitting your target. On the strike ball delivery your goal is to hit the 1-3 pocket if you bowl right handed and the 1-2 pocket if you bowl left handed. But, such a target is too far away from the point where the ball is released to be used as a point of aim. A closer target is needed.

Two techniques for aiming are used by almost all high average bowlers.

SPOT BOWLING: Aim at a spot or target out on the lanes, without looking at the pins. Your spot or target might be the dots imbedded in the lane about 7 feet beyond the foul line, or the arrows (range finders) imbedded in the lanes about 15 feet from the foul line, or some other spot such as a light or dark board on the lane.

LINE BOWLING: Imagine a line drawn from the point on the lane where the ball is released to the spot in the pin setup that you wish to hit — the pocket. Then roll your ball so it will follow this imaginary line. This method of aiming is sometimes called line/area bowling.

Spot Bowling is an accurate method of aiming or targeting, and is used by many top bowlers. The principle of spot bowling is that it is easier to hit a target 3 feet, 6 feet, or 15 feet out on the lane than it is to hit a pin or pocket target 60 feet from the foul line. And, if you hit your target or spot, you should hit the pin setup at the point of contact for which you are aiming. However, it is absolutely essential that you do not vary any other part of your delivery, such as speed, lift, extension, etc. Spot bowling will only work when you have developed a consistent and well-timed delivery.

Since many bowlers use spot bowling, you might want to start with this method right away. Rather than selecting a specific spot or board on the lane, you might select an area on the lane such as between the second and third arrows (from the right for the RHB and from the left for the LHB). This would make it easier for you to learn spot bowling.

The second method of aiming or targeting is called *Line Bowling*. An imaginary line is drawn from the point the ball is released on the lane to the pocket. Then two or more checkpoints are located on the path or line that the ball is supposed to travel. These checkpoints along the line might be the dots or arrows in the lanes, or could be light or dark boards. The principle of using a line with two or more checkpoints is that this will be more accurate than just hitting one spot.

For example, with only one spot as a checkpoint, you might hit it perfectly but at a different angle than you had planned and the ball would probably not hit the pocket. With two checkpoints along the line it would become obvious that you had done something differently, such as more or less speed, a different angle, more extension or reach, etc. With more than two checkpoints, you can get a more precise reading of the path of the ball to the pins.

The next time you go to a bowling center, notice the various dots on the lanes which are there to help you in your aiming. Dots are imbedded about 7 feet out on each lane on the 3rd, 5th, 8th, 11th, and 14th boards on both the left and right side of the lane. Arrows are imbedded in each lane about 15 feet in front of the foul line. There are 7 arrows spaced five boards apart, starting with an arrow on the 5th board, the 10th board, etc. The center arrow is located in the 20th board, which is the center of the lane.

Most right handed bowlers use the 2nd or 3rd arrow for aiming. Left handed bowlers often use the 1st arrow from the left side of the lane. (More details on these arrows and the use of them in targeting will be found in SECTION 2, READING THE LANES. At that time we will also present a more detailed discussion of the construction of the lane, from the approach through the pin deck.)

Dots are imbedded in the lanes at the foul line. These dots are often used for aiming, but they are slightly more difficult to use than the arrows since

they are so close to the foul line. Many bowlers find it too difficult to watch these spots and to maintain proper balance at the time of delivery and release of the ball. These dots are, however, useful for seeing if you are drifting left or right in your approach.

Notice also that dots are imbedded in the approach, sometimes two sets of them. One set is at the 12 foot mark (behind the foul line) and the other set is often located 15 feet in back of the foul line. These approach markers are useful for selecting the proper starting position on the approach, which is essential to proper aiming.

To improve your accuracy in hitting the pocket, you must develop an accurate method for aiming. Choose the system of aiming that is best for you; one with which you can develop confidence in yourself. Use all of the targeting and aiming features built into the approach and the first 15 feet of the lane. Practice both spot and line bowling methods, and any other system that appears to work well for you. If you can develop an accurate aiming system, you will get the ball into the pocket with a great deal of consistency. You will also be in a position to take advantage of other adjustment techniques, particularly angle changes.

GETTING UP TO THE POCKET

"Never up, never in."

The quote cited above was borrowed from the game of golf. If the ball does not get up to the cup, it cannot fall into the hole. The same is true in bowling. If your ball does not reach the pocket (sometimes referred to as *the hole*) then you cannot expect to make perfect strike hits. You may still get strikes on occasion, but you will not be able to build a high average on such hits.

If the ball hits to the right side of the 1-3 pocket (RHB), or the left side of the 1-2 pocket (LHB), then an adjustment is needed to get the ball *up to* the pocket. Such hits are called *outside hits,* meaning hits that are toward the outside of the lane.

Several angle, equipment or delivery adjustments are available to get the ball up to the pocket. Each adjustment could be used separately, or in combination with others, depending upon the results you achieve after making the adjustment. Exhibit 1-3 summarizes the normal types of adjustments that will bring the ball up to the pocket for both left and right handed bowlers. Since both types of bowlers are trying to get the ball toward the center portion of the lane, that is, into their respective 1-2 and 1-3 strike pockets, the adjustment techniques are similar.

Normally it is best to make a single adjustment to get the ball up to the pocket after hitting on the outside portion of the pin setup. If the adjustment is not sufficient (an underadjustment) or is too much (an overadjustment) then a further adjustment is needed. When two or more adjustments are made at the same time, and an over or under adjustment has occurred, it becomes slightly more difficult to determine which adjustment was not correct. Hence, the suggestion is to make only one adjustment at a time, if possible.

Exhibit 1-3 addresses the question of the backup ball delivery, and adjustments to get up to the pocket. *If you roll a backup ball, please refer to the note at the bottom of the exhibit.*

There is very little material written for the bowler who elects to use a backup ball delivery. Yet it is not easy for some people to change their delivery methods, nor do they always wish to do so. Because pin and ball deflection are better with the use of the *opposite pockets,* and educational material is now available for left as well as right handers (especially in this series of four books), there is a much better chance for the backup ball user to improve his or her average.

All angle, equipment and delivery adjustments needed to get the ball *up to* the pocket will be discussed in great detail in later sections. For the moment they have only been summarized to provide you with an overview of the types of adjustments needed to get the ball *up to the pocket* after it has failed to do so.

EXHIBIT 1-3
Adjustment Techniques to Get the Ball Up to the Pocket

ADJUSTMENT TECHNIQUES	FOR GETTING THE BALL *UP TO* THE POCKET
Strike Line or Angle	Move Toward Outside Lines or Angles
Ball Surface	Use a Softer Ball Surface
Ball Balance	Use More Positive or Less Negative Weights
Ball Speed	Use Less Speed
Loft	Use Less Loft
Lift (Turn, Action, Etc.)	Use More Lift

NOTE: Normally only one adjustment is made at a time.

Right Handed Bowlers: The objective is to hit the 1-3 pocket. Any hit to the right side (or light in the pocket) is considered one that did not get up to the pocket. The above adjustments are designed to get the ball into the pocket after such misses to the right.

Left Handed Bowlers: The objective is to hit the 1-2 pocket. Any hit to the left side (or light in the pocket) is considered one that did not get up to the pocket. The above adjustments are designed to get the ball into the 1-2 pocket after such misses to the left.

Backup Ball Users: *Right handed bowlers using a backup ball delivery, and the suggested 1-2 pocket for strikes, should use one or more of the following adjustments after missing the pocket to the left:* Move to the left on the approach; use a ball with a softer surface; use more negative or less positive weights; use less speed, less loft, or more lift. *Right side misses* would use the reverse of these adjustments.

Left handed bowlers who use a backup ball delivery, and who keep missing the 1-3 pocket to the right, should use one or more of the following adjustments to get the ball up to the pocket: Move to the right on the approach; use a ball with a softer surface; use more negative or less positive weights; use less loft, less speed, or more lift. *Left side misses* should use the opposite of these adjustments.

GETTING BACK TO THE POCKET

"Normally it is best to make a single adjustment to get the ball back to the pocket."

In the previous section we discussed those situations in which you missed the pocket on the outside portion of the lane. This meant a right side miss for the RHB and a miss to the left side for the left handed bowler. Misses requiring an adjustment to get back to the pocket are just the opposite, as explained below.

If the ball is too high in the pocket, or crosses over in front of the pocket or head pin completely, then we have what are called *high* or *crossover* hits. Both of these misses require adjustments to bring the ball *back to* the pocket because they have passed it by. Any adjustment technique might be used to make the correction, that is, a change in angle, equipment or delivery. Or, combinations of adjustments might be used to achieve the same objective.

Exhibit 1-4 summarizes the normal types of adjustments that will bring the ball back to the pocket. These adjustments apply for both right and left handed bowlers. Any adjustment could be made alone or in combination with other adjustments. For example, you could move to one of the inside angles (discussed at length in SECTIONS 3 and 6) and use more speed to get the ball back to the pocket.

As previously stated, it is best to make one adjustment at a time. If that adjustment is not sufficient or is too much then some further adjustment will be needed.

Exhibit 1-4 addresses the question of the backup ball delivery, and adjustments to get back to the pocket. *If you roll a backup ball, please refer to the note at the bottom of the exhibit.*

Previous sections have discussed the reasons why those of you who roll a backup ball should use the opposite-side pockets for strikes. You may have a little difficulty using some of the charts in this book because of your unorthodox approach, but you can significantly increase your average if you will make an attempt to relate the material to your style of bowling.

All angle, equipment and delivery adjustments needed to get the ball back to the pocket will be discussed in great detail in later sections of this book. For the moment, they have only been summarized to give you an overview of the types of adjustments needed to get the ball *back to the pocket* when you have made a crossover or high pocket hit.

EXHIBIT 1-4
Adjustment Techniques to Get the Ball Back to the Pocket

ADJUSTMENT TECHNIQUES	FOR GETTING THE BALL *BACK TO* THE POCKET
Strike Line or Angle	Move Toward Inside Lines or Angles
Ball Surface	Use a Harder Ball Surface
Ball Balance	Use More Negative or Less Positive Weights
Ball Speed	Use More Speed
Loft	Use More Loft
Lift (Turn, Action, Etc.)	Use Less Lift

NOTE: Normally, only one adjustment is made at a time.

Right Handed Bowlers: The objective is to hit the 1-3 pocket. Any hit to the left side (or high in the pocket) is considered one that passed by the pocket. The above adjustments will get the ball back to the pocket.

Left Handed Bowlers: The objective is to hit the 1-2 pocket. Any hit to the right side (or high in the pocket) is considered one that passed by the pocket. The above adjustments will get the ball into the pocket after such misses to the right.

Backup Ball Bowlers: *Right handed bowlers using a backup ball delivery should use one or more of the following adjustments after missing to the right of the suggested 1-2 pocket:* Move to the right on the approach; use a ball with a harder surface; use more positive or less negative weights; use more speed, more loft, or less lift. *Left side misses* would use just the opposite of these adjustments.

Left handed bowlers using a backup ball delivery, and the suggested 1-3 pocket, should use one or more of the following adjustments when continually missing the pocket to the left: Move to the left on the approach; use a ball with a harder surface; use more positive or less negative weights; use more loft, more speed, or less lift. *Right side misses* would use the reverse of these adjustments.

READING THE LANES

"Lane reading is a continuous process: keep reading, keep adjusting, and you should keep striking."

Basically, two skills are required for making strikes consistently, and under varying lane conditions: (1) the ability to read the lanes, to see how the ball and the lane are interacting, and (2) the ability to make angle, equipment or delivery adjustments to get the ball and lane working together for you. This section will briefly recap some of the principles of *reading* the lanes, while the following one covers principles of *adjusting* to lane conditions.

Properly reading a lane means that you know what the ball will do as it passes from one portion of the lane to the other on its path to the pins. Your reading of the lanes should start when the ball is placed on the lane and continue along its path to the pocket. *Keep watching the ball as it takes its path of deflection through the pins and off the back of the pin deck.* Any clues you can find, anything that tells you how the ball and lane are reacting, can be used to help you decide if any adjustments are needed to get the ball into a proper path to the pocket. Once you can hit the pocket, then you must continue to watch for signs that the lane is changing (drying out, oil patterns changing, etc.). Be alert to any unusual reactions of the ball which might be caused by wet (oily) spots, dry spots, high or low boards, etc.

For purposes of analysis we have divided the lane into four portions or sections: the approach; from the foul line to the arrows (called the headers); from the arrows to the pin deck (called the mid-lane); and the pin deck. *Each portion of the lane has information that you need.* Reading the lane will provide that information, thereby telling you what if any adjustments are needed to get the ball into the pocket correctly. (One professional stated that he felt like the lanes were talking to him. The lanes would say, "If you lay the ball down here, I will take it into the pocket. If you don't, then I will not let you get the ball in the pocket.")

Before we take a brief look at each of the four portions of the lane, we should ask ourselves: "What questions do we have to get answered by reading the lanes?" Essentially, three questions have to be answered. (1) What is the best strike line or angle to get the ball into the pocket? (2) What equipment will work best on this lane at this point in time? and (3) What delivery adjustments (if any) will I have to make to properly play this lane? A fourth question might be, "Is there anything unusual about this lane that might cause a problem or give me an advantage in playing it?"

For most bowlers, with only one bowling ball to their name, (or who are possibly using a house ball), the second question regarding equipment selection is not relevant. They must use whatever equipment they have or can find. For top bowlers, equipment selection is often considered the most important question they ask.

Selecting the proper strike line is perhaps the most important question for the once-a-week or average bowler. It is a very important question no matter what average you have. Incorporated into this question of strike line is a concern for the best *foul line angle* and the best *pocket angle* for the lane. These two angles make up an essential part of the path of the ball to the pins.

Delivery changes are of more concern for the professional or high average bowler than the average or league bowler. The average or league bowler will not normally be making changes in delivery, although to increase his or her average to higher levels this ability must be developed and used. Such changes normally revolve around changes in speed, loft or lift. These delivery adjustments are often needed to take advantage of a lane condition, overcome a lane condition, make small changes within a given strike line or angle, etc.

Keeping the above questions in mind, let's now look at the four portions of the lane and try to determine what each section offers in clues to reading the total lane.

The Approach: You must study the physical construction of the lane in order to find the proper starting position behind the foul line. How far back should you stand? Should you stand in the center of the approach, or toward the left or right side? Does

your normal walk pattern take you in a straight line toward your target? Or, do you drift to the left or right in your walk to the foul line? These questions should tell you why we have included the approach as a portion of the lane. What you do on the approach must be taken into consideration on each shot, since what you do during the delivery of the ball will affect the ball on its path to the pins.

The Headers (from the foul line to the arrows): If you can read this portion of the lane, you are well on your way toward reading the entire lane. Here you must take into consideration questions such as: What is the foul line angle? Do you need to open or close this angle? How much skid do you need through this portion of the lane? The answers to these kinds of questions give you some idea of how the ball and the lane are going to react from the foul line to the arrows.

The Mid-Lane (from the arrows to the pin deck): After the ball has skidded through the headers, it will begin its roll toward the pins. Now you need to know if there is a lane track, and how the ball reacts to it! How have the lanes been conditioned? Where does the conditioning stop? What pocket angle is being created, and what pocket angle appears to be the most advantageous to use? If you roll a curve, backup or hook ball, when does the ball begin its break or curve to the pocket? Is this break too soon or too late? Is the break too strong or not strong enough? These are some of the factors you must be considering as you try to read the mid-lane portion of the path of the ball to the pin deck.

The Pin-Deck: The first and most obvious clue provided by the pin deck is the exact contact of the ball with the pins. Did the ball hit in the pocket or miss to the right or left? Has the ball come up to the pocket, failed to come up to it, or passed it by? What pins were left if you did not get a strike? How did the ball go through the pins, what was the path of deflection? Where did the ball go off the end of the pin deck? Do the pins appear to be heavy or light? Was there good mixing of the pins? Did the ball appear to have proper action on it when it arrived at the pin deck? Was the ball too weak, or too strong, How was the speed of the ball? What was the pattern of pin and ball deflection? At what angle did the ball enter the pocket? You can readily see that here is where it all happens, on the pin deck. You must be alert to all of these signals from this portion of the lane so you will know what adjustments may have to be made.

In SECTION 2, READING THE LANES, we will try to point out the dots, arrows, and other physical characteristics of the lane that are provided to give you clues to read the lanes properly. These vital signs are an essential ingredient in developing your skill at reading the lanes.

It is essential that you determine the condition of the lane (read each of the four portions) as quickly as possible. Then you can make any needed adjustments to get the ball and lane working together for you. *Don't fight the lane.* You cannot change the condition of the lane, only adjust to it. You should not try to overpower the lane. Few bowlers can do this with any degree of consistent success.

You need a consistent, well-timed and natural delivery to read the lanes well. When anything unusual happens to the ball on its path to the pins, you want to be sure that it was not caused by an *un*intentional change in your delivery. If you do not do anything differently in your delivery (such as a change in speed, drift, early or late release, improper timing, etc.) then any reaction of the ball on the lane can be properly attributed to lane conditions, and an adjustment can be made.

In conclusion, properly reading a lane means that you know how the ball and the lane are going to interact from the time the ball is released onto the lane until it goes off the back of the pin deck. Since there is going to be some interaction between the ball and the lane, your task is to determine what the interaction means to your strike delivery. *Lane reading is a continuous process.* Once you have determined the proper angle, equipment and delivery adjustments to get the ball into the pocket consistently (and correctly), you must continue to monitor the path of the ball on the lane to look for any signs that the lane is changing. The lane will change with use, and as a result of atmospheric conditions (temperature and humidity). Keep reading; keep adjusting (when necessary); and you will keep striking.

ADJUSTING TO LANE CONDITIONS

"Few people can overpower the lanes; most bowlers have to adjust to lane conditions."

Reading the lanes and adjusting to lane conditions are directly related. The two are in fact like two sides of the same coin. Each is part of a total plan for playing the lanes properly.

The objective of adjusting to lane conditions is to get the ball and the lane working together for you to get the ball into the most favorable path to the pocket. Once you have located this ideal strike line, you must continue reading the lanes and continue adjusting as required. Lanes change with use, and as a result of atmospheric conditions (basically temperature and humidity). *Adjusting is therefore a continuous process.*

All adjustments can be classified into one of three groups: *Angle or line* adjustments; *equipment* adjustments; and *delivery* adjustments. Each group is covered in great detail in SECTIONS 3, 4 and 5 for right handed bowlers, and SECTIONS 6, 7 and 8 for left handed bowlers. For the moment we will only present an overview of these major types of adjustments.

Line and angle adjustments fall into five subcategories, called strike lines: *deep inside* line, *inside* line, *second arrow* line, *outside* line, and *deep outside* line. Essentially each strike line is composed of a set of foul line angles describing the path of the ball from the foul line to the arrows. All foul line angles fall within one of these five strike lines. Every line or angle adjustment is a shift to the left or the right on the approach. Such a shift will change the foul line angle and will generally change the pocket angle as well. As a rule of thumb, a movement to the center of the approach (toward the inside strike lines) is an adjustment for hooking lanes. It is an adjustment to get the ball back to the pocket after it has passed by the pocket or hit too high in the pocket. Conversely, movements toward the outside edges of the approach are used to adjust for lanes that are not hooking very much. These outside strike lines are used when the ball has failed to get up to the pocket, or has hit the pocket too lightly.

Other changes in your delivery might have to be made as you change your position on the approach. You may have to alter your method of aiming, moving your target in closer to the foul line with the outside lines and aim further down the lane on the inside angles and lines. Your drift pattern may change as you make an angle change. Objects may interfere with your normal delivery, such as the ball return, a wall, etc. In other words, line and angle changes are more than simple moves to the left or right on the approach. You may have to combine such adjustments with equipment or delivery adjustments to properly play a given condition.

Equipment adjustments fall into three subcategories: changing the surface of the ball (going from one with a hard shell to a soft shell, or vice versa); changing the fit or grip of the ball (such as making span or pitch changes); and altering the weights and balances in the ball (by changing from one with positive weights to negative weights, or the reverse).

Such equipment changes are not a normal part of the adjustment arsenal of the once-a-week or average bowler. He or she normally has only one ball, and may even be using a house ball. Given the importance of the equipment you use to your success in making strikes, you should learn how to insure that the ball you use fits you properly. A properly fitted ball is vital to consistent high scores. If you decide to become more serious with your bowling game, you should have your own ball, properly fitted and drilled to accommodate your style of bowling. Without access to the option of equipment adjustments, you can only resort to angle and delivery changes to adjust to the lanes.

Delivery adjustments also fall into three subcategories: changes in the speed of the ball; changes in loft (how far out on the lane the ball travels before it hits the lane); and changes in release related to the amount of lift, turn, spin, etc. you put on the ball. *Delivery adjustments are among the most difficult ones to make, and are not usually made by beginning or average bowlers.* High average bowlers *do* use such delivery adjustments, and you should

learn how to make such changes in the way you roll the ball if you wish to improve your percentage of strikes. This is particularly important if you only have one or two types of ball surfaces or ball balances to use. If you cannot change your equipment, and you cannot change your delivery, then only angle changes are available to you. Your adjustment arsenal is not well stocked.

Multiple adjustments are, of course, possible and often needed. You may have to change both the angle and the speed of the ball to play a given lane condition. Knowing how to make individual adjustments independently will put you in a good position to combine adjustments. This will place you in better shape for finding the right adjustment or combination of adjustments needed to adjust to any lane conditioning.

Throughout this book we will be talking about making only a single adjustment to get the ball into the pocket: a change in angle, *or* a change in equipment, *or* a change in delivery. This is normally the best strategy to use: *make only one change at a time.* However, there are times when you need to make two or more adjustments at the same time to properly play the lane. For example, you might move to the outside line *and* reduce your ball speed. Or, you could use an inside angle *and* increase ball speed at the same time.

Some adjustment methods have the *same effect* as other techniques. Other adjustments react in the *opposite manner.* Therefore, making adjustments to get the ball into the pocket becomes a far more complex subject than we may indicate as we discuss each adjustment technique separately. At this point in time we wish to put the whole subject of your adjustment arsenal into a comprehensive perspective, with full details to follow in the appropriate sections.

Five terms comprise the essence of *multiple adjustments: total* adjustment; *competing* adjustments; *complementary* adjustments; *over-adjusting*; and *underadjusting.* Let's examine each of these terms to see how multiple adjustments can be used to increase your percentage of strikes.

Total Adjustment: When you combine two or more adjustment techniques to get the ball into the pocket, you create a total adjustment. If the two adjustment techniques are *complementary*, that is, they have the *same* basic effect, then your total adjustment will be more than if you combined *competing* adjustments, which have the *opposite* effect on the ball. At times you may wish to combine complementary adjustments, at other times you may combine competing adjustments, and at other times you may use one of each type. *Reading and interpreting the effect of multiple adjustments is obviously more difficult than if only one change is made at a time.*

Normally it is best to make only one adjustment at a time. The reason for this strategy is that you can more readily interpret the result of a single change on the path of the ball, and you will have a good idea as to the next adjustment you may have to make. If you make two or more adjustments at the same time, and they do not get the ball into the pocket properly, you may have some difficulty in determining which of the adjustments caused the problem, and what further adjustment is needed to correct the situation.

To illustrate further, suppose you moved to the outside line and reduced your speed at the same time. But, the ball passed by the pocket. Which of the two adjustment methods caused the overadjustment? If you guess that the speed change caused the problem, you will want to make a further speed adjustment. If it turns out that the angle or line change was more of the problem, you may still need another shot to try to get back to the pocket. But, if you had only made one adjustment, and it did not work correctly, you are probably in a better position to get closer to hitting the pocket on the next shot.

Therefore, as a general rule, make only one adjustment at a time and you should be able to get the ball into the pocket much sooner. But, if you have to make two or more adjustments, by all means do so. For those cases, you need to know which adjustment techniques work together (complement one another) and which work against each other (compete against one another). Let's look at Complementary Adjustments first.

Complementary Adjustments: These are adjustments that have the *same* effect, working together to produce a greater total adjustment. One group of complementary adjustment techniques is designed to get the ball *back to* the pocket, and the second set is used to get the ball *up to* the pocket. Both sets of complementary adjustment techniques are combined in Exhibit 1-5.

One pair of complementary adjustments would be to move to the *outside line* and to *reduce ball speed.* Both of these methods are designed to get the ball to come *up to* the pocket when you have failed

EXHIBIT 1-5
A Summary of Complementary Adjustment Methods

Some adjustment methods have the *same effect* as other methods. This chart summarizes the various set of *complementary* adjustments. For example, moving to the inside line is the same as using a harder ball surface, negative weights, more speed, less lift, more loft, as indicated *down column 1* of this exhibit. You can read this chart either across the lines or down the columns.

	TO GET THE BALL *BACK TO* THE POCKET						TO GET THE BALL *UP TO* THE POCKET					
ADJUSTMENT METHODS	**Inside Lines**	**Harder Ball**	**Negative Weights**	**More Speed**	**Less Lift**	**More Loft**	**Outside Lines**	**Softer Ball**	**Positive Weights**	**Less Speed**	**More Lift**	**Less Loft**
Inside Lines		Same	Same	Same	Same	Same						
Outside Lines								Same	Same	Same	Same	Same
Harder Ball	Same		Same	Same	Same	Same						
Softer Ball							Same		Same	Same	Same	Same
Negative Weights	Same	Same		Same	Same	Same						
Positive Weights							Same	Same		Same	Same	Same
More Speed	Same	Same	Same		Same	Same						
Less Speed							Same	Same	Same		Same	Same
Less Lift	Same	Same	Same	Same		Same						
More Lift							Same	Same	Same	Same		Same
More Loft	Same	Same	Same	Same	Same							
Less Loft							Same	Same	Same	Same	Same	

to do so. If you roll a hook ball, these two adjustments will cause the ball to begin its break to the pocket sooner. Therefore, if you make both of these adjustments at the same time, you will be making a greater total adjustment than if you simply used either one of them. These two methods may work together and create too much of an adjustment (overadjustment), causing the ball to hit the head pin too full or cross over to the brooklyn side of the head pin. Or, they could work together exactly as you planned and create the total adjustment that gets you the perfect pocket hit. *Therefore, complementary adjustments are not inherently good or bad: they simply work together to create a greater total adjustment than either one makes independently.*

If you have made an adjustment, and it is not sufficient (an underadjustment), then any other complementary adjustment could be made to give you the additional adjustment you need. A knowledge of which adjustments work the same as other ones gives you the option to make one or several changes to make the total adjustment you need to get the ball in the pocket.

Competing Adjustments: These are adjustments that work *against* each other, such as *increased loft* and *less speed*. Increased loft is an adjustment to get the ball *back to* the pocket, but less speed is designed to get the ball *up to* the pocket. Another set of competing adjustments would be to combine a harder ball surface with more lift (turn, action, spin). A harder ball surface is an adjustment to get the ball back to the pocket, but increased lift on the ball is designed to get the ball up to the pocket. Exhibit 1-6 summarizes competing adjustments.

Competing adjustments produce a *lesser amount* of total adjustment than do complementary adjustments. And, you may wish to combine competing adjustments, just as you may wish to combine complementary adjustments. Once you become familiar with the various types of adjustments, and *the combined impact* of any set, then you are in a much better position to make the necessary adjustments to meet any lane condition you might find. When you adjust and you are still not in the pocket, you will know what adjustment options are open to you.

Not making the proper adjustment suggests the two additional terms that should be briefly mentioned here: overadjusting and underadjusting.

Overadjusting: If you have made an adjustment, and you have a result that is *more* than you needed to get the ball into the pocket, you have overadjusted. For example, you needed to get the ball up to the pocket, so you moved to the outside line and the ball passed by the head pin—too much of an adjustment. Of course, you could simply move a little more toward the center of the approach, that is, correct the angle adjustment you had made. But, *you could use any other competing adjustment* to solve your overadjustment situation.

Underadjusting: If you have made an adjustment, and you have a result that is still not what you need to get the ball in the pocket, you have underadjusted. For example, you needed to get the ball back to the pocket and you moved to the inside strike lines. Yet the ball still passes by the head pin and does not get back to the pocket—an underadjustment. *Any other complementary adjustment could be used* to increase your total adjustment, to get back to the pocket.

Study Exhibits 1-5 and 1-6 until you are familiar with all of the adjustment techniques available to you, and you are able to combine techniques when necessary. Practice making each type of adjustment until you feel comfortable with all of them. Then whenever the situation arises that calls for any one or more of these techniques to properly play the lanes, you will be ready to use whichever methods are most appropriate. Your adjustment arsenal will be well-stocked, and you should be able to get your fair share of strikes under all lane conditions.

EXHIBIT 1-6
A Summary of Competing Adjustment Methods

Some adjustment methods have the *opposite effect* of other methods. This chart summarizes the various sets of *competing* adjustments. For example, moving to the inside line is the *opposite* of the outside line, softer ball, positive weights, less speed, more lift and less loft, as indicated *down Column 1* of this exhibit. You can read the chart either across the lines or down the columns.

ADUSTMENT METHODS	Inside Lines	Outside Lines	Harder Ball	Softer Ball	Positive Weights	Negative Weights	More Speed	Less Speed	More Lift	Less Lift	More Loft	Less Loft
Inside Lines		Opp.		Opp.	Opp.			Opp.	Opp.			Opp.
Outside Lines	Opp.		Opp.			Opp.	Opp.			Opp.	Opp.	
Harder Ball		Opp.		Opp.	Opp.			Opp.	Opp.			Opp.
Softer Ball	Opp.		Opp.			Opp.	Opp.			Opp.	Opp.	
Negative Weights		Opp.		Opp.	Opp.			Opp.	Opp.			Opp.
Positive Weights	Opp.		Opp.			Opp.	Opp.			Opp.	Opp.	
More Speed		Opp.		Opp.	Opp.			Opp.	Opp.			Opp.
Less Speed	Opp.		Opp.			Opp.	Opp.			Opp.	Opp.	
Less Lift		Opp.		Opp.	Opp.			Opp.	Opp.			Opp.
More Lift	Opp.		Opp.			Opp.	Opp.			Opp.	Opp.	
More Loft		Opp.		Opp.	Opp.			Opp.	Opp.			Opp.
Less Loft	Opp.		Opp.			Opp.	Opp.			Opp.	Opp.	

CHECKPOINTS ON ALL STRIKES

"Bowl the frame and not the game. Concentrate on your delivery in each frame and you have concentrated on your complete game."

Although this is a book devoted totally to making strikes, you should *not* think about making a strike as you stand on the approach. The more you think about strikes, the less you can think about making a perfect execution of the delivery. Strikes are the goal and the result of perfect execution. Intelligent thinking and planning prior to stepping upon the approach will allow you to *focus your attention entirely upon executing the shot perfectly.* If you make the shot as well as you possibly can, you have done all you can do to get a strike.

If you think about making a strike, rather than thinking about making a good execution of the shot, you will be placing undue pressure on yourself. This is particularly true when you have a string of strikes going. Don't think to yourself 'If I could just get one more'. *Think about making the best delivery you can,* since that is the only thing you do when you bowl—you deliver the ball. Concentrate solely upon what it is you have to do: roll the ball the best way you can after you have carefully planned the angle and speed needed for the shot.

Concentration is essential on every delivery. In order that your efforts remain focused upon the essential elements of your delivery, it is best to establish several checkpoints—a countdown—prior to each delivery. We have developed a set of 10 items you should consider in each frame.

The following three items should be taken as preliminary planning before you step upon the approach and take your stance:

1. Select the board you wish to use as your target.
2. Determine the angle across that board that you will use. *(You have now defined the foul line angle you plan to use.)*
3. Select your approach position, taking into consideration your walk pattern, drift, etc. (Later we will give you a personal formula that will make it very easy to determine your stance location.)

Then step upon the approach and consider these additional checkpoints:

4. Face your target directly. Align your feet to the board on the approach that you have determined is your starting point.
5. Square your shoulders to the intended foul line angle along which you plan to roll the ball.
6. Align your ball to your intended path to the target on the lanes.
7. Pushaway: Push the ball through the intended line.
8. Continue to focus your eyes along your intended line.
9. Swing through the line. *Let your swing pull you through the line.*
10. Follow through in your swing and watch your ball as it rolls along its path to and through the pins. Determine what, if any, adjustments will have to be made in your next delivery.

It is important that you think through the first three items before you step upon the approach. This will prevent you from rushing your shot, since you will not have to decide these items while you are on the approach. The additional time on the approach can be devoted to the other items in the countdown, and you can concentrate more fully on them. Consistency can only be achieved by concentrating on each shot.

Remember what results you had on each shot, especially the pin and ball deflection that occurred on the pin deck. Such information will tell you what adjustments you may have to make on your next delivery. Each spare leave gives you some idea as to what your ball did when it *hit the pins,* which also gives you some clue as to what your ball did *on its path* to the pins.

Knowing what your ball did on each lane each time will allow you to make immediate adjustments. Watch to see if the lanes are changing (drying out, breaking down). Be prepared to change your angle, equipment, or delivery (or combinations of these three adjustment techniques) to keep the lanes working for you. Don't fight the lanes, adjust to them!

These 10 checkpoints should become automatic to you, similar to an airline pilot going through the checklist prior to takeoffs and landings. Practice these checkpoints on all your deliveries, including those for spares as well. When they become an automatic part of your game your success rate with strikes should increase rapidly. Concentrate on all your strike deliveries and you will improve your percentage of strikes, and that is the purpose of this book.

SECTION 2
READING THE LANES

"Read the lanes and adjust! Don't fight the lanes," Bob Lubin, Member, PBA.

CONTENTS PAGE

OVERVIEW

This section presents a comprehensive and detailed discussion of lane reading principles. *Reading a lane means determining what the ball and lane are doing together, how they are interacting.* Once you know what the ball is doing on the lane, then you can determine what angle, equipment or delivery adjustment you can make to get the ball into the pocket.

It is essential that you have a consistent, natural, and well-timed delivery in order to read lanes properly. SECTION 5 will discuss these aspects of the delivery for right handers and SECTION 8 will present them from the left hander's point of view. This present section will assume you are capable of delivering the ball in the same manner, on a consistent basis. (Volume 1 in this series, ***The Complete Guide to Bowling Principles,*** discusses methods for developing such a delivery!)

We begin the discussion of lane reading principles by looking at the lane as a total unit, indicating the *key factors* at each section of the lane. For purposes of analysis we have divided the lane into four portions: The approach; from the foul line to the arrows (called the headers); from the arrows to the pin deck (called the mid-lane); and the pin deck.

This is followed by a review of lane inspection and certification procedures. The emphasis of this discussion is a knowledge of the procedures used to inspect lanes to insure compliance with established criteria for lane maintenance. The purpose of the inspection and certification process is to insure uniformity in playing conditions throughout the bowling industry.

Once lanes have passed inspection and are certified for use, they must be conditioned (oiled) on a regular basis, and in accordance with guidelines set down by accrediting organizations. Some conditions are fair, others favor high scoring, while still others make scoring unnecessarily difficult. We will review all types of conditions, covering such topics as *a fair shot, lane blocking, reverse blocking,* etc.

Then we will begin our detailed discussion of the four portions or segments of the lane, beginning with THE APPROACH. We will attempt to point out, for each portion of the lane, the critical or key elements to look for as you begin to develop your ability to totally read a lane.

As a continuation of this overview section, we will now take a look at the total lane.

KEY FACTORS IN READING LANES: Exhibit 2-1 shows the lane from an overall point of view, but indicating the four segments or portions mentioned above. Within each lane portion there are specific clues you must look for, in order to completely read the lane.

We have included the approach as a portion of the lane. It is upon the approach that you take your stance, and it is here that the delivery takes place. A proper delivery requires some specific knowledge about the approach, particularly how you locate your stance location, how you align yourself for playing the various angles, how you determine your drift or walk pattern, etc.

Key phrases associated with each lane segment give a summary of the elements of the lane that are important for a proper understanding of lane reading principles. During the next few paragraphs we will summarize the main factors associated with each lane segment. Later in this section we will make a detailed analysis of all four portions of the lane. *This overview is provided as a frame of reference into which you can place all of the lane reading principles which follow.*

The Approach: Three key elements exist on the

EXHIBIT 2-1
Key Factors in Reading Lanes

The Pin Deck: The key terms in this portion of the lane include: the pocket; pin and ball deflection; the pocket angle; speed; action; clue pins; etc.

See Exhibit 2-7 The Pin Deck

From the Arrows to the Pin Deck: The key terms associated with this section of the lane include: lane track; conditioning line and pattern; break point and pocket angle; unusual lane conditions; etc. For purposes of discussion, we call this the *mid-lane* portion of the lane.

See Exhibit 2-6 From the Arrows to the Pin Deck

From the Foul Line to the Arrows: We refer to this lane section as *the headers,* or simply the *heads.* Key terms include: foul line angles; open and closed angles; skid; targeting; loft; etc.

See Exhibit 2-3 Foul Line to the Arrows

The Approach: We include this as part of the lane since all other lane factors are related to what you do on the approach. Key terms include: stance location (or sometimes called the *point of origin*); feet and body alignment; walk pattern (including drift); etc.

See Exhibit 2-2 The Approach

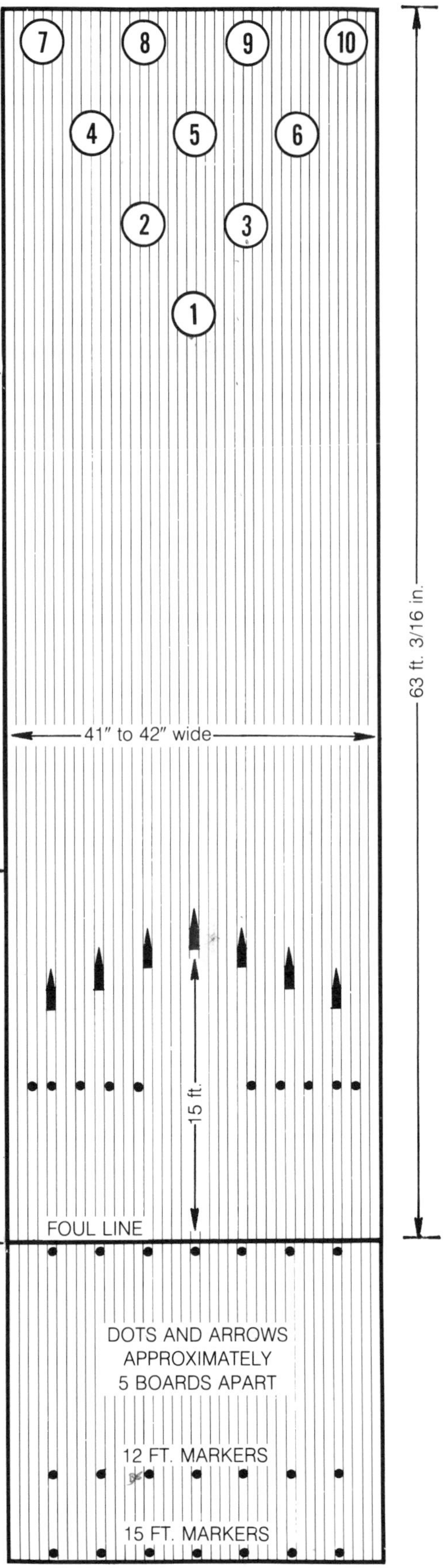

approach: The *stance location;* feet and body *alignment;* and your *walk pattern*. There is an exact place for you to take your stance for each foul line angle you play. This stance location (sometimes called point of origin) will depend upon the size and number of steps you take in your approach. We will indicate the proper procedures for determining exactly your stance location on every angle you play.

Proper alignment means that you are in a position to walk in a straight line, and deliver the ball in a straight line. You must align yourself to the intended path of the ball and not necessarily with the foul line. Your walk pattern should be straight in line with your target, but you might drift to the left or right. You must be able to calculate the amount and direction you drift. We will explain how this can be done. You must also know precisely the number of boards by which you miss your ankle with the center of the ball when you deliver the ball. We will also show you how to check this for yourself. Once you know your walk pattern and the number of boards by which you miss your ankle when you deliver the ball, you are in a position to make some very easy but accurate calculations for playing any strike angle.

From the Foul Line to the Arrows: This portion of the lane is sometimes called *the headers,* or simply the *heads*. Some of the key terms associated with this portion of the lane include: targeting or aiming; foul line angles; skid; open and closed angles; loft; etc. This 15 foot portion of the lane is considered by top bowlers to be vital to striking consistently. The ball should *skid* through this lane portion, and along an *angle* that you have decided is the best one to use on this lane at this point in time. Your targeting or aiming will occur within this lane segment, and you will loft the ball out on the lane at a variable distance, depending upon what you have decided about the lane.

At times you will play an angle that leads directly to the pocket. This is called a *closed* angle. At other times you will send the ball out to the side, and try to hook or curve it back to the pocket. Such an angle is called an *open* angle. Opening and closing your strike angle (adjusting the angle) is the major factor related to the portion of the lane from the foul line to the arrows. We will devote an entire section of this book to the subject of making angle adjustments to get the ball into the pocket (SECTION 3 for right handers and SECTION 6 for left handers).

From the Arrows to the Pin Deck: For purposes of discussion, we have called this section of the lane the *mid-lane*. Some of the key terms associated with the mid-lane are: the lane track; the break point; conditioning line; pocket angle; the back ends; pattern of conditioning; etc. This 45 foot section of the lane gives you many clues as to what is happening to the ball on its path to the pin deck. The lane track is an important feature of this segment of the lane for right handers, but is of far less significance to left handers. The break point, when the ball turns for the pocket, is of importance to both left and right handers. And both are concerned with the pattern of conditioning (the oil) on this portion of the lane, which includes an estimate of how far down the lane the oil has been placed (the conditioning line).

Many bowlers are very concerned with the last 15 feet of the mid-lane, the so-called *back ends*. What the ball does at this point down the lane will have a strong bearing on the pocket angle (the angle created when the ball makes its turn for the pocket). Thus, a proper reading of the mid-lane portion of the total lane is very important for a correct overall reading of the lane.

The Pin Deck: This is where everything happens, where the ball and the pins interact. Either all ten pins fall for a strike or you have a spare to convert. Key terms associated with this portion of the lane include: the pocket; the pocket angle; pin and ball deflection; ball speed and action; clue pins; etc.

You can learn much from watching what happens to the ball and the pins on the pin deck. Where did the ball contact the pins? From what angle? At what speed? With what action on the ball? Where did the ball leave the end of the pin deck? How did the clue pins (the 4, 5, and 6-pins) fall? What type of ball deflection occurred? What type of pin action happened? The answer to all of these questions can only be gained by following the path of the ball from the time it hits the pins until it leaves the end of the pin deck. Thus, reading the pin deck is an extremely important part of reading the lane. In fact, reading the pin deck properly, will practically suggest what angle, equipment, or delivery changes you will have to make if you are not striking.

These, briefly, are the four lane segments that will be presented in detail later in this section. Now, as a further part of our overall picture of lane reading principles, we will look at lane inspection and certification procedures.

LANE INSPECTION AND CERTIFICATION: All lanes undergo certification tests each year in order to get a *certification sticker.* Receipt of this sticker indicates that the lane has met certification standards, that the lane meets uniformity and tolerance levels. Some of the conditions for which lanes are tested include: the width of the lane; the depth of the pit; the width of the pit; the crosswise tilt of the pin deck; the lengthwise tilt of the pin deck; the level of the lane; the size of the pin spots; the thickness of the kickbacks; the location of the targeting arrows; and many other measurements.

Despite these tests to insure uniformity and consistency between lanes, lane conditions vary from bowling center to bowling center, and even within the same house. It might be safe to say that no two lanes are exactly alike, but there will be a great deal of similarity and uniformity among lanes that have been inspected and have passed the tests to which they were subjected.

After the inspection process is completed, the lanes are (hopefully) certified as meeting the standards set by the accrediting bodies. These groups or organizations are usually the American Bowling Congress (men); The Women's International Bowling Congress (women); or the women's or men's Professional Bowlers Association. Each organization assumes responsibility for the condition of the lanes upon which their sanctioned competitions are held.

Lanes must also be inspected periodically to insure that they are not falling into disrepair, or getting out of established tolerances. There is another time in which lanes are inspected. It is upon completion of any significant scoring activity, such as a perfect '300' game, an 800 series, a record high series, etc. After such occurrences, lanes are checked to determine if the scores were bowled upon *legal* or properly conditioned lanes. For a review of what constitutes *properly conditioned lanes,* we will now look at some of the methods used to prepare the lanes for play.

LANE CONDITIONING: Two distinct and different reasons exist for conditioning lanes: (1) to protect the lane surface from the pounding of a bowling ball, and (2) to provide a fair shot for the bowlers. A properly conditioned lane will meet both of these objectives.

A 16 pound bowling ball can sear or burn the wood in the lane. These burn spots are noticeable dark streaks found on lanes that have not been conditioned properly, or frequently enough to protect the lanes from such abuse. Proper lane conditioning provides a frictionless area, a skid area, a slide point on the header portion of the lane, to take the impact of the ball hitting the lane. This skid effect is directly related to the second reason for conditioning lanes.

A properly conditioned lane will provide a skid area of *at least* 15 feet. This skid will get the ball well down the lane before the ball begins to roll and then hook into the pocket. Getting the ball down the lane before the ball begins to hook gives the maximum opportunity to achieve the perfect pocket angle. If there is little or no skid, the ball will begin to roll and hook too soon, preventing an effective angle into the pocket.

The second reason for conditioning lanes brings us to the logical question: "What is a fair shot?" There may be varying answers to this question, but there are elements of an answer upon which there would be widespread agreement.

What is fair? The pattern of conditioning (oil) on the lanes will neither assist the bowler excessively in getting the ball into the pocket (a blocked condition) nor will it prevent the bowler from getting into the pocket when good shots are executed (called a reverse block). (Both types of conditions, blocked and reverse blocked, will be explained shortly!)

A fair shot is also one in which it is possible for the bowler to determine what his or her bowling ball will do under given conditions, such as increased speed, an angle change, more or less lift, etc. The ability of the bowler to read the interaction of the ball and lane is another ingredient in what we would describe as a fair shot.

A fair shot also exists when there are no erratic conditions on the lanes, such as an oil buildup, dry or wet spots, etc., other than those that occur because of lane usage. If the lanes are dressed properly, if a fair shot has been laid down, then the skill of the bowler is the major reason why he or she scores well. (Tom Kouros, author of *Par Bowling,* considers a fair shot to exist when both accuracy and action are required to score well.)

A wide variety of ways exist to condition lanes. But, there are three major types of lane conditions, three patterns of oil distribution commonly used. We will relate each oil pattern to its effect on the scoring potential of the lane.

Pattern A. (Realistic Scoring Potential) Oil is evenly placed across the width of the lane and taken down approximately 30 feet from the foul line. This means that about one half of the lane is oiled (conditioned), and the back ends are relatively free of oil. With such a pattern, scoring will be realistic, that is, you can score well if you are able to adapt to the lane, use the correct ball, select the proper angle, and deliver the ball well. If you bowl well, you should score well. If you bowl poorly, you should score poorly.

Pattern B. (High Scoring Potential) Oil is placed heavily in the middle of the lane and the outside portions are dry or contain very little oil. High scoring is very possible, and it is very normal to score well under such an oil pattern. The oil is taken down the same 30 feet, or about half the distance from the foul line to the pin deck. With this condition the ball will maintain the same path to the pocket for a long period of time, with only minor adjustments needed.

Pattern C. (High Scoring Potential) The oil pattern is blended or tapered across the entire lane. (This pattern is often called a *blend or tapered* condition for obvious reasons.) There is a *crown of oil* in the center of the lane, and the oil is tapered (lessened) toward the sides of the lane. You can get good ball reaction under this blended condition, and high scoring is a real possibility. The oil is also taken down about 30 feet, with the back end of the lane relatively dry.

These three patterns of oil distribution give rise to three additional conditions. The pattern *across the lane* is the same, but the oil is only placed on the first 15 or so feet of the lane, and *not* down to 30 feet. This creates 6 different oil patterns, the three mentioned above at the 30 foot mark, and each one with oil only down to the arrows (15 feet from the foul line).

When the oil only covers the first 15 feet of the lane, there are three specific adjustments you can make to improve your scoring potential (although you should expect lower scoring under such conditions). You can use a harder ball surface, move to the inside angles, or reduce the amount of lift you impart on the ball. These adjustments are designed to delay the break or hook of the ball, which will tend to occur too soon when only 15 feet of the lane contains oil.

Another factor contributing to the scoring potential of a lane, is the *amount* of oil or conditioner placed on the lane. The amount of oil could be heavy, moderate to heavy, light to medium, or very light to dry. And each of the amount variations could be combined with the six patterns described above to initially create a wide variety of scoring conditions. These *initial conditions* will change over time and with use of the lane.

When we say *the lanes are changing,* we mean the lanes are *drying up,* are causing the ball to hook more than the initial condition created. Thus lane reading becomes an effort to determine how fast the lanes are *drying up,* and what is causing the change in lane surface.

Four factors contribute to the *speed* with which lanes change and the *amount* of change that takes place. (1) *The Surface of the Lane:* Is the lane of a natural wood that will absorb the oil dressing? Is the lane of an artifical surface material that prevents absorption of oil, and causes the oil to spread on the top of the lane? Does the surface retard or prevent the spreading of the conditioner? (2) *The Initial Amount and Pattern of Lane Dressing:* How much oil is on the lane, how is it distributed, and how far down the lane does the condition extend?

Answers to these questions will tell you how to start playing the lane and will give you some indication of the way in which the lane will change during play. (3) *The Pattern of Use or Play:* Heavy use or play around the 2nd arrow or any other part of the lane will cause that part of the lane to lose its oil, and will re-distribute the oil on the lane surface. The lane track situation is created by heavy traffic of balls going over a small part of the lane. (4) *Atmospheric Conditions:* Temperature and humidity affect the rate of change in lane conditioning. Hot temperatures cause the oil to evaporate more quickly than cooler temperatures. Humidity will cause the lanes to dry out *less* rapidly, since there is already moisture in the surrounding air. Dry air on the other hand will cause the lanes to dry out more rapidly, as the air accepts the moisture from the lane dressing.

In summary, the lanes will change during play. How quickly or how slowly the lanes change will depend upon the four factors mentioned above. Lanes change most rapidly where there is a porous surface, with high heat and low humidity, and heavy ball traffic over a given part of the lane. Lanes change less rapidly under the opposite conditions.

It should be obvious that the time of the day, the day of the week, the season of the year, the location of the lanes with respect to air conditioning and doors, etc., all determine how the lanes will change. But the lanes *will* change, and this is the most significant factor to keep in mind if you are going to continue to play lanes properly. Keep reading the lanes and keep adjusting when you have to do so.

The above discussion suggests that lanes can be conditioned (or could change) in such a manner that the skill of the bowler is negated. That is, the lanes will *not* allow good scoring or *will* allow unnecessarily high scoring by anyone with a medium amount of skill in rolling the ball down the lanes. This is true! You can initially condition lanes that are favorable to high scoring, or *lay down a condition* that does not favor high scoring.

Conditioning lanes in either manner, giving or taking away the pocket, is called *blocking.* Many bowlers prefer to call taking away the shot as *reverse blocking* and giving the pocket as *blocking.* We will use these two terms (blocking and reverse blocking) since they identify both extremes in creating an unfair lane condition. Let's look at each term in detail.

Blocking can be created by laying a heavy (heavier than normal) streak of oil down the lane. This strip of oil would extend from the foul line to about 40 or more feet, and will cover boards 8 through 8 from the right side of the lane to the left side. Boards 1 thru 7 on the left and right would be relative free of oil or have a light coating. Such a blocked condition would favor both left and right handers. The first 7 boards may only be conditioned down to 30 feet beyond the foul line, enough to give the desired skid pattern through the heads (the first 15 feet of the lane). When the ball began to hook toward the pocket, the heavy oil strip would stop or slow down the hook, and guide the ball into the pocket, just as though a wall had been built down the 17th board. It would be extremely difficult to hit the pocket too high, or to cross over to either brooklyn side. The *wall of oil* would straighten out the shot and lead the ball to the pocket.

Reverse Blocking, on the other hand, is created in just the opposite manner from the block. The outside portion of the lane would contain a great deal of oil (be *flooded with oil*) and the inside portion would be *bone dry.* Perhaps the first 7 boards on the left and right sides would contain the oil and the inner boards (from 8 to 8) would be very dry. Under such a conditioning pattern it is difficult to get the ball into the pocket on any consistent basis.

If the ball is rolled *down the outside* of the lane it will not be able to hook effectively to the pocket. The heavy oil pattern will cause the ball to skid too much. If the ball is rolled *down the inside* portion of the lane (the dry portion) the ball will hook too soon and often too much. An effective skid is difficult to achieve. If the ball is rolled on *an open angle* (out to the side), the ball will not be able to get into an effective roll and hook pattern. Using *a closed angle,* and heading the ball directly toward the pocket is also ineffective. The ball will begin to hook strongly once it enters the dry portion of the lane, requiring an extremely accurate shot to the pocket to score with any degree of consistency.

Trying to adjust to a reverse block usually results in delivery changes, thereby making it difficult to consistently deliver the ball in the normal manner. High scoring under such adverse conditions is usually a matter of luck rather than skill. Lanes so conditioned are often referred to as *grave yards,* for obvious reasons. Your scoring potential is *dead* under such conditions.

Between the extremes of blocked or reverse blocked lanes are a wide range of alternative forms of lane dressing or conditioning. Strips of alternating oil and dry spots could be placed on the lane. Areas of the lane could be either flooded with oil or left bone dry. The amount of lane dressing could be of varying thickness. The distance down the lane that the oil is spread can be anywhere from 15 to 45 or more feet. The width of the area of conditioning across the lane can be narrow or could go from gutter to gutter. All of these lane conditioning situations can and do occur on occasion, either by accident or on purpose. Improper maintenance of lane conditioning equipment and poor training of lane maintenance personnel are two of the most likely causes for improper lane conditioning. Deliberate conditioning to give or take away the shot also occurs.

A knowledge of the vast range of conditioning patterns is essential to a good understanding of lanes. Your best clues as to the pattern that exists come from a careful reading of the interaction of the ball on the lane. In the next four parts of this section on lanes we will try to give you a sound basis for reading the lanes.

Following the discussion of these four portions of the lane, we will present a list of lane-related terms. These terms can increase your knowledge of this important aspect of making strikes.

THE APPROACH

"The approach is where it all happens for the bowler. It is where the ball and the bowler interact in what is called the delivery."

Any discussion of the lanes would normally begin at the foul line. To do so is to omit an important part of the total lane, the approach. The physical construction of the approach is of vital importance to the serious bowler. Knowing how to *read the approach* is critical to any effort to improve the percentage of strikes. That is why we include the approach as a part of the discussion of lane reading principles.

Three major factors are associated with the approach portion of the lane: (1) your stance *distance behind* the foul line; (2) your feet, body, and shoulder *alignment* with reference to the boards on the approach and your target on the lane, and (3) your *walk pattern* from the time you begin your delivery of the ball until you complete your slide at the foul line. Reading the approach means paying attention to these three important items.

The approach is where it all happens for the bowler. It is where the bowler and the ball interact together in what is called the delivery. It is the only time in which you, the bowler, are involved in the strike delivery. Once the ball is released, the ball and lane interact until the ball reaches the pin deck. On the pin deck the ball and the pins interact in what you hope will be perfect pin and ball deflection

EXHIBIT 2-2
The Approach

The approach is 15 feet in length, with dots imbedded in the boards at the Foul Line, 12 feet behind the Foul Line, and sometimes 15 feet as well. These dots are helpful in determining your stance location and walk pattern. Some lanes have 7 dots at the 12 and 15 foot markers, but others have only 5 dots.

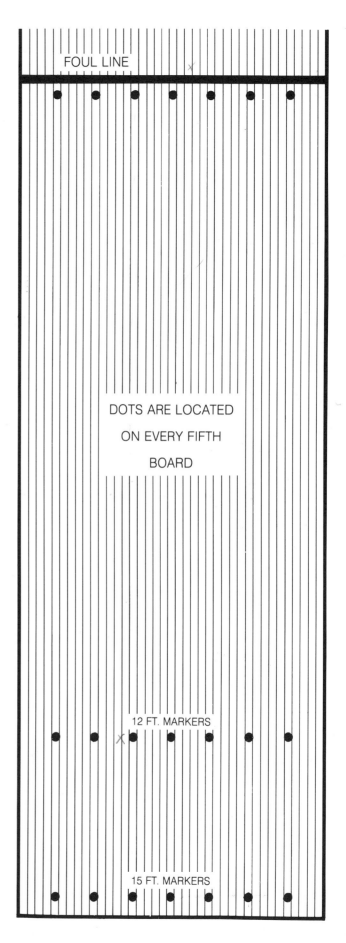

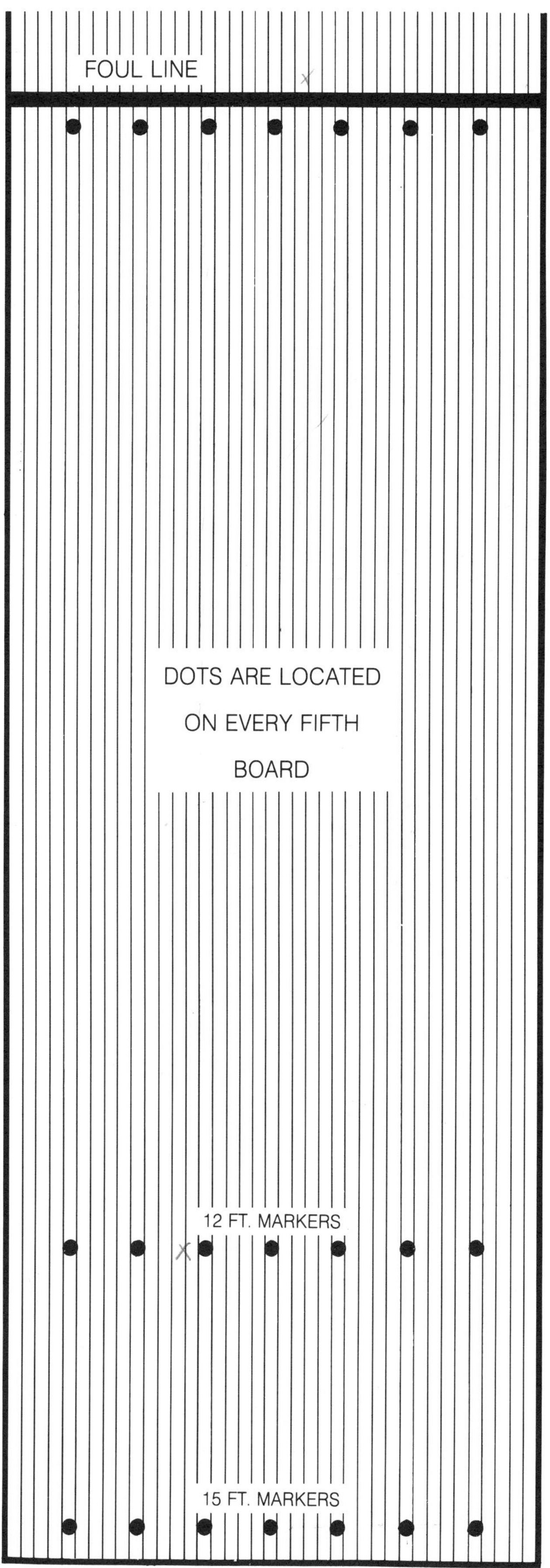

for a strike. There is no further human intervention once the ball leaves your hand.

Since there is nothing more you can do with the ball once it leaves your hand, you must decide *in advance* everything you want to happen to the ball while it is on the lane. All of this takes place, for you, on the approach. Therefore, this is where you should concentrate all your efforts, since delivery of the ball is all you ever do.

What do you need to know about the approach to aid you in a total understanding of the lane? You need to know exactly where and how to take your stance on the approach, and how to get the ball onto the lane properly. We will now take the three factors that help you do this, *stance, feet and body alignment,* and *walk pattern,* and look at each one in detail.

The Stance: For our purposes the stance location (sometimes called the point of origin) will be the exact distance you stand behind the foul line as you begin the delivery. It is concerned with alignment with the boards on the approach and your location with reference to the center of the approach. Either you are at the center, or to the left or right of center.

Your exact stance location consists of two distance measurements: How far behind the foul line you are, and how far you are away from the center of the approach (in number of boards). These are the two critical measurements you have to know so your stance on the approach will be correct and consistent from delivery to delivery. The horizontal distance with regard to the center of the approach will be covered in more detail in SECTION 3 (RHB) and SECTION 6 (LHB) under angle adjustments. These are moves to the left or right on the approach in order to create some angle into the pocket. Scientific methods are available for determining exactly how many boards you move on either side of the approach to properly play various strike angles. For now, we will focus on how far behind the foul line you should stand.

Basically, that distance is the *number of steps you take* in your normal delivery, *plus ½ of a step* to allow for the slide at the foul line. If you have a four step delivery, stand at the foul line, facing *away* from the pins. Take your normal four steps away from the foul line, and then take about ½ additional step to account for the slide. Turn around and face the foul line. This is *the first estimate* of your starting point behind the foul line.

To validate this distance, take your stance in the center of the approach at the spot you have just determined as proper for you. Align the inner side of your sliding foot (left foot for RHB and right foot for LHB) with the center dot on the approach, board 20. NOTE: Sliding on the foot that is the opposite from the arm you use is a widely accepted standard for scoring well. Proper balance is the benefit from doing this, although cases exist where LHB slide with the left foot and right handers slide with the right foot.

The location you have selected, the 20th board, should be marked by a small dowel or dot imbedded in the lane. You may be near that dot, or in front or behind it, depending upon the number and size of the steps you take in your approach. These locator dots are in the approach to help you locate your proper stance position each time.

Now, let's check to see if you have found the proper distance behind the foul line for you. From this centrally located stance position, deliver the ball in your normal manner. Do not be concerned with the result of the shot, only with the distance you have stopped behind the foul line. If you end as close to the foul line as you wish to be, then you have located the correct distance behind the foul line for your stance. If not, then make some forward or backward adjustment from that previous stance location and deliver the ball again. Repeat this process until you have found the exact distance behind the foul line that is correct for your delivery.

Use this distance for your stance each time you bowl unless something happens to cause you to move closer to or further away from the foul line. A slide that ends within three inches behind the foul line should be adequate, but there is room for variation, depending upon what feels comfortable to you. Once you have determined the correct stance location for you, try to keep it constant unless you make some basic change in your delivery (add or subtract steps, lengthen or shorten the steps, change the slide, change foot speed, etc.). It is important that you start your stance from the identical distance behind the foul line each time, unless you know why you are moving in closer or further back.

Alignment of feet, body and shoulders: This is the second major factor related to your knowledge of the approach. *Your feet should be pointed in a direct line with your target on the lane. Your body and shoulders should be squared to that line.* At times you will be lined up exactly alongside the boards on the approach. At other times you will be at a slight left or right angle to these boards. But at all times you should be pointed in a direct line toward your target on the lane and squared to that target with your body and shoulders.

If you are playing straight down any particular board, say the 10th board, then you align yourself parallel to the boards on the approach. Walk in a straight line to the foul line and release the ball down the tenth board (more on this later). It is only when you are playing straight down any particular board that you are lined up parallel to (alongside) the boards on the approach. At all other times, you will be at some angle to the approach boards.

If you are playing the ball to go out to the side of the lane before it begins its break to the pocket (for those of you using a curve, hook, or backup ball delivery) then you align yourself to the target on the lane and not the boards on the approach. You will be at some angle to the boards on the approach, but facing in a straight line toward your target on the lane.

If you are rolling the ball in a direct line toward the pocket from either side of the lane (left side for the LHB and right side for the RHB) you should face your target on the lane and take a stance that is at some slight angle to the boards on the approach. The key point is that you always *align yourself to face the target,* and only sometimes will you also be in alignment with the boards on the approach. This only occurs when you plan to roll the ball straight down one particular board.

Proper alignment is almost like being on a pivot point. When you are aiming to the left, you are aligned or facing to the left on the approach. When you are aiming to the right, pivot and align yourself to the right. When you are aiming straight down the lane, align yourself in a straight line with the boards on the approach.

We have now determined how far back from the foul line you should stand when you take your stance on the approach. We have shown you how to align your feet, body, and shoulders to the intended path of the ball down the lane, to the target on the lane. Now you must consider your walk pattern, from the time you leave your stance position until you have completed your slide at the foul line.

The Walk Pattern: Your walk pattern describes the path you take from your stance location to the foul line. It can be in a straight line, or you could *drift* to the left or right on your way to the foul line. *A straight line is generally conceded to be desirable,* but as with so many rules and guidelines, there are many exceptions to this one.

For the moment let's agree that the ideal walk pattern is a straight walk toward the target, *not necessarily the foul line.* This is an important point. You should walk in a straight line toward your target at all times, but you may be walking toward the foul line at a slight angle, if you are playing the ball out to the side of the lane or from a corner of the approach toward the pocket.

Walk directly toward your target, deliver the ball in what has been described as a *pendulum swing* in a straight line through your intended strike angle. The ball will be swinging by your side as you approach the foul line and slide. The center of the ball should miss your ankle by about 7 boards as it passes your sliding foot at the foul line. (More on this later). This straight-line walk pattern with a parallel pendulum swing is considered to be the ideal delivery, a natural or classic delivery. However, there is no reason to assume that your walk pattern is incorrect if you do not do this. Virtually any walk pattern or ball swing can be effective if you perfect it and incorporate it into a successful style for you.

If you drift either to the left or the right in your walk pattern (you do not walk in a straight line toward the target on the lane) then you need to know (1) *how many boards* and (2) in *what direction* you drift. You then have one of two choices: try to eliminate the drift and develop a straight walk pattern, or incorporate the drift into your normal style of bowling. With a drift pattern of 3 boards or less, you can incorporate the drift into your walk pattern with little or no difficulty. A drift of over 3 boards should be reduced to 3 boards or less, or eliminated altogether.

Again, as with all rules of thumb, almost *any drift pattern* can be incorporated into a successful style of ball delivery and walk pattern with sufficient practice. We suggest these guidelines only to help you assess what you wish to do with your drift pattern should you have one. As long as you have a drift that is (A) reasonable for your style, (B) incorporated into your natural game, and (C) kept in mind in making all angle and delivery calculations, then the drift should represent no problem for you.

How can you determine the amount of your drift, if you have one? Take your normal stance position, but align yourself with the 20th board on the approach. This is the center of the approach, and allows you to make the most natural delivery. Take your normal walk pattern to the foul line and deliver the ball as normally as you can. Use as your target the second arrow, or slightly to either side of it. Do not concern yourself with the result of the shot, but hold your stance at the foul line and mark the board you ended upon. If it is the 20th board (where you took your stance position) then you have no drift. Try this same delivery several times to see if you have a straight walk pattern or a left or right drift. Finishing on any board other than the 20th one will tell you *how much* and *in what direction* you drift. You can then decide whether you will incorporate the drift into your normal style, or try to reduce or eliminate it entirely.

You can determine *how many boards by which you miss your ankle with the center of the ball* in a similar manner. With the approval of the center manager or your instructor, tape a piece of paper on the lane at the foul line, covering boards 10 to 20. Take your same stance in the center of the approach, lined up with the 20th board. Walk to the foul line in your normal walk pattern. Release the ball so that it hits the paper, and hold your stance at the foul line. The inside of your sliding foot will give you one number (say it was the 20th board, no drift) and the board number where the ball ripped the paper will give you another number (say the 13th board). The difference between these two numbers tells you how many boards by which you missed your ankle, (in this example, you missed by 7 boards). Repeat this procedure several times to get the exact number of boards by which the center of the ball misses your ankle. This number is vital in aligning yourself to the various strike lines and angles, and in making adjustments from one angle to another. (We will use this number later.)

Your drift pattern (if you have any drift) and the number of boards by which you miss your ankle with the center of the ball are two very important numbers to know.

They will, quite obviously, vary for bowlers of differing walk patterns, drifts, body widths, arm swings, etc. They are *personal numbers* which are only important to you. If you do not know what your two personal numbers are, then you should make some effort in the near future to determine exactly what each one is. You will find that most bowlers miss their ankle by 6, 7 or 8 boards, but drift patterns vary too much to make general statements. A small amount of drift is neither good nor bad. It is something you have to keep in mind as you are making calculations for playing the lanes and aligning yourself for your strike ball deliveries.

These, then, are the key ingredients in reading the approach portion of the lane: (1) determine exactly how far behind the foul line you should stand; (2) properly align your body and feet for any angle you are playing; (3) develop a consistent walk pattern to the foul line; (4) know how many boards and in what direction you drift (if you must drift); and (5) know how many boards by which you miss your ankle with the center of the ball when you deliver it.

In summary, properly reading and understanding the approach means knowing exactly what you have to do to get the ball to the foul line and onto the lane exactly as you have planned to do. It means coordinating your steps in the delivery with swinging the ball through your intended line and angle. It means getting the ball out on the lane in exactly the correct strike angle that you have determined is the best strike line for this lane at this point in time, considering the nature of the equipment you are using. Once the ball is released there is nothing more you can do.

Now we move to the second portion of the lane, from the foul line to the arrows located approximately 15 feet beyond the foul line. Correctly reading this part of the lane will determine where you stand and your walk pattern to the foul line. In fact, a case could be made that the lane should be read from the pin deck back to the approach. However, for purposes of analysis only, we will continue to discuss the lane from the perspective of the approach to the pin deck. Once you have a knowledge of each portion of the lane, you will be able to integrate this information into a total reading of the complete lane.

HEADERS (From Foul Line to Arrows)

"If you can master the first 15 feet of the lane, then you can master the lane," Ernie Schlegel, Professional Bowler.

The portion of the lane from the foul line to the arrows imbedded in the lane is often referred to as *the headers,* or simply *the heads.* It is this 15 or so feet of the lane which starts the ball on its path to the pins. Once the ball is on the lane, you are out of the picture. The ball and the lane are going to interact, and there is nothing more you can do to influence the ball to the pocket. It is therefore, very important to study the headers to get a proper reading of what the ball and lane are going to do together, and decide what you must do to get the ball into the right path to the pins.

The *interaction* of the *surface of the ball* with the *surface of the lane* is considered by many students of bowling to be the most important aspect of both the strike and spare deliveries. There is no human intervention after the ball leaves the hand of the bowler. Once on the lane, the ball surface and lane surface interact in what you hope will bring the ball into a path to the pocket with the correct speed, angle and action for the perfect strike. Since ball surfaces and lane surfaces vary in their degree of hardness (or softness), and lanes can be conditioned in a number of ways, the opportunity exists for a wide range of reactions between the two surfaces.

EXHIBIT 2-3
The Headers (From the Foul Line to the Arrows)

This 15 foot section of the lane has Arrows imbedded on every fifth board, and dots on boards 3, 5, 8, 11, and 14. These lane features can be of assistance in locating the proper line and angle for all lane conditions.

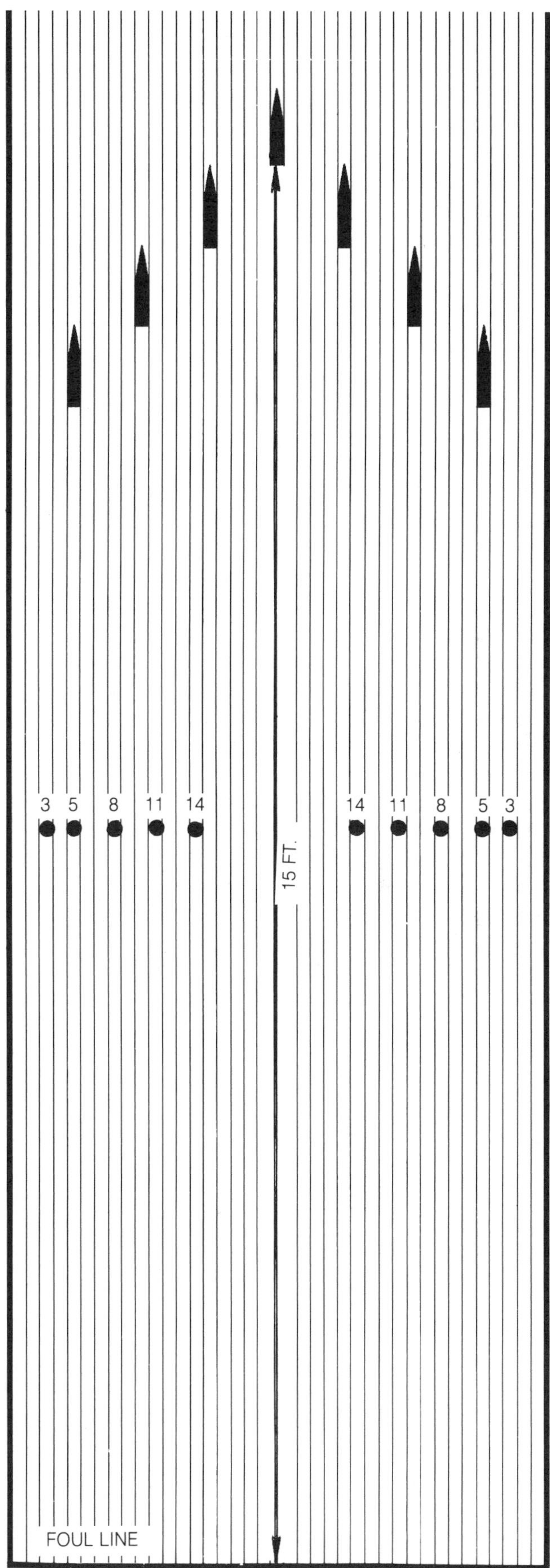

Moreover, the lane surface changes with use, as the conditioner is either removed from the lane by the ball or is spread around to form patterns of dry or wet spots. Equipment selection (ball surfaces, weights and balances, fits, etc.) and lane reading are therefore the major concerns of those who aspire to higher bowling averages. And actual lane reading begins with the headers.

This portion of the lane must be constructed of a very durable material. It has to take the pounding of 16 pound bowling balls thrown on it over and over again. Where natural wood is used (not artificial lanes) the headers are made of very hard maple. Beyond the arrows there is a splice where the pine begins, and this continues to the pin deck, which is made of the same hard maple. The impact of a bowling ball on the lane surface may generate enough heat to actually create burn marks on the lane. If a softer wood were used, many dents would be placed in the lanes.

The wood at the headers is covered with a substance to protect the surface, such as lacquer. Recently many types of protective surfaces have been developed, as well as artificial substances to be used for the headers or the entire lane.

In addition, a surface conditioning program is an on-going process in any bowling center. The conditioning program is designed to protect the lane surface, and to give the bowler a fair shot (one that does not give the bowler undue help in getting the ball into the pocket, nor does it make it difficult to get the ball into the pocket). On occasion, the header portion of the lane will be *double oiled* to protect the lane surface. This creates a highly slick surface, one that allows for maximum skidding of the ball from the foul line to the arrows.

In reading the headers, several terms will be discussed. These include: *Skid, Loft, Foul Line Angle,* and *Aiming.* We will begin the discussion with the first item, *Skid.*

Skid: The ball is supposed to skid, roll and then hook on its path to the pocket. Therefore, the headers should be conditioned to permit this early skid, and the conditioner or oil should be placed down the lane far enough to permit the proper amount of skid. Skid delays the hook of the ball until it is further down the lane, creating a situation in which the hook can be delayed until it is ideal for the perfect pocket angle.

If the headers are not conditioned (oiled) properly, the ball will not skid as much as it should, and may even begin its roll or hook well in advance of the ideal break point down the lane. Either the ball hooks too much and hits too high into the pocket or crosses over to the brooklyn side, or the ball *rolls out* by the time it reaches the pocket. (The ball loses its drive or pocket action because it has rolled or hooked too soon.)

Getting through the heads properly is a phrase you will often hear around high average bowlers. It means, among other things, the ball has been delivered in such a manner that it will not begin its roll and hook until it is well down the lane, perhaps 30 feet or so. The hook will break for the pocket anywhere from 10 to 15 feet in front of the pin deck. When you cannot get through the heads properly, you have to make some other adjustment to get the ball to delay its break point (such as moving to inside strike angles, using a ball with a harder surface, increasing the speed of the ball, increasing loft, etc.). Such adjustments, if they have to be made when the headers are not conditioned properly, often cause you to become inconsistent and to alter your game, thereby reducing your chances for scoring well. Properly conditioned headers will allow you to get through the heads well, and to use your normal style of bowling.

Loft: This is the next term associated with the header portion of the lane. The term loft refers to the distance out on the lane that the ball travels before it makes contact with the lane. This might be from 12 to 18 inches, or it could be as much as 5 or 6 feet. The full uses of loft will be discussed in the DELIVERY ADJUSTMENTS section of this book, so we will only briefly touch upon it here.

The ball should be lofted *gently* out on the lane beyond the foul line. It may only travel 12 to 18 inches as a general rule, a distance sufficient to provide the proper amount of skid. Too little loft may cause the ball to skid less than desirable, causing the ball to begin its roll and hook too early. Too much loft would, of course, have the reverse effect, causing the ball to skid more than necessary and create a late-breaking situation.

The conditioning on the headers, as well as the conditions found on the entire length of the lane, will dictate how much loft is correct. On dry headers, or dry lanes, more loft might be necessary to prevent an early roll and hook. On extremely wet or oily headers, less loft may be correct.

Under no circumstances should the ball be lofted in a high arc out on the lane. Not only is this bad for the lane, but it is difficult to maintain control of such a ball. *A gradual and gentle arc out on the lane is the best kind of loft,* both for control and for care of the lane.

Aiming: All aiming or targeting begins at the headers, and in many cases it ends there too. The only exception is in the case of those who use the pins for their aiming. But line and spot bowlers always use the headers for their aiming.

To assist in this aiming or targeting process,

arrows (rangefinders) are imbedded in the lane approximately 15 feet beyond the foul line. There are 7 such targeting arrows, located on the 5th board, 10th, 15th, etc. across the lane. The fourth arrow is located on the 20th board, the center of the lane and it is the farthest arrow from the foul line. (See Exhibit 2-3.)

Each arrow is separated from the adjoining one by four boards. *But, this is not always the case.* In many instances there may be five or six boards between some of the arrows, particularly with artificial lanes. Check for this condition where you bowl. A one board difference in aiming or targeting is a very big difference at the pin deck. (It means a possible miss of 3 boards at the pin deck.)

A related problem exists with some lanes: the boards do not align at the splice just beyond these targeting arrows. This can also create a problem in your aiming. Therefore, you should examine this portion of the lane carefully, since all of your aiming will be based upon what you see or think you see on the lane.

Another assist in your aiming is a set of dots or dowels imbedded out on the lane at about the 7 foot mark. These dowels are located or positioned on boards 3, 5, 8, 11 and 14 on both the left and right sides of the lane. These can be particularly useful for those of you who like to pick a target relatively close to the foul line. Such a method of aiming is often used with the outside strike angles.

Once the ball is placed on the lane, its path to the pins has been determined. If you have aimed and targeted properly, you should get the results you want at the pin deck. If you have made an error in your aiming, or have failed to hit your target on the lane, there is nothing further you can do with the ball. So let's discuss the next factor associated with the headers, one directly related to aiming—the Foul Line Angle.

The Foul Line Angle: This is an angle created by drawing a straight line between the board the center of the ball crosses over *at the foul line* and the board *at the arrows.* Even if you loft the ball out over the foul line, its center will pass over a specific board at the foul line. And this board is the one used in calculating the foul line angle.

Exhibits 2-4 and 2-5 illustrate the foul line angle concept for right and left handers. (This angle is sometimes called a *header angle.*) *In the examples which follow, boards will be numbered from the right side of the lane for RHB and the left side of the lane for left handed bowlers.*

The foul line angle can be *straight down* the lane (called a straight angle) or the angle could be headed *toward the pocket* or *away from the pocket.* Which angle you decide to use will be largely determined by the condition of the lane. Angles toward the pocket are called *closed* angles, and those heading away from the pocket are called *open* angles. Closed angles are normally used when the lanes are not hooking and open angles are used when the lanes are hooking.

Every foul line angle is referred to by two numbers: the first number indicates the board at the foul line and the second number refers to the board at the arrows. To clarify this concept, we will look at examples of *straight, open* and *closed* foul line angles.

A *straight* angle is created when the board at the foul line is the same as the number of the board at the arrows, such as in the 10-to-10 angle. *The first number refers to the board at the foul line and the second number is the board at the arrows.* Since both numbers are the same, this angle describes a path straight down the 10th board. (To repeat, if you are a left hander, this refers to the 10th board from the left side of the lane. If you are right handed, it refers to the 10th board from the right side.) A 9-to-9 foul line angle is still a straight angle, directly down the 9th board.

Any time the two numbers in the angle are different, an open or closed angle is indicated. When the *first number* (the board at the foul line) *is larger* than the second number (the board at the arrows) the angle is said to be *open.* For example, the 12-to-10 foul line angle is open and describes the 12th board at the foul line and the 10th board at the arrows. Other open angles would include the 11-to-9 angle; the 15-to-10 angle; the 20-to-18 angle; etc.

When the *first number is smaller* than the second, then a *closed* angle is indicated. The 8-to-10 angle is closed, indicating that the ball travels from the 8th board at the foul line to the 10th board at the arrows. Other examples of closed angles would be: 9-to-11; 3-to-5; 5-to-7; etc.

Another way to look at foul line angles is related to how you move on the approach. When you move toward the center of the approach you will be rolling the ball out to the side of the lane, thereby opening the angle. The ball will be heading away from the pocket instead of toward it. When you move toward the outside portion of the approach, you are closing the angle. The ball will be heading more directly toward the pocket. (In a later section we will return to a discussion of foul line angles, in reference to a personal formula for adjusting your position on the approach for playing any foul line angle you select to play.) But, why would you want to open or close the foul line angle? Closing the angle is an adjustment to get the ball up to the pocket when you have failed to do so. Opening the angle is an adjustment to get the ball back to the pocket after you have hit the pocket too fully, or have crossed over to the

EXHIBIT 2-4
Straight, Open and Closed Foul Line Angles (RHB Only)

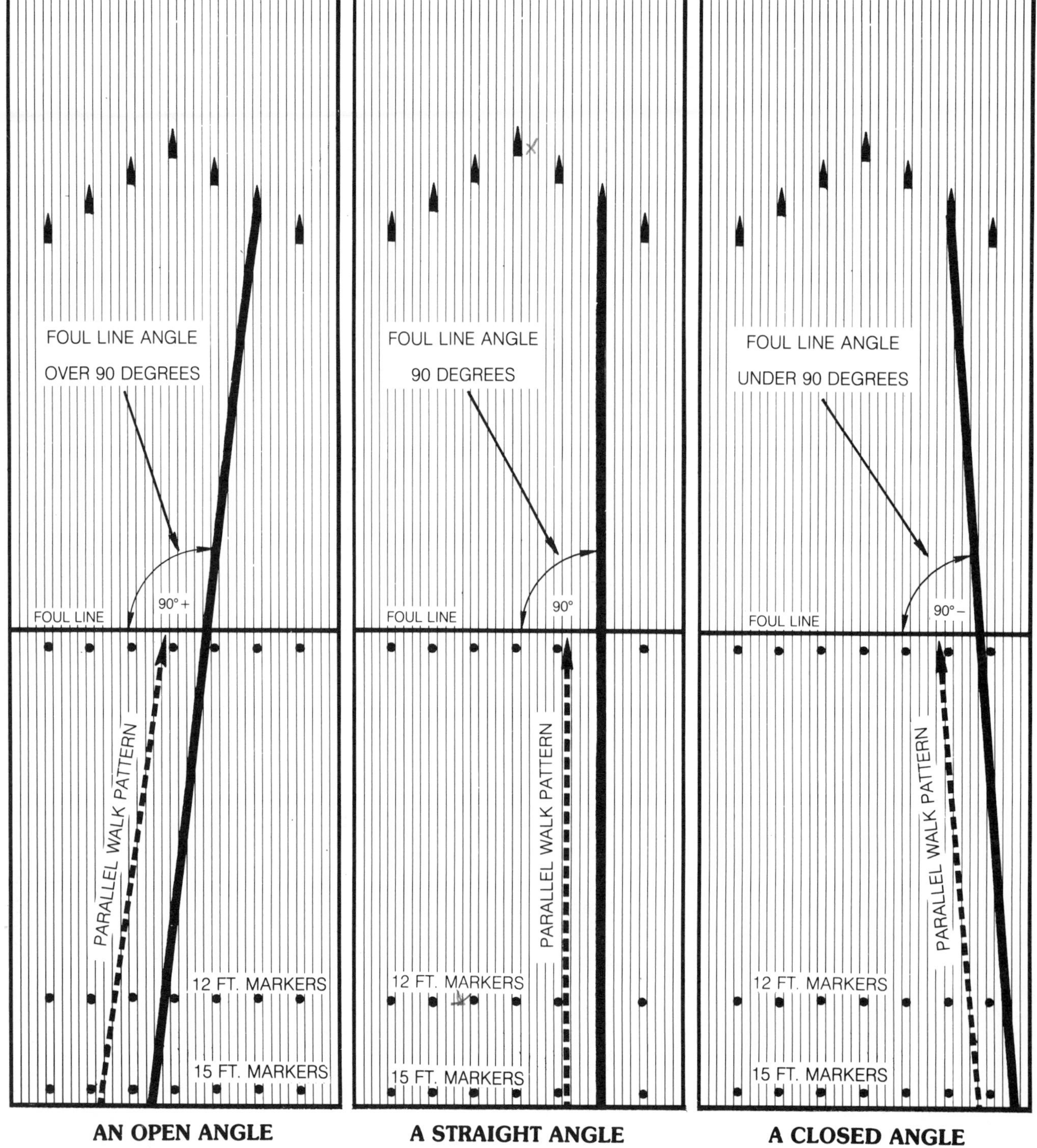

AN OPEN ANGLE **A STRAIGHT ANGLE** **A CLOSED ANGLE**

EXHIBIT 2-5
Straight, Open and Closed Foul Line Angles (LHB Only)

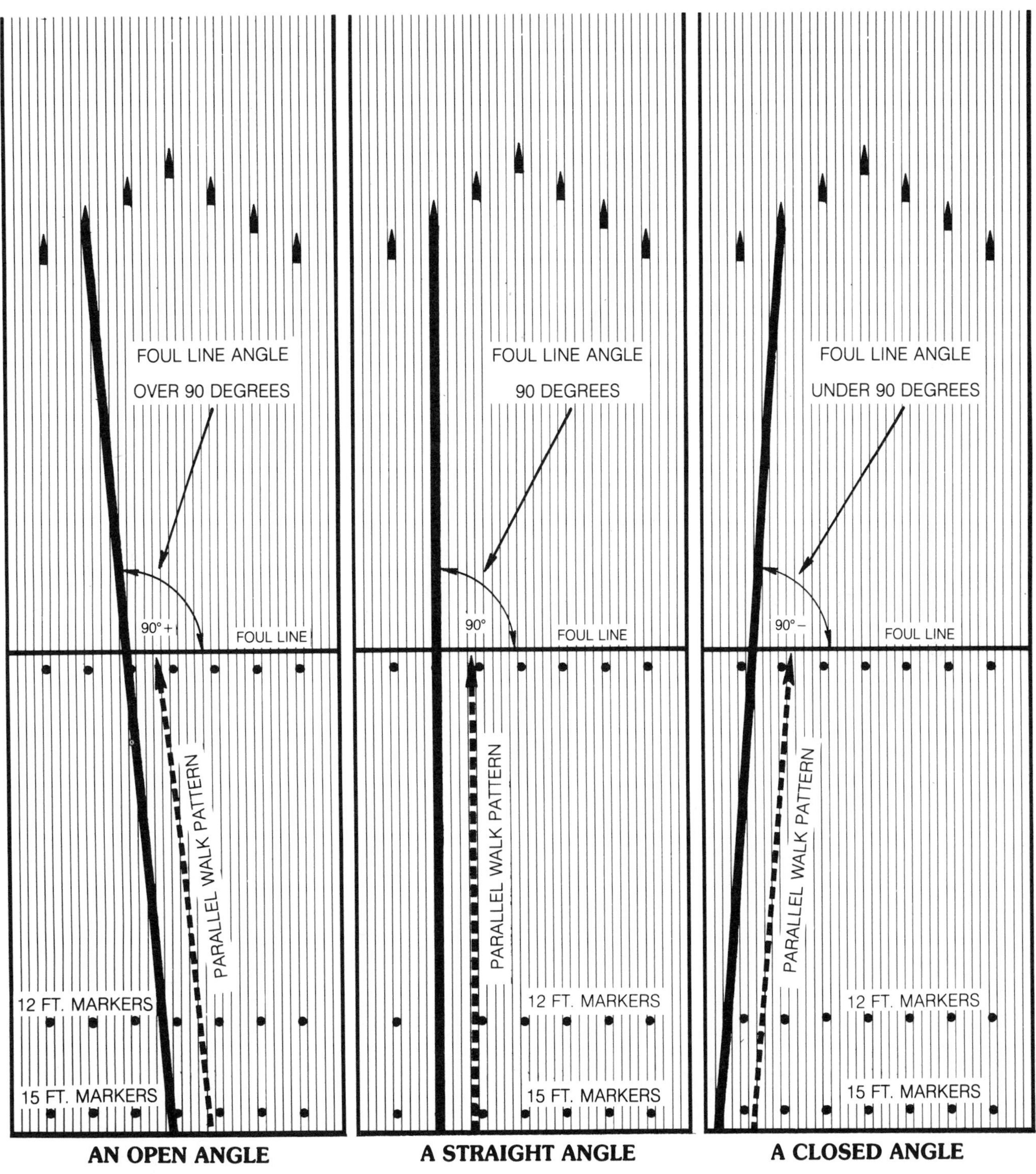

brooklyn side of the head pin.

If the lane is not hooking very well, then you might wish to roll the ball more directly toward the pocket. Therefore, you would close the angle of the shot. If the lane is hooking too much (is very dry), then you would open the angle to get the ball further down the lane before it began its break toward the pocket. (Of course these two adjustments assumed that you decided upon an angle change, instead of changing your equipment or delivery.) The foul line angle adjustment is, therefore, directly related to the condition of the lane, and whether you have to adjust to get the ball *up to* or *back to* the pocket. If you use the 12-to-9 angle and hit the pocket too fully, you might decide to open the angle slightly by playing a 13-to-9 angle. If the 12-to-9 angle is too light in the pocket, then closing the angle slightly to the 11-to-9 foul line angle might get the ball up to the pocket.

The *foul line angle* is different from, but related to, the *pocket angle* which we will discuss next under the mid-lane portion of the lane. The two angles represent the beginning and the end of the path of the ball to the pins. As such, these two angles are very important parts of the lane reading process. And, although we have separated the lane into four portions for purposes of analysis, it should be evident that you must consider the total lane in every delivery you make. Now we will move to a discussion of the next portion of the lane, from the arrows to the pin deck.

MID-LANE (From Arrows to Pin Deck)

"Watch the path of the ball for the entire lane. See what the ball and lane are doing."

This 45 foot section of the lane would normally be called the *pine portion*. It is generally made of pine, as contrasted to the much harder maple used for the headers and the pin deck. However, with the advent of artificial lanes and synthetic lane surfaces, such a name would not be accurate. Therefore, for purposes of discussion we have called this the "Mid-Lane" portion of the lane bed. (Thanks to Lyle Zikes for this term.)

Several critical factors must be understood if you are to read this portion of the lane properly. These include: *Lane Track; Conditioning Line and Pattern; Break Point; Pocket Angle;* and any other *Unusual Conditions* that might exist on the lane. We will now look at each of these aspects of the mid-lane, and what each one contributes toward our overall reading of the lane.

Lane Track: This is one of the most important aspects of the mid-lane, especially for right handed bowlers. Since only 15 or so percent of all bowlers are left handed, the lane track is far less of a factor for them.

The lane track is a worn area, generally found between the 8th and 12th boards from the right side of the lane. Such a *track,* or *area of wear,* is created by the normal use of the second arrow strike line by the majority of bowlers, most of whom are right handed.

EXHIBIT 2-6
Mid-Lane (From the Arrows to the Pin Deck)

This 45 foot section of the lane is where the ball surface and lane surface interact to create the final portion of the path of the ball to the pins.

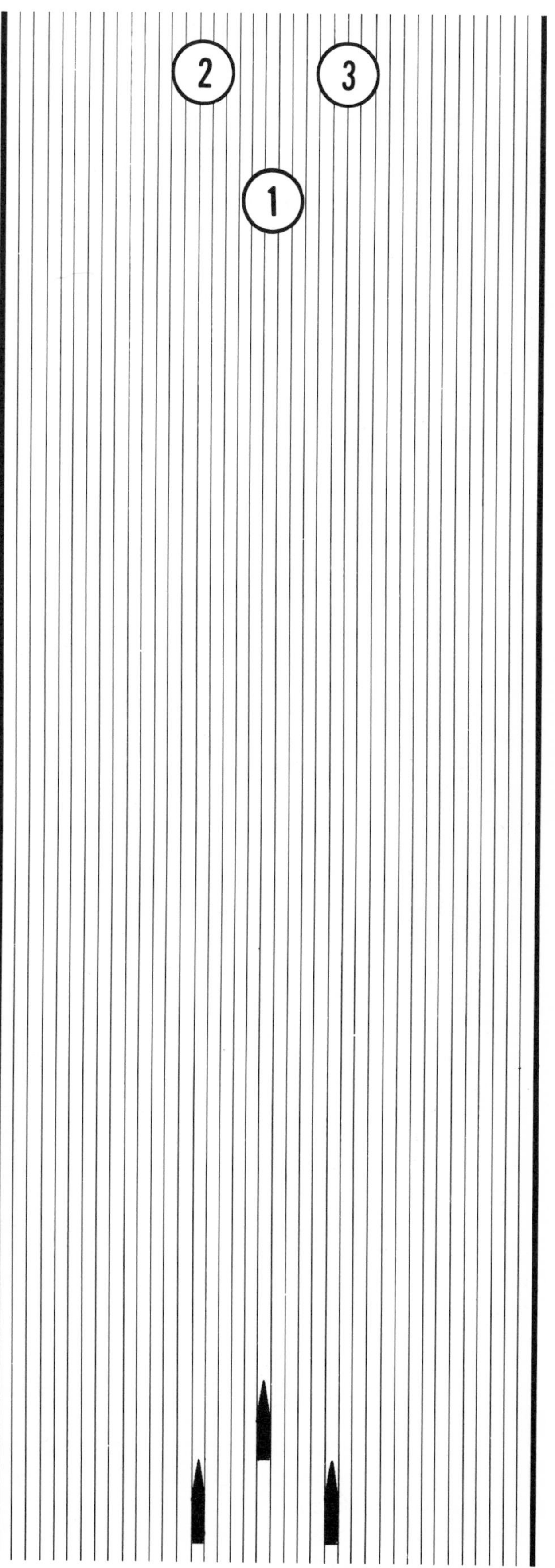

What problems or opportunities are created by the existence of the lane track? The lane track creates a *friction zone or area* that will cause the ball to grip the lane and hook more than when it is in a non-track portion of the lane. If the friction zone works for you, that is, directs or guides the ball into the pocket from the correct angle, then you have no problems with it. You are helped by the track.

If the ball is hooking too strongly by the ball track, you will have to get the ball into the track a little later, further down the lane. This can be achieved by moving to one of the inside strike lines or angles, which you do by moving to the inside of the approach. Or, you could increase ball speed to overcome the additional friction (hook) created by the lane track. A harder ball surface would have the same effect. Any adjustment designed to get the ball back to the pocket will help overcome a lane track that is causing the ball to hook too sharply or too high into the pocket.

Should the lane track be keeping the ball out of the pocket, that is taking the ball too far down the lane before the hook begins, then you will have to make adjustments opposite to those mentioned above. This is not a normal occurrence with the ball track. Usually the track becomes a friction zone which causes the ball to hook too much, and adjustments to get the ball back to the pocket are needed.

If it is necessary to avoid the lane track, you may play either to the left or the right side of it. The inside strike angles will allow you to get the ball further down the lane before it enters the track, and the outside lines may achieve the same purpose or avoid the lane track completely. Either adjustment can help overcome the lane track problem.

The important item to keep in mind when considering the lane track is that it represents a heavy ball-traffic pattern. As such, the lane will break down more rapidly in the track area, and you will have to be alert to make adjustments when you are playing the track. With no track to contend with, you can take a more open shot to the pocket. With a lane track, a more direct shot is best.

As previously mentioned, the lane track is normally not a problem for left handed bowlers. But, if there are several left handers bowling on the same lane at the same time, and all are using a similar angle to the pocket, then a lane track condition could develop. However, the problem will not be as severe as for the right handers, simply because there are fewer left handers.

Some centers are known as *track houses.* This means that the best scoring condition exists for those who play the track to the pocket. If you know a house has such a reputation, by all means try to use the track for your strike line.

The existence of the lane track is neither good nor bad. But it is a major item on the mid-lane portion of the lane. Watch for the reaction of the ball in the track to see whether you can use the track or have to avoid it.

Conditioning Line and Pattern: Lane conditioning is *not* placed on the entire lane, from the foul line to the pin deck. The back end of the lane (about 15 to 30 feet) is not normally conditioned for play. The line which marks the end of the conditioning, beyond which the lane is essentially dry, is called the *conditioning line.* When the ball gets beyond this point on the lane, it should begin its roll and break to the pocket.

Lanes are generally conditioned for 30 to 35 feet beyond the foul line. This is a general rule, and lanes may be dressed anywhere from as little as 15 feet to as much as 42 or more feet beyond the foul line. (At one time the entire lane was conditioned with oil.)

What is the effect of a *conditioning line* that is either short (15 feet) or one that is further down the lane (30 to 42 plus feet)? If the oil ends near the arrows or the splice slightly beyond the arrows, then the ball may begin to roll and hook much sooner than you would like. The ball may tend to be high in the pocket or to cross over in front of the head pin. You must make adjustments that will bring the ball *back to* the pocket: inside lines and angles, a harder ball surface, more speed, less lift, etc.

When the conditioning line is further down the lane, the reverse is true. The ball will not hook as much, or as soon as you might want it to break for the pocket. Adjustments to bring the ball up to the pocket are called for: outside lines and angles, softer ball surface, less speed, more lift, etc. These adjustments are the same for both left and right handers, assuming that the lanes are conditioned the same on both the left and right sides.

There are an enormous number of initial lane *conditioning patterns* which can be created as the lanes are prepared for play. Oil could be heavily applied, very lightly applied, or anywhere in between these two extremes. The conditioning can be placed across the entire width of the lane, or any portion of that width. And, as previously mentioned, the oil can extend as short as 15 feet down the lane to any distance from that point to the pin deck. These three dimensions, *thickness, width,* and *distance* represent the major variables in determining what pattern of oil is placed on the lane.

The initial pattern of conditioning will change over time and with use. How this pattern changes will depend upon atmospheric conditions (temperature and humidity, primarily) as well as the amount and type of play the lane receives. The change will also be a function of the type of initial condition that existed. If very little oil is laid down, the lanes will dry up (by evaporation and use) much faster than if a heavier pattern of conditioner had been applied. An initial heavy application of oil will spread more quickly than a lighter pattern, and puddles will occur more frequently when there is a lot of oil initially on the lane.

The ball will pick up oil as it rolls down the lane, thereby leaving the lane with less oil where the ball has traveled. Also, the ball will push aside the oil on its way to the pins, causing a build-up of oil along the path of the ball. If several bowlers use the same general area of the lane, the oil in that area will disappear and be spread around much more rapidly than will occur when bowlers are using many different paths to the pin deck. (As oil is removed from an area of the lane, the lane is said to be *breaking down,* beginning to hook more.)

Oil is also carried down the lane by the ball, extending the initial conditioning line beyond its original distance from the foul line. Over time the back end of the lane may contain a great deal of oil or conditioner, and the ball will react differently than when it was initially relatively free of oil.

As the pattern of oil changes by use or atmospheric conditions, you must be alert to any changes you have to make to keep the ball on a favorable line to the pocket. Usually this will mean making an angle change to the inside as the lane *dries up.* But, any other adjustment method could be used that has the same effect as the inside line (a complementary adjustment, such as a harder ball, more speed, etc.).

Check your ball after it returns from the pit. Is there a streak of oil on it? If so, wipe this off before your next shot so you keep the ball surface as near to the same as possible for each shot. This will help you read the reaction of the ball on the lane. Also, the amount of conditioning *on the ball* will give you some idea as to how much oil is *on the lane.* This may give you a clue as to the angle, equipment or delivery changes you should make to properly play the lane.

As a general rule, as the pattern of lane conditioning changes, the lane will cause the ball to hook more than you want. The ball will be high in the pocket, or cross over to the *brooklyn* side. To get the ball *back to* the pocket, use any adjustment designed to do that: inside angle, more speed, etc. As your strike line is changing, you should be adjusting too. In this way, you can keep your strike line to the pocket, no matter what initial conditioning pattern was laid down and no matter how it changes.

Break Point: At some point down the lane the ball will begin its break or turn toward the pocket. With the straight ball, the angle into the pocket begins from the foul line. With the curve, hook or backup ball the break occurs somewhere in the mid-lane portion of the lane. *The break point is the beginning of the pocket angle.*

The ideal break point is somewhere between 10 and 15 feet in front of the pocket (or closer if you can delay the break that long). Lane conditions will dictate what the ideal breaking point is for a given lane at a particular point in time. This break point is of utmost importance if you are to achieve the ideal pocket angle.

If you roll a curve, hook, or backup ball, every adjustment you make in your strike delivery can be related to this break point. You will be trying to get the ball to break *sooner* or *later,* or *more* or *less.* These decisions can be related to our previous discussions concerning getting *up to* or *back to* the pocket.

If the ball breaks too soon or too much, then a high pocket or crossover hit will normally result. You will have to make an adjustment to get the ball *back to* the pocket. This might suggest the use of an inside strike angle, a harder ball surface, more speed, less lift, more loft, etc.

If the ball breaks too late or not enough, a light pocket hit or failure to reach the pocket may occur. You will have to adjust to get the ball *up to* the pocket, such as using the outside angles, a softer ball, less speed, less loft, more lift, etc.

The timing of the break point determines the pocket angle. Get the ball at the correct break point and you should achieve the ideal angle into the pocket.

Unusual Mid-Lane Features: Unusual conditions could exist on the mid-lane or any other portion of the lane. The term refers to *anything out of the ordinary* that might influence the path of the ball to the pins, either in your favor or against you.

A *high or low board* on the lane is an example of such an unusual lane feature or condition. Such a condition could cause the ball to straighten out, hook badly, not hook at all, or force you to use another line or angle into the pocket. Normally, such a condition is unfavorable, and you have to take measures to avoid it. (Mis-aligned boards at the splice could also be classified as an unusual lane condition.)

Spotty lane conditions would also fall into the category of unusual lane features. On occasion the oil will create a *puddle* on a portion of the lane, causing the ball to skid when it hits the buildup of oil. The hook might be stopped, or at least not be as effective as it might have been had it not hit the puddle of oil. On the other hand, *dry spots* may be created on the lane. These could occur as a result of normal ball play or because some mistake was made when the lane was conditioned. The normal hook or roll of the ball would be altered by the presence of a dry spot on the lane.

The presence of wet or dry spots can be detected by noting any unusual reaction of the ball in its path to the pin deck. That is why it is important to keep your eye on the ball for the entire path to the pocket. If such unusual lane conditions exist, you will be alerted to them and can make the appropriate angle, equipment, or delivery adjustment to compensate for them.

The presence of either a *block* or *reverse block* could be considered an unusual lane condition. If the block exists (a *wall* is provided to the pocket) then by all means use it! If a reverse block exists, and keeps you from hitting the pocket, then make the best shot you can and hope for the best. You cannot change the condition of the lane, only adjust to it. Besides, if a reverse block does occur on occasion, all other bowlers will be facing the same condition. Since they all have the same handicap, scores will be uniformly low and skill will determine who scores the best under such conditions.

Sometimes the lane will contain an *erratic condition* which will give you no realistic shot for the pocket. Under such circumstances, bowl as well as you can and concentrate on your spare shots. If you can't be striking, then at least be converting your spares. After all, there will be other times when the lanes favor your game and you will be able to make up for the *graveyard* (low scoring) lanes. As long as you do everything you can do, as well as you can do it, then you should bowl well under any lane condition. Over the long run, your skill will prevail.

The lanes will tell you how to play them, if you will only listen. Watching the reaction of the ball for the entire length of the lane (and even off the end of the pin deck) is the only way you can determine if there are any unusual lane conditions. Watch for them and adjust as needed.

These, then, are the critical factors associated with the mid-lane, from the arrows to the pin deck: lane track; conditioning line and pattern; pocket angle and break point; and unusual conditions that might exist on the lanes. Now we will conclude our discussion of lane reading with a look at the key factors on the pin deck.

THE PIN DECK

"The pin deck is where it all happens. Either all ten pins go down for a strike, or you have a spare to convert."

This is where everything happens, on this 36-inch triangle of ten pins called the pin deck. If the ball hits the 1-3 pocket (RHB) or 1-2 pocket (LHB) from the correct angle, with the proper amount of speed, and with the right amount of action on the ball, the maximum chance exists for the perfect strike hit. But both pin and ball deflection must work properly for the strike to occur. Of course, you may miss the pocket but get lucky pin action that results in a strike. You cannot rely upon such good fortune to build your average and to raise your percentage of strikes. Your objective must continue to be a perfect pocket hit for a strike. Professional or high averages are based upon consistently accurate shots into the strike pocket.

As with other portions of the lane, we will look for the critical elements on the pin deck that will let you read what is happening there. Several words or terms are descriptive of the activities on the pin deck, and tell you what adjustments, if any, you must make in your strike ball delivery. These include, *The Pocket; Pin and Ball Deflection; Pocket Angle; Pocket Action; Pocket Speed;* and *Clue Pins* (the 4, 5 and 6-pins. How they fall will give you some indication of what the ball is doing on its path through the pins.) We will look at each of these terms in order to understand the pin deck portion of the lane.

The Pocket: This term was discussed in detail in SECTION 1 under PRINCIPLES OF STRIKES. Therefore, we will only briefly review the concept here.

The pocket is the 1-3 pin contact area for the RHB and the 1-2 pin contact area for the left handed bowler. In fact, the point of contact is only on the 1-pin, immediately after which the ball will deflect into the 3-pin (RHB) or 2-pin (LHB). This contact area on the 1-pin will send the pins into a pattern of pin fall that was previously described as pin and ball deflection on a perfect strike hit. (Exhibit 1-1 has illustrated this pin fall pattern.)

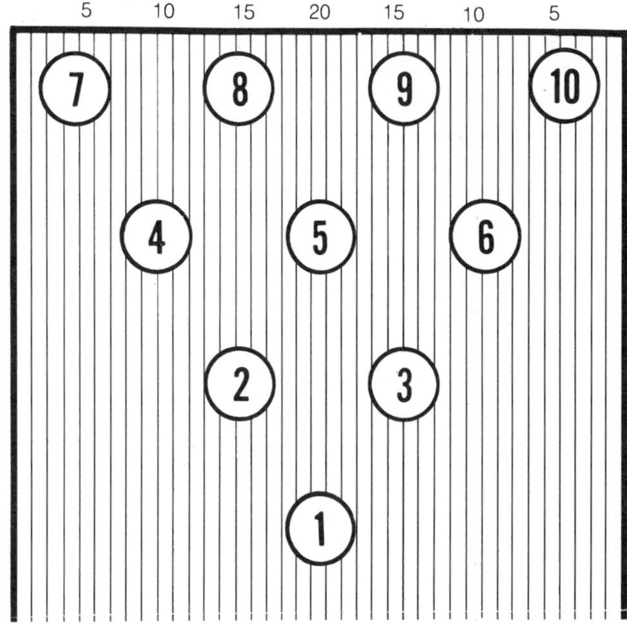

EXHIBIT 2-7
The Pin Deck

The 10 pins are arranged in a 36 inch triangle, with a 12-inch gap from the center of each pin spot to the center of the adjacent pin spot. In this exhibit we have marked every fifth board so you can determine the exact location for any portion of the pin deck. The complete pin deck area should include the kick backs, located on both sides of the pin area. On many strikes, pins will bounce off the kick backs and take out pins, instead of the pattern of pin and ball deflection covered in SECTION 1, under THE PERFECT STRIKE.

Pocket Angle: The ideal entry into the pocket can only be achieved by a ball which starts to turn into the pocket when it is within 15 or so feet from the pin deck. If you drew a straight line from the center of the perfect pocket angle back toward the approach, the line would go off the lane before it reached one third of the way back to the foul line, or about 15-20 feet in front of the pin deck. (This perfect pocket angle is beautifully illustrated in *The Perfect Game*, referenced in the bibliography.)

Since the ball cannot possibly be rolled from the adjoining lane, it is necessary to get the ball as far down the lane as possible before it makes a turn (break) for the pocket. That is the reason why almost every top bowler uses some form of the hook or curve ball, rather than use a backup or straight ball. *The hook ball gives the best pocket angle to produce perfect strikes on a consistent basis.* It is still possible to get strikes with the other types of deliveries, but not as many strikes and not as consistently.

There is a best pocket angle to play any lane at a given moment in time. This angle may and often does change, as the amount of play on the lane increases, or after the lane is conditioned. A lane changes with use. Therefore, you must not only determine what strike pocket angle is best for the lane at a given moment in time, but continue to read the lane to see if the angle you have selected is still the correct one. (The clue pins will help, as we discuss a little later in our coverage of the pin deck).

Once you have determined that the pocket angle must be changed, to keep the ball going into the pocket, several methods are available to you. The pocket angle can be changed by increasing or decreasing the speed of the ball. Increasing ball speed will straighten out the pocket angle. Reducing ball speed tends to create more of an angle into the pocket.

You could also change the pocket angle by altering the amount of lift or turn on the ball at the moment of release. More lift will increase the pocket angle; less lift reduces it. Still another delivery change that can be used to alter the pocket angle is to use more loft (to reduce the pocket angle) or less loft (to increase the pocket angle).

Yet another method of changing the pocket angle, one that is perhaps the most widely used technique, is to change the foul line angle. Moving to the center of the approach, opening the foul line angle, tends to reduce the pocket angle. Moving toward the outside portion of the approach tends to create more of a pocket angle. The inside strike lines, discussed in SECTION 3 (RHB) and SECTION 6 (LHB), are adjustments to straighten out the shot, to reduce the pocket angle. Outside strike lines are designed to create more of a pocket angle.

And there is the whole range of equipment adjustments available to alter the angle of the ball into the pocket. Although more details will be given in the equipment adjustment sections (4 and 7), the general pattern is: positive weights and imbalances will cause the ball to create more of a pocket angle, and negative weights and imbalances create less of a pocket angle. A harder ball surface (generally speaking, and depending upon lane conditions) will reduce the pocket angle, and softer ball surfaces increase the pocket angle.

Why is the pocket angle so important, and how can you tell if the angle is too much or not enough? The answers to these questions are related to the discussions of pocket action and pocket speed. But some general statements can be made at this time. With light pins, a reduction in the pocket angle is best, since the ball will not deflect out of the pocket as readily against light pins (3 pounds 2 ounces, or 3 pounds 3 ounces, called 3-2's and 3-3's). Heavier pins often call for more of a pocket angle since they tend to deflect the ball out of the pocket more than lighter pins.

Spare leaves also give clues as to the nature of the angle needed to make strikes. If the ball appears to be *diving through* the pins, then less of an angle is suggested. A RHB leaving the 4-pin, the 4-9, or the 9-pin indicates that the angle may be too steep. Leaving the 10-pin, the 5-pin, the 5-10 pins and similar spares suggest more of an angle is needed. The corresponding leaves for the LHB are the 6-pin, the 6-8 split, and the 8-pin on pocket angles that are too steep, and the 5-pin, 5-7-pins, and 7-pin for an angle that needs to be increased.

When you are hitting the pocket and not making strikes, you *could* conclude that the angle to the pocket is not correct. However, the problem *may be* in the speed of the ball, or the action on the ball. These three factors, *pocket angle, pocket speed,* and *pocket action* are so interrelated that any one or more could create the problem. If you are not making strikes on your pocket hits, you *can* conclude almost without exception that one or more of these three pin deck factors is the problem. Therefore, let's discuss the other two items, *pocket speed* and *pocket action.*

Pocket Speed: There is a correct ball speed for any given lane condition and for the angle you are playing at the time. Most high average bowlers roll with moderate speed, with the ball traveling from the foul line to the pin deck in about 2.2 seconds, plus or minus .2 of a second. The correct speed will work well with the lane, will create the correct amount of skid through the headers (the first 15 feet of the lane), will cause the ball to make its turn to the pocket at the appropriate time for the lane conditions, and will keep the ball in its path of deflection through the pins. A ball with proper speed will contact the 1-3-5-9 pins correctly (RHB) or the 1-2-5-8 pins for the LHB.

Speed control is an essential element in your adjustment arsenal. You should practice changing ball speed so you will be able to change when lane conditions or pin weights (or other factors) dictate such a change. Please note that you will normally be changing ball speed by about .2 of a second, one fifth of a second. You will either be slowing down from 2.2 to 2.4 seconds, or increasing ball speed from 2.2 to 2.0 seconds. (Although these are approximate times, they are very realistic estimates of the range of ball speeds used by high average bowlers. Time them, and have someone time you.)

If ball speed is excessive, the ball will drive through the pins. A slow ball, however, will deflect out of the pocket. Noticing where your ball contacts the 5-pin, what spares you are leaving, and where the ball leaves the end of the pin deck will give you some insights into your ball speed. When ball speed is proper, the ball will maintain its ideal path of deflection and will leave the pin deck somewhere between where the 8 or 9-pins were standing. (In the delivery section we will present methods for altering your ball speed.)

Pocket Action: The term action often refers to the spin, lift, turn, etc., that is *imparted to the ball* at the moment it is released on the lane. *Pocket action is our term for the action on the ball at the moment it hits the pocket.* Action is considered by many people to be *the driving force of the ball,* that is, the force that permits the ball to continue into the pin setup after contacting the 1-3 or 1-2 pocket. The ball should drive, or force its way, into the 18½ board, which is 1½ boards inside of the pocket (the 17th board from the right for the RHB and 17th board from the left for the LHB). Too little action will not get the ball this far into the pocket. Too much action will take it into the 19th or 20th boards. Too much pocket action on the ball causes it to hit the 5-pin too fully, and too little action creates a light hit on the 5-pin. Pin and ball deflection are less-than-ideal when pocket action is less-than-ideal.

Although action is *put on the ball* at the release point in the delivery (sometimes called the explosion point), the lane and ball surface interact to determine what action is *still on the ball* when it arrives at the pocket. Pocket action is often determined by the timing of the break point, for those who roll a hook, backup or curve ball. If the ball starts its turn to the pocket too soon, it will lose some of the action imparted at the release point. The ball will lose some of its drive, will have *rolled out* before it gets to the pocket. If it makes its break or turn too late, then the ball will not have developed its optimum action by the time it hits the pocket. In either case, an early or late break, pocket action is not at the optimum level for penetrating the pocket and maintaining the path of deflection through the pins.

Therefore, the timing of the break point is a crucial decision for those who roll a hook ball. At times you will want to get the ball to break sooner, and at other times you want a later break. These may be the two most important decisions a bowler using a hook has to make. (Since the *break point* was discussed in the previous mid-lane portion of the lane, we will not duplicate the material here.)

These three terms, *pocket angle, pocket speed,* and *pocket action* explain why more than a pocket hit is needed to produce strikes. They also outline the three clues you can look for if you are hitting the pocket and not making strikes. One of these three items, or a combination of them, will be depriving you of your strikes. Once you are able to hit the pocket, every adjustment you make will be related to one or more of these three factors. However, there is another set of clues available to help you read the activity on the pin deck. They concern the clue pins.

Clue Pins: How can you tell when ball and pin deflection are not working perfectly? The pattern of pin fall gives some insight, with three specific pins important in your reading of the pin fall: the 4-pin, the 5-pin, and the 6-pin. The manner in which these pins fall will give you further insight into your strike ball. They tell you if you are striking well, not striking, or are losing your strike pattern.

You will recall from previous discussions of the perfect strike hit that the 4-pin takes out the 7-pin, the 6-pin takes out the 10-pin, and the 5-pin takes out the 8-pin (RHB) or 9-pin (LHB). When these clue pins *are* doing their jobs well, there is little doubt about the 7, 8, 9 and 10-pins falling. When these clue pins *are not* doing their jobs, then pin and ball deflection are not perfect, and some slight adjustment might be in order. In other words, you may even be striking, but are losing your strike hit.

When the pattern of pin fall for our clue pins is less-than-perfect, a change in pocket speed, pocket action, or pocket angle is suggested. A late-10 or late-7 strike, trip-4 or trip-6, or similar strike hit suggests that pin and ball deflection are less than perfect. Sliding the 5-pin in front of the 8-pin (RHB) or 9-pin (LHB) suggests that the ball is not hitting the 5-pin fully. When the 4-pin hits the 7-pin on the left or right side and barely takes it out, pin deflection is not as good as it could be. When the 6-pin barely takes out the 10-pin on the left or right side, you have the same situation. Watch how these clue pins are reacting and you will get a very good reading of pin and ball deflection, pocket speed, pocket action, and pocket angle on the pin deck.

Two other factors are important in determining the number and frequency of strikes you get: the *kickbacks* and the *pins.* Sometimes the kickbacks are lively and you can carry some of the *wall shots.* At other times the kickbacks are *dead* and you get no help from them at all. When they are helping you, and you are carrying the wall shot consistently, you may decide to make no change in your delivery. Keep rolling the same kind of ball and continue to accept your good fortune. There may be some reason why this particular strike shot is successful on this lane: the pins, your delivery, or the ball you are using. As we mentioned previously, trying to be *too perfect* can cause you to lose the strikes you are getting. When you are striking consistently with the use of the kickbacks, or on a light or heavy hit, you may wish to make no change at all. Nothing can be more perfect than consistent strikes, and if that is what you are doing, then you are bowling as well as you can. Bad luck will come along sometime, so accept the good luck while it is here. There is probably some reason for it (weight of the pins, lane conditions, etc.) so think carefully before you make any adjustment.

The Pin: Yet another very obvious factor on the pin deck, perhaps the most important element there, is the set of pins you are bowling against. Not all pins are alike, either in weight, in amount of use they have been subjected to, in their state of repair, etc. These are all very important factors in what happens to the pins after the ball arrives at the pocket.

Pins weigh from 3 pounds 2 ounces to 3 pounds 10 ounces (referred to as 3-2's and 3-10's). Heavy pins cause the ball to deflect more, suggesting a change in angle, speed, or action to keep the ball in its path of deflection through the pins. Light pins deflect the ball less, requiring some adjustment in one of these three factors as well. As a general rule, light pins call for less speed, less action, and less of an angle to the pocket. Heavy pins call for the reverse: more speed, more action, and more of a pocket angle.

A controversy over the pins concerns the velocity at which pins move after being hit by the ball or other pins. This controversy has been the result of major changes made in pin manufacturing processes and the type of materials used in pin construction. Since pins are undergoing changes as much as other facets of bowling (lane surfaces, ball surfaces, etc.), there will probably always be some concern for the *velocitating* action of the pins.

Professional bowlers usually bowl against 3-5's or 3-6's. A set of ten pins cannot differ by more than 4 ounces between any two pins in the set. High scores on such mixed pins would be disallowed by some of the sanctioning organizations concerned with the integrity of the game. The purpose of this ruling is rather clear. If pins are of the same weight and construction, then pin and ball deflection will not be erratic. With mixed pins, the pattern of pin fall and ball deflection would depend upon the location of the heavier or lighter pins.

How can you tell if you are bowling against heavy or light pins? You can look for clues on the pin deck or you may even ask the center manager. Ball deflection is perhaps the best indicator of the weight of the pins. Watch what happens to the ball on its path through the pins, noting particularly where the ball goes off the back of the pin deck. If the ball is driving through the pins, they could be light pins (or the angle could be too steep, or ball speed could be too fast). If the ball is deflecting off the pins too sharply, the pins could be heavy (or the angle could be not enough, or ball speed could be too slow). It could also be that ball action at the pocket was too much or not enough in both of these situations. You must be alert to all of these factors, so you can determine which one is the likely cause for the activity you see on the pin deck.

Once you have determined what kind of pins you are bowling against, you can decide how to alter the speed, angle, or action to get the ideal deflection for your strikes. To ignore the weight of the pins as a factor in reading the pin deck portion of the lanes is to unnecessarily deprive yourself of a valuable piece of information that may permit you to score well.

These, then, are the key elements in reading the pin deck section of the lane: the pocket angle; the pocket; pin and ball deflection; pocket speed; pocket action; clue pins; the kickbacks; and the weight and condition of the pins. Each item gives you some information that will help you read the pin deck.

Study Exhibit 2-7 very well, particulary noting the location of the pins by board number on the pin deck. A knowledge of the pin deck will help when you are missing the pocket, indicating the board the ball was on when it hit the pin setup. That piece of information is vital in determining adjustments which are needed to either get *back to* the pocket when you have passed it by, or *up to* the pocket when the ball has failed to do so.

Everything that you are trying to do, to make a strike, is happening on the pin deck. Get every clue, every piece of information you can, and you will be reading this portion of the lane as well as possible. What you see hapening on the pin deck will often provide you with the exact information you need to make some adjustment for playing the lanes properly.

Exhibit 2-8, on the following page, summarizes many of the terms we have been using to describe the lane reading process. This exhibit can increase your knowledge of the lanes.

EXHIBIT 2-8 Lane-Reading Terms

Back ends: The last 15 feet of the lane, in front of the pin deck.

Block: An artificial lane condition which guides the ball into the pocket, creating a high scoring potential. Usually created by placing a heavy oil strip down boards 8 through 20 on both sides of the lane, if the block is for both left and right handers.

Breaking down: The lanes are drying up, more friction is being created, and the ball begins to hook more.

Crowning: A conditioning pattern with high oil on both sides of the lane track.

Doctoring a lane: Conditioning a lane so an artificial scoring condition is created, favoring or disfavoring the bowler.

Fair shot: A lane condition where scoring is based upon skill and performance of the bowler and not the condition of the lane.

Dress the lane: Apply oil to the lane in preparation for play.

Flood the lane: Apply oil heavily. Sometimes the headers are double oiled, or flooded with oil.

Finger smear test: One of three tests to determine the pattern of conditioning on the lane. By sliding your finger across the lane you can determine the presence or absence of oil. Making three parallel lines give you a good idea of the pattern and amount of oil on the lane.

Friction zone: A dry portion of the lane, usually the lane track.

Give a shot: Condition the lanes so there is a reasonable shot for the pocket.

Grabbing lane: A lane that hooks a great deal. (See Sand Trap.)

Grooved lane: Where a track or rut exists on the lane.

Heads: The first 15 or so feet of the lane. Also called the headers. Approximately from the foul line to the targeting arrows.

House condition: The way lanes are conditioned for league play.

Inside house: A bowling center where inside strike angles are generally best for high scoring.

Lane analyzer: An instrument for measuring friction on the lane. Lack of friction indicates the presence of oil, and a lot of friction means there is very little oil.

Lane conditioning: Preparing the lanes for play, or the substance put on the lane to protect the surface and provide a shot for the bowler.

Lane finish: The surface of the lane before oil is placed on it, such as a lacquer, urethane, or artificial surface.

Lane track: A worn area on the lane, usually on the right side and between boards 8 through 12.

Mid-lane: From the arrows to the pin deck, a distance of about 45 feet.

Oil barrier: A heavy strip of oil down the lane, either preventing the ball from hooking too high, or from getting up to the pocket.

Outside house: A bowling center where outside strike angles are generally best for high scoring.

Pre-reading a lane: Trying to determine the best way to play a lane before you roll your first ball on it. This is often achieved by watching others.

Pin deck: The back portion of the lane, on which the pins are standing.

Put down an inside shot: Condition the lane so inside angles are best for hitting the pocket.

Put down an outside shot: Condition the lane so outside angles are best for hitting the pocket.

Reverse block: An artificial lane condition which keeps the ball out of the pocket, creating a low scoring potential. Usually created by placing a heavy strip of oil down the first 8 to 10 boards on both sides of the lane, if the reverse block is for (against) both left and right handed bowlers.

Sand trap: Extremely dry lane, with a great deal of friction. Severely hooking lane.

Splice: Where the maple portion of the lane joins with the pine portion.

Spotty condition: Alternating wet and dry spots on the lane. Erratic conditions.

Synthetic lanes: Lanes not made of maple and pine, but of an artificial surface material.

Tactile lane test: A test to determine the presence or absence of oil. Touching the fingers to the lane will create a sticky feeling if the lanes are lacking in oil, or a slick feeling if oil is there.

Take away the pocket: Same as take away the shot. Condition the lanes so there is no reasonable chance for hitting the pocket consistently.

Taper the lane: A conditioning pattern where the oil is gradually reduced in amount, either down or across the lane.

Targeting dots: Dots imbedded in the lane in boards 3, 5, 8, 11, and 14 on both sides of the lane.

Targeting arrows: Seven arrows imbedded in the lane about 15 feet beyond the foul line, and used for aiming or targeting.

Tour condition: The way lanes are conditioned for professional tournaments.

Unfair shot: A lane conditioning pattern which either makes scoring very easy or very difficult. Skill plays a small part in scoring.

Uniform playing condition: A fair playing condition that rewards good bowling, but is neither a block nor reverse block. Not an erratic condition.

Visual lane test: By standing on the lane and looking at the reflection of the house lights, you can determine where oil has been applied.

Wall: A heavy strip of oil down the lane which guides the ball into the pocket similar to what would happen if an actual wall were built on the lane.

Wet condition: A heavy oil concentration or buildup.

SECTION 3
ANGLE ADJUSTMENTS
(Right Handed Bowlers)

"There is one strike angle that will let you play the lane well. Find it; use it; and you will score well," Ellenburg.

CONTENTS PAGE

OVERVIEW

The most common adjustments made by all bowlers are line or angle adjustments. Such adjustments call for a movement to the left or the right on the approach. However, as you will see shortly, the proper way to play any angle requires more than a simple movement on the approach. Some changes occur naturally as you move from one strike angle to another. Other changes must be made deliberately.

This section presents a complete description of the proper methods for playing all strike lines and angles. We begin with a definition of the terms *line* and *angle*. Then we discuss the methods of finding *the correct angle* to play any lane at a given point in time. Our material includes *a personal formula* that will allow you to play any angle, and to *calculate the new stance location* when you change angles.

This section concludes with illustrations of the five strike lines and guidelines for properly playing any angle within any line.

The terms *line* and *angle* are frequently used interchangeably. They are, however, different but related types of angle adjustments. Since there may be some confusion as to the meaning of these two terms, we will begin by defining each term as it is used in this book.

DEFINITION OF LINE: There are five commonly accepted strike lines that a bowler might use at one time or another, largely depending upon lane conditions and the type of equipment (ball) being used. These five strike lines are called: the deep inside line; the inside line; the second arrow line; the outside line; and the deep outside line. All of these strike lines are illustrated on Exhibit 3-1.

Each strike line describes a general path from the foul line to the pins through a specific set of boards at the foul line and the arrows. For example, the deep inside strike line is one that starts from the center of the lane (approximately boards 20-27 at the foul line) and travels through boards 18-22 at the arrows. Exhibit 3-1 shows the path going through the fourth arrow, which is the 20th board at the arrows.

Similarly, each strike line is described by an area of the foul line (in specific boards) and an area of the lane at the arrows (also stated in specific boards).

There is general agreement upon the existence of these five strike lines. However, disagreements exist as to the *specific names* given to each line and to the *exact board numbers* at the foul line and arrows contained in each line. These two areas of disagreement do not in any way restrict the usefulness of the material in this section. The disagreement is usually within a single board one way or the other. And, whether the 12th board (for example) is considered to be in the second arrow line or the inside line makes no difference in playing any angle over that board.

DEFINITION OF ANGLE: Within each strike line there are a *set of foul line angles* that make up the entire strike line. For example, foul line angle 12-to-10 refers to the 12th board at the foul line and the 10th board at the arrows. The 11-to-10 foul line angle refers to the 11th board at the foul line and the 10th board at the arrows. However, both of these angles are within the second arrow strike line. (Foul Line Angle is explained in SECTION 2, FROM FOUL LINE TO ARROWS.) Therefore, *any angle is defined as the path a ball takes from the foul line to*

EXHIBIT 3-1
The Five Strike Lines for Right Handed Bowlers

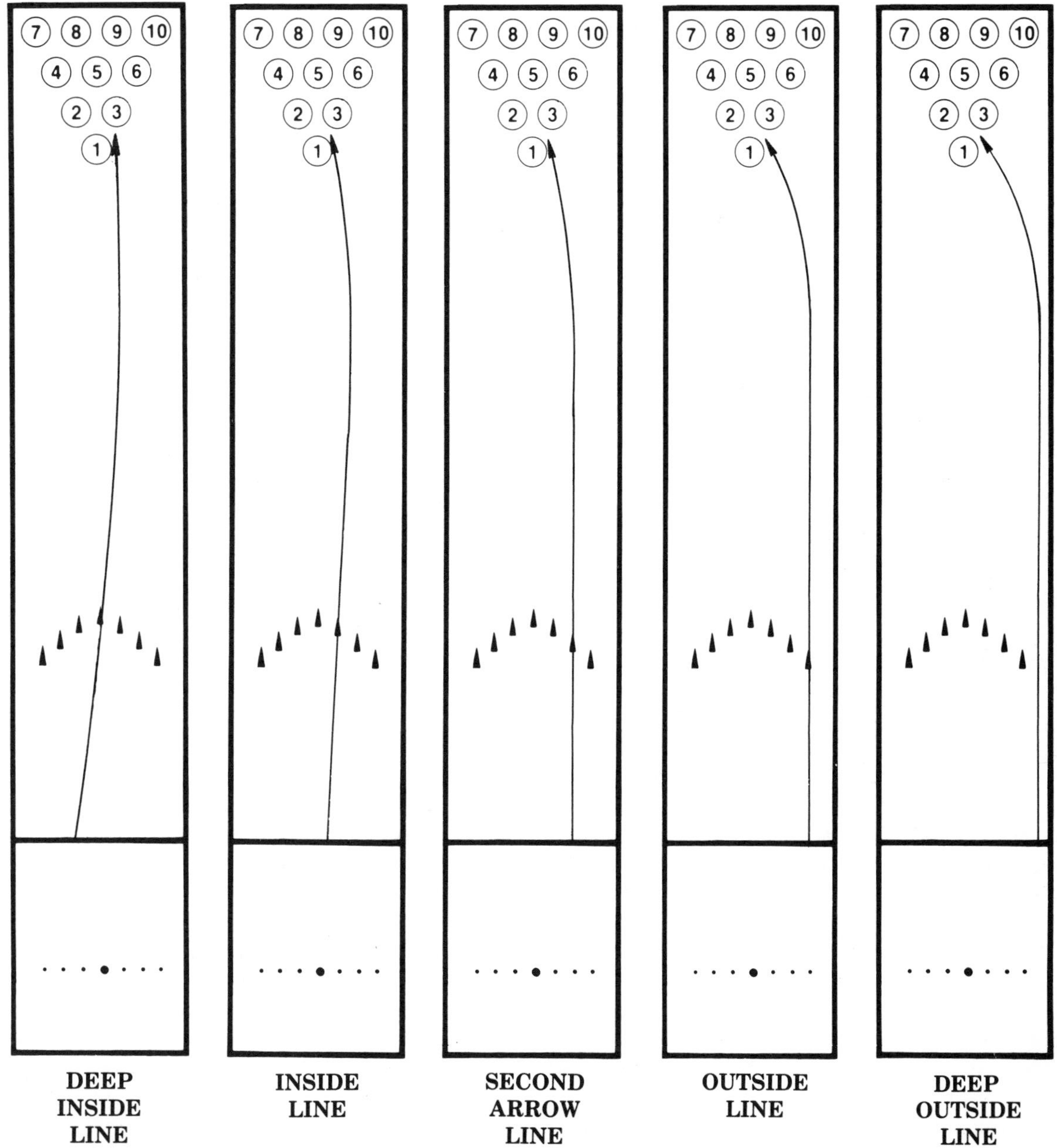

DEEP INSIDE LINE | INSIDE LINE | SECOND ARROW LINE | OUTSIDE LINE | DEEP OUTSIDE LINE

DEEP INSIDE LINE	*Approximately Boards 18–22 at the Arrows
INSIDE LINE (3RD ARROW)	Approximately Boards 13–17 at the Arrows
2ND ARROW LINE	Approximately Boards 8–12 at the Arrows
OUTSIDE LINE (1ST ARROW)	Approximately Boards 4–7 at the Arrows
DEEP OUTSIDE LINE	Approximately Boards 1–3 at the Arrows

*Boards are numbered from the right side of the lane. Although there may be differences of opinion as to the exact boards contained in any given line, there is general agreement upon these five strike lines.

the arrows, and is described by giving the board number at both locations. Notice that the *first number* in the foul line angle refers to the board at the *foul line,* and the *second number* refers to the board at the *arrows.* Since every ball has to pass over some specific board at the foul line (even if it does not hit the lane until it is 18 or more inches beyond the foul line) and it must also pass over a specific board at the arrows, the path taken by any ball can be described by two numbers that define the angle the ball takes down the lanes. Any foul line angle can be classified within one of the five strike lines previously described.

Now I think you can see why the two terms (line and angle) are used as though they were the same thing. On closer examination it becomes clear that the term *ANGLE is more specific,* whereas the term *LINE is more general.* When you make an *angle* change you are normally making a *small* adjustment. When you make a *line* change you are normally making a *larger* adjustment, moving from one strike line to another. In both cases you are changing your approach position. However, in the line change you are generally also making a change in your target boards at the arrows. In an angle change you are normally keeping the same target board at the arrows but changing the board you cross over at the foul line. (However, you could change from a 10-to-10 foul line angle to the 11-to-11 angle and still be within the same second arrow strike line, yet you have changed both your target board and the board your ball crosses at the foul line!)

FINDING THE ANGLE TO THE POCKET: Your objective, each time you bowl on a given lane, is to find the correct strike line and angle that will get the ball into the 1-3 pocket. And, you want to find that angle as quickly as possible, with a minimum of mistakes (splits, low counts, or very difficult spares).

Before you ever roll your first ball, you can gather a great deal of information about the lane. You may even be able to determine what strike line is most likely to be the correct one to use on this lane *at this point in time.* Many clues are available to help you *pre-read the lanes.*

What strike line and angle are some of the *high average bowlers using,* especially those who bowl with a style similar to yours, and who use equipment similar to yours? Are they using the deep inside line, the deep outside line, etc.? Are they scoring well with the line they are using? If so, then you may be able to use the same line or angle. If they are not scoring well, this might tell you not to use the line they are using. Any indication, before you bowl your first ball, that a line *may* or *may not* be the best one to use is a valuable piece of information.

Next, consider the *time of day* and the *amount of play* the lane has received prior to your session. If you are in a league that begins, for example, at 6:30 in the evening, and the lanes have just been conditioned for play, you can assume the *oil pattern* is unaltered by play. That is, the track has not been developed by play, the lanes have not been *broken down,* the oil has not been spread around by others, etc. Since you will get a few practice rolls, you will be able to determine for yourself what the lanes are doing. You can begin with the normal strike line and angle you use, and adjust from there. (Later on we will give you a personal formula for finding the correct line and angle into the pocket.)

But, if you are bowling in a later league, and a previous league has just completed their session, you know the lane track may have broken down. The pattern of conditioning has also been changed, and there may be wet or dry (spotty) conditions on the lane. You have to take previous lane play into consideration in determining the best line and angle to use.

If you are bowling in a tournament, watching other high average bowlers who have a style similar to yours is a good way to get a pre-reading of the lanes. What you are trying to do is find the best way to play the lane without wasting precious frames of your games. Some centers have a reputation as an *inside house,* a *track house,* an *outside house,* etc. Knowing this tendency for centers to favor or disfavor one strike line or another may also give you clues as to how you can determine the proper strike line and angle *before you begin* your game.

Often, if a tournament lasts for several days or a few weeks, the lanes *may* be conditioned differently at different times during the tournament. Keep this in mind when it is your time to bowl. In the early part of the tournament, scoring conditions *may* be difficult. This occurs, infrequently, when the tournament director does not wish to have large scores posted early in the tournament. (This might cause other bowlers to stay out of the tournament when they see scores already posted that they feel they cannot match.) Such a deliberate pattern of difficult scoring conditions during the early part of a tournament is seldom found, since most directors try to keep the same scoring conditions throughout the entire tournament. But, you should be aware of both situations, since each may occur. So no matter what conditions exist, watch what strike line and angle others are using successfully. This may help you align yourself quickly.

Ask other bowlers about the type of condition that exists. This is another way to determine the condition of the lanes and what line or angle might be best for you. As with all of the previous methods for pre-reading the lanes, this one is not guaranteed. But, each clue you get can be assessed when you get on the lanes. At least you will not be starting from zero information.

At this point you should be ready to step on the approach with an idea of the best strike line to play, although the actual angle within that strike line may be less certain. You will have to find the correct angle and approach position that is best for you at this time. To assist you in this search, one you must face each time you bowl, we have developed a *personal formula* that can help you find the correct angle and line into the pocket.

A PERSONAL FORMULA FOR PLAYING ANY ANGLE: It is possible to develop a personal mathematical formula for playing any angle. This formula will help you determine the exact stance location on the approach for every foul line angle. You may recall that *a foul line angle is the path taken by the ball from the foul line to the arrows.* Each foul line angle is described by two numbers, such as a 12-to-10 foul line angle. The *first number* always identifies the board at the *foul line* and the *second number* describes the number of the board at the *arrows.* A 10-to-10 foul line angle describes a ball that travels straight down the 10th board from the foul line to the arrows.

To properly play any foul line angle, it is necessary to determine the precise board on the approach where you take your stance. It is also necessary that you *align yourself* properly, *facing your target* on the lanes, and have the ball *swing along the intended angle.* The personal formula which we will present at this time will give you the exact board on the approach for your stance location. In every case we will assume that you align yourself properly once you have calculated the location for your stance.

This formula, which we call your *personal formula,* takes into account your walk pattern (drift) and the distance (in number of boards) by which you miss your ankle with the center of the ball when you deliver the ball. SECTION 2, THE APPROACH, explained how to determine both of these numbers for yourself. Since these two numbers are directly related to your personal game, the formula is tailored for you. Hence the title *personal* formula.

Your personal formula can be combined with other adjustment formulas to assist you in playing the various strike lines and all angles within these lines. However, before we discuss methods of adjusting from one foul line angle to another, we will explain *the formula for determining the exact stance location for any given foul line angle.*

It is necessary to use four numbers to determine the board to which you align yourself for your stance location. Later, we will reduce the requirement to only 3 numbers as we combine drift and the number of boards by which the center of the ball misses your ankle, into one personal number.

Two of the four numbers describe the foul line angle, giving the number of the board at the foul line and the number of the board at the arrows, or targeting zone. The third number relates to your drift pattern, and the fourth number describes the distance (in boards) by which the center of the ball misses your ankle when you deliver the ball onto the lane.

For purposes of illustrating the formula, we will select a specific foul line angle and show the method for determining the number of the board you use to take your stance. Keep in mind that after you have that board number, you must align yourself properly, face your target on the lane, and swing the ball through the intended foul line angle (path of the ball from the foul line to the arrows). Once we work our way through a specific angle, we will expand the discussion so that you can calculate the stance location for any foul line angle.

For illustrating the concept, we will select foul line angle 10-to-10, or the 10th board at the foul line (first number) and the 10th board at the arrows (second number). This is a straight line angle, and is perhaps the easiest to use to explain the concept of a personal formula.

The four numbers needed to determine the stance location for the 10-to-10 angle are as follows:

#1 Select a *board at the arrows* that you wish to use as your target. (For our example, we have chosen board *10 at the arrows.)*

#2 Select *the angle* you wish to play over that board. (For our example, we have chosen board *10* at *the foul line.)*

#3 Consider your normal *drift* pattern. (Assume that you normally drift *1* board to the right when you deliver the ball.)

#4 Consider the number of boards by which you *miss your ankle* with the *center of the ball* when you deliver it. (Assume that the center of the ball normally misses your ankle by 7 boards. Most bowlers will miss the ankle with the center of the ball by 6, 7 or 8 boards.)

The four numbers stated above can be used to determine exactly where you stand on the approach to play the 10-to-10 foul line angle. Later, we will show you how to combine #3 and #4 into a single personal number, and how to decide *if* this foul line angle is the correct one to use for getting the ball into the pocket. *For now, we are only trying to determine where you should stand on the approach to play this particular foul line angle.*

To recap, these are the four numbers needed to locate the proper stance location:

#1 The 10th board at the arrows (your target board),
#2 The 10th board at the foul line (the angle over that board),
#3 The 1 board drift to the right (we assumed for you),
#4 The 7 boards by which the center of the ball missed your ankle (we assumed for you).

If you wish to roll the ball down the 10th board at the foul line, and the center of the ball misses your ankle by 7 boards when you release the ball, then you have to slide at the 17th board at the foul line. If you slide at the 17th board, and miss your ankle by 7 boards, the ball will roll down the 10th board. BUT, we assumed that you drifted 1 board to the right in your approach. Therefore, to end up at the 17th board at the foul line for your slide, you have to start 1 board further *to the left* to compensate for this 1 board drift *to the right.*

Now to the formula. To determine the stance location on the approach for playing our selected 10-to-10 angle, follow this procedure. Subtract the number of the board at the arrows from the number of the board at the foul line. In this case; 10 minus 10, for a difference of zero. Add the difference (zero) to the number of the board at the foul line, (10 plus zero = 10). To this you must add the number of boards by which you miss your ankle, (10 plus 7 = 17). Finally, add to this number the number of boards you drift to the right, (17 plus 1 = 18). This gives you the number of the board on the approach with which you should align yourself for your stance location, board number 18.

Take your stance on board number 18; align yourself so you face your target on the lane and the ball will swing along your intended line; walk toward the foul line in your normal manner; you should drift to the right by 1 board and slide on the 17th board; miss your ankle by the 7 boards we assumed for our example; and roll the ball down the selected 10th board at the foul line. It should head straight down the 10th board, and roll over the 10th board at the arrows. You have now played the 10-to-10 foul line angle.

If you had *drifted to the left,* you would have to *subtract* one board from your starting position to end up at the foul line on the correct board. To compensate for drift, you always move in the opposite direction on the approach. This suggests that there must be some way to incorporate drift patterns and the number of boards by which the center of the ball misses your ankle, into a single number to simplify the formula. This is true, and the method for doing this is shown on Exhibit 3-2.

Exhibit 3-2 provides three charts which give you a way to determine your *personal number.* Each chart combines both a drift pattern and a specific number of boards by which the center of the ball misses your ankle. The result is a single number, your personal number, reflecting these two critical elements of your delivery. With this number you can make a very quick calculation to locate the exact board for your stance location for any angle you wish to use.

Locate your personal number by consulting one of the three charts on Exhibit 3-2. You may have to review the material in SECTION 2, THE APPROACH, to determine your drift pattern and the number of boards by which the center of the ball misses your ankle when you release it. But, once you have these two numbers, locate your personal number and mark it in the place indicated on the exhibit.

For purposes of illustration only, we will assume that you drift one board to the right and you miss your ankle by 7 boards as in our previous illustration. Chart #2 gives your personal number as 8. Now we can return to our previous example and use the personal number of 8 instead of concerning ourselves with drift and the number of boards by which you miss your ankle with the center of the ball. Both of these two items are taken into account with your personal number.

To play the same 10-to-10 foul line angle, subtract one number from the other (10 minus 10 = zero) and ADD the difference to the number of the board at the foul line (10 plus zero = 10). Then add your personal number (8) to get the number of the board to which you align yourself for your stance. (10 plus 8 = 18). Notice we still get board number 18 as the location for the stance for playing the 10-to-10 angle. This proves that the personal number is the same as taking into consideration both drift and the number of boards by which you missed your ankle with the center of the ball.

Any time you are playing a straight angle, when the board at the foul line and the board at the arrows are the same (12-to-12, 9-to-9, 8-to-8, etc.), your stance location is calculated by adding your personal number to the number of the board at the foul line. (Since both numbers are the same, it does not matter which one you add to your personal number; you will get the same result. But, for later calculations you will find it easier to *always add to the number of the board at the foul line.* This pattern will work for any

EXHIBIT 3-2
(RHB) Determining Your Personal Number

Your personal number is determined by two factors: the number of boards you *drift*, and the number of boards by which you *miss your ankle with the center of the ball when you release it*. The following charts allow you to determine your personal number by referring to the chart which corresponds with the second factor indicated above. For most bowlers this will be 6, 7 or 8 boards. Also, although zero drift is ideal, you can incorporate a drift of from 1 to 5 boards into an effective delivery. SECTION 2, THE APPROACH, illustrates how to calculate these two numbers for yourself. After calculating them, use the two numbers to find your personal number in one of these three charts. Then place it in the box that follows.

YOUR PERSONAL NUMBER IS: ☐

If you miss your ankle with the center of the ball by 6 boards, then use this CHART #1			If you miss your ankle with the center of the ball by 7 boards, then use this CHART #2			If you miss your ankle with the center of the ball by 8 boards, then use this CHART #3		
Personal Number is	**If your drift is:**	**Personal number is:**	**Personal number is**	**If your drift is:**	**Personal number is:**	**Personal number is:**	**If your drift is:**	**Personal number is:**
6	0	6	7	0	7	8	0	8
5 LEFT	1	RIGHT 7	6 LEFT	1	RIGHT 8	7 LEFT	1	RIGHT 9
4 LEFT	2	RIGHT 8	5 LEFT	2	RIGHT 9	6 LEFT	2	RIGHT 10
3 LEFT	3	RIGHT 9	4 LEFT	3	RIGHT 10	5 LEFT	3	RIGHT 11
2 LEFT	4	RIGHT 10	3 LEFT	4	RIGHT 11	4 LEFT	4	RIGHT 12
1 LEFT	5	RIGHT 11	2 LEFT	5	RIGHT 12	3 LEFT	5	RIGHT 13

EXAMPLES: If you miss your ankle by 7 boards, and drift 3 boards to the left, your personal number is 4.

If you miss your ankle by 6 boards, and drift 2 boards to the right, your personal number is 8.

If you miss your ankle by 8 boards, and drift 0 boards, then your personal number is 8.

If you drift more than 5 boards, either to the left or the right, you should make an effort to eliminate the drift, or reduce it to 3 boards or less. The less you drift, the more accurate you can be.

angle.)

What happens when the number of the board at the foul line is not the same as the number of the board at the arrows? This occurs when you play anything but a straight angle. It happens when you roll the ball across the boards on an angle to the right (called opening the angle) or when you roll the ball directly toward the pocket (called closing the angle). The formula can be used, with only *one minor modification*. But, you must know the relationship that exists for various strike angles, in reference to boards at the foul line and boards toward the back end of the approach where you take your stance.

Exhibit 3-3 illustrates the relationship that exists between boards at the foul line and boards on the approach, using the 10th board at the arrows as the target board. *A chart similar to this could be prepared for each target board at the arrows, and the relationship would remain the same.*

Notice that *for each 1 board angle change at the foul line, there is a 2 board change on the back of the approach.* The 11-to-10 foul line angle leads directly to the 12th board on the back end of the approach. The 12-to-10 foul line angle leads toward the 14th board. The 13-to-10 angle points toward the 16th board on the back end of the approach. NOTE: *The difference between the number of the board at the foul line and the number of the board at the arrows, when added to the board at the foul line, gives the board on the end of the approach.* The 13-to-10 angle (a 3 board difference) leads to the 16th board on the end of the approach. The 12-to-10 angle (a 2 board difference) leads to the 14th board on the end of the approach, etc. This relationship always exists when the angle is open, when the board at the foul line is higher in number than the board at the arrows.

When the angle is *closed,* the board number at the foul line is *lower* than the number of the board at the arrows. The same 2 board relationship exists, but you have to *subtract the difference* between the two numbers to locate the number of the board on the back end of the approach. The 9-to-10 angle leads to board number 8 on the end of the approach. The 8-to-10 angle leads to board number 6. The 6-to-10 angle leads to board number 2, etc. For all angles such as these (that point toward the pocket) you must take the difference between the two numbers describing the foul line angle, and *subtract* this from the number of the board at the foul line. This will give you the initial stance location board, to which you must still add your personal number. This *subtraction,* rather than addition, *is the minor change in the formula* which allows you to precisely calculate the stance location for any foul line angle.

Now we will summarize the use of the personal number, for both closed and open angles, and pull together all of the material related to our formula for calculating the stance location for any angle you might have to play. Perhaps a few specific examples will clarify all aspects of the formula.

Example #1 The 10-to-10 angle (a *straight* angle). The difference between the two numbers is zero.

Assume your personal number is 8.

A) Add the difference to the foul line number (10 + 0 = 10)

B) Add your personal number (10 + 8 = 18)

C) Align yourself with board 18 to play the 10-to-10 angle.

Example #2 The 12-to-10 angle (an *open* angle). The difference between the two numbers is 2.

Assume your personal number is 8.

A) Add the difference to the foul line number (12 + 2 = 14)

B) Add your personal number (14 + 8 = 22)

C) Align yourself with board 22 to play the 12-to-10 angle.

Example #3 The 20-to-15 angle (an *open* angle). The difference between the two numbers is 5.

Assume your personal number is 6.

A) Add the difference to the foul line number (20 + 5 = 25)

B) Add your personal number (25 + 6 = 31)

C) Align yourself with board 31 to play the 20-to-15 angle.

Example #4 The 8-to-10 angle (a *closed* angle). The difference between the two numbers is 2.

Assume your personal number is 6.

A) *Subtract* the difference from the foul line number (8 minus 2 = 6). NOTE: For a closed angle, we subtract.

B) Add your personal number (6 + 6 = 12)

C) Align yourself with board number 12 to play the 8-to-10 angle.

Example #5 The 6-to-10 angle (a *closed* angle). The difference between the two numbers is 4.

Assume your personal number is 7.

A) *Subtract* the difference from the foul line number (6 minus 4 = 2)

EXHIBIT 3-3

(RHB) Calculating The Stance Location on the Approach

There is a direct relationship between the number of the boards at the foul line, arrows, and back end of the approach. *For a 1 board angle change at the foul line, there is a 2 board change on the back of the approach.* This is shown by the sample foul line angles off board number 10 at the arrow zone. A chart similar to this could be prepared for each board number at the arrows, and the 2 board relationship would still be true. This relationship, combined with your personal number, allows you to calculate the stance location for playing any foul line angle. For example, *if your personal number is 6,* you would play foul line angle 12-to-10 from the 20th board on the approach. The 12-to-10 angle shows board 14 on the approach, to which you add your personal number of 6 to get stance location of board 20.

OPENING THE FOUL LINE ANGLE

Take the difference between the board at the arrows and the board at the foul line, and *add* it to the number of the board at the foul line. This gives the *initial* stance location, to which your personal number must be *added.*

CLOSING THE FOUL LINE ANGLE

Take the difference between the board at the arrows and the board at the foul line, and *subtract* this from the number of the board at the foul line. This gives the *initial* stance location, to which your personal number must be added.

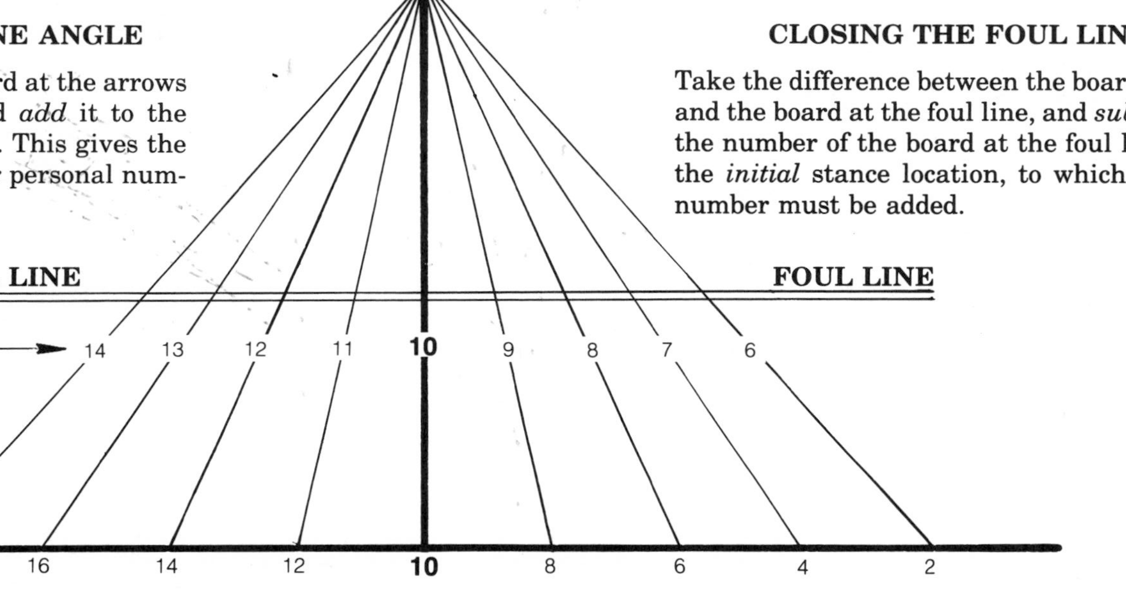

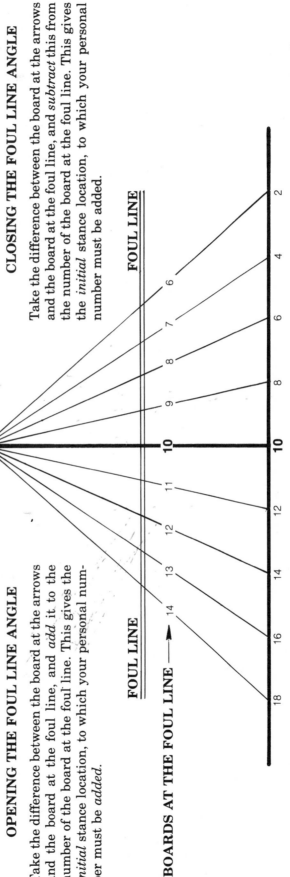

The *initial* stance location at the back of the approach, to which you must *add* your personal number. This gives you the board number on the approach which will allow you to play the appropriate foul line angle.

B) Add your personal number (2 plus 7 = 9)

C) Align yourself with board 9 to play the 6-to-10 angle.

These 5 examples cover the three types of angles you might have to play: straight, open, and closed. For *straight* angles, simply *add your personal number* to the foul line number to get the number of the board you use for your stance location. For open or closed angles, use this procedure: Calculate the difference between the number of the board at the foul line and the number of the board at the arrows. For *open* angles, *add this difference* to the foul line number and then *add your personal number*. For *closed* angles, *subtract this difference* from the foul line number, and then *add your personal number.*

To reinforce the formula into your thinking, the following table provides additional examples of foul line angles and the corresponding location to take your stance, assuming different personal numbers. *Keep in mind that the sole purpose of the calculation is to find your stance location on the approach.*

the principle of the formula, you should be able to adjust it to your backup delivery with little difficulty.

During our discussion of how to play the various strike angles, we assumed the angle was the correct one to get the ball into the pocket. But, suppose you did not hit the 1-2 pocket? Instead, you hit the head pin head-on and left a split. If you delivered the ball exactly as you had planned, then it is obvious this angle is not the one to use at this time.

Here is where you need another mathematical formula to help you find the correct angle to the pocket. Of course, you could simply *guess* how many boards to move your approach position, your target, and/or your angle. But that may take several frames of trial and error to find the correct angle, and you may run into splits or difficult spare leaves in the meantime. A mathematical formula can help you make angle adjustments and simplify the process of finding the correct angle to the pocket.

THE 3-1-2 MATHEMATICAL FORMULA: This is a mathematical formula that can help you make adjustments to find the correct angle or line

Foul Line Board		Arrows Board	Difference	Personal Number	Stance Location
17	-to-	15	+2 open	7	*17* plus 2 plus 7 equals 26.
16	-to-	14	+2 open	6	*16* plus 2 plus 6 equals 24.
12	-to-	8	+4 open	8	*12* plus 4 plus 8 equals 24.
10	-to-	10	straight	7	*10* plus 0 plus 7 equals 17.
8	-to-	8	straight	8	*8* plus 0 plus 8 equals 16.
8	-to-	9	−1 closed	7	*8* minus 1 plus 7 equals 14.
3	-to-	5	−2 closed	8	*3* minus 2 plus 8 equals 9.

As the preceding examples indicate, *the personal number is always added* in the formula. The *difference* between the two board numbers identifying the foul line angles is *added for open angles,* and *subtracted for closed angles.* If you keep these few rules in mind, and you properly determine your personal number, you can calculate the precise location for playing any angle.

SPECIAL NOTE TO BACKUP BOWLERS: If you roll a backup ball, and use the opposite side 1-2 pocket, you can still use the formula explained above. The only change you make in your calculations is to subtract your personal number at all times instead of adding it. You will, of course, be using boards and angles numbered from the left side of the lane. For example, to use the 10-to-10 angle into the 1-2 pocket (a straight angle), subtract your personal number (assume it is 7) from 10 and you end up on the 3rd board on the approach. Once you understand

into the pocket. The three numbers in the formula refer to three reference points.

a) The 3 refers to 3 boards at the *pin deck.*

b) The 1 refers to 1 board at the *foul line.*

c) The 2 refers to 2 boards at the *approach.*

The formula states: *For every 3 boards you wish to adjust the impact point of your ball at the pin deck, move your angle 1 board at the foul line, and move your approach position 2 boards.* The angle and approach moves will be in the *opposite direction* from the direction you want to adjust the contact point of the ball. In our example, to move the ball contact point back to the *right by* 3 boards (explained below) your angle move of 1 board and approach position move of 2 boards would be to the left, the opposite direction. If you wish to adjust to get the ball to hit more to the left, the angle and approach moves would be to the right.

In our illustration above, you hit the 1-pin head-on and left a split. From your knowledge of the pin deck (SECTION 2, THE PIN DECK) you know the center of the 1-pin is on the 20th board. The 1-3 pocket is the 17th board at the pin deck, you have missed the pocket by 3 boards to the left. You need to move your contact point back to the pocket, to the right by 3 boards. The 3-1-2 system can help you make this adjustment.

On our illustration you started the approach from the 18th board at the end of the approach. We assumed a 1 board drift to the right and missing the ankle by 7 boards. The angle was the 10-to-10 foul line angle, and we missed the pocket by 3 boards to the left.

To bring the ball back to the pocket (3 boards) using the 3-1-2 adjustment system, move the target at the foul line by 1 board to the left, and move 2 boards to the left in the approach position. The target and approach moves were in the same direction as the contact point on the pins. This is in accordance with the 3-1-2 formula, and follows a long standing statement in adjusting . . . *follow the ball.* If the ball is hitting to the left, move to the left in your target and approach. If the ball is hitting to the right, move your target or approach to the right.

Our new starting position on the approach is the 20th board. Our new board to hit at the foul line is the 11th board. Therefore, we are now using the 11-10 foul line angle. The angle has been opened slightly, since the new angle sends the ball slightly away from the 1-3 pocket to the right.

Now, face the target by slightly turning the feet to the right, square your shoulders to the intended line or path of the ball, and walk toward the foul line in your normal walk pattern. This slight angle change will cause you to walk back approximately ½ of the amount of movement in your approach position (½ of the 2 boards we moved) and you should drift to the right the same 1 board that we previously assumed for our example. You will therefore slide on the 18th board, miss your ankle by 7 boards, and the ball should be released on the 11th board (our 1 board foul line change that we used based upon the 3-1-2 system). Theoretically, you should hit the pocket after this adjustment, unless you made some change in your delivery (such as a speed change, loft, lift, etc.).

If, in our previous example, you had missed the pocket completely to the left, and had crossed over into the brooklyn side, you could still have used the 3-1-2 adjustment formula. The brooklyn side is board 23 from the right side of the lane. This represents a 6 board miss of the 1-3 pocket (the 17th board). The foul line target would then have been moved to the left by 2 boards, and the approach position would have been moved by 4 boards to the left.

The formula calls for a 1 board angle change at the foul line for *each* 3 boards you miss at the pin deck. And it calls for a 2 board shift of the approach position for each 1 board angle shift at the foul line. If the miss is by 6 boards *to the right,* then our foul line adjustment would be 2 boards to the right, with a 4 board change in the approach position (also to the right).

In summary of the 3-1-2 adjustment system, if you miss to the right, move your foul line angle and approach positions to the right. If you miss to the left, move both to the left. And, move your foul line angle 1 board for each 3 boards you miss at the pin deck. You move your approach position 2 boards for each 1 board change in foul line angle. Stated another way, if you want the ball to hit more to the left, move your target and approach positions to the right. If you want the ball to hit more to the right, then move your target and approach positions to the left.

This adjustment system will work consistently for you, if you deliver the ball in a well-timed and consistent manner. With practice, you can modify the formula slightly to suit your style of bowling, and to make adjustments that are not exactly in 3 board units.

THE FIVE STRIKE LINES: With this brief introduction to a system for finding the pocket, and a personal formula for adjusting your angle, we can now start to discuss the five strike lines that contain any angle you will ever have to play. *The ability to use each of these strike lines is a talent that should be in the adjustment arsenal of every serious bowler.*

The pattern for discussion is as follows: First there will be an exhibit illustrating the general nature of the strike line. This chart will indicate the specific boundaries of the line, including the boards at the foul line, and the boards at the arrows which comprise the line. The chart will also contain general information about the strike line, such as the two boundary foul line angles which separate one line from another. Keep in mind that these are somewhat arbitrary boundaries for analysis only. Whether a specific angle is within one strike line or the immediately adjacent one is not a material factor in the discussion. There is agreement on the existence of these five general areas for playing various types of lane conditions, even though there are minor differences in names for the lines, and the exact boundary from one line to another.

Following the illustration, the line is discussed from the point of view that more than a movement on the approach is needed to properly play any given strike line. You must face your target on the lane, which means that sometimes you are walking parallel to the boards on the approach, and at other times you are walking at an angle to these boards. You may have an unintentional change in your walk pattern (drift) as you go from one line to another. Your method of targeting or aiming may change. As you move to the inside lines, you might make a small change in your targeting or aiming, looking a little further out on the lane. As you move to the outside strike lines, you might bring your aiming in a little closer to the foul line. How much you alter your aiming is a matter of personal preference.

Try to maintain the same walk pattern as you move from one strike line to another. One way to help you achieve this, is to *let the ball guide you or pull you through the line.* Don't pull the ball! *Let it pull you to and through the foul line angle you have selected to play.* By starting the ball in the direction of the line you are playing, the ball can help you walk in a straight pattern. This action will help you overcome the tendency to drift which is often associated with the inside and outside lines.

Still other factors have to be taken into consideration when you move from one strike line to another. You may move to the extreme outside line and find that the ball return or a wall interferes with your approach and delivery. For some bowlers these items are a problem, but for others they are no cause for concern.

Lane conditions are the major reason for changing from one strike line to another. As lanes break down, as they begin to hook, you will find yourself moving to the inside strike lines. If you find that the lanes are not hooking very much, you may go to the outside lines. If the lane track is a benefit to you, the second arrow strike line might be the one to select. If the lane track presents a problem, you may have to go either to the inside or outside strike lines to avoid the problem. If you find an erratic lane condition, (high or low board, dry spot, spotty condition, wet spot, etc.) you will have to move from one strike line to another to get around the situation. *You should practice every one of the five strike lines,* and many foul line angles within each line, so you can use any line or angle to adjust to any lane condition you find.

A complete knowledge and understanding of each strike line is essential if you are to take full advantage of the adjustment opportunities each one offers. One strike line will be best to use on a given lane at a particular time. If you can find that strike line, and play it properly, you will significantly increase your chances for making strikes.

We will begin our discussion with the deep inside strike line, and proceed through the other lines to the deep outside line. Remember, all five general strike lines were summarized on Exhibit 3-1.

DEEP INSIDE ANGLES (Right Handed Bowlers)

This strike line is the only one in which you cannot roll straight down the boards, or even from the right side of the approach. The 18th board at the arrows (the right-most board in this line) is already to the left of the 1-3 pocket (board 17).

All angles within this strike line are left-to-right angles; such as 20-to-18; 25-to-22; etc. The two boundary angles in this line are the 20-to-18 and 27-to-22 foul line angles.

Although this strike line does not include boards beyond 22 at the arrows, you may have to go to the left of board 22 to get the ball into the pocket. Some lane conditions require going as deep as the 5th arrow from the right side of the lane, or the 25th board. This extreme inside line is used on lanes that are very dry and hooking a great deal.

If you are playing the 25-to-22 line, and the ball is still high in the pocket, don't hesitate to move even further to the left side of the approach and use a much deeper angle. The need to go much deeper than a 27-to-22 angle is a condition that the league bowler will not normally have to play.

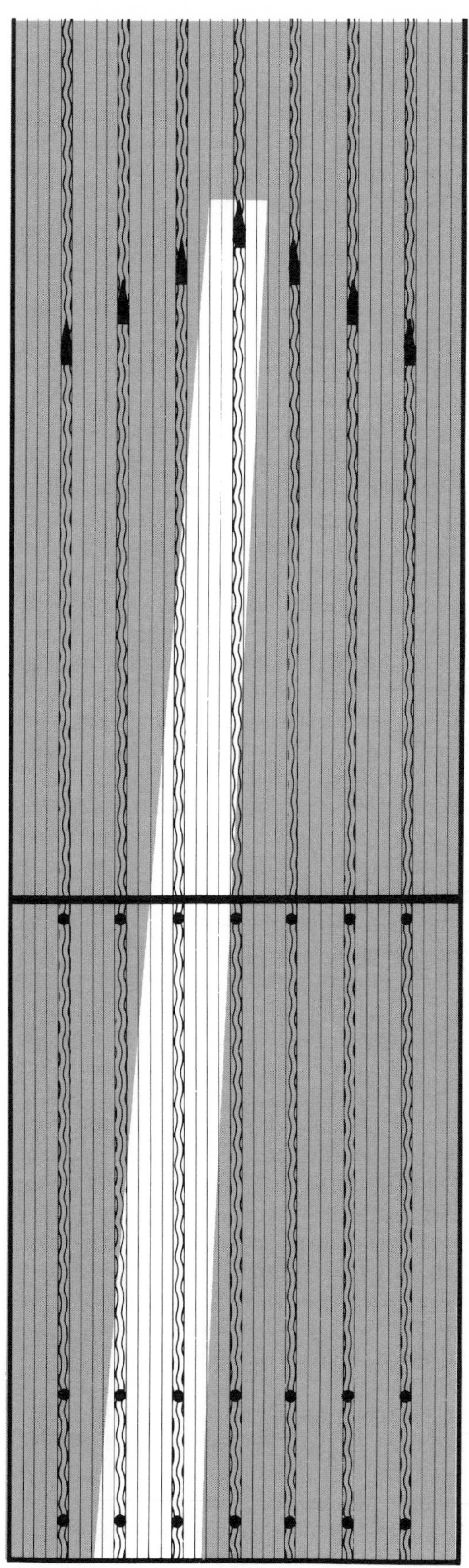

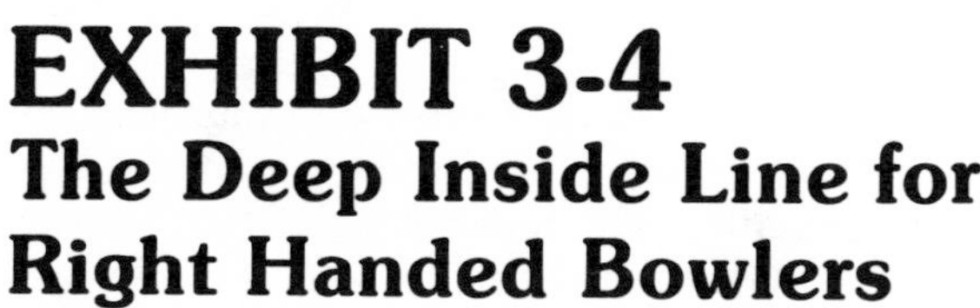

EXHIBIT 3-4
The Deep Inside Line for Right Handed Bowlers

BOARDS 18–22 AT THE ARROWS

BOARDS 20–27 AT THE FOUL LINE

PLAYING THE DEEP INSIDE LINE: In the next few paragraphs we will describe the conditions under which you might elect to use the deep inside strike line. First we will look at lane conditions that suggest the use of this line. Then we will cover aiming, alignment/walk patterns, and other factors related to the use of this strike line.

Lane Conditions: The deep inside line is used when the lanes are very dry and hooking a great deal. Under such lane conditions it is desirable to get the ball further down the lane before it begins its break to the pocket, and it is often necessary to cut down on the amount of the hook. Both of these objectives can be achieved by moving to the inside of the approach and using this strike line.

Another possible lane condition that could dictate using the deep inside line is when the lane track is so strong that it takes the ball into the pocket too quickly. Moving to the inside of the approach and using this line will get the ball further down the lane before it gets into the lane track. This late entrance into the track has two influences which will cut down on the hook. First, the ball will be angling away from the pocket, making it more difficult for the ball to hook strongly back to the left. And, secondly, the ball is in the track portion of the lane for a shorter time, giving the track less time to allow the ball to grip the lane. Thus, the existence of a strong lane track might be overcome by moving to this deep inside strike line.

Still another lane condition that might be played best from the deep inside line is when the lane has been conditioned with more oil (dressing, conditioning) to the left side of the lane track. This additional conditioning can be used to get the ball through the heads with enough skid to delay the hook for a proper pocket angle for strikes. Perhaps the outside of the lane (toward the right hand gutter) is so dry that it is impossible to get enough skid (delay the break point) to prevent the ball from breaking too soon. Therefore, whenever you want to get the ball further down the lane before it breaks to the pocket, or whenever you wish to reduce the strength and intensity of the hook, this deep inside angle adjustment may work well for you. This assumes, of course, that you wish to reach these objectives by an angle adjustment instead of an equipment or delivery change.

Aiming: A general rule concerning the strike line you are using and the distance beyond the foul line that you aim states: As you move toward the inside of the lane (toward the center of the approach) you should move your target further down the lane; as you move to the outside of the lane (toward the right gutter) you should move your target closer to the foul line. Therefore, the point of aim for this deep inside line should be further down the lane than any other strike line, since this line is more *inside* than any other.

The reason for moving the target further down the lane for this deep inside line is that you will be better able to *extend* yourself and get the ball further down the lane before it breaks for the pocket. Since the target is further down the lane, you may automatically loft the ball slightly further out on the lane, a delivery adjustment that goes hand-in-hand with the use of the deep inside line.

Alignment/Walk Pattern: As you open the angle of your strike ball delivery, which you do when you use this deep inside line, you must align your feet toward your target on the lane. Your shoulders should be square to your target and not to the foul line. Then you walk in a straight line toward your target, which means you will be walking at a slight angle to the foul line and the boards on the approach. *It is this angled path to the foul line which causes some bowlers to drift, or to slightly alter their walk pattern.* Let's take each of the three conditions regarding drift and analyze them separately as they relate to this deep inside strike line: (1) you have no drift in your approach, (2) you drift to the left, or (3) you drift to the right.

If *you have no drift* in your normal walk pattern to the foul line, using this deep inside line might cause you to drift a little either to the left or the right. A right drift is possible since you are walking slightly to the right toward the foul line and you might walk a little too much to the right, creating a slight drift. You might, on the other hand, drift left by trying to walk in a straight line parallel to the boards on the approach, rather than the slight angle required to properly play this strike line. In either case, you need to be aware of what is happening, since this drift may make it difficult for you to hit your target on the lane. If any change in your drift pattern occurs because you are now approaching the foul line from an angle (and you can't correct it) you will have to incorporate this drift pattern in your calculation of where to stand on the approach to begin your shot.

If you have *a slight drift to the left* in your natural delivery, the use of the deep inside line may cause you to drift slightly less than normal. This reduced amount of drift is caused by the fact that you are angling toward the right when you play this line properly, and it is more difficult to drift left while angling to the right. Keep in mind, however, you may *not* drift any less while using this line, but the tendency is that you will.

If you have *a drift to the right* in your normal delivery, the use of the deep inside strike line *may* cause you to drift slightly more to the right. This additional drift is created because you are angling to the right and drifting to the right. It is easier to increase the amount of your normal drift under these circumstances. Again, you *may not* drift more to the right, but the tendency will be to do so. And if you do drift a little more, you will need to make some correction in lining up for the shot, or work to eliminate the additional drift from your approach and delivery. *Letting your swing bring or guide you through the line can help insure a straight walk pattern, even when you are angling to the right.*

Whether your drift pattern is altered by the use of this strike line, or any other strike line, is not the important point. What *is* important is that you are aware of what *might* happen to your normal walk pattern as you use the various strike lines. Then you can decide whether you will try to eliminate the extra drift (through practice sessions), or to make some other correction in your game to use the drift properly. It is important that you end up at the foul line on the correct board at the moment of release, and that you place the ball on the correct board at the foul line. Therefore, observe your drift and walk pattern in this deep inside line (and all other strike lines) so you will be able to adjust accordingly.

Try to let the ball guide you to and through the foul line angle you have selected. When you start the swing properly, directly in line with the angle, the ball can help keep you in a straight-line walk pattern.

Other Factors Related to the Deep Inside Line: Changing your angle or strike line is more than a simple move to the left or right on the approach. We indicated that your drift pattern may change, and your method of aiming may be altered. There are even more factors you should keep in mind as you use the deep inside line.

Sometimes the use of a deep inside angle will put you nearer to obstacles that might not affect you from another line. If you are on the side of the lane where the ball return is located, or you are near a wall, these obstacles might cause you to deliver the ball in other than a normal manner. Some bowlers are afraid of hitting the ball return or wall with the free foot during the delivery. Others consciously or unconsciously walk away from the obstacles during the delivery, causing a change in their natural drift pattern and/or putting them at the foul line in a sideways position. This could cause a number of problems with the delivery or release of the ball. If such obstacles concern you, then you should either practice where such conditions exist, or make some other adjustment in your game to eliminate the possible problem. You might increase the speed of your delivery, therefore giving you the opportunity to reduce the angle slightly, and keep you away from the obstacles. (Delivery adjustments will be covered in a later section.) Or, you might make a change in your equipment to require less of an angle. However, it may be best to just practice until the problem is eliminated, so you can take full advantage of this strike line when conditions dictate its use.

Still another factor to consider when using the deep inside line is that you may be using a portion of the approach that has not been used much. This means you may either stick or slip at the foul line. Test this portion of the approach before you use it and there should be no problem. And if you are using the same deep inside line on both lanes you will have to test the condition on both approaches, since there is no way you can assume that the condition on one approach is the same on the other.

You may also wish to change your equipment or delivery (or both) in conjunction with the use of the deep inside strike line. Some of these possible adjustments will *complement* your move to the inside line, and others will *counteract* the move. Although these two major classifications of adjustments were fully discussed in SECTION 1, here are examples of additional adjustments you might wish to make. You could *increase your speed,* which goes along with the move to the inside line. Both are designed to get the ball further down the lane before the break to the pocket. Or, you could *reduce the amount of lift* you put on the ball, also delaying the break point. And, of course, you could change your equipment to a *different ball surface* or *balance.* All of these adjustments could be made in conjunction with the change to the deep inside line. Now you can see how many variables are at work as you try to find the proper strike line, equipment, and delivery technique to get the ball and lane working together for you.

The deep inside angle is designed to get the ball further down the lane before it heads toward the pocket. It is an adjustment to get the ball back to the pocket after it has passed by on the left side of the head pin. For those who use the hook ball, such an angle will get the ball further down the lane before the break begins to the pocket. This will delay the timing and intensity of the hook. These changes in the *timing* and the *intensity* of the hook are obvious methods for playing dry and hooking lanes.

INSIDE ANGLES (Right Handed Bowlers)

This strike line gives you the chance to play open (right to left), closed (left to right), and straight angles. The two boundary angles are the 21-to-17 shot, and the 11-to-13 closed angle. Between these two foul line angles are a variety of angles, all part of the inside line.

Notice the wide area of the approach covered by this line. This provides a great deal of options for getting the ball into the pocket. Most of these angles or options are needed whenever the lane is hooking too much, and it is necessary to roll the ball to the right so the hook will be delayed until the ball is further down the lane.

As with all five strike lines, the boundaries of this line may be extended one or more boards to the left or right at the arrows or foul line.

Normally, no more than a five board angle is played over a given board at the arrows. This is not a hard-and-fast rule, but is a guideline to follow when moving from one angle to another.

The purpose of illustrating all five strike lines, including this one, is to give you a more precise method for adjusting to lane conditions by changing your angle of entry into the pocket. Changing the angle from the foul line to the arrows will change the pocket angle.

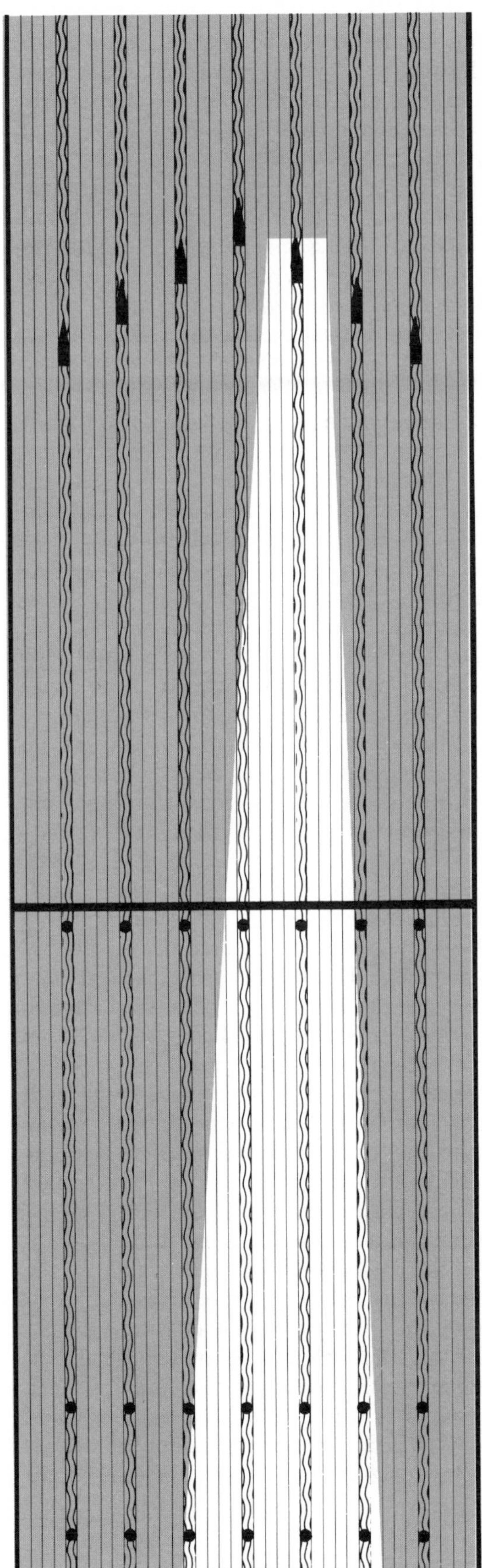

EXHIBIT 3-5
The Inside Line for Right Handed Bowlers

BOARDS 13–17 AT THE ARROWS

BOARDS 11–21 AT THE FOUL LINE

PLAYING THE INSIDE LINE: In the next few paragraphs we will describe the conditions under which you might elect to use the inside strike line, and the various foul line angles within that line. First we will look at the types of lane conditions suggesting the use of this line. Then we will follow the same pattern as used for the previous strike line (the deep inside line), by covering such topics as aiming, alignment/walk pattern, and other factors related to the use of the inside strike line.

Lane Conditions: The inside line is often used when the lane is a *little* dry and the ball is hooking a *little* more than you would like. Under such a condition it is desirable to get the ball a little further down the lane before it breaks to the pocket. High pocket hits suggest you might move in to this strike line, if you were using the second arrow strike line.

The lane track might also cause you to move to this inside strike line. The track might be *grabbing* the ball too soon, and taking it high into the pocket. Moving in slightly on the approach and using this inside strike line may be just enough to get the ball back to the pocket.

You may also be able to find more oil on this portion of the lane, thereby giving you more opportunity to get the ball *through the heads* and delay the hook or break point until the ball is further down the lane.

In summary, lane conditions suggesting the inside line are somewhere between conditions suggesting the deep inside strike line and those conditions which make the second arrow strike line the best to play. Therefore, we will not dwell too much on lane conditions for this strike line. The topic is covered fairly well in the discussions of those other two strike lines.

Aiming: The general rule regarding aiming and strike lines is used in deciding how far out on the lane you will target for this inside strike line. (This rule was explained under the deep inside strike line. Basically, it states that you might move your target out on the lane as you move to the inside lines, and target closer to the foul line as you move to outside lines.)

The exact distance for aiming while using the inside line will, of course, depend upon personal preferences. But the distance should be slightly closer than you would use for the deep inside line, and slightly further out on the lane than you would use for the second arrow strike line (discussed next).

Since you are still on the inside lines, you want to get yourself to extend properly, to perhaps loft the ball slightly further out on the lane than you would with the second arrow line (yet a little closer than you might for the deep inside line). By moving your point of aim, your target, these delivery adjustments should occur naturally, with no conscious effort on your part.

Alignment/Walk Pattern: The inside strike line contains straight, open and closed foul line angles. Therefore, depending upon which portion of the line you are using, you will have to be sure you are properly aligned to your target on the lane. At times you will be parallel to the boards on the approach (straight angles); at times you will be angling to the right (open angles); and at other times you will be aligned toward the pocket (closed angles).

In each case you must *square yourself to your target, walk in your normal pattern* to the foul line, and *let your swing pull you through the line.* The ball should be in line with the foul line angle you are playing.

Your drift pattern should not be affected by playing this inside line. When you are playing a closed angle within the line, you will be angling slightly to the left, and this may cause you to drift a little to the left when you have no normal drift. It may, however, cause you to drift less if you have a normal right drift, or to drift slightly more to the left when you already have a left drift in your approach.

On the other hand, playing open angles within the line might cause you to: (A) drift slightly to the right; (B) drift less to the left if you have a left drift; or (C) drift more to the right if you already have a drift to the right.

These changes in drift are *tendencies only.* Watch for these possible changes in your walk pattern so you can correct them, or incorporate *small* walk pattern changes in your adjustment calculations.

Other Factors Related to the Inside Strike Line: The inside line is used to get the ball back to the pocket after you have been using the second arrow strike line and hitting high or crossing over in front of the pocket. This strike line will often come into play when you notice the lanes are beginning to *break down* slightly as a result of play on them.

Of course, you could have been using the deep inside line, and not be getting up to the pocket. In that case, moving to the right on the approach, and using this inside strike line would give you a better angle into the pocket, bringing the ball up to the pocket.

You should encounter no obstacles (ball return, wall, etc.) when you use this strike line. Moreover, you might wish to use other adjustment techniques with this strike line. Less lift, a harder ball surface, and more speed are also adjustments designed to get the ball further down the lane before breaking for the pocket, which this strike line is designed to do.

We suggest that you only make one adjustment at a time, and preferably only the angle change. That way you will be in a better position to understand the result of the adjustment you have made.

SECOND ARROW ANGLES
(Right Handed Bowlers)

This is the most commonly used strike line, the one that most bowlers learn to bowl upon. Several reasons account for its wide use: it is located in the center of the right side of the lane, which appears to be a natural location for the right hander to select and use; it feels comfortable for the right hander because he or she can use the center portion of the approach for the stance location; it permits a use of a wide area of the approach for many angles within the strike line; it is consistent with a normal desire to avoid extremes, that is, not to play too near the gutter; most high average bowlers develop a 6 or 7 board hook, and the line is about that number of boards to the right of the pocket (the 17th board at the pin deck).

Because this strike line is used so often by right handed bowlers, and because almost 85% of those who bowl are right handed, a track or groove is often worn into the lane, usually at boards 8 through 12 from the right side of the lane.

This lane track presents special situations for the right handed bowler that left handers do not have to face. At times the lane track will assist the RHB in getting into the pocket, and at other times the track will get the ball hooking too soon, or make it difficult to get the ball into the pocket properly.

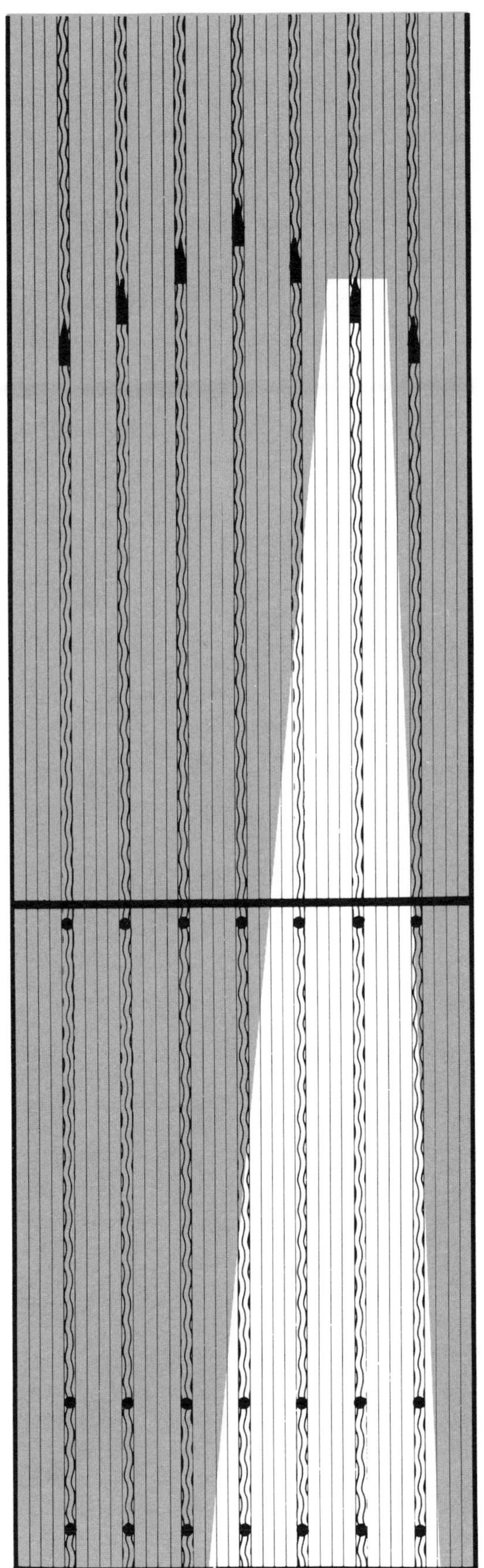

EXHIBIT 3-6
The Second Arrow Line for Right Handed Bowlers

BOARDS 8-12 AT THE ARROWS

BOARDS 6-17 AT THE FOUL LINE

PLAYING THE SECOND ARROW LINE: On the following page we state why this strike line is so popular and frequently used. In the paragraphs that follow we will take into consideration other factors you must also think about when you play this line, including: lane conditions; aiming; alignment/ walk pattern; and other factors. It should be obvious at this point that an angle change is more than simply a movement to the left or right on the approach. Each time you change your angle you have to be aware of other needed changes, or accidental changes that may occur.

Lane Conditions: The second arrow strike line is used when the lanes are what most bowlers consider *normal,* that is, the lanes are not too dry and hooking nor are they too wet and not hooking. They are just right for you. Someone else bowling with you at the same time might conclude that the lanes are hooking too little or too much for them, but that is not important. They may be using a different delivery, different equipment, etc. Or they could just prefer another strike line and have made some other adjustment to allow them to use that line.

A second reason why the second arrow strike line might be recommended, or work well for you, is that the lane track is helping to guide the ball into the pocket. In that case it is best to get the lane and the ball working together for you. Rather than make a move to the inside of the lane and enter the track further down the lane, or move outside and enter the track on a more direct angle into the pocket, it may be best (under some lane conditions) to get the ball in the lane track immediately, and let them both work for you.

Still another reason why lane conditions might favor this second arrow strike line is when the pattern of oil or conditioning is erratic on both sides of the lane track. Playing on either side of the lane track might cause an unpredictable reaction of the ball. Or it could be that the pattern of conditioning on either side of the lane track is too dry, making it difficult to get the ball through the heads from those strike lines. When the lane is too dry from the foul line to the arrows the ball will tend to break too soon. You may be forced to increase your speed (a delivery adjustment) to prevent this early break. However, anything that gets the ball to skid further down the lane before the break begins, without requiring any change in your approach, release or delivery, will give you an advantage in hitting the pocket correctly. Finding the proper amount of oil on the heads is the easiest way to achieve this delay in the break point. And when this is found in the second arrow strike line (around boards 6-17 at the foul line and boards 8-12 at the arrows) then you should try to use this line. It is more difficult to bowl consistently when you are forced to make a change in your delivery.

In summary, the two types of lane conditions suggesting the second arrow strike line are either a good lane track condition, or an improper lane condition on either side of the track.

Aiming: Your aiming pattern for this second arrow strike line should be the normal one you use, since this is the most commonly used strike line. Any movement in your aiming, toward or away from the foul line, should be made with reference to your point of aim for this strike line.

The general rule regarding the strike line and aiming distance applies to this line, as it does to all others. As you use the inside portion of this second arrow line you might move your point of aim slightly further out on the lane. As you use the middle portion of this strike line (for example, the 10-to-10 angle) you might aim your normal distance. But when you use the outside portion of this strike line (for example, the 6-to-8 angle) you would move your point of aim closer to the foul line.

These adjustments in aiming are all designed to get you to use the proper amount of extension or reach in your delivery. The differences in aiming points are also related to the amount of loft you use. You are more likely to use more loft when you aim at a point further down the lane than if you aim at a point closer to the foul line. Additional extension and loft are helpful in getting the ball further down the lane before it begins its break to the pocket. Thus, the purpose of moving your point of aim is, in effect, to cause you to make a small change in your delivery without any conscious effort on your part. (In a later section we discuss delivery adjustments in more detail.)

Alignment/Walk Pattern: Your alignment and walk pattern is probably least affected by this second arrow line than any other. The alignment and walk pattern you normally use is what you should have when you use this line, the normal strike line for many right handed bowlers.

There are several open angles within this strike line (those in which the ball is headed away from the pocket) as well as closed angles (where the ball is headed on a more direct line toward the 1-3 pocket). You will have a slight change in your feet alignment, and you might tend to have a small change in your walk pattern, as you use the boundary angles *within* this strike line.

The alignment of your feet should be straight toward your target. This is true in every case, with every strike line, but is worthy of repeating. *Face your target squarely, align your feet and shoulders toward the target and you are ready for your approach.* In the center of this line you will align your feet parallel to the boards on the approach, but for the outside angles within this line, your feet will be parallel to your intended path of the ball. *Then, let your swing guide you or pull you to and through your line.*

As before, let's take each possible walk pattern and look at how each might be affected as you use different strike angles in this second arrow line. We will begin with a zero drift walk pattern.

If *you have no drift* associated with your walk pattern to the foul line, you will have little if any tendency to drift by using this strike line, especially the middle portion of the line. As long as you are walking in a relatively straight line toward the foul line (such as when you are using a 10-to-10 or 11-to-11 angle), you will be walking parallel to the boards on the approach. No drift tendency should occur, other than any normal drift you might have in your walk pattern. When you elect to use an angle to the inside or outside portion of this strike line, you might develop a slight tendency to drift one way or the other. Using the inside portion of the line (toward the center of the approach) might cause you to drift slightly to the right (because your walk pattern is angled slightly to the right). Using the outside of this strike line (toward the right side of the lane) might cause you to develop a slight drift to the left (because you are angling slightly toward the left). In either case, you should be aware of the *possibility* that a drift *might* develop in your walk pattern, or your normal drift *could* be altered. If any change should occur in your drift pattern, you can either take this drift into consideration when you align yourself on the approach, or practice to eliminate the *drift tendency* when you use this strike line.

If your normal walk pattern includes *a drift tendency toward the left,* using the inside portion of this line might decrease your drift pattern, and using the outside portion of this line might increase your drift. Both of these possible changes in drift pattern are consistent with this thought: When you angle to the right in your approach you may *tend to* increase any normal drift to the right, and decrease any normal drift to the left. When you walk on an angle to the left in your approach, any left drift might be increased while a right drift in the walk pattern might be reduced. It is possible to develop or increase a drift pattern that is in line with the way you walk from your stance position to the foul line. Any drift opposite of the line you take to the foul line may tend to be lessened. Therefore, if you normally have *a drift to the right* in your walk pattern, the effect of using this second arrow line is as follows: It may increase when you use the inside of this strike line, or decrease when you use the outside. Using the center portion of the strike line (a 10-to-10 angle) should have little or no effect on your normal walk or drift pattern.

As previously stated, a small amount of drift is neither good nor bad. It is just something you have to be aware of and make whatever change is needed to use it effectively. As long as the drift pattern is constant for you, you can incorporate the drift into your natural game. *(However, you are much more likely to improve your bowling skills by eliminating drift completely.)*

Other Factors Related to the Second Arrow Line: The second arrow strike line may be used to either get back to the pocket after missing it to the left, or to get up to the pocket when you miss to the right. The inside portion of this line is an adjustment to get back to the pocket, whereas, the outside portion of the line is designed to get up to the pocket after having failed to do so.

Of course, this strike line can be used in conjunction with other delivery or equipment adjustments to get the ball into the pocket properly. You could combine the outside portion of this line with: less speed, a softer ball surface, more positive weights, less loft, or more lift on the ball. The inside portion of the line is similar to these types of adjustments: more speed, a harder surface on the ball, negative weights, more loft, and less turn on the ball. Later sections will look at each of these other adjustments independently, and in conjunction with each other.

OUTSIDE ANGLES
(Right Handed Bowlers)

This is the first of two strike lines toward the right side of the lane. Both lines contain angles that give the ball more opportunity to grab the lane and hook.

The range of angles in this line is much more narrow than the *second arrow* or *inside lines.* The boundaries for this line are the 8-to-7 angle on the inside and the 3-4 angle on the right side of the line. These are much tighter and straighter angles than the other lines since there is less area for the ball to go to the right side of this outside line. A more direct shot is needed to properly play this strike line.

As a general rule, as you move your strike line to the outside, you are forced to use a narrower range of angles. This occurs because you are using a relatively small portion of the lane. From the inside angles you are able to use the full width of the lane to execute the shot.

This narrower shot may cause you to feel constrained or tight in your approach and delivery. If you keep this potential problem in mind when you practice using this strike line, you should be able to develop the same free and relaxed swing that is normally a very natural part of using a wider line. You may also feel obliged to pull the ball away from the gutter. This problem can also be minimized with practice.

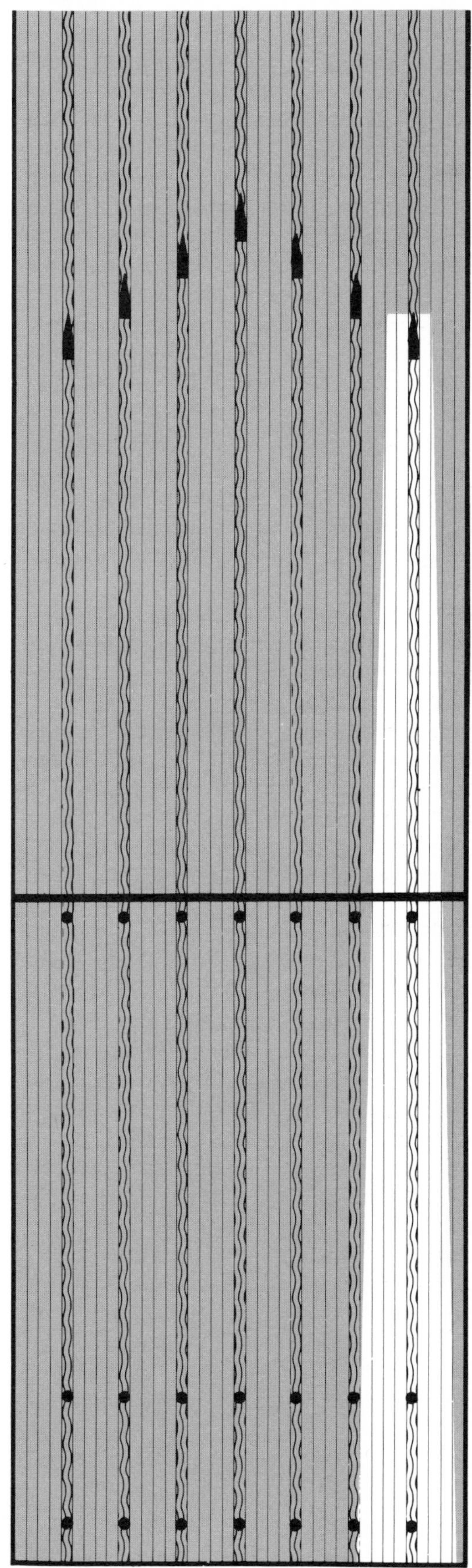

EXHIBIT 3-7
The Outside Line for Right Handed Bowlers

BOARDS 4-7 AT THE ARROWS

BOARDS 3-8 AT THE FOUL LINE

PLAYING THE OUTSIDE LINE: In the next few paragraphs we will describe the conditions under which you might decide to use the outside strike line, and the various foul line angles within that line. First we will look at the types of lane conditions suggesting use of this line. Then we will follow the pattern used for the other strike lines, covering such topics as: aiming; alignment/walk pattern; and other factors related to the use of the outside line.

Lane Conditions: The outside line is often used when the lanes are a little wet, and the ball is not hooking as much as you would like. Under such conditions it is desirable to get the ball rolling or hooking a little sooner, and this outside line will do that for you. Missing the pocket to the right is an indication that you might want to move to this outside strike line.

You may also find the oil on this portion of the lane is the proper amount to get the ball through the header portion of the lane and into a roll leading to the pocket.

The lane track might also cause you to consider using the outside strike line. Moving out on the lane may get the ball into the track at just the right time and angle to get a good pocket angle.

In summary, the type of lane conditions suggesting the use of the outside line are somewhere between those dictating either a second arrow or deep outside line. Therefore, we will not need to cover lane conditions too deeply here, since the topic is covered fairly well in the discussions of those two other strike lines.

Aiming: The general rule regarding aiming and strike lines is used for this line as well. The exact distance for aiming while using this outside line will depend upon personal preferences. But the distance should be slightly closer than you would use for the second arrow strike line, and slightly further out on the lane than you would use for the deep outside line (discussed next).

When you are using the outside line, you will probably loft the ball slightly less than you would for the second arrow line, and slightly more than you would if you were using the deep outside line. By moving your point of aim, this change in loft should occur naturally, with no conscious effort on your part.

Alignment/Walk Pattern: Most of the foul line angles contained in the outside line are relatively straight. There is not enough room in the line for very open or very closed shots. This situation is true of all outside shots. There is less room to open the angle since the gutter is so close to the right side of the line.

As with all strike lines, you must be certain that you square yourself to your target and walk in your normal pattern to the foul line. *Let the ball and your swing pull you through the strike line you are playing, keeping the straight pendulum swing, so essential to an effective delivery.* (More on this later.)

Your drift pattern should not be affected by playing this outside line. There may be a tendency to alter the drift pattern as you play the boundary angles in this line (either open or closed angle), but the shot is so straight that your walk pattern should not change. Be alert to the tendency for a walk pattern change, and take measures to eliminate the change. Or, if the change is small, you might be able to incorporate it into your walk pattern and adjustment calculations. However, a much better objective is to strive for no change.

Other Factors Related to the Outside Strike Line: The outside line is used to get the ball up to the pocket after missing to the right. Usually, these misses are not too far to the right, or else the deep outside line would be suggested. This strike line often comes into play when the lane is not hooking very well, usually the result of a heavy oil pattern around the second arrow.

Obstacles such as the ball return or a wall should not interfere with your approach when you use this strike line. This will occur, however, when you have to use the deep outside line, which we will discuss next.

Since you are usually not missing the pocket by much when you switch to the outside line, you might make other adjustments instead of using this line. For example, you could use more lift, a softer ball surface, or less speed to achieve the same objectives which the outside line allows you to reach. Or, you could combine one of these adjustments with a move to the outside line.

We suggest you make only one adjustment at a time, and preferably only the angle change, but you should be aware of other adjustments that have the same effect as the angle change to the outside strike line.

DEEP OUTSIDE ANGLES (Right Handed Bowlers)

This is probably the most uncomfortable to play of the five strike lines. That is why it is not used by many bowlers, even though it may be the best line to use to get the ball into the pocket.

This is best when the lane will not hook at all and you must give the ball as much of the lane as possible for the ball to hook across into the pocket. Sometimes the inside portion of the lane is such that any shot to the right from that angle will not get back to the pocket. Or, this may be the line that will allow you to get the ball as far down the lane as possible before it begins to hook for the pocket. Sometimes this is called the *gutter shot,* since it is right next to the gutter. This can be an extremely good angle into the pocket, but you can leave some very unusual and rare spares on occasion.

Notice how straight the shot has to be to use this strike line. There is almost no opportunity to open or close the angle of the shot. There are only 3 boards to use. As you move to the outside lines, this will happen. You are forced to play a much straighter shot down the lane. There is little margin for error on this line, and often you will see some of the best bowlers in the world roll a gutter ball while using this strike line.

Although this strike line is perhaps the most difficult to master, you should practice and develop it to give yourself that added flexibility to change the angle as the lane dictates.

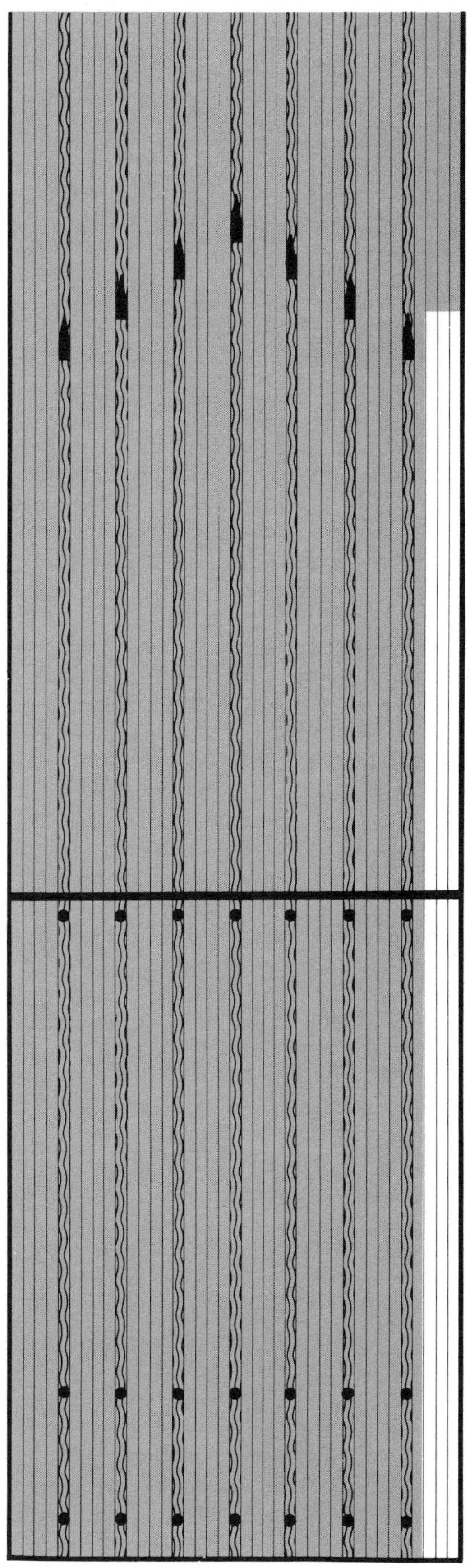

EXHIBIT 3-8
The Deep Outside Line for Right Handed Bowlers

BOARDS 1-3 AT THE ARROWS

BOARDS 1-3 AT THE FOUL LINE

PLAYING THE DEEP OUTSIDE LINE: In the next few paragraphs we will describe the conditions or situations under which you might decide to use this deep outside line. First we will describe lane conditions which suggest using this strike line; then we will cover aiming, alignment/walk pattern, and other factors to consider.

Lane Conditions: The primary lane condition suggesting the use of the deep outside line is when the lane is heavily dressed (having a lot of oil) and not hooking very much at all. Moving to the deep outside strike line will allow you to get the ball into the pocket at a more favorable angle than any of the inside lines.

The inside portion of the lane may also be spotty, with intermittent wet (oily) and dry spots. Such an inconsistent lane condition creates a very difficult condition in which to create a consistent and reliable shot to the pocket. Such an erratic path to the pins makes it difficult to read the lane well. Therefore, under such lane conditions it is usually best to move to the outside angles and strike lines.

The inside area of the lane may also have received heavy use or play. Perhaps the lane track has broken down too much, making it difficult to use this portion of the lane. There may be no consistent lane surface upon which you can find a good angle to the pocket. You may have to roll the ball across oil, through dry spots, into oil, and back into the drier areas as the ball follows a path to the pins. Under such varying lane conditions it is also difficult to produce a consistent shot to the pocket.

Finally, many times the only smooth lane condition can be found in this deep outside portion of the lane. This situation could arise because of the lack of play on this area, or it could be a result of a rougher lane surface created by constant use in the track area. A smooth lane surface will permit you to find the best and most consistent shot to the pocket, with no unusual or unplanned reactions between the ball and the lane.

Aiming: The proper distance for targeting or aiming while using this deep outside line may only be 5 feet in front of the foul line, depending upon personal preferences. This distance represents the closest method of targeting of all five strike lines, since this is the most extreme outside line. You will recall that the targeting rule states to bring the target closer to the foul line as you move to the outside lines.

This closer aiming distance may be uncomfortable to those who are not used to using it, and there is little room for error when you are laying the ball down so close to the gutter. However, as with all of our general rules, you must modify it to suit your style of bowling. Select the targeting distance which allows you to play this deep outside line comfortably. If it works well, and consistently, then it is right for you.

Other Factors Related to the Deep Outside Line: This strike line gives you a stronger angle to the pocket. You can get a great deal of action on the ball even if you give it only a little bit of lift at the release point. Therefore it is very useful to practice this strike line so you will be prepared when some of the following situations arise.

If the pins are on the heavy side, above 3 pounds 6 ounces (3-6's), you may need the additional strength of this deep outside strike line to prevent the ball from deflecting too much to the right and into the 3-pin. Heavy pins cause more deflection than light ones. It is easier to compensate for heavy pins by a line or angle change than to make an equipment or delivery change.

On occasion you will need more action on the ball, and do not wish to change your delivery or equipment. In that case, you can get more action on the ball by simply moving to the right on the approach and using the deep outside line. Even a little lift on the ball will be sufficient to create a lot of action if it is combined with the use of this strike line.

There are some difficulties in using this particular strike line, as there are special problems associated with each strike line. The ball may hook too much because of the deep angle created by this line. As we mentioned previously, a small amount of lift or turn on the ball will often result in a strong hook. Just a little mistake in your release could result in a big error in the path of the ball. Some very difficult leaves are often the result of using this deep outside line.

The ball return, or a wall, may interfere with the use of this line. You may feel uncomfortable and constrained in the use of this area of the approach. The gutter is close, and there is often a tendency to pull the ball in front of the body instead of releasing it naturally in a straight line down the intended path of the ball. Therefore, it is important that you practice the use of this deep outside strike line in order to develop your natural delivery from this portion of the approach. Get used to laying the ball down on the 1st through 3rd boards, and doing it without any concern for the nearness of the gutter, the ball return (if it is located on this side of the approach), or a wall, if you are on a lane next to one.

You may also wish to make other changes in your game when you play this strike line. You may slow down your speed slightly, since this strike line is used when the lane is not hooking, and a slower ball speed facilitates the development of a hooking action. You may also loft the ball slightly less, which is another adjustment to counteract a non-hooking lane. Or, you may make any one of a number of adjustments which assist in the use of this deep outside line.

The deep outside line can be used to get the ball further down the lane before it breaks toward the pocket. This line will get the ball into a pocket angle that will either give you a lot of strikes or some of the most difficult spare leaves you will ever face. Sometimes this line is used to get the ball back to the pocket, and at other times it is used to get the ball up to the pocket, depending upon the condition of the lane. On occasion, two bowlers on the same lane will use both the deep inside and deep outside line at the same time. Equipment or delivery changes might have to be made to accommodate the two strike lines. Some bowlers favor this line, and will use it whenever lane conditions permit them to do so. Used properly, this can be an extremely effective strike line.

SECTION 4
EQUIPMENT ADJUSTMENTS
(Right Handed Bowlers)

"Proper equipment is essential for high scoring."

CONTENTS PAGE

OVERVIEW

This section addresses the three major types of equipment adjustments for right handed bowlers: ball *balance* adjustments, ball *surface* adjustments, and ball *fit* adjustments.

Prior to a discussion of these techniques for adjusting to various lane conditions, it is necessary to explore several topics directly related to equipment adjustments.

The first topic will be *total ball weight.* Since a bowling ball may be as light as 8 pounds or as heavy as 16 pounds, selecting the proper ball weight is a very important part of any equipment adjustment strategy. A choice of ball weight is generally no problem for most adult males, since they normally select the maximum weight of 16 pounds. *This is often a mistake,* since a ball of less weight may often be a better choice.

For young boys and girls, senior bowlers, and often for adult females, the decision regarding total ball weight is significant. Moreover, the decision is *not* a lifetime decision. You may wish to change to a ball of more or less weight at various times during your bowling career, and in fact you should do so in most cases.

Next we will begin our discussion of how weight imbalances are created when a bowling ball is drilled. We start with a look at several types of weight blocks, which permit drilling the ball so that the *center of gravity* is *not* located in the center of the ball.

An imbalance is created by drilling the thumb and finger holes closer to or further away from the weight block. Imbalance is *not* created by adding weight to a portion of the ball. Thus, it is necessary to understand the concept of a weight block, and the part it plays in creating ball imbalances.

Guidelines have been established regarding the *maximum imbalance* that can be created when a ball is drilled for use. These maximums will be reviewed from time to time by accrediting agencies. It is important that you understand the relative advantages and disadvantages of each type of weight imbalance that can be created.

Then we will discuss and illustrate the five typical types of *ball tracks* (the portion of the ball surface which contacts the lane as the ball skids, rolls, and hooks to the pocket). Any discussion of weights and imbalances as an adjustment technique must consider the ball track. The effect of a given amount of ball imbalance is directly related to the location of this imbalance relative to the ball track.

As part of the discussion of ball tracks, we will briefly explore the concept of *axis weight* as a ball imbalance adjustment technique. This is one of two common methods for changing the center of gravity of the ball, thus creating imbalances which can be useful for influencing the action of the ball. The other technique for creating imbalances is called *top weight* or *label weight,* in which the top half of the ball weighs more than the bottom half after drilling is completed. Top weight usually refers to creating an imbalance in the ball by positioning the thumb and finger holes relative to the weight block. Axis weight, on the other hand, usually means changing the balance situation after the thumb and finger holes are already drilled in the ball. (Of course, you can take into consideration the positioning of the holes prior to creating axis weight imbalances).

Label weights will be discussed extensively under the section titled BALL BALANCE ADJUSTMENTS. Axis weights will only be discussed in this introductory section following the coverage of ball tracks.

Equipment selection and adjustment is both an

art and a science. Selecting or creating proper weights and imbalances, the correct fit, and differing ball surfaces cover a complex subject. For example, any discussion of ball weights and imbalances must also cover such topics as total ball weight, ball tracks, and both label and axis weights. All of these factors have some influence on the roll of the ball and its ability to create proper pin and ball deflection patterns. To compound the subject of equipment selection and adjustment even further, we must consider lane conditions, the five strike lines and related angles, and the different types of ball releases and deliveries.

We cannot make you an expert on all aspects of equipment selection and adjustment in this section. We can, however, help you understand some of the fundamentals of equipment adjustments, and make it easier for you to *communicate with an expert ball driller.* Armed with this information, you should be able to get the best equipment, properly fitted and matched to your style of bowling. You should be able to avoid many errors associated with bowling equipment.

Most of the material in this section assumes that you roll a curve or hook ball. If you roll a straight ball you can still benefit from much of the material, especially on ball fit, ball surfaces, etc. You may decide to convert to a hook or curve delivery at a later time. In fact, the availability of so many equipment adjustment techniques to those who roll a curve or hook ball should be a further incentive to convert to one of those styles of bowling.

If you roll a backup, then you should refer to the equipment section for the left handed bowler, SECTION 7. As previously mentioned and discussed in more detail in SECTION 5, (DELIVERY ADJUSTMENTS), we suggest that you use the 1-2 pocket for strikes and roll the ball as a left hander would roll it. Therefore, you should read the material on equipment adjustments as though you were left handed. All translations of the material will have been made for you, and it should be possible for you to take advantage of these equipment adjustment techniques.

Lists of ball *surface,* ball *balance,* and ball *fit* terms have been prepared for each appropriate section. These terms are part of an extensive strike-related glossary of terms appearing in this book. Appendix A includes additional terms to assist you in learning the vocabulary related to making strikes. You might wish to review these three special lists of terms prior to reading the detailed material in this equipment adjustment section. They serve as good reference points for some of the terminology and discussion which follow. (Each list appears at the end of the related section.)

This OVERVIEW section will now continue with our discussion of *total ball weight.* Following this topic we will cover *the weight block, ball tracks,* and *axis weight,* in that order.

TOTAL BALL WEIGHT: A bowling ball will weigh from about 8 pounds to a maximum of 16 pounds after it is drilled. Most bowling balls will weight 10 pounds or more, with a majority of adult bowlers using the maximum 16 pound ball.

What weight is best for you? In general, the answer to that question is: "A ball that is as heavy as you can comfortably control during the swing and delivery stage of bowling." The two problems associated with total ball weight relate to your normal strength, and pin and ball deflection at the pin deck.

As you develop your overall strength you will be able to handle a ball of increasing total weight. Thus, young bowlers should start out with a ball that feels comfortable to them, one they can control instead of a ball that controls them. Adults should favor a ball of 15 or 16 pounds, since this weight can normally be handled by them. As you increase in age, your strength and ability to control a heavy ball begin to diminish, and you should consider using a ball of less total weight. There are no benefits, and many disadvantages to using the maximum ball weight when you are no longer able to control it properly. Change to a lower ball weight, one that you can still control.

Too many adults continue to use the maximum ball weight because they do not want others to know that their ball is less than a full 16 pounds. How foolish; scoring is bound to suffer. If you need a lighter ball, then by all means get one. You will still be able to bowl well (perhaps better) and can make other adjustments to compensate for the lighter ball. For the average bowler who must normally convert 7 spares per game, the lighter ball is almost certain to help maintain or improve his or her average. And, as for strikes, the lighter ball can be more effective since it will be rolled with more control. Let's look at some of the adjustments you can make to overcome some of the minor disadvantages of the lighter ball.

Pin deflection and ball deflection are the two major areas for consideration when you change to a lighter ball. Actually, ball deflection is of more concern, since the difference between pin deflection with a heavier or lighter ball will normally not cause you any problems. (In fact, the velocitation could be better with the lighter ball.) Ball deflection is another matter altogether.

A lighter ball will deflect more when it hits the pins, and may be deflected out of the ideal path through the pins. Therefore, as you reduce the total weight of the ball you can make a number of adjustments to keep the ball in the correct path of deflection.

Increased speed will keep the ball in the proper path of deflection. *More lift,* turn, action, etc. on the ball will keep it driving into the pocket. And it may be easier for you to put more action on a ball that you can control well. *A deeper angle* into the pocket will also overcome the deflection problem. The use of *top or axis weight* can also give the ball more drive and reduce deflection. Any one or more of these adjustment techniques can overcome any problems with the lighter ball, and will probably cause your average to increase.

With so many adjustment techniques available to you, it makes no sense to continue using a ball that is too heavy for you to control. You will probably develop problems in your delivery, release, timing, etc. There is no merit in using a ball too heavy to control properly.

If you are *not* using a fingertip or semi-fingertip grip, then you might consider changing your span when you change to a lighter ball. You could go from a conventional grip to the semi or full fingertip. The added span will permit you to get more action on the ball, therefore giving the ball more of a chance to hold its line in the path through the pins.

In summary, the total weight of the ball is an important factor in determining how well you bowl. There is an ideal weight for you, depending upon your ability to control the ball. Find the ideal weight for you. Do not be afraid to drop to a lighter ball (or increase to a heavier ball) if that is called for. *Many people should be using a ball that weighs less than the maximum 16 pound limit.* Still others, but a lesser number, are using a ball that is too light for them, which can also cause control and deflection problems.

Take care in relying upon the stated weight found on most bowling balls. Often the ball will weigh as much as one pound *more or less* than the weight appearing on the ball. This is particularly true when you purchase a ball from any place other than a bowling center or pro shop. Have your bowling ball accurately weighed by an expert ball driller who has the correct equipment for doing this.

Increased control and comfort in delivery by having the proper ball weight could mean a significant increase in scoring ability. This is particularly important on spare leaves, where accuracy and not action (pin or ball deflection) is the key to success. Continue to assess the total weight of your bowling ball to determine if it is a factor contributing to your success or lack of success. Be ready to change to a heavier or lighter weight when the change is needed. Your scores should improve, and you will have added another valuable technique to your adjustment arsenal.

THE WEIGHT BLOCK: Thumb and finger holes must be drilled into the top half of the ball. It is illegal to drill holes into the bottom of the ball, opposite the manufacturer's mark. Such a ball could not be used in sanctioned competition. Since holes represent weight taken out of the top half of the ball, the manufacturing process has to make the top half of the ball initially weigh more than the bottom half. To do this, a weight block of some type is used.

Exhibit 4-1 illustrates the form or shape that a weight block might take. Other forms and shapes are used, but these illustrate some of the more common types of weight blocks. In each case, *the purpose of the block is to add weight to the top half of the ball during the manufacturing operation in preparation for weight removal caused by drilling the thumb and finger holes.*

To get this additional top weight, the ball is manufactured with an added portion of material which weighs more than the normal substance from which the core of the ball is made. The size, shape, location, etc. of the weight block will vary from manufacturer to manufacturer. There will be more research into the impact of weight blocks of various sizes, shapes, and locations (multiple weight blocks) within the top half of the ball. However, the purpose of the additional weight provided by the block or blocks will remain essentially the same, to make the top half of the ball weigh more than the bottom half in preparation for drilling, and to stabilize the roll of the ball.

If the top and bottom halves weighed exactly the same prior to drilling, then after drilling the bottom half would always weigh more than the top.

Ball drilling experts agree that top weight may be desirable to cause the ball to react differently (and beneficially) on the lane. Bottom weight, on the other hand, is considered an undesirable situation. Therefore, weight blocks will continue to provide sufficient additional top weight to more than compensate for the weight loss due to drilling the thumb and finger holes. The result will be excess top weight after drilling.

Drilling the holes with reference to this excess top weight is what causes ball balance (or imbalance, if you prefer) situations. Holes that are drilled close to the excess top weight have the least imbalance. Holes that are drilled away from the excess weight have the most imbalance. Imbalance is created by removing weight from the ball, not by adding weight anywhere. *Weight blocks give you the opportunity to create ball imbalances.*

BALL TRACKS: As the ball rolls down the lane, only a small portion of the surface of the ball actually comes into contact with the lane. That portion of the ball which touches the lane will, over

EXHIBIT 4-1
Four Examples of Weight Blocks

Weight blocks provide excess top weight. When the thumb and finger holes are drilled (removing some top weight) the top portion of the ball will still weigh as much as or more than the bottom half. Excess top weight may be very desirable, but excess bottom weight is rarely used.

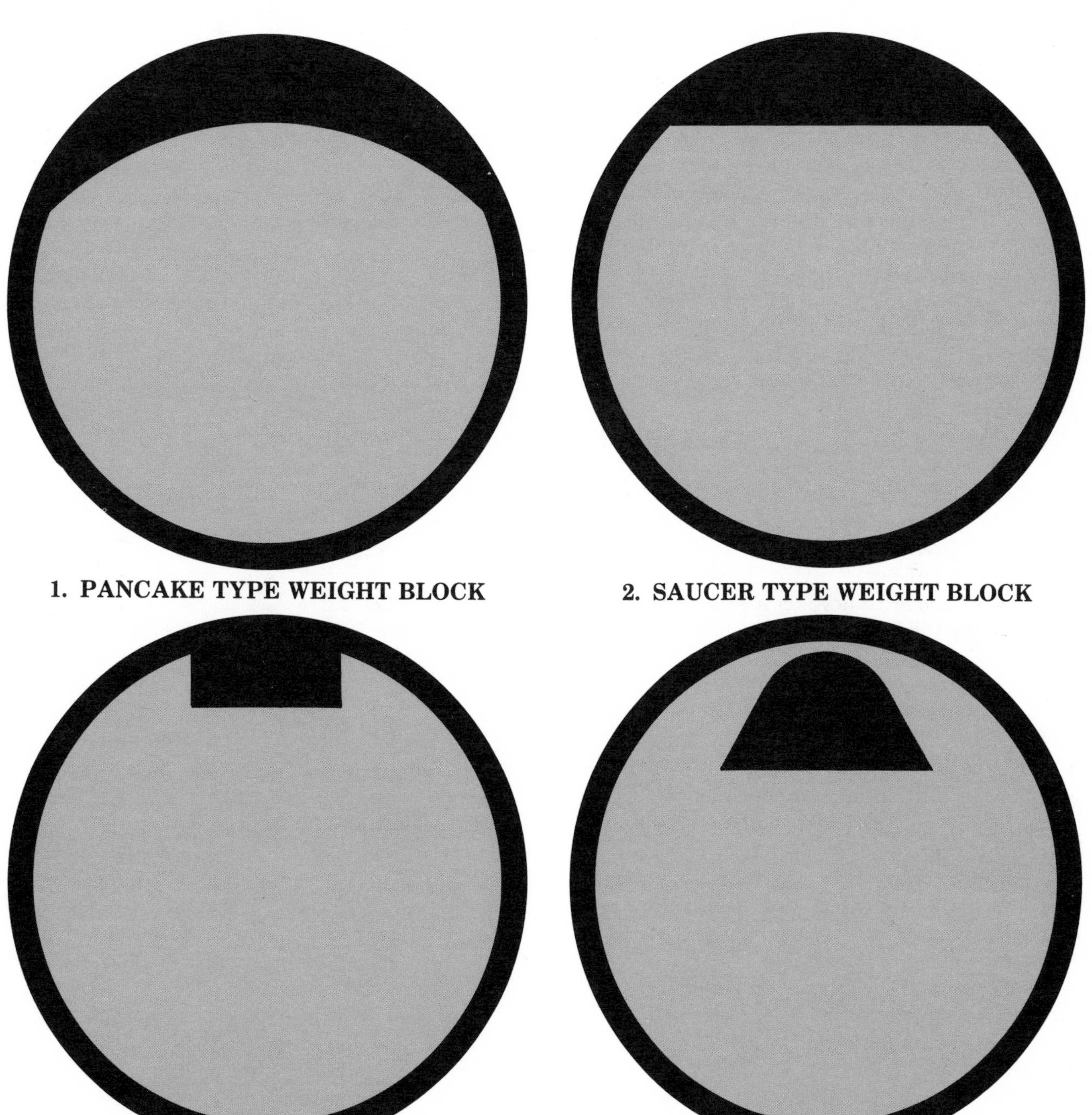

time, scratch a ring or circle around the entire ball, or some smaller portion of the circumference. *This circle or ring of wear is called a ball track.*

You can readily see the ball track by looking closely at the surface of the ball. A narrow ball track indicates a steady consistent ball release. A wide ball track indicates just the opposite situation.

Each pattern of scratch marks or tracking identifies a certain type of ball roll. With some ball tracks the ball rolls around the entire circumference of the ball. With other ball tracks, only a very small circle is created.

What is the significance of the ball track? Each type of ball track indicates how the ball might react on the way to the pins, and what impact the ball may have in terms of pin carry, ball deflection, etc. The ball track is also related to the utility of ball weights and imbalances. A given amount of ball imbalance will have more or less impact on ball roll, depending upon where the imbalance is located relative to the ball track.

Some ball tracks are more effective than others. Therefore, a knowledge of ball tracks will give you some idea of the potential scoring effectiveness of the ball. We will review the impact of each ball track on the action of the ball.

Over the years ball tracks have been called by various names, such as the full roller, high roller, ¾ roller, spinner, etc. Very little standardization exists in the names and means for distinguishing one ball track from another.

Bill Taylor, author of many bowling publications, has attempted to develop a set of standards for determining the measurements which define the most common types of ball tracks. His purpose is "to attempt to standardize the definitions for efficiency and accuracy in the exchange of information regarding bowling ball tracks." (From *Balance,* by Bill Taylor, referenced in Appendix C. This is an excellent book containing enormous detail on ball balance, ball tracks, and many other concepts for the serious bowler.)

Exhibit 4-2 contains the chart for standardization of ball tracks by name, size, description, and other characteristics separating one ball track from another. This chart was developed by Bill Taylor, and represents the best attempt at standardization of ball track terminology that the authors have seen.

In the following material, we will describe the characteristics of the five types of ball tracks, and identify the scoring effectiveness of each one. We will also relate the use of top weight (sometimes called label weight) to the tracks, in addition to discussing lane conditions related to ball tracks. *In SECTION 5 we will outline types of releases which produce each type of ball track.*

The five ball tracks are, by name: *full roller, high roller, low roller, high spinner,* and *low spinner.* Each name is descriptive, indicating in descending order the percentage of the circumference of the ball covered by the track, as indicated in Exhibit 4-2. The *spherical diameter* of the full roller is 13½ inches, or a ball track that covers the entire circumference of the ball. On the other hand, the spherical diameter of the low spinner is the smallest of the five ball tracks, only 7½ inches. (Spherical diameter is measured by a tape measure across the full diameter of the track, and is curved by the shape of the ball. See Exhibit 4-2.)

The total distance between the ball track and the thumb and finger holes is another identifying characteristic separating the five tracks. These two dimensions, spherical diameter and distance from the thumb and finger holes, are the most important elements in separating one type of ball track from another.

Before discussing each type of track separately, it is important to keep in mind one essential element of ball balance (or imbalance) as it relates to ball tracks. The closer the ball imbalance is to the ball track the LESS effect it has on ball action. The further away from the ball track the imbalance is, the MORE effect on ball performance you can get. This relationship will become clearer after you read the material regarding BALL BALANCE ADJUSTMENTS. The usefulness of weights and balances is dependent upon the type of ball track.

The following paragraphs will only summarize the essential features and potential scoring effectiveness of the five types of ball tracks. If you wish to read a great deal more about each one, we refer you to *Balance* by Bill Taylor as referenced in Appendix C.

The Full Roller (Spherical Diameter of 13½ inches). This ball track has the largest spherical diameter of the five types of tracks. It travels between the thumb and fingers, and covers the full circumference of the ball. Traction is good on the full roller, but it is not possible to get any real benefit from the use of top or label weight with this ball track. The full roller normally does not get many ball revolutions and is inferior to some of the other ball tracks in this respect.

The High Roller (Spherical Diameter of 12 inches). This is the second largest of the ball tracks, and has been called by various other names in different parts of the country. Semi-roller, three quarter-roller, and high three-quarter-roller are some of the more common names. They suggest that the ball track covers approximately three fourths of the circumference of the ball. Because the track of the high roller does not intersect the top of the ball, and

EXHIBIT 4-2
Standardization of Ball Tracks (Right Handed Bowlers)

This chart represents an attempt to standardize the terminology of bowling ball tracks for right handed bowlers. It provides illustrations and descriptions of the five major types of ball tracks. It also characterizes each one by name, spherical diameter, angle of the ball track to the lane, distance between ball track and thumb and finger holes, and other pertinent features of each type of ball track.

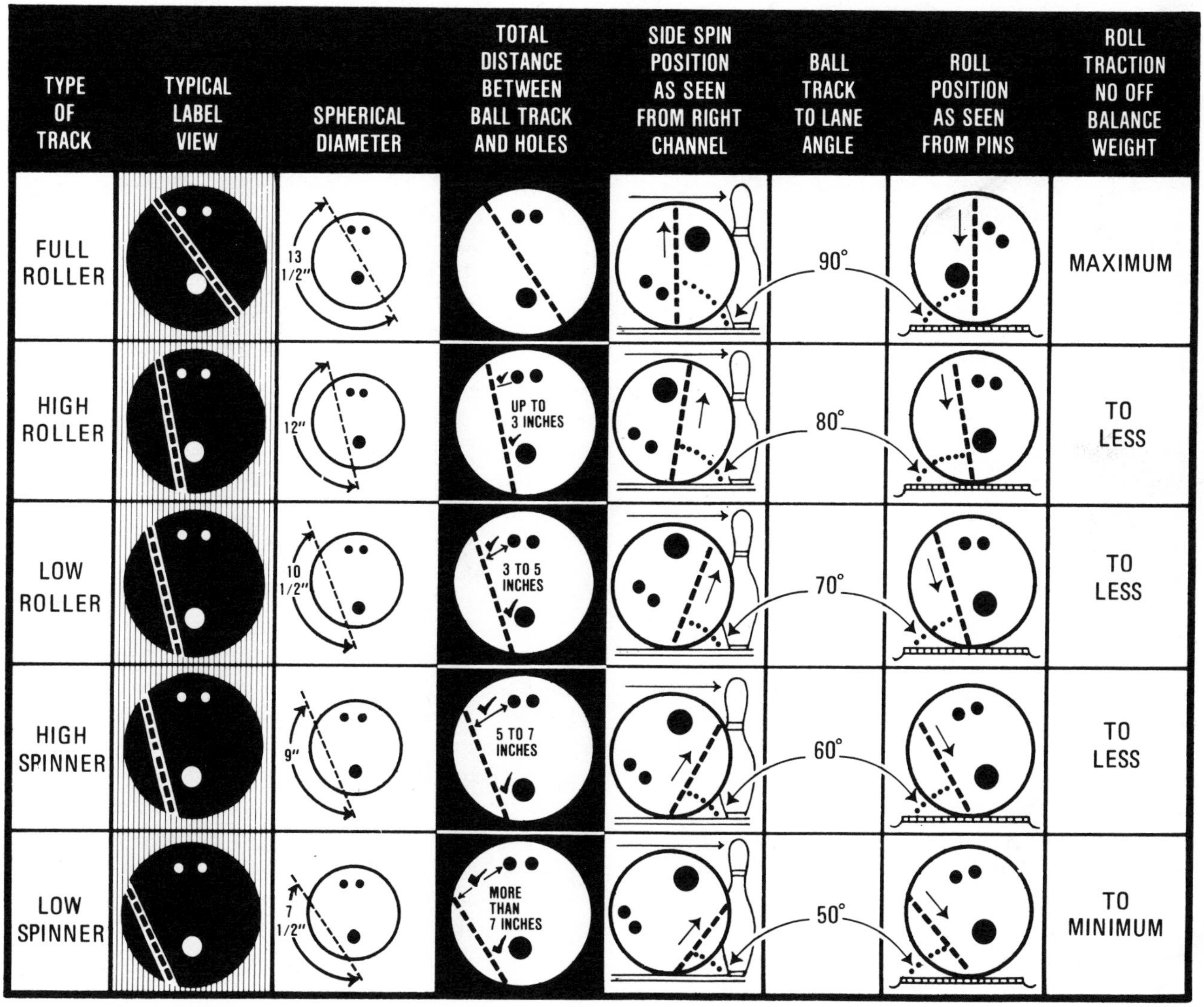

TYPE OF TRACK	TYPICAL LABEL VIEW	SPHERICAL DIAMETER	TOTAL DISTANCE BETWEEN BALL TRACK AND HOLES	SIDE SPIN POSITION AS SEEN FROM RIGHT CHANNEL	BALL TRACK TO LANE ANGLE	ROLL POSITION AS SEEN FROM PINS	ROLL TRACTION NO OFF BALANCE WEIGHT
FULL ROLLER		13 1/2"			90°		MAXIMUM
HIGH ROLLER		12"	UP TO 3 INCHES		80°		TO LESS
LOW ROLLER		10 1/2"	3 TO 5 INCHES		70°		TO LESS
HIGH SPINNER		9"	5 TO 7 INCHES		60°		TO LESS
LOW SPINNER		7 1/2"	MORE THAN 7 INCHES		50°		TO MINIMUM

SOURCE: from *Balance,* by Bill Taylor. (Reproduced by permission.) For more details on this very useful book, consult the material in Appendix C.

misses the weight block area by more than an inch, it is possible to use top weight to affect the hooking of the ball. Since the track is relatively close to the fingers, top weight can be used to provide a relatively stable or steady path into the pins. Many top average bowlers effectively use the high roller ball track.

The Low Roller (Spherical Diameter of 10 to 11 inches). The next smallest ball track is the low roller, which tracks closer to the thumb but further away from the fingers. It is also called by names similar to the ball track we have labeled the High Roller, such as: the semi-roller and the three-quarter roller. Since the ball track is still further away from the top center portion of the ball, weight imbalances can be used with the low roller even more effectively than either the full or high rollers. However, the effect of the weight imbalance is less steady, and creates more of a *wobble and loping action,* as the imbalance revolves around the ball. As top weight gets further away from the ball track, the impact is greater as we have indicated, but the roll is less steady. The low roller can be used very effectively for many types of lane conditions, but is perhaps best from these three strike lines: inside line, second arrow line, and outside line.

The High Spinner (Spherical Diameter of 9 inches). The next smallest ball track, next to last of the five, is the high spinner. This ball track has also been called the semi-spinner, meaning it is near to the low spinner, but not quite there. Top weight can be used to advantage with the high spinner, and this type of ball track can be used effectively on most strike lines, but particularly on the deep inside and deep outside strike lines. Many high average bowlers use the high spinner ball track.

The Low Spinner (Spherical Diameter of 7 to 8 inches). This ball track is located farther away from the center of the ball than any of the other four tracks. It is not a very effective track to roll because of the poor traction it has with the lane. Negative weight imbalances might help the low spinner go into an effective roll. However, on normally conditioned lanes the pocket effectiveness of this ball track is not very good. The low spinner could be useful on very dry lanes where it can get good traction.

In summary, the most prevalent ball tracks are the high roller, the low roller, and the high spinner. These ball tracks allow you to use top weight (or axis weight) to increase the effectiveness of the ball. Yet the traction with the lane is still good. With the full roller, traction is better than with any other ball track, but you cannot use top weight or axis weight effectively to affect the roll and hooking power of the ball. With the low spinner, traction is greatly reduced as the ball spins down the lane.

Your ball track indicates your normal, natural release of the ball. Check your ball track. What kind is it? Is it the best for the conditions upon which you normally play? Perhaps your local ball driller or instructor can tell you whether your *ball track* and *ball balance* are helping or hindering your scoring potential. (SECTION 5 will show the release changes which create the various ball tracks.)

Speaking of ball balance, we will now discuss one of the two methods for creating ball imbalances to assist you in scoring: *axis* weight. Following this discussion of axis weight we will begin a lengthy discussion of the second way to create ball imbalances: *top* weight. But now let us look at axis weight.

AXIS WEIGHT: A bowling ball will rotate around an axis line roughly perpendicular to the ball track (at a 90 degree angle, and passing through the center of the ball). By drilling a hole somewhere along this axis line, you can create an imbalance in the ball on the side opposite the hole. This imbalance can influence the roll of the ball, the timing of the curve or hook, and the deflection pattern after it hits the pocket. Exhibit 4-3 gives three illustrations of axis weight, and shows the 90 degree relationship between the ball track and the axis line.

Axis weight is one of the two most common forms of creating ball imbalances. The other method is top (label) weight, which will be discussed later in this section on equipment adjustments. Both methods are designed to affect the timing and amount of curve and to have the proper strength when entering the pocket to maintain an ideal path of deflection through the pins.

The major advantage claimed by advocates of axis weight is that you can get the imbalance as far away from the track as possible, and therefore you can get the maximum influence from a given imbalance condition. As you will recall in our previous discussion on ball tracks, the influence of any imbalance is increased as the imbalance gets further away from the ball track. In label or top weight imbalancing, it is not possible to get the imbalance very far away from the ball track when that track is close to the label weight (weight block). This situation is particularly evident in the full roller and high roller, which run across the weight block (full roller) and very close to it (high roller).

Another advantage to axis weight is that you can create it *after* the thumb and finger holes have been drilled. With label weight, you create the imbalance by positioning the thumb and finger holes relative to the weight block. Of course, you can take into consideration placement of the thumb and finger holes in preparation for creating axis weight. For example, you can create 2 ounces of right side weight by drilling the holes to the left of the weight

EXHIBIT 4-3
(RHB) Illustrations of Axis Weight

A bowling ball rotates around an axis line roughly perpendicular to the ball track, and passing through the center of the ball. By drilling a hole along this line, you can create an imbalance on the side of the ball that is opposite of that hole. This imbalance can influence the roll of the ball and the pattern of deflection after it hits the pins.

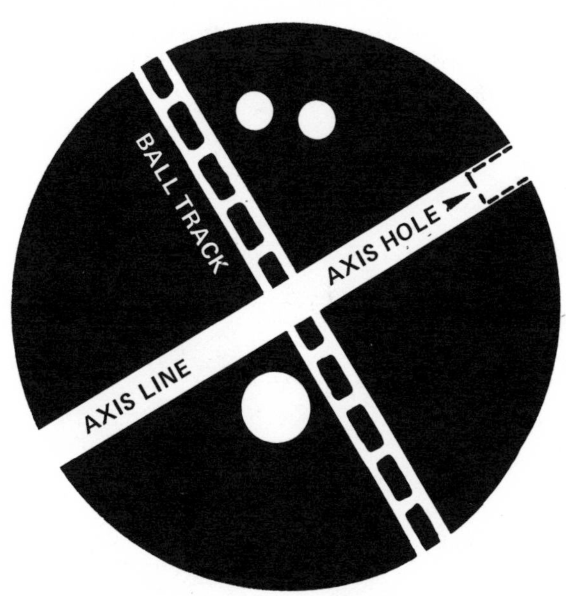

A. FULL ROLLER

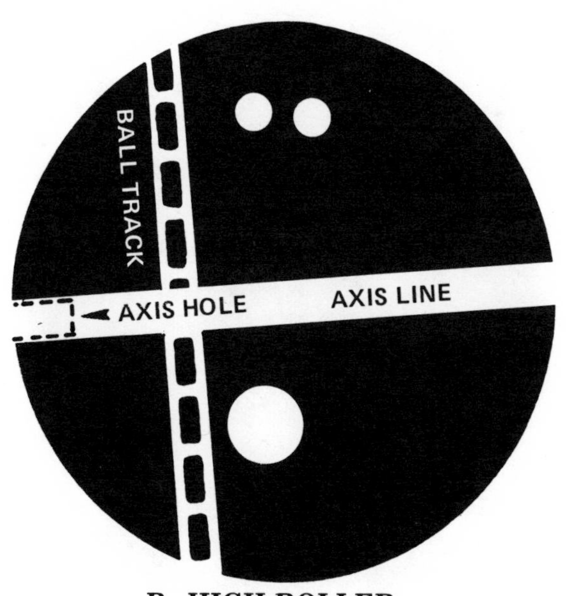

B. HIGH ROLLER

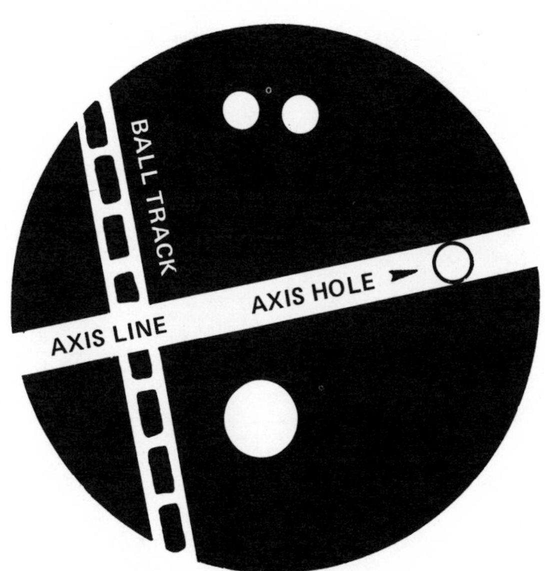

C. HIGH SPINNER

block, and then take 1½ ounces out of the right side to leave only ½ ounce of right side weight completely away from the ball track.

There are an enormous number of ways to create axis weight. Placement of the thumb and finger holes relative to the ball's weight block, combined with holes of various sizes along the axis line, make for limitless possibilities for creating axis weight. Of course, only one axis line hole would be legal in a ball, but through experimentation you could find the best axis weight for your style and ball track. Simply drill one axis hole; try it; and if it is not right plug it and drill another one. Eventually you will find what is best for you. Notice that you are not changing the thumb and finger holes, although you could do so.

Both label (top) weight and axis weight techniques have their advocates. Both methods for creating ball imbalances, to influence curve and deflection patterns, have their advantages. And both methods can be used in conjunction with one another to get the benefits of each.

This concludes the OVERVIEW section of equipment adjustments for the right handed bowler. We have discussed total ball weight, the weight block, ball tracks, and axis weight in preparation for the discussion of the three major types of equipment adjustment techniques. We begin that discussion with BALL BALANCE ADJUSTMENTS.

BALL BALANCE ADJUSTMENTS
(Right Handed Bowlers)

"Ball weights and balances will only work for you if you are a consistent shooter," Larry Lichstein, PBA Player Services Director.

After a bowling ball has been drilled, it must be subjected to a set of tests to determine if it falls within acceptable limits of ball imbalance. These tolerance limits determine what equipment can and cannot be used in sanctioned league and professional competition.

Two sets of weight or imbalance tolerance levels have been established: one set applies to bowling balls weighing 10 pounds or more, and the other applies to those weighing less than 10 pounds. Maximum ball weight is, of course, limited to 16 pounds.

Exhibit 4-4 illustrates maximum ball weights and imbalances for both the lighter (under 10 pounds) and heavier bowling balls. Briefly, limits for a ball weighing 10 to 16 pounds are:

A) The top half of the bowling ball cannot weigh more than 3 ounces heavier than the bottom half. Or conversely, the bottom half of the ball cannot be more than 3 ounces heavier than the top portion.
B) The weight of the left side of the ball cannot exceed the weight of the right side by more than 1 ounce, or vice versa.
C) The front half of the ball (the finger hole portion) cannot exceed the back half of the ball (thumb hole portion) by more than 1 ounce, or vice versa.

If the ball weighs less than 10 pounds, then the side portions (item B) and the front and back portions (item C) cannot differ by more than 3/4 ounce, instead of the 1 ounce tolerance permitted for the heavier ball. The top and bottom imbalances are still the same 3 ounces.

A ball that exceeds these imbalance limitations would be declared illegal for use in sanctioned competition. Within these established maximums, or ranges, a multitude of imbalance situations could be created by positioning the thumb and finger holes at various locations on top of the ball.

You could, for example, have 2 ounces of top weight, 1/4 ounce of finger weight, and 1/2 ounce of right side weight. Or, you could drill the ball to create this imbalance situation: 3 ounces of top weight, 3/4 ounce of thumb weight, and 1 full ounce of left side weight. The variations are enormous, since normal imbalances are created by *fractions of an ounce.*

How do you get these imbalance situations? Why would you decide to have a particular imbalanced ball situation after drilling? To answer these very important questions, we will have to study top weight, look at ways to create various types of ball imbalances, and determine what each type means in terms of the action or reaction of the ball on the lane. First we will discuss top weight.

Top Weight: If the top half of the ball weighs more than the bottom half, the ball is said to contain top weight. For a ball to have top weight *after* drilling, excess weight must be in the top half of the ball which is greater than the weight removed by drilling the thumb and finger holes. Maximum allowable top weight *after drilling* is 3 ounces.

The impact of top weight, as with all other imbalance conditions, is largely dependent upon the type of ball track you use. The closer the imbalance is to the ball track, the less influence it has on the ball. The further away from the track it is located, the more impact it has.

For the full roller, with a ball track around the circumference of the ball, top weight will have very little effect on ball roll. The track goes directly across the weight block. The ball may tend to pulsate or oscillate (wobble) as the top half of the ball rotates on its roll down the lanes.

As the track moves away from the full roller type, toward high roller and then spinner, the impact of top weight is increased. Top weight will cause the ball to hook slightly more than will the absence of such an imbalance condition. This may cause the ball to break sooner, getting up to the pocket more than another ball without top weight. Such an imbalance would be favorable under lane conditions where the ball was breaking too far down the lane. Of course, excess top weight might cause the ball to

EXHIBIT 4-4
(RHB) Maximum Ball Weight and Balance Tolerances

After a ball is drilled, it must meet certain weight and balance standards, or it will be declared illegal for sanctioned competition. The indicated weights are for bowling balls weighing 10 or more pounds. Those weighing less than 10 pounds permit only ¾ ounce tolerance each place the chart shows 1 ounce.

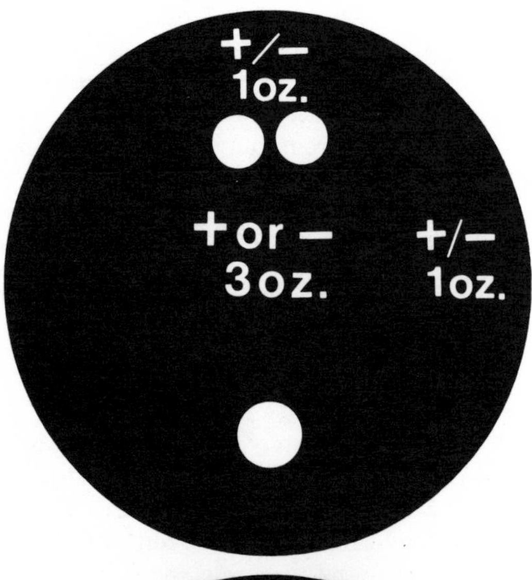

TOP weight can be plus or minus 3 ounces. hooks sooner

LEFT or RIGHT SIDE weight can be plus or minus 1 ounce.

FINGER or THUMB weight can be plus or minus 1 ounce.

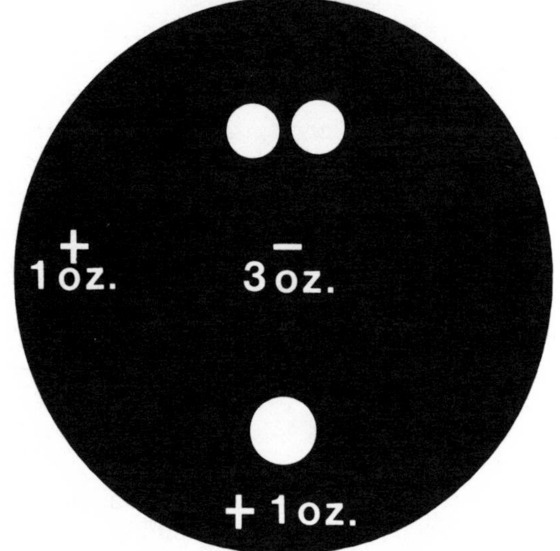

NEGATIVE WEIGHTS
The maximum imbalance permitted to cause the ball to begin the roll sooner and to curve less are:

3 ounces of bottom weight
1 ounce of thumb weight
1 ounce of left side weight

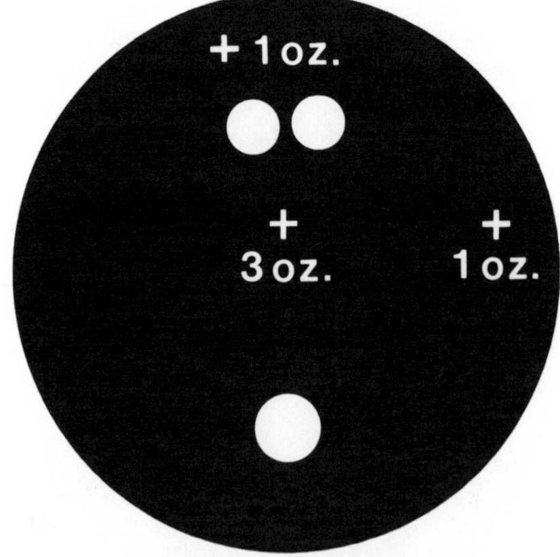

POSITIVE WEIGHTS
The maximum imbalance permitted to cause the ball to curve more and to deflect less are:

3 ounces of top weight
1 ounce of finger weight
1 ounce of right side weight

begin its break too soon, therefore losing some of its power upon impact with the pins, or causing the ball to cross over to the brooklyn side if the hook is too strong.

Top weight is a *source* of the other types of weight imbalances we will be discussing, such as finger or thumb weight, left or right side weight, etc. Many people are under the impression that there are three kinds of weight imbalances: side weight, finger weight, and thumb weight. But, top weight is a *source* of all three of these imbalance conditions. Without top weight there would be no side, finger, or thumb weight imbalances. This concept should become clearer as the section on weights and balances progresses, but let us digress for a minute to cover this idea in more specific terms. Later discussions might be more understandable after this explanation of how weight imbalances are created.

Imagine that the ball could be weighed in various segments: the top half versus the bottom half; the left side and the right side; the front half (where the finger holes are drilled) and the back half (where the thumb hole is located). In fact, *the ball can be weighed in such a manner.*

Now, if you remove any portion of the ball (as you do when you drill into it), an imbalance is created. Those portions of the ball where the holes are drilled will weigh less than the side of the ball opposite from the holes. This is how imbalance conditions are created: by removing weight from one section of the ball, you cause the opposite section to be heavier *by comparison.*

If a ball is perfectly balanced prior to drilling, that is, the center of gravity of the ball is exactly in the center of the ball, then all portions of the ball would weigh equally. The top and bottom half would weigh the same. The left and right side would weigh equally, and the finger and thumb portions of the ball (front and back) would also weigh equally.

After drilling our perfectly balanced ball, the ball's center of gravity would be located somewhere other than the absolute center of the ball. And, the portions of the ball would weigh unequally. Those portions with holes drilled into them would weigh less than those still undrilled. The new center of gravity of the ball could then be defined with reference to the previous center of the ball.

Three measurements or directions are needed to locate the *new center of gravity* of the ball. From the center of the ball you would measure: either up or down (top or bottom); left or right (the two sides of the ball) and front or back (finger or thumb portion). These three dimensions, these three directions, describe where the new center of gravity of the ball is located. Up or down, front or back, and left or right side. This is why many people think there are three types of imbalance conditions: *to locate the center of gravity of a drilled ball requires three measurements or directions.*

A ball that has a center of gravity at the absolute center of the ball will roll relatively true, in a straight direction. One that is imbalanced will not roll in such a manner, but will tend to roll in the direction of the imbalance. A bowling ball that is rolling will tend to favor the portion of the ball that has the center of gravity, the imbalance. Knowing this reaction pattern of an unbalanced ball, we are able to create such conditions and use them in our adjustments to various lane conditions. (For more details on this concept of center of gravity, and for the concept of the bowling ball as a functioning gyroscope when it is in motion, please see *Balance,* by Bill Taylor, as indicated in Appendix C.

Top weight alone would mean that the center of gravity of the ball is straight up from the exact center of the ball, and not toward either side or front or back. *Finger weight* means the center of gravity is up toward the top half of the ball and then forward toward the portion of the ball in which the finger holes are drilled. *Thumb weight* is the opposite of finger weight, with the center of gravity toward the top and back portion of the ball. *Right side weight* is an imbalance condition where the center of gravity of the ball is toward the top and right side of the ball. *Left side weight* is, of course, just the opposite condition, up and to the left side. *Bottom weight* means the center of gravity is down from the exact center of the ball.

Another way to look at these imbalance situations is to look at the ball in sections, comparing the relative weight of each section. *Top weight* means the top half of the ball weighs more than the bottom half. *Finger weight* means the half of the ball containing the finger holes weighs more than the half containing the thumb hole. *Left side weight* means the left half of the ball weighs more than the right half. *Right side weight* means the right side weighs more than the left side.

Placement of the thumb and finger holes determines the weight imbalance of a drilled ball. Since there is wide latitude as to where these holes can be drilled, and over the *initial weight* of the ball, a wide range of imbalance conditions can be created. Some imbalances will be favorable or unfavorable, depending upon the ball track, lane conditions, type of delivery, etc. This section looks at the various types of imbalances and the effect each has on the action of the ball.

Bottom Weight: Any discussion of top weight is by its very nature a discussion of bottom weight. A change to either the top or bottom half of the ball affects the other half. Taking weight out of the top half will change the *relative* difference between the two halves. If, after drilling the thumb and finger holes, the bottom half of the ball weighs more than the top half, then bottom weight exists.

Such a condition will only occur when the *initial* excess weight of the top half of the ball does *not* exceed the weight of the material removed in the drilling operation. For example, if the top half weighs 2 ounces more than the bottom half of the ball, and 2½ ounces are drilled out for the thumb and fingers, then the bottom half will be ½ ounce heavier than the top half. Bottom weight, excess bottom weight, will exist.

The maximum allowable bottom weight is 3 ounces, just as the top half cannot weigh over 3 ounces more than the bottom. And what is the value of bottom weight? There are no known advantages to having excess bottom weight, although this situation could change in the future as ball drilling and weights and balances are explored further. Bottom weight is rarely drilled intentionally; it usually happens by mistake. This occurs when the top and bottom halves of the ball *initially* are about equal in weight, prior to drilling.

It is currently illegal to drill into the bottom half of the ball. And virtually all bowling balls contain excess top weight (the weight block) when they are manufactured. Therefore, when the thumb and finger holes are drilled, excess top weight will exist, and not excess bottom weight.

Finger Weight: This weight imbalance is created when that portion of the ball into which the finger holes are drilled (often called the *front* of the ball) weighs more than the portion containing the thumb hole (often called the *back* of the ball). To create this type of ball imbalance, it is necessary to drill the finger holes close to the weight block. Or, stated differently, the thumb hole is drilled further away from the weight block.

As you may recall, to create excess weight in one portion of the ball it is necessary to remove weight from the opposite portion. Since thumb weight is opposite of finger weight, drilling the finger holes closer to the weight block places these holes closer to the thumb or back side of the ball. Therefore, excess weight is created in the finger portion.

This concept is illustrated on Exhibit 4-5. It shows that excess weight is created by the positioning of the thumb and finger holes relative to the center of gravity of the ball, which is somewhere near the weight block. All weight imbalances, in reality, are only changes in the center of gravity. In a perfectly balanced bowling ball, the center of gravity would be the exact center of the ball.

The maximum amount of allowable finger weight is 1 ounce for 10 to 16 pound bowling balls, and ¾ ounce for those weighing less than 10 pounds. But, what is the impact or utility of having a ball with excess finger weight? It causes the ball to hook or curve slightly more than if the weight were perfectly centered. This means that the ball may start to roll and break to the pocket later, but it will drive stronger into the pocket. The ball is less likely to be deflected out of its path through the pins. If, however, the roll or break begins too soon, then the ball may lose some of its drive upon reaching the pin deck. It will have *rolled out.*

Of course, the impact of a given amount of finger weight (for example, ½ or ¾ ounce) is dependent upon the ball track you use. As the ball track moves further away from the full roller (to the low spinner), the impact of finger weight increases. With the full roller, finger weight has little or no significant impact on ball roll.

Thumb Weight: Thumb weight is just the opposite in impact of finger weight. It is created by drilling the thumb hole close to or into the weight block, near the manufacturer's label.

The maximum legal thumb weight is 1 ounce for bowling balls weighing 10 to 16 pounds, and only ¾ ounce for those weighing less than 10 pounds. The impact of this imbalance is still dependent upon its position relative to the ball track.

As a general rule, thumb weight will cause the ball to curve sooner, to hook less, and deflect more. Such an equipment adjustment would be helpful when the lane is dry and hooking strongly. It is the type of adjustment to get the ball back to the pocket when the lane is taking the ball too strongly to the left.

Often thumb weight will be combined with other types of negative weight imbalances, such as left side and bottom weight. *The ultimate influence on ball action would be the sum of the combined negative weights.*

Left Side Weight: You can create another ball imbalance, left side weight, by drilling the thumb and finger holes in a certain location relative to the weight block.

By drilling the holes more toward the right side of the ball, excess weight will result in the opposite or left side. The maximum allowable left side weight is 1 ounce for 10 to 16 pound bowling balls, and ¾ ounce for those weighing under 10 pounds.

The effect of this aspect of negative weight is to cause the ball to skid less before it starts to break for the pocket. Also, the hook will be less than if no left side weight imbalance existed. The overall result is a ball that will bring you back to the pocket after high or crossover hits.

The effect of left side weight is still dependent upon the nature of the ball track you use. The fur-

EXHIBIT 4-5

(RHB) Creating Finger, Thumb, Left and Right Side Weight

The location of the thumb and finger holes relative to the weight block determines what ball imbalance is created. Removing weight by drilling into one portion of the ball shifts the center of gravity of the ball toward the opposite portion. The impact or utility of a given amount of ball imbalance is largely determined by the location of the imbalance relative to the ball track. One ounce of imbalance near the ball track has less impact on ball roll and deflection than an ounce further away.

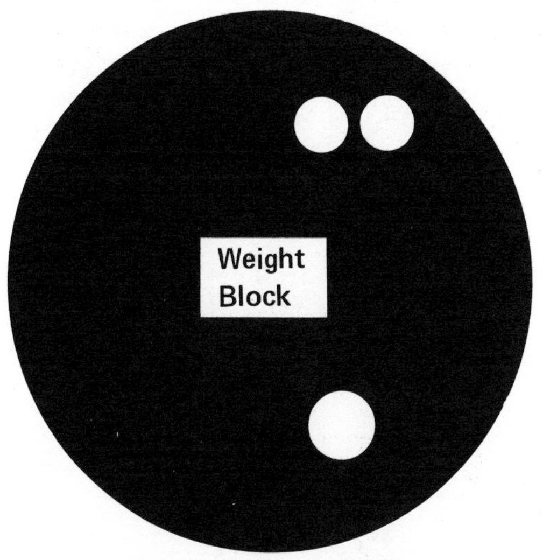

1. LEFT SIDE WEIGHT IMBALANCE

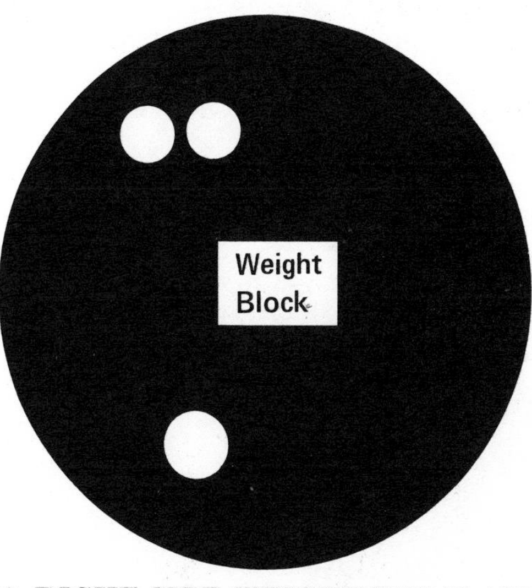

2. RIGHT SIDE WEIGHT IMBALANCE

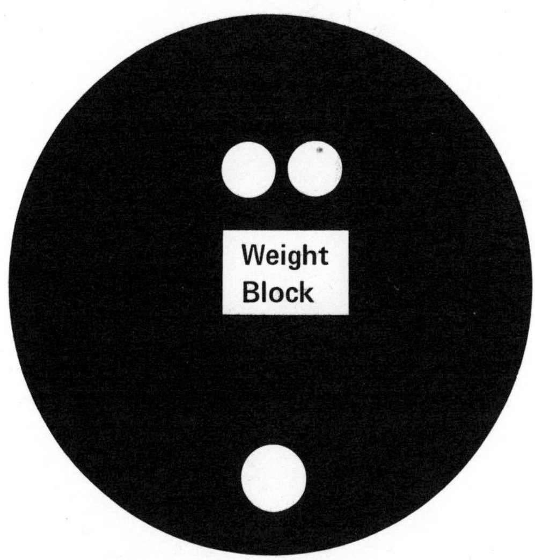

3. FINGER WEIGHT IMBALANCE

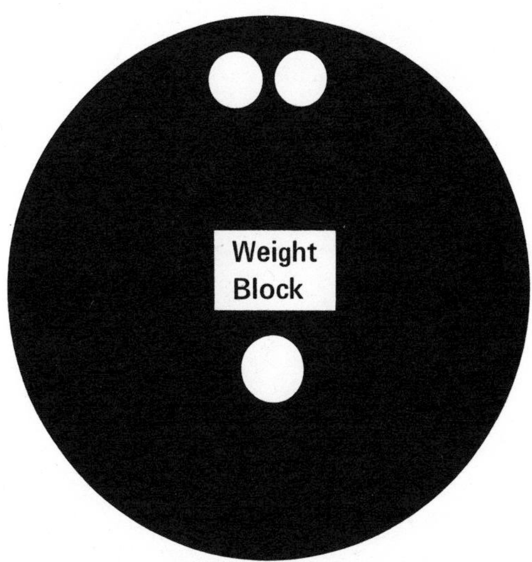

4. THUMB WEIGHT IMBALANCE

ther away from the ball track the imbalance is located, the more impact left side weight will have.

Negative weight is a term associated with excess left side weight. The term actually refers to three types of ball imbalances: *bottom* weight, *left* side weight, and *thumb* weight. These imbalances are grouped together since the impact of each is similar. All cause the ball to skid less and to advance the point at which the ball starts to roll. The ball curves less and deflects more at the pocket.

Right Side Weight: The last of our six ball imbalance situations is right side weight. Obviously the utility of this imbalance is just the opposite of left side weight. By drilling the holes more toward the left side of the ball, right side weight is created.

The maximum legally allowable right side weight is 1 ounce for bowling balls weighing 10 to 16 pounds, and 3/4 ounce for those weighing less than 10 pounds.

The effect of this type of *positive weight* is to cause the ball to skid more, begin its break to the pocket later, and break more strongly toward the pocket. All of these adjustments are designed to get the ball up to the pocket when it continually fails to do so. The effect of right side imbalance is stronger as the ball track moves from a full roller to a spinner.

Positive Weight is a term associated with excess right side weight. The term actually refers to three types of ball imbalances: *right* side weight, *finger* weight, and *top* weight. These imbalances are grouped together since the impact of each one is similar. All cause the ball to skid more, begin to roll later, curve more and deflect less. This group of imbalances is, quite obviously, just the opposite from the negative imbalances previously discussed under left side weight.

This concludes our discussion of weight and balance adjustments. Exhibit 4-6 summarizes many of the concepts relating to this type of equipment adjustment technique.

EXHIBIT 4-6
(RHB) Ball Balance Terms

Ball weight: Refers to the total weight of the ball. The range of ball weight is from about 8 pounds to 16 pounds. Most high average bowlers use a 16 pound ball, but many also use one slightly more than 15 pounds.

Bottom weight: A ball that weighs more on the bottom half than on the top half where the thumb and finger holes are drilled.

Center of gravity: The point within the ball around which the total weight of the ball is distributed. If an undrilled ball had no weight block, then the center of gravity would be in the exact center of the ball.

Finger weight: A ball that has been drilled in such a manner that the top half of the ball weighs more than the bottom half, and the portion of the ball toward the finger holes weighs more than the portion toward the thumb hole.

Imbalance: A situation created in drilling the ball in which the center of gravity of the ball is *not* located exactly in the center of the ball.

Left side weight: A ball drilled so that the top half of the ball weighs more than the bottom half, and the side to the left of the holes (as you look at the ball) weighs more than the side to the right of the holes.

Maximum weights: The maximum imbalance allowed in a legally drilled ball. (See Exhibit 4-4 for complete details.)

Maximum weight tolerances: The outer limits (maximums) allowed in a legally drilled bowling ball. (See Exhibit 4-4 for details.)

Negative weights: Weight imbalance in these three areas: left side, thumb, and bottom (for the right handed bowler). These are defined in a different way for the left handed bowler.

Positive weights: Weight imbalances in these three areas for the right handed bowler: right side, finger, and top. The left handers' definition of positive weights are different, as explained in the appropriate section for LHB.

Right side weight: A ball drilled in such a manner that the top half of the ball weighs more than the bottom half, and the side to the right of the holes (as you look down on the ball) weighs more than the side to the left of the holes.

Side weight: A ball in which either the right side or left side contains the extra weight, in other words, the center of gravity is not in the center of the ball, but is off to the right or left.

Thumb weight: A ball that has been drilled in such a manner that the vertical half of the ball which contains the thumb hole weighs more than the half of the ball into which the finger holes are drilled.

Top weight: A ball that weighs more on the top half (where the thumb and finger holes are drilled) than the half which is opposite the holes. The top half of the ball is indicated by the label of the manufacturer.

Weight block: A segment or substance found within the ball and located in the top half of the ball which causes the top half to weigh more than the bottom half prior to drilling. This situation is created to compensate for the weight loss that occurs when the thumb and finger holes are drilled in the top half of the ball. (See Exhibit 4-1 for sample weight blocks.)

BALL SURFACE ADJUSTMENTS
(Right Handed Bowlers)

"The ball and the lane will always interact. You must select the proper ball surface to match the lane surface and conditioning."

The surface of the ball and the surface of the lane will always interact. There is nothing you can do about this interaction, except that you have some choices as to the surface hardness or softness of the ball you use. *There is a best ball surface for a given lane surface and condition, and the way you roll your ball.* Some lane conditions dictate a ball with a hard surface. Other conditions call for a softer ball surface. Reading the lanes properly will tell you which degree of hardness or softness to select. Once you have made your selection, the lane and the ball are going to interact in some manner. Your objective is to get both lane and ball surfaces working for you to get the ball into the pocket at the correct speed, angle and action to produce strikes.

Ball surfaces can generally be classified into two different but related categories: Hard Surfaces and Soft Surfaces. Of course, within each category there are varying degrees of hardness or softness. To measure the precise degree of hardness, a DUROMETER is used. This device measures the amount of pressure required to penetrate the outer shell of the ball. The more pressure required, the harder the ball. The less pressure needed, the softer the ball.

Legal standards have been developed for the degrees of hardness or softness that are acceptable for organized, sanctioned competition. In effect, the standard really refers to the degree of softness, since only a soft ball might be declared illegal for competition. (Of course, other factors such as weights and balances could cause the ball to be declared illegal for play.)

Ball surface standards for ABC, WIBC, WPBA, PBA, and AJBC may differ slightly, and these standards may change over time. But for sake of clarity in the subject of ball surfaces, the following exhibit gives the *general range* of relative hardness or softness of bowling ball surfaces, as indicated by the use of a durometer.

EXHIBIT 4-7
Ball Surface Hardness Classifications

Durometer Reading	Classification
Under 72	Illegal by some standards*
72-75	Very Soft
76-80	Soft
81-85	Medium
86-90	Hard
90-Above	Very Hard

*Standards of illegality differ among the organizations listed above. Check your appropriate organization to find out what lower limit is currently considered illegal!

To repeat a very important point, the above table is a *general* classification of the relative degree of hardness or softness of bowling ball surfaces. *Current rules and policies of each organization sanctioning bowling competitions should be consulted for current requirements needed to conform to legal and acceptable standards.*

Before we get into a discussion about what degree of hardness or softness is best under given lane surfaces and conditions, let's look at another way in which bowling ball surfaces are classified: (1) Rubber shell or surface, and (2) Plastic shell or surface.

It is possible to manufacture a ball of not only different material (basically plastic or rubber) but of widely varying surface characteristics, such as hardness and porosity. (More on porosity a little later.) You could, for example, have both hard and soft surfaced rubber bowling balls, and both types of surfaces in a plastic ball as well. So to compare a rubber versus a plastic ball, you must also take into consideration the surface hardness of each type. A rubber ball could be either softer or harder than a plastic ball, or vice versa. To simplify our analysis, we will discuss soft rubber and plastic surfaces first, then hard rubber and plastic.

A *soft rubber* bowling ball will, generally speaking, grip the lane more than a similar plastic ball. Therefore, when you need a ball surface that will grip the lane (when lanes are heavily oiled and more hook or roll is desired) a soft rubber ball would be the choice. Since rubber is generally softer than plastic (or is more porous) a greater portion of the ball track will contact the lane and the added friction will permit the ball to grip the lane for more hook.

A *soft plastic* bowling ball will, generally speaking, be more apt to skid further down the lane than a soft rubber ball under similar lane conditions. Therefore the hook will be delayed until the ball is closer to the pins. When the ball begins to hook it will hook less than a comparable rubber ball. The soft plastic ball should be used when lane surfaces and conditions are medium to heavily oiled.

A *hard rubber* ball will skid more and hook less than a plastic ball of similar hardness. When the lane is very lightly oiled, you might select a hard rubber ball and use a relatively straight angle down the lane.

A *hard plastic* ball, on the other hand, will skid less and hook more than a rubber ball of similar hardness. When the lane is lightly oiled, you might use a hard plastic ball and a relatively straight angle down the lane. Or, if the lane is very dry, very lightly oiled, you could use the hard plastic ball but a more open foul line angle.

Exhibit 4-8 illustrates, in general terms, the relationships that exist among hard and soft rubber and plastic ball surfaces, and the angles most likely to get the ball into the pocket under certain lane conditions.

The type of *lane surface,* in addition to the amount and pattern of *lane conditioning,* must also be taken into account when trying to select the proper ball surface to fit the playing condition. The lane surface might be of lacquer, urethane, or other artificial surface. This is the permanent aspect of the lane. *Conditioning* refers to the oil or conditioner used to prepare the lane for play. As a general rule, plastic ball surfaces react best on plastic coated lanes, and rubber ball surfaces are better for lacquer coated lanes. These are only generalizations. The hardness or softness of the surface of the ball is more important than the plastic or rubber content. And your style of bowling (as related to the ball track you generate, and other release factors) combined with the kind of lane conditions you normally find in the centers where you regularly bowl will also be determining factors. Consult a knowledgeable professional or ball driller where you bowl for more specific help on this subject. He or she can give you guidance to aid you in selecting the best ball surface to use.

The initial degree of hardness of your ball is subject to change. It is *not* a fixed, permanent condition. Of course, you could soak your ball in a variety of solutions to change the surface hardness, but such a process is both *illegal* for most competition and *extremely dangerous* to your health! What we are talking about is the effect of *temperature* and *use* on the surface hardness of the ball.

Ball *use* creates surface heat. This heat can drop the surface reading on a bowling ball. If your ball registers close to the lower end of the durometer scale (such as a 72 or 73 reading), the added heat from normal use of the ball could drop the hardness level. This might drop your ball into the illegal range if a measurement is required both before and *after* competition.

Temperature can also affect the surface hardness of the ball. Cold temperatures cause the ball hardness to rise to harder readings. Warm temperatures melt the surface of the ball and produce softer readings. This temperature effect is an important point to consider when storing your ball. Try to keep the ball stored in the same temperature range that will occur when you bowl. Keeping the ball stored in the trunk of your car for extended periods of time can affect the surface readings, and affect the interaction of the ball and lane during use. Taking the ball out of a storage place with a temperature higher or lower than you will encounter when you bowl, could cause the ball to act irregularly until the surface warms or cools to the normal bowling temperature. Keep

EXHIBIT 4-8
(RHB) Ball Surfaces and Lane Conditioning Relationships

The amount of oil suggests a given ball surface hardness or softness. Solid lines on the charts indicate the most desirable ball surface (plastic or rubber) and the degree of hardness. Dotted lines give alternative types of surfaces and hardnesses. *These are general patterns and guidelines only.*

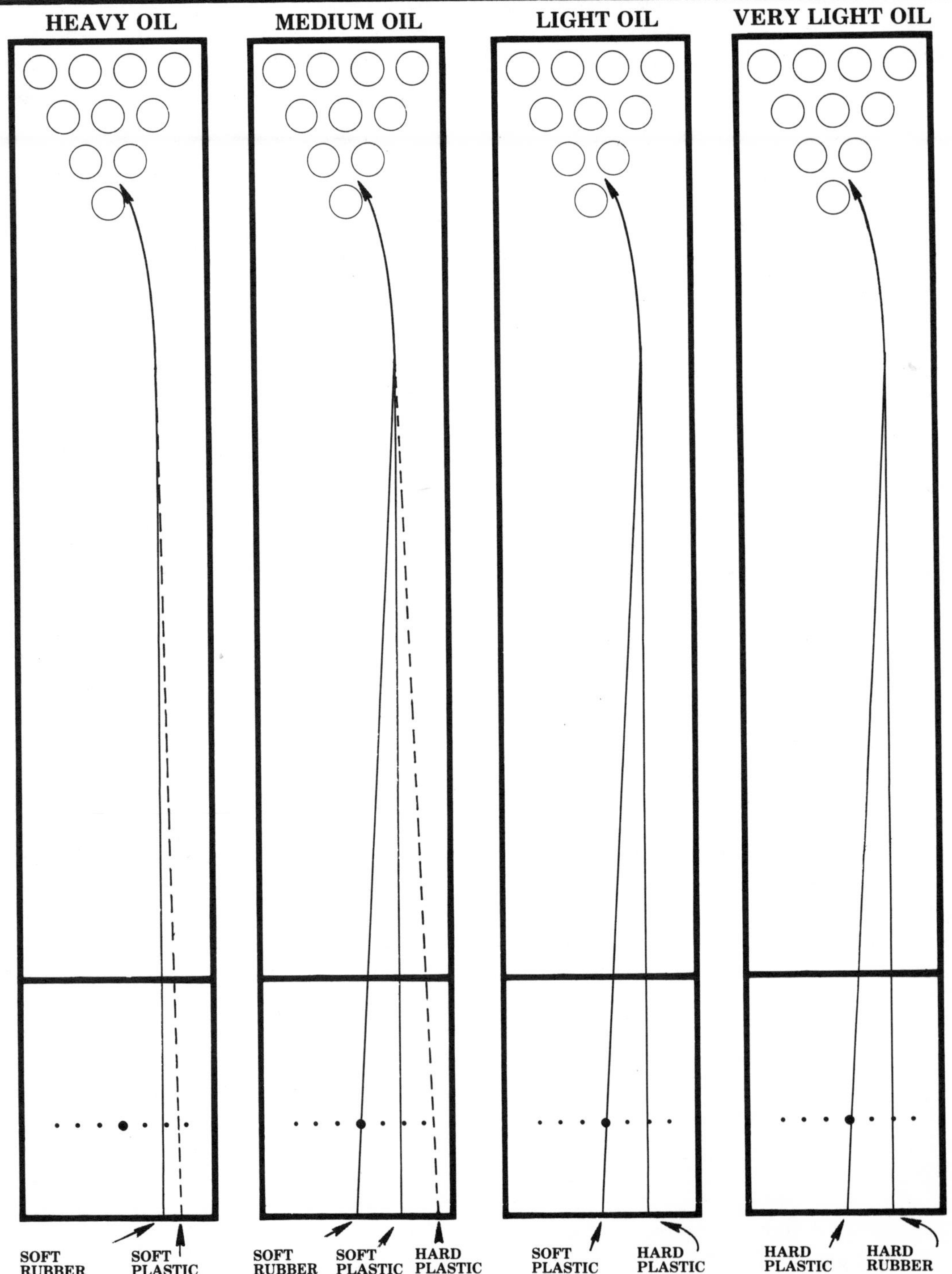

The conditions on which you normally bowl will dictate the exact type of ball surface you need. For full adjustment potential, you should have one soft and one hard surface bowling ball.

this temperature effect on the ball surface in mind at all times.

Now we can return to the concept of ball porosity mentioned before. *Porosity refers to the ability or tendency of the ball surface to absorb the oil found on the lanes.* A very porous surface will absorb more oil than a less porous surface. You will often see better bowlers cleaning the ball surface between each shot. This is one way to keep the surface of the ball as near to the same on each shot as possible. If the ball picks up oil from the lane, as it will with varying degrees of porosity, then the ball surface will be changing as you bowl. Keep the ball surface clean so you will know what the ball should do on each delivery. With a very porous surface, the ball will absorb oil in the ball track and cause the ball to act as if the lane surface were harder than it is. You should wipe the oil off the ball after each delivery. It is better and more consistent to bowl with the same surface on the ball than to have a constantly changing condition occurring as oil builds-up on the ball track.

In SUMMARY, to change the ball surface as an adjustment to certain types of lane surfaces and conditions can be very effective and beneficial. When you want the ball to hook sooner, to grab the lane sooner, to come up to the pocket, then a softer surface on the ball is the correct type of adjustment. On the other hand, when you want the ball to hook later, to grab the lane further down, to come back to the pocket, then a harder ball surface can help you.

It should be obvious at this point that, if you intend to include ball surface changes as part of your adjustment strategy and arsenal, you would be well advised to have two different bowling balls, with varying surface hardnesses—one toward the soft end of the durometer scale, and the other toward the hard end of the scale. It is not unusual for touring professional bowlers to have several types of ball surfaces from which to choose in a given tournament. The center in which they are to bowl, the surface of the lanes, plus the playing condition that has been created, all dictate which ball surface they will select for that competition.

For the once-a-week bowler, having such a large selection of equipment is not very practical. But having two bowling balls is a very good idea if you wish to have the full range of equipment adjustment options open to you. Having this additional degree of adjustment flexibility may well mean the difference between scoring that is average, or well above average. Ball surface adjustments can influence the number of strikes you get.

This concludes the discussion of Ball Surface Adjustments. Exhibit 4-9 summarizes many of the concepts relating to this type of equipment adjustment technique.

EXHIBIT 4-9
(RHB) Ball Surface Terms

Ball track: The portion of the ball surface that contacts the lane as the ball rolls toward the pin setup. The ball track is usually marked by slight scratches on the ball surface, and forms the figure of a ring around some portion of the ball surface.

Breaking-in period: Usually refers to the time required to create a ball track on the ball. The term might also refer to the time needed to get used to a newly drilled ball, especially if some change has been made in the fit, grip, pitches, etc.

Durometer: An instrument for measuring the surface hardness of a bowling ball, or other item. A durometer measures the amount of pressure needed to break the surface of the item being tested. The more pressure required, the harder the surface; the less pressure, the softer the surface.

Hard ball: A ball whose surface hardness reading registers high on the hardness scale, approaching 100. (See Rock, below.)

Hardness scale: A means of classifying ball surfaces in terms of surface hardness. A low number on the scale (such as a reading of 72) indicates a relatively soft surface. A high number on the scale (such as 90) is an indication of a harder surface. (See Illegal Ball.)

Illegal ball: A ball whose surface hardness has been declared below the level of acceptable hardness, as determined by the appropriate sanctioning organization. Such a reading is now near 72 on the hardness scale.

Plastic ball: A bowling ball constructed of a plastic type material, as opposed to one made predominantly of a rubber substance.

Porosity: The degree to which a bowling ball surface will absorb or not absorb the lane conditioner. A very porous ball will absorb the oil on the lane more readily than one with a less porous surface.

Rock: A term for a bowling ball whose surface hardness is 90 or more, indicating a very hard surface.

Rubber ball: A bowling ball constructed of a rubber type material, as opposed to one made predominantly of a plastic substance.

Soft ball: A ball whose surface hardness reading registers low on the hardness scale, generally less than 80 on the scale.

BALL FIT ADJUSTMENTS
(*Right Handed Bowlers*)

"A correctly fitted ball will feel very comfortable and allow you to release it properly."

Drilling a bowling ball is both an art and a science. The size and placement of the holes drilled into the bowling ball should feel comfortable during the swing and should permit good execution of the delivery. How the ball feels in your hand from the stance to the delivery is critical to the effectiveness of your game.

The two key terms related to ball fit are: Comfort and Release. A ball that has been measured and fitted correctly will be able to achieve both of these objectives well. If the ball is comfortable to the feel and can be held securely during the approach, it is possible to develop a natural, consistent, and well-timed delivery.

Some of the hand measurements needed to drill the ball are more related to one of these terms than to the other. That is, some aspects of ball fit are primarily designed to get the ball to feel comfortable, and to fit the structure of your hand, thumb, and fingers. Other measurements are more closely related to the type of release you wish to have, your style of bowling. This suggests still another way to look at ball fit: measurements that are *requirements* imposed by the structure of your hand, as opposed to *options* available to adapt the ball fit to your style of bowling. For example, the flexibility of the thumb (or lack of flexibility) requires you to do certain things in drilling the thumb hole. (More specifics will be given later in this section.) Yet, you can alter the forward pitch (an option) to affect the nature of your release. Another more obvious example relates to the span, the distance between the thumb and finger holes. If you choose to use a conventional grip, then the structure of the hand will determine the proper length of the span. Should you elect another type of grip, the fingertip, then the structure of the hand will again determine the length of span required. You could select either type of grip, but once you make your choice the structure of the hand determines the other measurements and adjustments needed to get the correct ball fit.

Exhibit 4-10 illustrates a sample Ball Measurement Chart giving guidelines to drill bowling balls. All of the normal measurements are indicated. Exhibit 4-16 at the end of this section on BALL FIT, gives definitions of each type of measurement. This set of definitions also covers other terms that will be used throughout this discussion of ball fit. It might be helpful to review these terms so the following material will be more meaningful to you.

The Ball Measurement Chart indicates five (5) measurement categories related to ball fit: (1) *width* of the thumb and finger holes; (2) *depth* of the holes; (3) *pitch,* or angle at which the holes are drilled into the ball; (4) *span,* or distance between the thumb and finger holes; and (5) *alignment,* or location of the holes. These five items define *ball fit.* Each one will be discussed in this section. But before that discussion, two questions need to be answered: Why is it important to understand how to fit the ball? And, what are the characteristics of a properly and improperly fitted ball?

Why is it important to understand how to fit the ball? A fundamental knowledge of ball drilling principles can be beneficial to you in many ways, and can greatly improve your overall adjustment strategy.

First, your current ball fit might *not* be correct for your hand and for your style of bowling. You can determine this by learning some of the principles of measuring the hand for the ball, and by knowing what options are open to you in the way your ball fits your hand and game. You need not be an expert at ball drilling, and this book will *not* qualify you to drill bowling balls. But the information concerning ball fit will be of assistance to you in evaluating how well your ball has been drilled.

Second, you will be able to communicate much better with a knowledgeable ball driller. This will help you explain to him or her your problems and desires in a ball fit. You should also understand more fully any comments or suggestions the ball driller has to make concerning ball fit. In this way a much greater chance exists to get the most comfortable fit for you, and to incorporate the best fit-options into your specific game.

EXHIBIT 4-10
Ball Measurement Chart

This chart is used to record your individual hand measurements in preparation for properly drilling the ball.

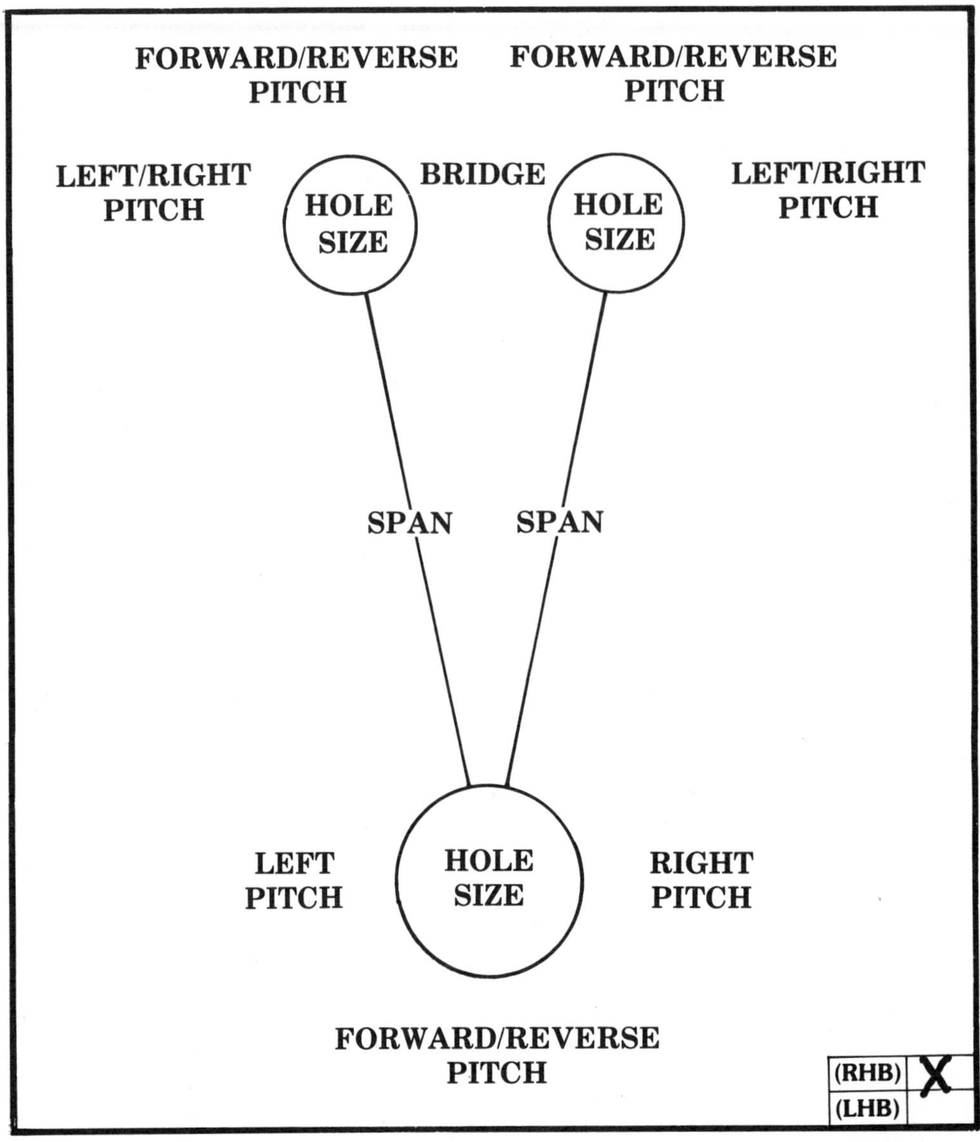

Several of these measurements are dictated by the structure of the hand. Others are the result of decisions you make: the way you elect to bowl; the bowling style you use; the skill level you have reached; and a number of other factors. Are you using a ball that fits properly? Do you know the correct measurements for your hand and bowling style? Why not get these measurements tested to see if they are correct for your ball?

Third, and closely related to the second item, is the knowledge of the full range of options in ball fit available to assist you in your game. If you wish to make a small change in ball fit, for example, to avoid making a change in your basic delivery, you will be aware of both the techniques for doing so and the expected results of the change. Two such ball fit adjustments will be discussed later in this section.

What are the characteristics of a correctly and incorrectly fitted ball? In general, a *correctly fitted* ball will be comfortable and will permit you to release it naturally for your game. More specifically, a correctly drilled ball will have, among other things: thumb and finger holes that are neither too small nor too large, and neither too deep nor too shallow; a span that is neither too short nor too long; proper pitches to fit your hand structure and the type of game you choose to play; bevels on the holes that are neither too sharp nor too rounded; an alignment of thumb and finger holes that fits the style of bowling you use and the structure of your hand and fingers; and holes located in the position to give you maximum advantage of weights and balances in the ball.

On the other hand, an *incorrectly drilled* ball will not meet the criteria stated above. Without a correct fit, here are a few problems you may have:

1. The hand, fingers or thumb may be strained, resulting in inconsistent deliveries, forced deliveries, poor timing, or sore portions of the hand.
2. You may be unable to achieve a natural rhythm to your steps and your swing, making it difficult to read the action of the ball on the lane.
3. You may be forced to squeeze the ball excessively during the delivery, resulting in improper and ill-timed releases. This situation often arises when the span is too short or the holes are too large (especially the thumb hole).
4. You may drop the ball during the swing or backswing, or just prior to the correct moment for releasing it. Dropping the ball is usually caused by (A) too short a span, (B) too large a thumb hole, (C) an incorrectly pitched thumb hole, or (D) the finger holes are too large.
5. You may not be taking advantage of the weight block, and in fact the weight may be working against you. (This area was discussed under BALL BALANCE ADJUSTMENTS.)
6. You may have to use a ball that is not the ideal weight for you, causing you to lose pin count and marks.

Of course, you might encounter many other problems with a poorly fitted ball. But, with a correctly fitted bowling ball most or all of these problems can be eliminated entirely. Therefore, it is important for you to know what measurements and techniques are available to correctly fit *your ball* to *your hand* and to *your game*. Like fingerprints, handprints are unique and require skill in measuring and interpreting the results.

A skilled ball driller can do this. And, since ball grip is one aspect of your game that can be completely controlled by you, it is not necessary to use any ball unless it fits your hand and your game. Your present ball can be plugged and redrilled so it will fit properly.

Now we will discuss the five categories of measurements related to ball fit. First we will begin by discussing the *width* of the thumb and finger holes. This will be followed by analyses of *depth, pitch, span,* and finally, *hole alignment.*

Width of Thumb and Finger Holes: It is vital that the width of the thumb and finger holes be correct: not too snug, causing soreness or making release of the ball difficult; nor too loose, causing the ball to be lost in the swing or creating an ineffective ball.

Perhaps the most important width measurement is the thumb. The role of the thumb during the swing and delivery is to help carry the ball to the point of release. At the moment of release the thumb should leave the ball first, in a smooth and natural manner. This will give the fingers time to impart lift to the ball.

Timing of the thumb release is very important, and is directly related to the width of the thumb hole. If the thumb comes out of the ball too soon, the ball may be dropped and the correct lift cannot be imparted by the fingers. If the thumb hangs-up in the hole, or drags during the moment of release, it will exit the ball later than it should and will interfere with the fingers imparting their lift. Also, this late release may cause you to miss your target on the lane.

When the thumb hole is too wide, there may be a tendency to grip the ball firmly. This causes the release to vary considerably from time to time since the ball cannot be released by relaxing the *un*natural grip on the ball. This situation—too wide of a thumb hole—is the major potential problem with the thumb hole.

Most ball drillers initially make the thumb hole a little smaller than they think it eventually will have to be. It is easy to enlarge a hole, but a lot more difficult to re-plug and re-drill! Since the smaller hole can be easily enlarged, and since it is usually obvious to the bowler that the thumb hole is too small, this method of drilling the width of the thumb hole is advisable, and should result in a hole that will allow you to barely touch the sides of the hole with your thumb when you insert and remove it repeatedly.

The *width of the finger holes* is relatively simple to measure and drill properly. The width may vary slightly depending upon the type of ball fit or grip you use: the conventional grip; the fingertip grip; or the semi-fingertip grip. The conventional grip calls for the finger holes to accommodate up to the second joint; the semi-fingertip, up to the first joint and half the distance to the second joint; and the full fingertip must accommodate the finger only up to the first joint. The finger holes can be slightly snug, but should not be too loose, especially as you move to the longer span grips.

In short, the width of the finger and thumb holes should be measured and drilled carefully. The thumb hole is slightly more important since it has the most impact on the timing and relative ease of the release. Yet both types of holes should be comfortable and fit your hand structure.

Depth of Thumb and Finger Holes: Two points are important in regard to the depth of the thumb and finger holes: The depth should provide for a consistent grip on the ball; and the depth is directly related to the type of ball fit or grip you select from among the three most common ones. Of course, the depth of the holes must take into account the size of the thumb and fingers and the structure of the hand.

If the holes are not deep enough, the fingers or thumb will not be able to be inserted properly. This may cause problems in the swing and in the release. There might be a tendency to squeeze or grip the ball too tightly with the thumb or fingers.

On the other hand, if the holes are too deep, the thumb and fingers may be inserted to varying depths during different deliveries. This could affect the swing and release. It could also create a situation in which the lift imparted on the ball would differ, resulting in inconsistent deliveries and also making it more difficult to properly read the action of the ball and the lane.

Once you select the type of fit or grip you will use, and the span you wish to use, the depth of the finger holes is largely determined. For the conventional grip, the shortest span, the fingers are inserted up to the second joint. This influences both the width and the depth of the holes, as already indicated in the section on *width* of the holes. Should you select the semi-fingertip grip, the depth will have to accommodate the fingers up to the first joint and half way to the second joint. And, of course the fingertip grip will require a hole depth sufficient enough to insert the fingers to the first joint.

The fingers should barely touch the bottom of the hole when the holes are at their proper depth. This will create the correct feel when the thumb and fingers are inserted, and should insure that you are getting the same grip on the ball from delivery to delivery. This may not be possible if you need to take top weight out of the ball by drilling the holes deeper.

Span: This term refers to the distance between the thumb hole and the finger holes. The span can be relatively short, commonly referred to as the conventional grip, or it could be relatively long as in the fingertip grip. Also, the span from the thumb and the middle finger need not be the same as the span (distance) between the thumb and the ring finger. When there is a difference between the two spans, the difference is often referred to as *offset.*

Each span length has certain advantages and disadvantages. Of course each is related to the *structure of your hand* and *your style of bowling*. But each is also related to the amount and type of lift you can impart on the ball, and the degree of security you feel in the grip during the delivery. After discussing the three types of spans, we will look at the relative merits of all three.

Exhibit 4-11 illustrates the three most common spans, or ball fits, or ball grips. (All three terms are used interchangeably, but can mean different things in different parts of the country! Consult the Glossary of terms in Appendix A for clarification.) We will begin our discussion with the conventional grip, the one most often suggested for the beginning to average bowler.

In the *conventional* span the fingers are inserted to the second joint, and the thumb is fully inserted. This relatively short span provides the most comfortable and secure grip and feel to the beginning bowler. The ball does not feel as if it is going to slip off the fingers (if the span is proper) and the full strength of the fingers and thumb can be used to carry the ball during the delivery. Since the fingers are not stretched as in the longer spans, the ball can be carried in a more relaxed, natural manner. This will allow you to use a ball of the maximum weight for you. The added weight will give better carry and keep the ball in the path of deflection through the pins. In addition, any mistake you make in your delivery with the conventional span will *not* be magnified, as it would be with longer spans. This is a very important point. Since the beginning or low average bowler *will* be making mistakes, it is best to keep the magnitude of these mistakes to the lowest possible level. This is one strong point in favor of beginning your bowling career with this span. (Arguments for and against the use of the conventional span to begin your bowling career will be pre-

EXHIBIT 4-11
(RHB) Conventional, Semi-Fingertip and Fingertip Fits

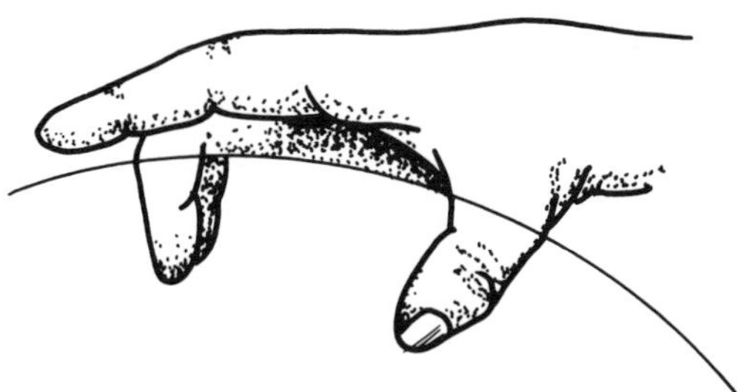

CONVENTIONAL FIT: FINGERS INSERTED TO SECOND JOINT.

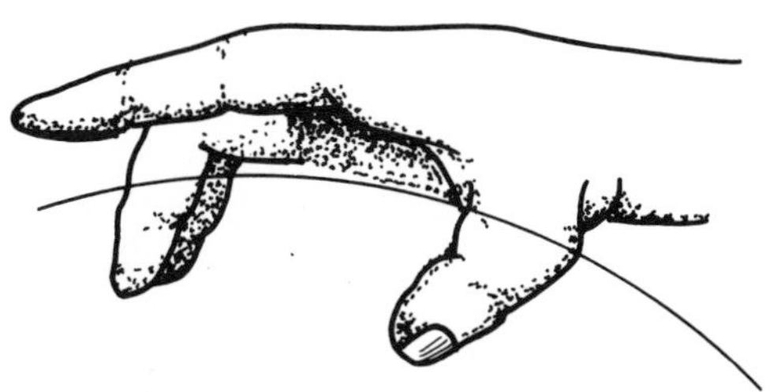

SEMI-FINGERTIP FIT: FINGERS INSERTED TO BETWEEN 1ST AND 2ND JOINT.

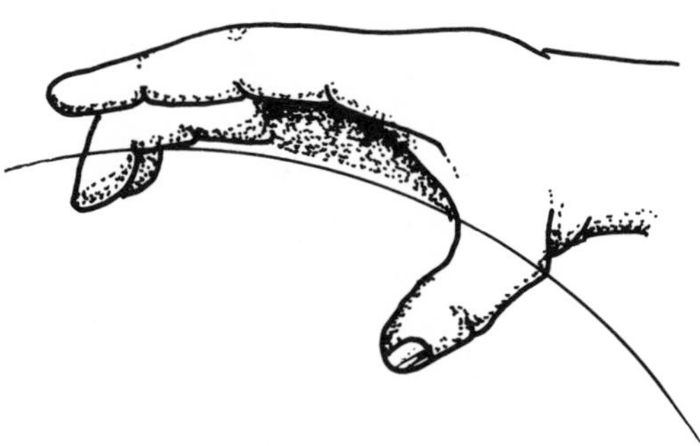

FINGERTIP FIT: FINGERS INSERTED TO FIRST JOINT.

sented a little later in this discussion.) Moreover, it is not necessary for you to ever go beyond this conventional span. You could develop a very high average using the conventional grip, and many bowlers have done just that. However, the vast majority of top bowlers use a longer span. You should be familiar with the other spans, and decide if and when you might want to change to one of them.

Let's jump from the conventional grip to the *fingertip* span, skipping for the moment the intermediate span, the semi-fingertip. The fingertip grip or fit is the longest of the three normal spans. In it, the fingers are inserted only to the first joint. The thumb (as always) is fully inserted. Such a long span will cause you to feel you are stretching your fingers to get them into the holes, as indeed you may have to do. Also, some bowlers refer to a *relaxed fingertip* and a *stretched fingertip* grip, indicating the degree of stretching required to insert the thumb and fingers into the holes. Some people also use the term relaxed fingertip to refer to the *semi*-fingertip which we will describe next. Regardless of the name used, any grip beyond the conventional span will require some degree of stretching in the hand and fingers.

Unlike the shorter conventional grip, it takes a little time to get used to the fingertip fit. It feels uncomfortable at first because it is less natural than the conventional grip. The ball does not feel as secure in the hand since only the first joints of the fingers are holding the ball, rather than up to the second joint with the conventional grip. This means a certain amount of *strength* and *confidence* are needed to use this span. These two terms are critical to your decision as to *if* and *when* you might decide to use this longer span. A certain amount of strength is needed to handle wider spans with ease and comfort.

The major reason for selecting the longer fingertip span is the added amount of *action* you can get from the ball. It is easier to create a hook ball with the longer spans than with the shorter spans—to some degree. With more hook and action on the ball as it hits the pocket, it is easier to keep the ball in the path of deflection through the pins. You are able to play all 5 of the strike lines and the angles within these lines when you are able to hook the ball. (You can still play all of them with the shorter conventional grip, but some of the deep inside angles may be less effective with less action on the ball.) Since you are able to get more hook on the ball with the wider span, it is also true that a small error in your delivery will be magnified with the fingertip grip! Thus, you should be relatively consistent in your delivery when you are using it. Your mistakes will be more exaggerated, and this could have a detrimental impact on your scores.

Despite the disadvantages of the longer span, most top bowlers use this grip to give them the maximum potential for scoring. The added lift they can achieve is a benefit that far outweighs the possible problems associated with the fingertip grip. And once you get used to the fingertip fit, it feels just as natural as the conventional or semi-fingertip grips.

The *semi-fingertip* grip is between the smaller conventional span and the longer full fingertip grip. It is created by drilling the finger holes deep enough so the fingers can be inserted to a point between the first and second joint. The utility of this grip is similar to that of the fingertip: you can get more leverage at the moment of release and therefore get more action on the ball.

Some bowlers refer to the semi-fingertip as a relaxed fingertip. Still others see the relaxed fingertip as a span falling between the semi and the full fingertip. The difference in concepts is not important. The only important fact is that you can lengthen or shorten the span to accommodate a grip that feels comfortable to you, fits your hand structure, and gives you the amount of lift and resulting action you desire. What you call the grip does not matter.

These then, are the three most common types of span or grip: the Conventional grip; the Semi-fingertip grip; and the Fingertip grip. Which is best for you? Which should you start with? Should you lengthen your span as your skill level increases? These are personal questions, but general guidelines can be given to guide you to a correct choice for you.

One school of thought suggests that you start with the conventional grip first. Then, move to the semi or full fingertip grip after your skill level has developed to a point where you have a fundamentally sound delivery, and can consistently and confidently roll the ball. The reasons for using the conventional grip first are sound and include: The conventional grip is the most comfortable, most secure, easiest to use, can be used for your entire career, does not magnify the inevitable mistakes a low to average bowler will make, allows you to concentrate on the development of a sound delivery without undue concern for losing the ball in the delivery, permits you to develop your strength in rolling a ball at the maximum weight for you, will not put a strain on your hand or fingers, and has no major disadvantages for the beginning or average bowler. Given the many stated advantages, and few, if any, disadvantages, it is easy to see why many bowlers feel it is best *to start with* the conventional grip.

However, there is another school of thought on the matter. Virtually all top bowlers use a span in the range of a semi or full fingertip. Therefore, if you plan to use such a span at some time in your bowling career, you might just as well learn how to use it when you start so you will have no adjustment period when you make the conversion. Many people are able to handle the full or semi fingertip grip from the start, or early in their bowling career. Since they are able to handle the longer span grip, why not learn this first? Thus, this argument in favor of the longer span is plausible, but not as persuasive as that which suggests using the conventional grip when you first learn to bowl.

The decision could be handled in this manner: *if* you think you will want to switch to the longer span grip at some time in your future, and *if* you are able to handle the longer span grip at the present time, and *if* the longer span presents no special problems for you, then perhaps you should start with the semi or fingertip. If you have difficulty handling the longer span after trying it, or you are not sure you will want to use it in the future, start with the conventional grip.

Since the decision is largely a personal one, why not discuss the matter with a local bowling instructor or knowledgeable ball driller?

Hole Alignment: Several issues are involved in the decision of the correct alignment of the thumb and finger holes. First, there is the obvious issue of the structure of the hand. The holes should be aligned to provide the correct bridge size (the gap between the two finger holes). And the distance or span between the thumb and middle finger and the thumb and ring finger must contain the correct amount of offset (the difference between these two measurements, dictated by hand structure). Still further, hole alignment is related to your ball track and the ball imbalance you wish to create. The term imbalance, (concerned with locating the thumb and finger holes with reference to the weight block) was discussed under BALL BALANCE ADJUSTMENTS earlier in this section.

Each of the issues related to hole alignment will be covered under the appropriate categories. For now, we will limit our discussion to the three standard ways in which the holes are aligned, as illustrated on Exhibit 4-12

The standard way to align holes, if there is such a thing as a standard, is the one in which the thumb aligns with the bridge (gap, web) between the two finger holes (#2 on Exhibit 4-12). This is sometimes called the *standard offset.*

Still another method of alignment is to arrange the thumb and middle finger as illustrated in #1 on Exhibit 4-12. This type of alignment is often referred to as the two-by-one method.

And the third common method for alignment of the thumb and finger holes is to align the thumb with the ring finger. This is shown as Item #3 on Exhibit 4-12. This method is often called the middle finger offset, since the middle finger is off to the left side of the line between the thumb and ring finger.

Of course, there are other methods of alignment, such as using any one of the three we have mentioned but combining it with some slight angle between the two finger holes. This situation is largely dictated by the structure of the hand, specifically the length of the middle finger in relation to the ring finger. These measurements create the need for offset as explained above.

One item that could be varied in the hole alignment is the width of the gap or bridge between the finger holes. If the bridge is too narrow, it may break. If it is too wide it may be uncomfortable, and it may prevent the two fingers from working effectively together as a unit. Therefore, the span should be kept at a width that is comfortable, fits the hand structure, and allows the two fingers to work as a team to impart lift and turn at the moment of release. The exact measurement will largely be determined by the structure of the hand.

Many of the other items of ball fit are directly related to the alignment of the holes, including pitch, depth, width, and the type of ball track you have decided to use. In aligning the thumb and finger holes for your particular fit, try for comfort and fit that will give you a natural release.

Pitches: Each ball is manufactured with an emblem or manufacturer's label embossed on it. This area is referred to as the top of the ball, and the thumb and finger holes are drilled into this portion of the ball. It is illegal, from a sanctioning point of view, to drill holes into the bottom portion of the ball.

Imagine a bowling ball in front of you, with the label facing you. This will allow you to visualize the direction of the pitches which will be described below.

Pitch refers to the angle at which the holes are drilled into the ball, all with reference to the center of the ball. Three kinds of pitch exist: *zero* pitch; *lateral* or side pitch; and *vertical* or forward/reverse pitch. In zero pitch the holes are angled directly toward the center of the ball. Lateral pitch exists when the holes are angled toward either the left or right side of the center of the ball. And, vertical pitch exists when either (1) the hole(s) angle above the center of the ball (forward pitch), or (2) the hole(s) angle below the center of the ball (reverse pitch).

Exhibit 4-13 illustrates the various types of pitches, giving a top and side view of both thumb and finger pitches. Notice how all the pitches are shown in relationship to the center of the ball.

What is the purpose of pitch? Actually there are two objectives to be reached by drilling the correct

EXHIBIT 4-12
(RHB) Three Types of Hole Alignment

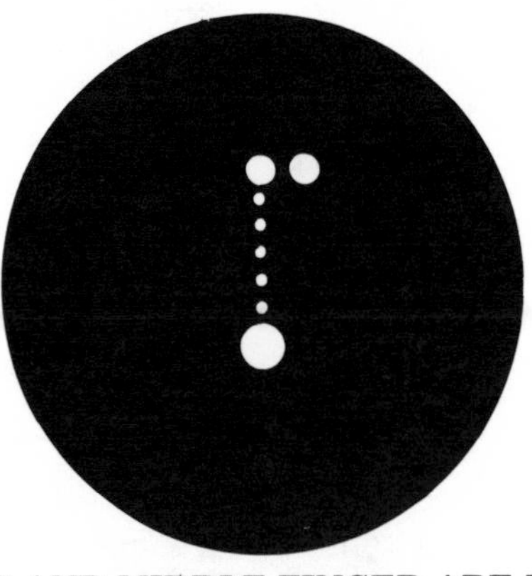

1) THE THUMB AND MIDDLE FINGER ARE IN ALIGNMENT

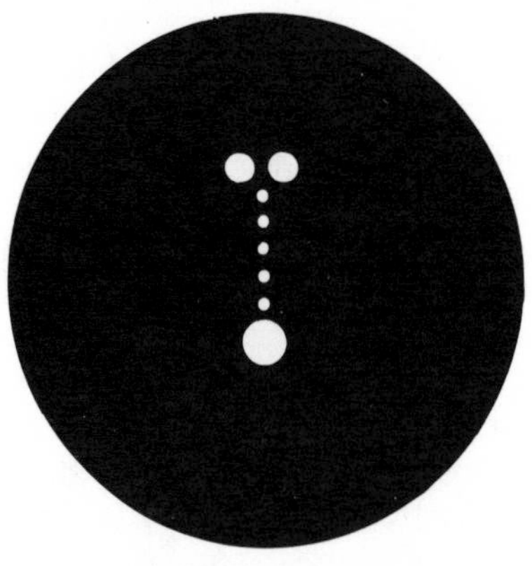

2) THE THUMB AND BRIDGE ARE IN ALIGNMENT

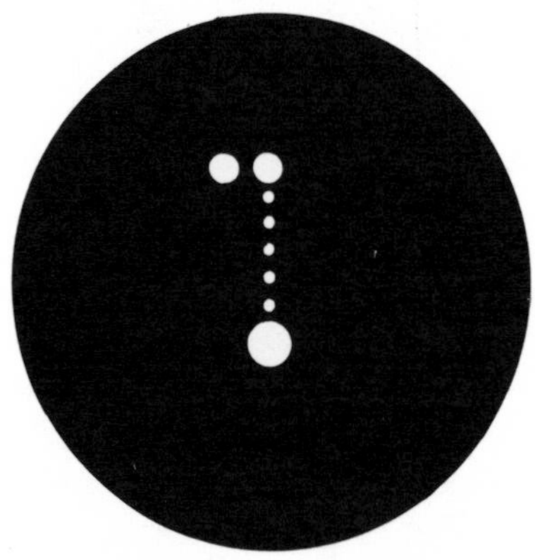

3) THE THUMB AND RING FINGER ARE IN ALIGNMENT

EXHIBIT 4-13
(RHB) Illustrations of Thumb and Finger Pitches

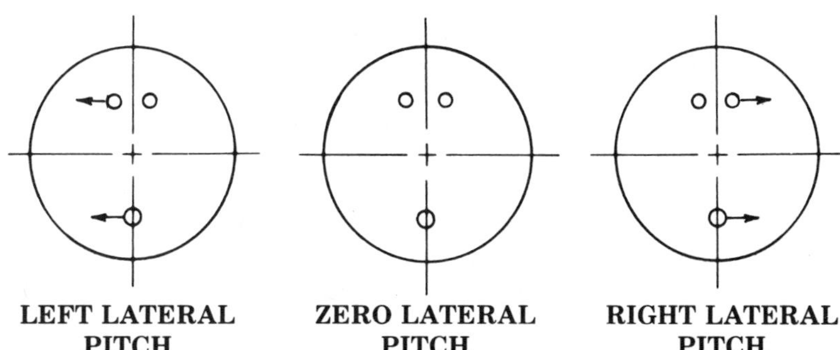

TOP VIEW: FINGERS AND THUMB

LEFT LATERAL PITCH | ZERO LATERAL PITCH | RIGHT LATERAL PITCH

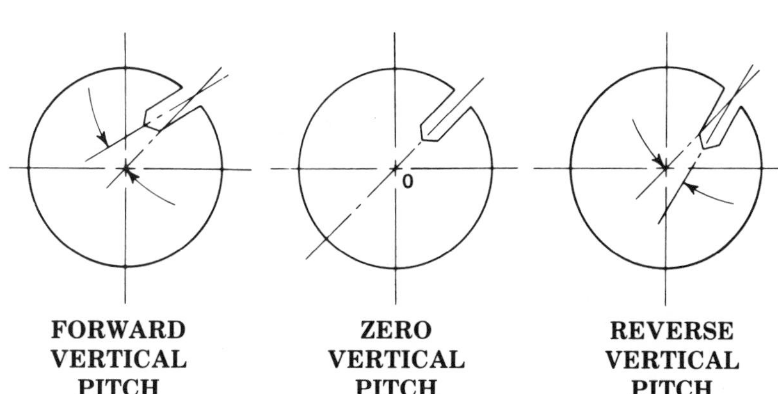

SIDE VIEW: THUMB

FORWARD VERTICAL PITCH | ZERO VERTICAL PITCH | REVERSE VERTICAL PITCH

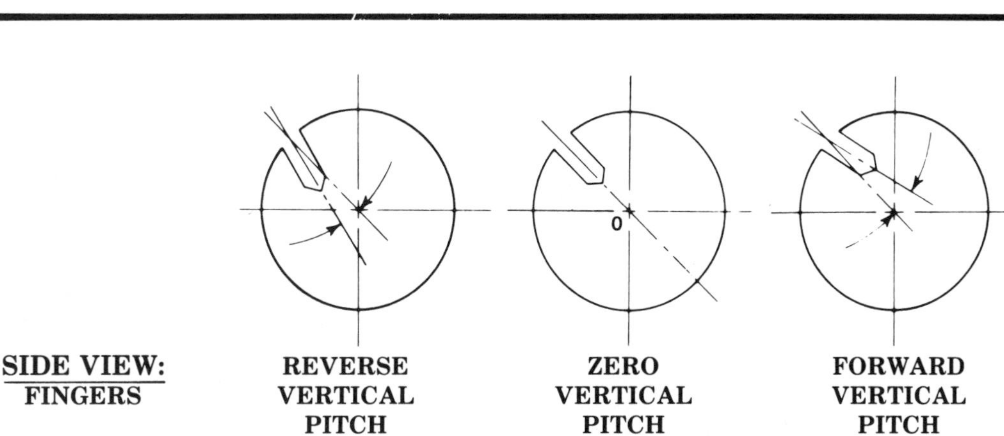

SIDE VIEW: FINGERS

REVERSE VERTICAL PITCH | ZERO VERTICAL PITCH | FORWARD VERTICAL PITCH

pitch for the finger and thumb holes—*comfort* and *lift*. Some forms of pitch are designed to permit the ball to fit the structure of your hand so the ball will feel comfortable during the entire delivery. Still others are designed to give you more or less lift and turn at the moment of release.

Exhibit 4-14 indicates the major types of pitch that might be drilled into a bowling ball. This exhibit relates each type of pitch either to improving the comfort of the ball in the hand, or to affect the degree or amount of lift imparted at the moment of ball release.

Two general statements about pitch are in order at this time. (1) Those pitches that are related to providing a comfortable fit as their *primary* objective are (A) side pitch in the finger holes, and (B) vertical pitch in the thumb hole. (2) Those types of pitches more directly related to affecting the amount of lift or turn created by the release are (A) lateral or side pitch in the thumb hole and (B) vertical or forward/reverse pitch in the finger holes. These are generalizations only, since a pitch that is changed from uncomfortable to comfortable will probably improve the lift and bring about a more consistent release. One that gives you more lift may cause you to be slightly uncomfortable until the change has been incorporated into your game.

The relationship between vertical and lateral pitch in the thumb hole further illustrates this connection between comfort and lift. If you alter the side-ways pitch in the thumb hole (to raise or lower the ball track), the vertical pitch should be changed proportionately to keep the same degree of comfort in the fit. As a general rule, when you move the lateral (side pitch) of the thumb hole ⅛ inch, the vertical pitch should be changed by 50% of that amount, 1/16 inch. Left side thumb pitch should be accompanied by increased reverse pitch or less forward pitch. Right side pitch should be accompanied by forward pitch or less reverse pitch.This concept can be illustrated by the following exercise. (Exhibit 4-15.)

Hold your hand in front of you, with your palm facing away from you. Close your thumb and fingers until your thumb touches one of your fingers. (Which one it touches and where it touches will depend upon the degree of flexibility in your thumb!) Then, open and close your fingers and thumb several times, noticing the direction that your thumb moves. It will move at an angle, to the left and back at the same time. If there were no relationship, the thumb would move either straight back, or directly to the side. Since it moves both to the side and back at the same time, there is a relationship between these two pitches. So, when you increase the left lateral pitch in your thumb hole, you have to add some more reverse pitch to keep the same degree of comfort in your grip. When you move your pitch for the thumb to the right side, you have to take your current vertical pitch and move it more toward the front, increasing forward pitch.

This may be slightly confusing to you at first, but a closer examination of the movement of the thumb and fingers during the above exercise should help clarify this concept of thumb pitch. It should also suggest that as you lengthen or shorten the span in your grip, *there is a relationship between pitches and span*. Forward pitch on the thumb hole (like closing your hand) would create a shortening of the span. Reverse thumb pitch creates the need for a longer span. These complex interrelationships merely serve to illustrate that the art and science of ball drilling requires a great deal of knowledge about the structure of hands, and also about the influence of pitches on how you deliver the ball. (See Exhibit 4-15.)

EXHIBIT 4-14
(RHB) Relating the 12 Pitches to Comfort or Lift

Pitches may be used to (A) fit the structure of the hand in a comfortable manner, or (B) influence the amount of lift generated the moment the ball is released. This chart indicates the *primary* function of the 12 types of pitches that may be drilled into the holes of the ball.

TYPE OF PITCH	THUMB	FINGERS
Vertical-forward	Comfort-lift	Lift
Vertical-*zero* pitch	Either	Either
Vertical-reverse	Comfort-lift	Lift
Lateral-right side	Lift-comfort	Comfort
Lateral-*zero* pitch	Either	Either
Lateral-left side	Lift-comfort	Comfort

NOTES: Vertical and lateral thumb pitches are related, as indicated in later discussions. But vertical thumb pitch is primarily related to comfort, and lateral thumb pitch is primarily related to lift. Vertical finger pitches are primarily used to influence the amount of lift generated. Lateral finger pitches are more related to comfort and fitting the structure of the hand.

Changing from an incorrect (uncomfortable) to a correct (comfortable) pitch could also result in a change in the amount of lift you generate.

EXHIBIT 4-15
(RHB) Relationship Between Vertical and Lateral Thumb Pitches

A direct relationship exists between vertical and lateral pitches that are drilled for the thumb hole. Once a proper fit has been determined, any change to one should be accompanied by a change in the other. The dotted line indicates the approximate path of the thumb as the hand is opened and closed. It shows that the thumb moves on an angle, neither straight back nor from left to right. Any movement of the thumb is both a movement to the side and the front or back at the same time.

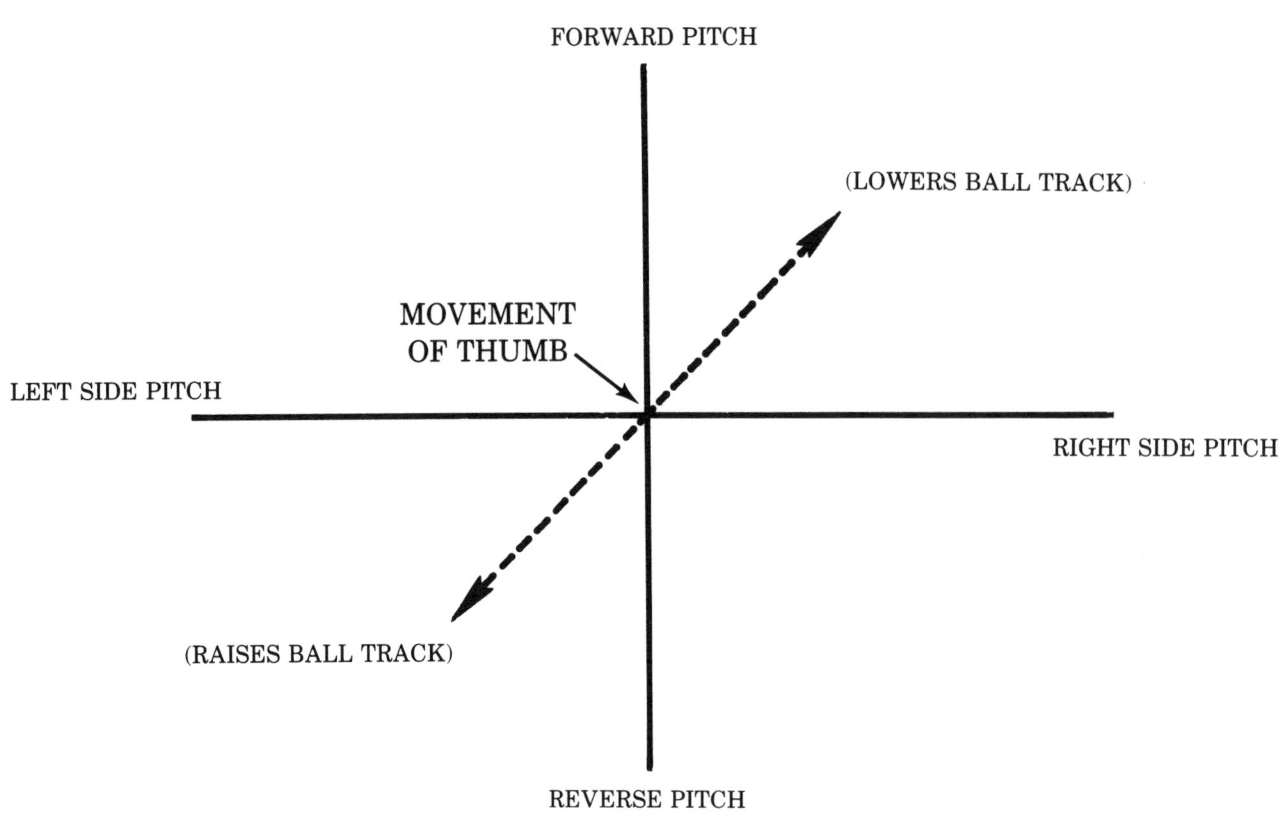

Notice that forward and right side thumb pitch will cause the ball track to go lower on the ball. Left side and reverse pitch will raise the ball track. Should you wish to move the ball track up or down on the ball, this is the type of ball drilling adjustment that could be used. Of course, the exact angle that would apply to a given bowler is related to the flexibility of the thumb and the structure of the hand. And the span may have to be changed to accommodate the change in thumb pitch.

EXHIBIT 4-16
(RHB) Ball Fit Terms

Bridge: The small area of the ball directly between the two finger holes.

Conventional fit: A method of gripping or fitting the ball so the finger holes are deep enough to insert the fingers to the second joint, and in which the finger and thumb holes are located relatively close to one another. This is a narrow span grip. The conventional fit is the easiest to learn to use and is the most common grip or fit among beginning or low average bowlers.

Fingertip fit: A method of gripping or fitting the ball so the finger holes are only deep enough for the fingers to be inserted to the first joint, and in which the thumb and finger holes are located far apart. This is a wide span fit or grip. The fingertip fit is very common among high average bowlers, since it provides the maximum opportunity to impart lift on the ball.

Forward pitch: Drilling the ball so the angle of the hole is above the center of the ball, instead of being angled below center, or toward the center.

Grip: A term which defines the total way the holes are drilled, including span, pitches, size of holes, location, alignment, etc. Sometimes the term grip is used to describe one of the three most common types of ball fit: conventional, semi-fingertip or fingertip.

Hole alignment: Describing the way in which the thumb and finger holes are aligned after drilling is completed. The thumb can be in line with the middle finger, the ring finger, or with the bridge or gap between the two finger holes. Other variations are also possible.

Left side pitch: Drilling a hole so it slants to the left side of the ball, instead of toward the center or right side.

Offset: The difference in span between the thumb and one finger and the thumb and the other finger.

Pitch: The angle at which a hole is drilled into the ball. There can be forward, reverse, side or zero pitch. These pitch angles are illustrated in Exhibit 4-13.

Reverse pitch: Drilling a hole into the ball so the hole angles below the center of the ball, instead of toward the center or above it.

Right side pitch: Drilling a hole so it slants to the right side of the ball, instead of toward the center or left side.

Semi-fingertip: A method of gripping or fitting the ball so the finger holes are drilled deep enough for the fingers to be inserted mid-way between the first and second joint. A medium span fit or grip that is between the conventional and fingertip fit.

Span: The distance between the thumb hole and the finger holes. A wide span is considered a fingertip grip, and a narrow span is called a conventional fit or grip.

Stretch fingertip: A term implying that the span for the fingertip is rather long, causing the hand to be stretched for proper insertion. Often the regular fingertip is called a relaxed fingertip to separate it from the stretch fingertip.

Thumb-middle-finger alignment: Drilling the holes so the thumb hole and the middle finger hole are in alignment. (Sometimes called two-by-one.)

Thumb-ring-finger alignment: Drilling the holes so the thumb hole and the ring finger hole are in alignment.

Thumb-bridge alignment: Aligning the thumb with the bridge or gap between the two finger holes. (Sometimes called a standard offset.)

Zero pitch: Drilling the holes directly toward the center of the ball, as opposed to angling them to the top, bottom, left or right side.

SECTION 5
DELIVERY ADJUSTMENTS
(Right Handed Bowlers)

"A consistent, natural, well-timed delivery is the foundation for high scoring."

CONTENTS

OVERVIEW

The purpose of this section is threefold: to discuss the essentials of an effective delivery; to describe the four most normal paths the ball takes to the pin deck; and to present the three most common delivery adjustments.

Deliveries can be classified in a number of ways, including: (1) by the hand you use (left or right); (2) by the nature of the ball track; or (3) by the path the ball takes from the foul line to the pin deck (straight ball, curve ball, hook, or backup).

Other methods of classification exist, but we will limit our discussion of deliveries to the three types outlined above.

The first classification, left or right handed, has been addressed throughout this book. All material has been presented from both the left and right handed points of view. We have tried to make all translations of the material in each section.

In this way, each style is treated equally. (Volume 3, ***The Complete Guide to Bowling Spares,*** is also written in this manner, as are all volumes in this series.) *These may be the only books on bowling that treat left and right handed bowlers on an equal basis.*

The second classification of deliveries, by the path the ball takes from the foul line to the pin deck, will be covered extensively in this section. We will begin discussion of the straight ball, curve, backup and hook ball after covering the elements of an effective delivery.

Delivery adjustments are without a doubt the most difficult adjustments to make. *Most high average bowlers agree that delivery adjustments should not be made unless a change in angle or equipment cannot be found to meet lane conditions.* Yet there are times when you will have to make some change in the way you deliver the ball to capitalize on, or accommodate lane conditions. Therefore, you should add delivery adjustments to your adjustment arsenal.

A delivery change often upsets timing, rhythm or tempo. Those who have practiced making changes in the way they deliver the ball will make such adjustments very quickly and easily. As with all adjustments, the more you practice, the easier they are to make. Therefore, you should practice making at least three types of delivery adjustments: increasing or decreasing the ball *speed;* using more or less *loft* of the ball out over the foul line; and giving the ball more or less *lift* (turn, action, etc.)

Before we begin our discussion of these three delivery adjustments, it is necessary to review the fundamentals of a sound and effective delivery. *High scoring on any long term basis is dependent upon the development of a sound delivery.* Without an effective delivery of the ball it is not possible to take advantage of many of the scientific systems of adjusting that are covered in this and other volumes in the series. (Volume 1, ***The Complete Guide To Bowling Principles,*** concentrates almost exclusively upon the development of a consistent, natural and well-timed delivery.) For example, you cannot tell what your ball and lane are doing (how they are interacting) until you have control of your delivery.

ELEMENTS OF AN EFFECTIVE DELIVERY: What are the essential ingredients of a delivery upon which high scoring can be developed? Three elements stand out as most important, despite the particular type or style of delivery: Your delivery should be (1) consistent, (2) natural, and (3) well-timed.

Consistent: Your walk pattern from the stance

position to the foul line should be consistent. Your arm swing should be the same each time you deliver the ball. All elements of your delivery should be consistent. Inconsistency creates errors.

You can drift in your walk pattern, or walk in a perfectly straight line. You can take large or small steps, or shuffle to the foul line. You can do any number of things that may be considered poor form, so long as you do them with a high degree of regularity. You can be successful with any style of bowling, if it works well for you on a continuous basis, as attested to by the variety of styles displayed by the top bowlers in the world. But, whatever they do, they do in a consistent, predictable manner. It is part of their game.

Natural: Your delivery is influenced by your body build, your strength, and the way you learned to bowl. How you bowl feels comfortable to you since you have been doing it for some time. The things you do in your delivery may be similar to what others use, or they could be completely different. *There is no single perfect style of delivery that can be used by every bowler.* Any individual style, one that is natural to the person, can be developed into one that produces high scores on a regular basis. It may be easier or harder for you to overcome some natural tendencies you have, but with practice most delivery styles can be groomed into successful ones.

Observe the natural styles of some of the more successful bowlers. Notice the wide range of individual characteristics displayed. Yet we can say that their style of delivery feels natural to them. And, that is the important point. You do not need to become a carbon copy of anyone else. You should be you. *You should develop a game that is natural to you.*

It may be natural for you to take 3 steps, or 4, 5, or 6, or more. You may drift by 5 boards to the left or right in your walk pattern. You may bend your elbow during the swing. You may have a style that is unlike the classic styles often recommended. But, what you are doing may not be wrong *for you.* The result determines whether anything is wrong. If you can score well, on a regular basis, and you are able to adapt to changing lane conditions, then whatever you are doing is correct. You must determine what type of delivery will work for you, what feels natural to you, and develop your delivery along those lines.

Well-Timed: When you take your stance on the approach, there are two things you have to do to get the ball on its way to the pins. You have to (1) take a series of steps toward the foul line (although the number and size of these steps will differ from bowler to bowler); and you have to (2) swing the ball from its initial position in the stance until the moment it is released. These two factors, your steps and your swing, have to be well-timed.

Within this broad guideline of being well-timed, there is wide latitude as to how many steps you take, of what size, at what speed, and in what actual direction (with or without drift). Your ball could be held down at your side, waist level, higher or lower, and your swing could include a backswing of any height. As long as you are able to keep these elements of your delivery in the proper timing *for you,* in the right rhythm and tempo *for you,* you should be able to take advantage of all the adjustment techniques for getting the ball into the pocket correctly.

Your ball speed may be moderate, slow, fast, or very fast, as compared to other bowlers. But, as long as your timing in the delivery is such that you are able to score well, on a regular basis, then it must be that what you are doing is correct, and well-timed.

In summary, an effective delivery is consistent in every way, is natural for you, and is well-timed in steps and swing. Once you have such a fundamentally sound delivery, you are in a position to make small adjustments to accommodate various lane conditions.

Although there are a wide range of changes you could make in your delivery as you try to get the ball either up to the pocket, or back to it, three types of delivery adjustments are most frequently used: changes in ball speed; changes in lift imparted at the release point; and changes in the distance the ball is lofted out over the foul line. One or more of these delivery adjustment techniques may have to be made to properly play the lane. Following the discussion of the four common types of ball paths to the pins, we will explain how these three types of adjustments can be made. But, now, let's look at the straight ball, curve, backup, and hook deliveries.

FOUR PATTERNS OF BALL ROLL: All four paths to the pin deck are illustrated on Exhibit 5-1. Each type of ball can be effective under given circumstances. Each delivery has advantages and disadvantages, and it is possible to improve your average with any of them.

The path of the ball to the pocket is largely determined by the position of the thumb and fingers at the moment the ball is released onto the lane. Rotation of the ball *prior* to release, and altering the degree of firmness of the fingers at the time of release, will also affect the path to the pins.

The thumb is supposed to come out of the ball first, followed a split second later by the fingers. For this split second that the ball is held by the fingers, there is an opportunity to impart lift (turn, spin, fingers, action, etc.) on the ball. An early or late release of the thumb, rigid or limp fingers at the explosion point (the moment the ball is released by

EXHIBIT 5-1
(RHB) Four Common Paths to the Pocket

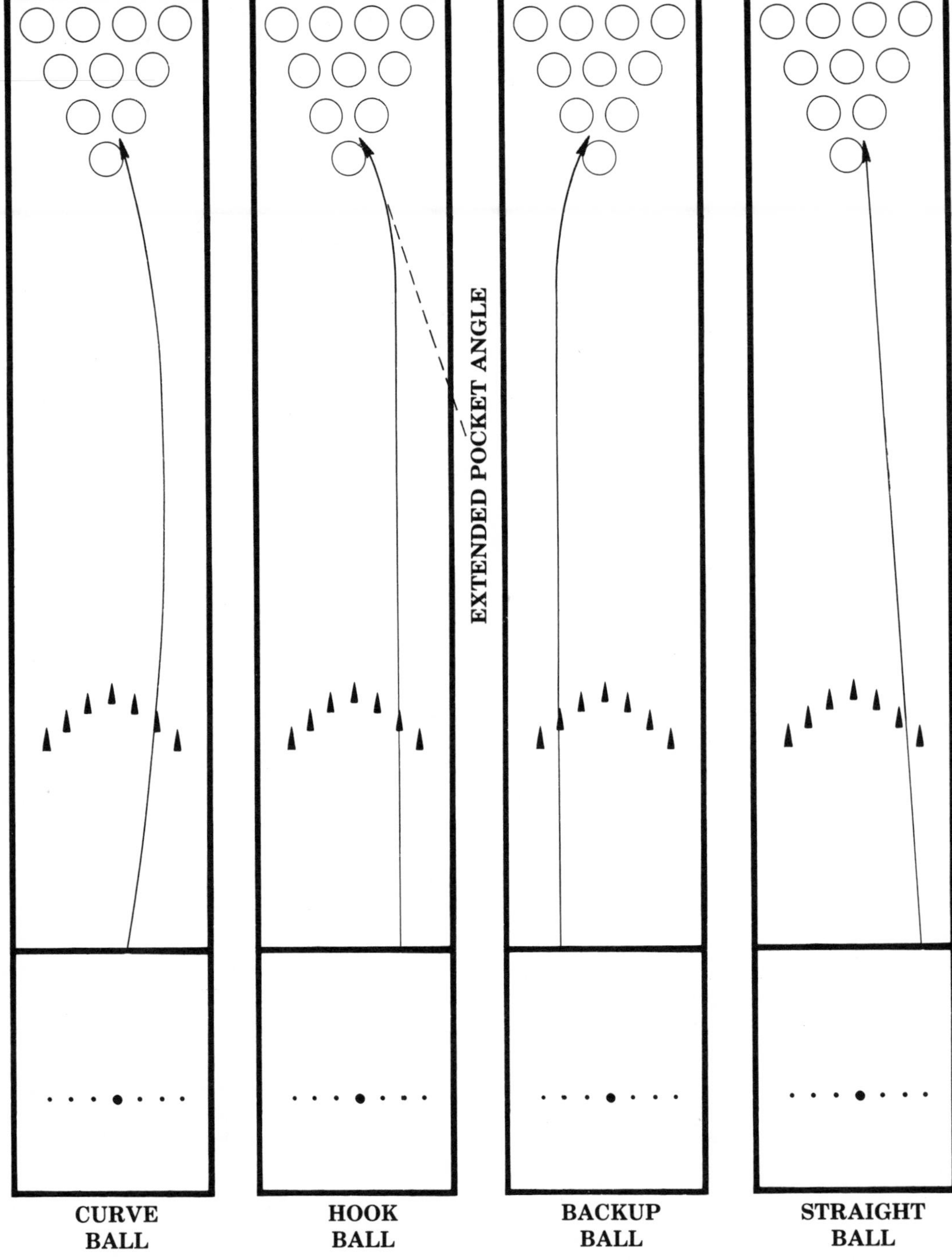

Most bowlers will roll the ball along a path similar to one of the four illustrated above. Notice that the backup ball pattern is similar to the hook ball rolled by left handed bowlers. Also, the pocket angle indicated for the hook ball would, if extended, go off the side of the lane about 20 or so feet in front of the pin deck. This correct pocket angle can only be achieved by rolling either a curve or hook ball, or a backup ball into the 1-2 pocket.

the fingers), or a strong or weak follow-through, are all factors that determine what path the ball will take. However, most bowlers will roll the ball along a path similar to one of the four general patterns shown on Exhibit 5-1.

Perhaps the best way to describe the position of the fingers at release time is with reference to an imaginary clock laid across the foul line on the right side of the lane. Imagine such a clock positioned with 12 o'clock facing straight down the lane, 6 o'clock to the rear, and 3 and 9 o'clock directly on the foul line.

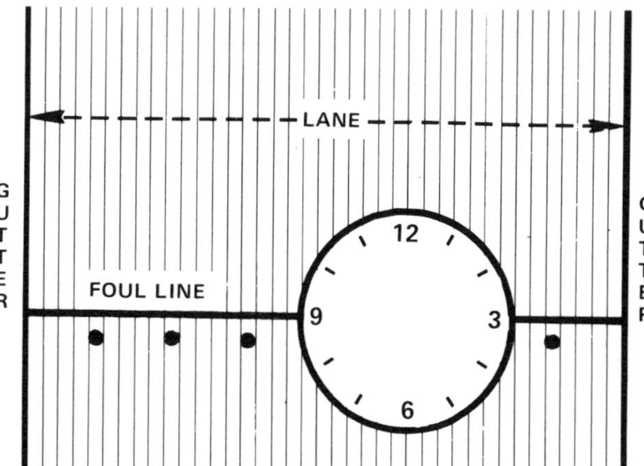

The four paths to the pin deck illustrated in Exhibit 5-1 are created by locating the fingers in these positions: the *straight* ball is created by having the fingers at a position at 6 o'clock; the *curve or hook* is rolled by having the fingers at a position somewhere between 4 and 5 o'clock; and the *backup* ball is rolled by having the fingers at about a 7 or 8 o'clock position as the ball is released.

Rotation of the fingers in a counter clockwise manner at release will tend to create a curve or hooking pattern. A rotation of the fingers in a clockwise manner at release tends to produce a full roller or a backup ball delivery, depending upon how far the fingers are rotated. Combining such rotations with other delivery changes will affect the eventual path of the ball to the pins. These generalizations should help you understand the relationship between finger positions at time of release and ball paths to the pins.

Since the fingers are naturally on the opposite side of the top of the ball (from the thumb) you could refer to the position of the thumb at the moment the ball is released to determine the eventual path taken by the ball. But, since the fingers are used to impart lift to the ball, attention should be focused upon their position at release time.

What are the relative merits of each of the four general paths to the pin deck? Which one is the most effective for making strikes, and why? To answer these and other related questions, we will review all four types of deliveries, starting with the straight ball.

The Straight Ball: The straight ball, as the name implies, follows a direct path from the foul line to the pins. Since the pocket is located on the 17th board at the pin deck, it is possible to roll a straight ball directly down the 17th board at the foul line. However, it is usually rolled from the extreme right side of the lane, from any one of a number of right-to-left foul line angles.

Pin and ball deflection represent the problem associated with using the straight ball for making strikes. A straight angle into the pocket is far less effective than the ideal angle created by the hook ball (to be discussed later). A ball rolled straight for the 1-3 pocket from the foul line is too easily deflected out of the pocket, causing the ball to hit the 3-pin too fully, and hitting the 5-pin either too lightly or not at all. Usually the ball will not hit the 5-pin because the ball is being deflected away from it, rather than driving into it, as is the case with either a curve or hook ball. The straight ball cannot penetrate into the 18½ board after contacting the pocket, unless the hit is slightly high or the speed of the ball will permit such penetration to take place.

The straight ball can, however, be effective in producing strikes. The key to successful bowling at the higher average levels is a consistently high percentage of strikes (50% or more). This is more difficult to achieve with the straight ball than it is with the curve or hook, because of less-than-ideal pin and ball deflection.

Three adjustments can be made that will allow you to use the straight ball and increase your percentage of strikes. First, use as much of an angle into the pocket as you possibly can. Roll the ball from the deep outside foul line angle position. This will permit the ball to penetrate the pocket more than one rolled from a straighter angle. Second, roll the ball with sufficient speed to keep the ball driving into the pocket after contact with the 1-pin. This will give the ball a chance to contact the 5-pin properly. And, third, hit the pocket slightly high on the head pin, so the ball is not deflected into the 3-pin too sharply. A slightly high pocket hit will permit the ball to maintain its path of deflection through the pins.

Of course, these suggestions mean you have to be a little more accurate with your strike hits, and you will run the risk of splits or high-pocket leaves. The result is a lower than 50% average in number of strike deliveries. But, using the above three adjustment suggestions should increase your number of strikes on the straight ball delivery.

There should be no overall disadvantage to you if you use the straight ball for your spare conversions. Some spares will be easier for you, and others will be more difficult. But as a general rule, there will be no noticeable problems with your spares. In fact, many high average bowlers try to straighten out their shots for spares, since accuracy (not action) is the key ingredient in making spare conversions. (Just the opposite is true on all strike attempts!) Since these high average bowlers deliberately elect to use a straighter ball for their spares, to reduce the possibility for errors, it follows that the straight ball *may* even be more advantageous over the hook ball for spare conversions. This is definitely true in many instances (such as the 3-10 split).

If you converted almost all of your makeable spares, but were not able to produce a high percentage of strikes, your top average potential might be limited to about 175. This is a respectable average, and would place you very high in the standings in most leagues. But such an average is 25 pins below the 200 average level generally used to establish the cutoff point for separating the top bowlers from all others.

Therefore, if you are willing to accept a theoretical maximum attainable average around 175, then by all means continue using the straight ball. You can still roll some big games, enjoy the game more than if you held a much lower average, and *you could even go beyond this stated maximum.* But if you wish to move to higher plateaus, to as high as your skills will permit, then you should consider learning how to roll the hook ball. With the hook ball, there is no practical limit to how high you could increase your average. *To date the highest league average is a 240 season average by John Johns. The record for women stands at 227, set by Patty Ann of Arlington Heights, Illinois.*

The Backup Ball: The general path of the backup ball is similar to the path of a hook rolled by a left handed bowler. That is, the ball hooks or curves from left to right. This is an important fact, since it suggests that the backup ball delivery might be effective if it is rolled into the 1-2 pocket instead of the normal 1-3 pocket for the right handed bowler.

The backup ball is also known as a reverse hook, although there is a slight difference between these two deliveries. Both the backup and reverse hook follow a left-to-right path to the pins, but the reverse hook has a sharper turn to the right than the backup delivery.

To assess the effectiveness of the backup ball delivery, it is necessary to recall the pin and ball deflection required for a perfect strike hit. The ball should be driving *into* the pocket, contacting the 1-3-5-9 pins on its path through the pins. The ball should contact the 5-pin rather firmly and send it into the 8-pin.

A backup ball rolled toward the 1-3 pocket deflects *away* from the pocket, and particularly away from the 5-pin instead of toward it. The backup ball hits the head pin in a left-to-right manner, which causes the ball to deflect more toward the 6-pin than the 5-pin. A backup ball rolled for the 1-3 pocket by a right hander is exactly like a LHB rolling for a brooklyn strike! The hit and the angle of the ball are very similar.

It is easy to conclude that if you wish to continue rolling a backup ball, and you want to increase your percentage of strikes, then you should roll for the 1-2 pocket. Pin and ball deflection will be working for you when you use this opposite pocket. *In effect, you should roll your strike delivery similar to a left handed bowler.* You may not be able to get as much drive on the ball as a left hander would, but your possibilities for making strikes will definitely be greater than if you use the 1-3 pocket.

There is no major disadvantage associated with the backup ball delivery for spare conversions. Some spares will be easier for you, but others will be more difficult. On any spare in which the LHB has an advantage (because of favorable pin or ball deflection) you have the same advantage with the backup ball. Where the RHB has the advantage, your backup delivery would put you at a disadvantage. For example, the 10-pin is a most difficult non-split spare for the RHB, but the 7-pin is relatively easy to make. Just the opposite would be true with your backup delivery; the 10-pin should be very easy since you are rolling *into the pin.* The 7-pin might be difficult since the backup ball is moving *away from the pin.*

Since accuracy (not action) is the most important factor in making spares, the backup ball can be very effective. You can be just as accurate with the backup ball (with the correct amount of practice) as you can with a hook, curve, or straight ball delivery. Pin and ball deflection are *not always critical on spare* leaves, but they are *always critical on every strike try.*

Therefore, if you wish to improve your average significantly, and you want to continue rolling a backup ball, you can and should do so. Simply use the 1-2 pocket for your strike ball, and bowl the entire game as if you were left-handed. Do not use the 1-3 pocket for strikes, since a backup ball will produce fewer strikes using that pocket.

Don't be ashamed, concerned or embarrassed by using the so-called opposite pocket. You are increasing your percentage for strikes and bowling intelligently by doing so. If you wish to achieve the highest average possible for your potential skill level, then you should try to develop a hook ball. Your local bowling instructor can help you develop this type of delivery. Also, Volume 1 in this series ***(The Complete Guide to Bowling Principles)*** goes into great detail on that subject.

The Curve Ball: This type of delivery is rolled or created in much the same manner as the hook ball. The fingers are to the right of the 6 o'clock position at release time. The ball is rolled slowly with an exaggerated counter clockwise rotation of the hand at the moment of release.

The path of the curve ball is similar to that taken by the hook ball, but there are essential differences between the two paths to the pocket. The curve ball is rolled slowly and follows a gradual arc or curve to the pins, almost in the shape of an archer's bow. It goes out to the right in a gradual arc and then slowly makes a turn toward the pins. The curve ball crosses many boards on its path to the pins. On the other hand, the hook ball usually takes a more direct and straight path from the foul line until it reaches a breaking point, where it makes a sharp turn to the pocket. The hook ball crosses fewer boards than the curve ball. (More on the hook ball in the next part.)

Although the curve ball can be effective on occasion, it is difficult to be consistent with it. You *can* contact the pocket at the ideal pocket angle. But the ineffectiveness of the curve ball is a result of its gradual turn to the pocket and the excessive number of boards it crosses. As a general rule, the more boards a ball crosses on its path to the pins, the less accurate it is. There are too many chances of hitting erratic lane conditions over the wider surface of the lane. In addition, the gradualness or gentleness of the turn to the pocket may not leave the ball with enough action to drive into the pocket properly.

Still another disadvantage of the curve ball is that it is less useful for lane conditions suggesting strike lines other than the ones toward the inside of the lanes (the inside and deep inside strike lines). It can be used with the second arrow line, but this may call for entering the lane track twice on the way to the pocket. When lane conditions dictate the outside or deep outside strike lines, it may not be easy to get the curve ball to follow the proper or ideal path to the pocket. Thus, the curve ball presents a reasonable path to the pins under some types of lane conditions, but is less likely to provide a good shot at the pocket under all types.

Speed control is another disadvantage of the curve ball. It is difficult to maintain a consistent speed throughout the shot, and adjusting ball speed might be difficult. Although speed control could be developed with sufficient practice, altering ball speed is difficult to master with the curve ball without affecting the timing of the approach.

If you roll a curve ball, and wish to continue doing so, you can still develop a high average. Lane conditions may limit your ability to adapt, and you may only be able to score well when you hit your condition, but you can do fairly well with the curve ball. With a little practice, you could convert to rolling a hook ball, and that is what we suggest you do if you wish to raise your average to the highest possible level. So, let's look at the hook ball delivery.

The Hook Ball: Virtually all high average bowlers use some form of the hook ball. They roll the ball so that it takes a sharp break or turn toward the pocket, usually when it is within 10 to 15 feet of the pins. To create this hook ball, the fingers are situated between 4 and 5 o'clock at the moment the ball is released, although the fingers might have been rotated in a counter clockwise manner to get to this release point. Precise finger location determines to a large degree how much the ball will hook, as does any rotation of the ball during the swing. Lane conditions, the strike angle used, and ball weights and balances also play a part in the timing and intensity of the hook.

When and *where* the ball hooks are very important points to consider in reading the lanes. At times you will want the ball to hook sooner or later (timing of the hook) and at other times you will want the ball to hook more or less (strength or intensity of the hook). These are the major decisions which any hook ball bowler has to make: do I want the ball to break sooner or later, and more or less?

Our previous discussions about the perfect strike hit and the pocket angle give us an insight into why the hook ball is the most effective delivery for making strikes. Pin and ball deflection are best for carrying all ten pins when the ball enters the pocket from an angle that allows the ball to contact the 3 and 5-pins properly after hitting the 1-3 pocket. Too much of an angle will have the ball contacting the 3-pin too far on the left side, and hitting too much of the 5-pin. Not enough angle will cause the ball to hit the 3-pin too fully and hit the 5-pin too lightly on the right side. In both cases pin deflection will generally not result in a strike.

The correct pocket angle, extended back toward the bowler, would go off the right side of the lane less than 20 feet in front of the pin deck. Carried all the way back to the foul line, the extended line would be perhaps two lanes to the right! (See Exhibit 6-1 for an illustration of this point. Extend the hook portion of the hook ball pattern away from the pins in a straight line. It will go off the lane and cross over into the adjacent lane on the right side very quickly.)

The only way to get the ball into this ideal pocket angle is to delay the hook point (the breaking point) until the ball is well down the lane, perhaps to within 10-15 feet of the pocket. Breaking either too soon or too late will put the ball into the pocket at a less-than-ideal pocket angle.

A backup or straight ball cannot hit the 1-3 pocket from this ideal pocket angle. The curve ball could, as previously mentioned. Therefore, only a hook ball that begins its break toward the pocket after it is more than 45 feet beyond the foul line, can enter the pocket at the correct angle to produce strikes *consistently*. The backup ball, if rolled for the 1-2 pocket, could enter that pocket from the optimum angle to produce strikes consistently, as discussed in the previous section on the backup ball.

From this brief discussion of the ideal pocket angle, and the pin and ball deflection required for the perfect strike, it should be clear why almost every high average bowler uses some form of hook ball for strikes. This is the only type of ball pattern that has a consistent chance to keep its path of deflection through the pins, and which creates the proper pin and ball deflection to take out the six pins not taken out by the ball. Although there are many ways to strike, including the occasional strike which results when the head pin has been missed, the hook ball gives the best chance to strike *consistently*.

Consistency in striking is one of the two major ingredients in the game of top bowlers, making about 50% of their strike deliveries (averaging about 5 strikes per game). The second ingredient is making about 95% of their spare leaves. These two goals represent a standard to set for yourself if you wish to achieve the status of a 200 or better average bowler. Rolling the hook ball delivery would be the best way to help you achieve this objective.

Summary: To summarize the merits of the four types of deliveries, the major disadvantage to every type of ball roll except the hook ball and curve ball is the problem associated with pin and ball deflection on the pin deck. A backup, or straight ball can be effective on occasion, and you can raise your average and enjoyment of the game. But it will be difficult for you to approach the effectiveness of the hook ball and curve ball even under the best of circumstances. Only a hook ball or curve ball allows you to get the ball to hit the pocket from the correct pocket angle, with the right hit on the-1-3-5-9 pins, and with the correct amount of action on the ball to maintain its path of deflection through the pins.

Any one of the four types of deliveries may be effective for spare conversions, since accuracy and not action is the key to making spares. In fact, many high average bowlers try to straighten out their spare shots, indicating that the straight ball might be advantageous for many spares. But for making strikes consistently, the hook ball is far superior to the curve, backup or straight ball.

And now we will cover the three major types of delivery adjustments which should be a part of the adjustment arsenal of every bowler who wishes to increase his or her average to higher levels: speed adjustments, loft adjustments, and lift adjustments.

SPEED ADJUSTMENTS
(Right Handed Bowlers)

"Incorrect ball or foot speed is the biggest enemy of making strikes," Jeff Morin, Member, PBA.

The ability to adjust ball speed is an important skill to add to your adjustment arsenal. Very often you will have to increase or reduce ball speed to properly play the lane conditions you find.

A ball is supposed to skid, roll and then hook as it heads toward the pins. Too much speed increases the amount of skid and prevents the ball from getting the correct number of revolutions before it hits the pocket. (More on ball revolutions in a later section on LIFT ADJUSTMENTS.) The result is an ineffective ball, one that does not work for you by getting the pins to mix with the other pins for proper carry. Pins fly almost upright back into the pit and do not take out as many pins as they would if they were heading for the pit in a horizontal manner. Also, excessive speed drives the ball too deeply into the pocket and does not allow the ball to follow the ideal path of deflection through the pins.

Too little speed is equally ineffective, but of course in the opposite manner. A slow ball is too easily deflected out of the ideal path of deflection through the 1-3-5-9 pins. Pins do not velocitate sufficiently to give you good pin carry. It is difficult to take full advantage of the kickbacks when ball speed is insufficient.

Once you have established your normal and natural ball speed, you must develop the ability to increase or reduce ball speed to meet lane conditions. Since your ball speed will approximate 2.2 seconds, you should be able to roll the ball plus or minus 10% of this figure, or from 2.0 to 2.4 seconds. (Speeds far outside of these ranges are *not* common among high average bowlers.) Three very common methods are used for altering ball speed.

The first method for changing ball speed is to *change the height* at which you hold the ball in your stance. Holding the ball slightly higher will create a higher back swing and automatically raise ball speed. Holding the ball lower in the stance has the opposite effect, reducing the speed of the ball.

The second way to alter ball speed is to *apply slight pressure* in the pendulum swing to increase the height of the back swing. Or you could apply the pressure from the top of the back swing through the point at which the ball is released on the lane. Both methods will increase ball speed. The pressure should be from the elbow down, not from the shoulder, and should be gradual, not forced. Applying less pressure has the opposite effect, lessening ball speed. This ball speed adjustment is slightly more difficult to make than the one for increasing pressure. The ball should be applying all of the pressure during the swing, and therefore you should not be able to reduce this pressure, except by holding back slightly on the pull of the ball through the swing.

The third method for changing ball speed is to *alter the tempo or length of your steps.* A faster pace or longer steps will increase body speed to the foul line, thereby resulting in faster ball speed. A slower tempo or shorter steps will have the opposite effect, slowing down the speed of the ball.

A word of caution is in order at this time. Whenever you attempt to change a part of your delivery there is a chance you will affect your timing and rhythm. It is imperative that you keep your natural and proper timing when you attempt to change ball speed.

It is difficult to change your natural ball speed and to keep your timing. This ability will require long hours of practice to perfect. However, this skill can be very advantageous. In many instances speed control is the key element in making strikes. Other adjustments will just not do the trick.

Under what circumstances would you want to consider altering ball speed? If the lane is hooking too strongly, and you are hitting the pocket too fully, you may elect an increase in ball speed to overcome the situation. Increased ball speed is a delivery adjustment designed to bring the ball back to the pocket. If the ball is beginning its break too soon, or is breaking too strongly, then increased ball speed is an adjustment to correct either situation. Any one of the three methods of altering ball speed could be used to achieve the objective.

If the lane is not hooking as much as you would

like, and you wish to alter your ball speed to increase the amount of the hook, or to get the ball to start hooking sooner, reduced ball speed can achieve these corrections.

It would be helpful to have someone time your ball speed during league or practice sessions. Try to slow the ball down, or increase ball speed, by using any or all of the speed adjustment techniques mentioned above.

You should be able to vary ball speed to fit within the 2.0 to 2.4 second range. A speed slightly higher than 2.4 seconds could still be correct for you. Your normal speed might be 2.4 seconds, and your range could be from 2.2 to 2.6 seconds. A .2 of a second increase or decrease in ball speed is probably the most realistic speed adjustment to incorporate into an effective delivery.

Keep in mind that whether you roll the ball fast or slow is neither good nor bad, as long as it is near the general speed range given above. But the ability to change the speed of the ball as an adjustment technique for certain lane conditions is an ability you should develop if you wish to improve your percentage of strikes. It would be essential for you to develop such a skill should you decide you would like to become a high average bowler.

Develop a ball speed appropriate for your strength, your body build, your height and the particular style you have developed as natural for you. If your ball is always rolled the same way, with the same speed, you are in a very good position to control its path to the pins and to read lanes properly. Once you know what your ball will do on the lanes, and how to change the speed to suit changing lane conditions, you should be far more accurate on both your strike and spare deliveries. And you will have added a valuable adjustment method to your game.

LOFT ADJUSTMENTS
(Right Handed Bowlers)

"Proper lift and proper loft go hand-in-hand," Tom Baker, Member, Professional Bowlers Association.

There is a direct relationship between the timing of the release and the amount of loft you get on the ball. If you release the ball slightly sooner than you normally release it, you will place the ball on the lane much closer to the foul line than you usually do. If you release the ball slightly later than you normally do, you will loft the ball further out over the foul line than is true in your normal delivery. To properly play some lane conditions you may want to alter or change the amount of loft on the ball. This affects the timing of your release and the distance the ball travels out over the foul line before it contacts the lane surface.

A normal release of the ball is either just at the bottom of the pendulum swing, or just as the ball would be on the upturn if the swing were to be completed and the ball not released at all. It is at this moment of the release that you can get maximum lift (turn, action etc.) on the ball. But, there will be times when you want to give the ball more or less opportunity to grip the lane, hence altering the action on the ball. Adjusting the amount of loft can help you do this (as will other techniques which will be discussed under LIFT ADJUSTMENTS).

When the lane is hooking more than normal, and you wish to make a slight change in your delivery to correctly play the lane (instead of making an angle, equipment, or other delivery change), you might loft the ball slightly further out on the lane, perhaps to a distance of 36 to 48 inches, or more. Such an additional amount of loft will cause the ball to skid further, and will take the ball further down the lane before it makes its break toward the pocket. This type of delivery adjustment is designed to bring the ball back to the pocket after it has passed by, or hit high in the pocket.

When the lane is not hooking very much, or less than you consider normal for your delivery, you might reduce the amount of loft by placing the ball on the lane much closer to the foul line. (Remember, you cannot foul with the ball!) For a moderately conditioned lane you might loft the ball about 18 to 36 inches beyond the foul line. This amount of loft will give the ball more time to grab the lane and hook into the pocket. It is the type of delivery adjustment that will get the ball up to the pocket after it has failed to do so.

Loft adjustments can be combined with speed adjustments. Increased speed and increased loft are both delivery adjustments designed to get the ball to come back to the pocket. Reduced speed and reduced loft go hand in hand to get the ball to grip the lane and come up to the pocket. Therefore, you may have to combine these two adjustments for given lane conditions.

You should never loft the ball too far out on the lane, since this will alter or destroy the effectiveness of your ball. (Plus, it will not help the lane surface!) Also, you should not try to make any other changes in your delivery when you are making loft adjustments. Such changes will have an effect on the path of the ball to the pins.

When you are practicing loft adjustments, pretend there are three foul lines: the real one, and two others located 24 and 48 inches beyond the foul line. Then practice lofting the ball, in *a gradual arc,* out over the foul line to various distances.

If the center manager will permit you to do so, tape a towel on the lane at the foul line, and practice lofting the ball over the towel. Such practice will be beneficial to you when you decide a loft adjustment is the best way to make an adjustment to lane conditions.

In summary, more loft is used as an adjustment to get the ball back to the pocket after high pocket or crossover hits. Less loft is used to get the ball up to the pocket when it fails to do so. You may also use more speed with more loft, or less speed with less loft. These are complementary sets of adjustments, both working together to achieve the same objective.

LIFT ADJUSTMENTS
(Right Handed Bowlers)

"The location of the fingers at the moment of release determines the lift imparted on the ball."

Lift is an upward pressure applied by the fingers at the moment the ball is released. This release point should occur a split second after the thumb has cleared the ball. If the thumb is released too soon, the fingers will not have time to impart lift to the ball. If the thumb is released too late, the lift of the fingers will be minimized by the *drag* of the thumb in the ball. Therefore, to get the proper lift on the ball the release must be timed very precisely.

Although the fingers apply lift, other factors associated with the delivery also have an influence on the amount of lift the fingers can impart. If the ball is released in the downswing, the pressure of the ball will also act as force to increase the amount of lift. Raising up with the sliding foot at the moment the ball is released will pull the hand up and increase the amount of lift. A strong or weak follow through will determine how much lift is put on the ball. And a bending of the elbow will, of course, bring the hand up sharply, creating more lift. All of these factors, and the timing of the release of the thumb, determine the amount of lift.

More lift is needed when you want to get the ball up to the pocket after it has failed to do so. Less lift is an adjustment to bring the ball back to the pocket after a high pocket hit or a crossover to the brooklyn side. Since finger position is the most important factor influencing lift, let's review changes in finger location as they relate to lift.

Strong lift is created, or can be created, when the fingers are *under* the ball at the time it is released onto the lane. Very little lift can be imparted if the fingers are on the upper side of the ball. In between these two extremes are various locations for altering the amount of lift on the ball.

During your practice sessions you should alter the location of the thumb and fingers to see how lift is affected. Try to vary the amount of lift and turn on the ball. Try to alter the number of revolutions, either increasing or reducing the number of times the ball rotates around its ball track.

How many revolutions are needed to create an effective and working ball? The answer depends upon two factors: the type of ball track you are using and the condition of the lane. If a lane is non-hooking, you may only be able to get 5 to 7 revolutions. On a hooking lane, you may be able to increase this to more than 13 revolutions.

On a hooking lane you want the ball to skid further down the lane before it breaks for the pocket. A revolving ball will skid more than one making less revolutions. But, on non-hooking lanes you want to reduce the skid and get the ball rolling much sooner. Fewer revolutions are the result of non-hooking lanes. More revolutions are possible and desirable when the lanes are hooking.

The number of revolutions on the ball influences the action on it at the moment it hits the pocket. Ideally, the ball should still be gaining momentum in its revolutions (revs) when it hits the pocket. This gives the ball drive to keep it in the path of deflection and imparts a mixing action or velocity to the pins. The ideal number of revolutions should be in the 11 to 13 range, but on non-hooking lanes you may only be able to get 5 to 7 revolutions on the ball.

The ball track influences the number of revolutions. The smaller the ball track, the more revolutions you can get. The larger the ball track, the less revolutions you can get. For example, a full roller covers the entire 27 inch circumference around the ball, so you get fewer revolutions than with a high and low spinner, which have smaller ball tracks.

Rotating the fingers at the moment of release will determine what type of ball track is created. The amount and direction of the rotation will decide what kind of track the ball will have. The full roller is created by rotating the fingers in a clockwise manner, but all others are created by a counter clockwise rotation upon release.

Referring to our imaginary clock located at the foul line, here is the way ball tracks are created:

Full Roller—Rotate the fingers from 4 to 6 o'clock at release. This is a clockwise rotation.

EXHIBIT 5-2
(RHB) Rotating the Fingers to Alter Lift

Rotation of the fingers *at the moment the ball is released* will affect the lift imparted on the ball. Assuming a "normal" position for the fingers at 4 to 5 o'clock, rotating them in a counter clockwise manner will delay the break point and increase the sharpness of the break. Three methods of rotation are illustrated here, from 6 to 4 o'clock; from 7 to 4 o'clock; and from 8 to 4 o'clock. The more rotation, the later and sharper the break.

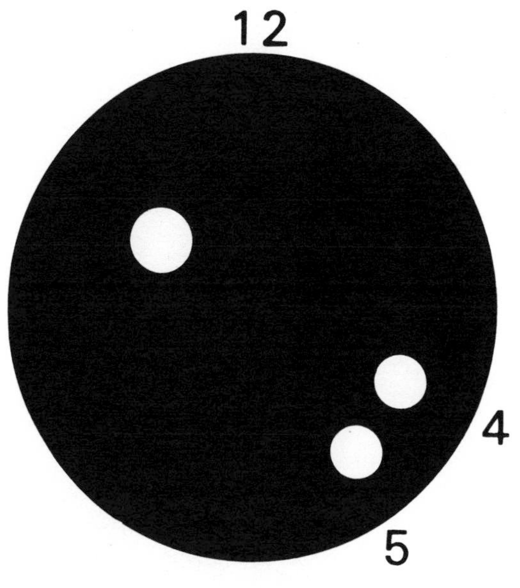

"NORMAL" 4-5 O'CLOCK POSITION

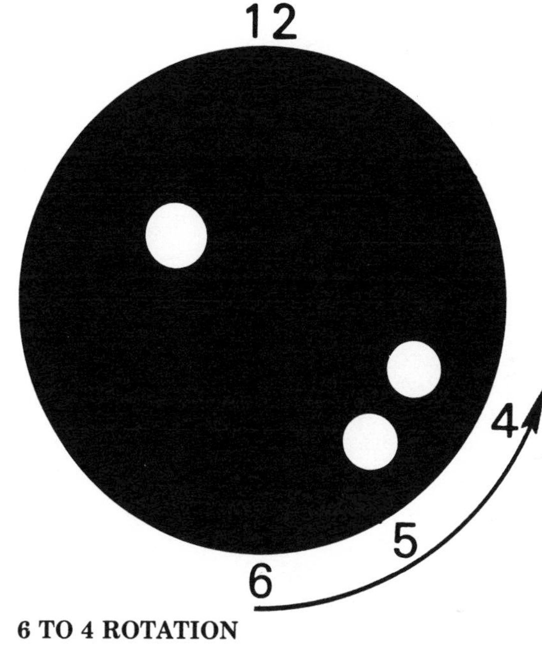

6 TO 4 ROTATION

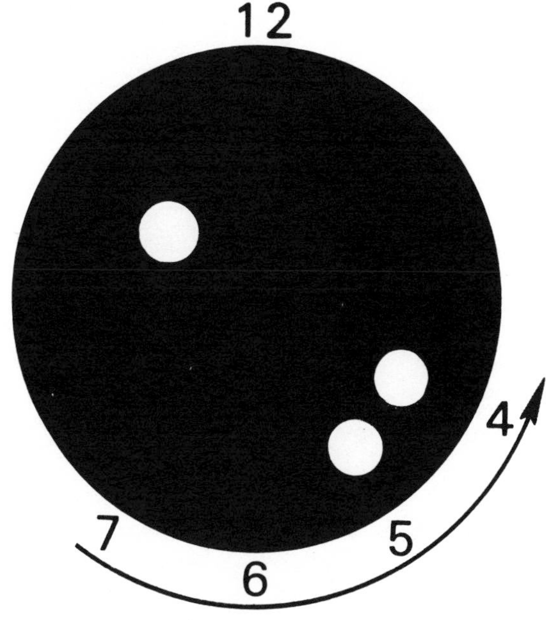

7 TO 4 ROTATION

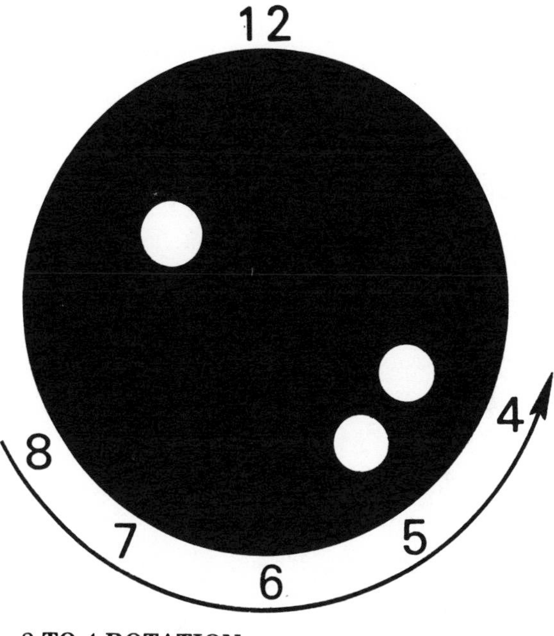

8 TO 4 ROTATION

High Roller—Rotate the fingers to a 4 or 5 o'clock position, and then lift straight up to create this ball track. This is a counter clockwise rotation.

Low Roller—Rotate the fingers from 6 to 4 o'clock, but not beyond. This is a counter clockwise rotation, as in the high roller.

High Spinner—Rotate the fingers from 6 to 3 o'clock, counter clockwise. Here you are rotating around the ball, turning as well as lifting.

Low Spinner—Rotate the fingers from 6 to 2 or 1 o'clock to create this ball track. Here you are almost topping the ball, almost overturning it. This is generally an ineffective ball track.

The rotation of the fingers can start at 7 or 8 o'clock, instead of the 6 o'clock position indicated above. *Where you stop the rotation dictates what type of ball track is created.* Also, as you increase the amount of rotation beyond 4 o'clock, you lower the ball track, going from a high roller to a low spinner.

The two extremes, full roller and low spinner, are the least effective ball tracks. High roller, low roller and high spinner are the three types of ball tracks most frequently used by high average bowlers.

Other delivery adjustments, affecting the amount of lift imparted on the ball, relate to the timing and intensity of the hook. At times you will want to *advance the break point,* and at other times you will want to *delay the point at which the ball breaks for the pocket.* You may also want to cause the ball to *break stronger* into the pocket, or with *less strength.*

To delay the break point and to reduce the strength of the hook, either an angle or a speed change could be used. Moving to the inside strike lines will delay the break point until the ball is further down the lane. Also, the ball will be at a much straighter pocket angle, and will hit the pocket with less strength than a ball with the same amount of lift but coming from the outside strike lines. Similarly, increasing ball speed will delay the break point and will generally reduce the strength of the hook after the ball does break.

To delay the break point by making a release change, simply rotate the fingers at the moment the ball is released. This rotation should be in a counter clockwise manner, as shown on Exhibit 5-2. Within the range indicated on this exhibit, increased rotation delays the break point and increases the strength of the hook. Such delivery adjustments will bring the ball back to the pocket after high or crossover hits, which frequently occur on hooking lanes.

Advancing the break point is simply a reversal of the above adjustments. Slower ball speed and the use of the outside strike lines will advance the point at which the ball breaks for the pocket. Reducing the amount of rotation of the fingers at the moment of release will also advance the break point. Such adjustments bring the ball up to the pocket after it has failed to do so, a frequent occurrence on a non-hooking lane.

At this point it should be obvious that delivery changes are difficult to make and require a great deal of practice to successfully incorporate into your adjustment arsenal. Each time you make a delivery change, you must be careful you do not create problems with your timing, rhythm or tempo. As a rule, make delivery changes only after you have tried angle and equipment changes first and have not been able to make a successful adjustment.

Wrist Positions: The position of the wrist is yet another factor to determine how much lift is put on the ball. *Minor* changes from a straight wrist can be an effective way to increase or reduce lift.

The most highly recommended and fundamentally sound position for the wrist is in a relatively *straight* line. (See Exhibit 5-3, for illustrations of *straight, broken,* and *cocked* wrist positions.) The straight wrist position is least prone to error, allows you to get the most natural feel and consistent lift on the ball, and creates less chance for developing an improper swing. This position is also the easiest of the three types to maintain in a natural manner. Also, many types of wrist aids are available to assist in maintaining the straight position.

If you wish to develop a little more roll on the ball, a little less skid, then the wrist can be *broken* ever so *slightly.* (See Exhibit 5-3.) This wrist position will place a small amount of weight on the thumb and the balance on the fingers, something that will give you a little less feel with the fingers. Because the fingers are now higher on the ball, and less underneath it (as with the straight wrist) there is less chance to impart as much lift. But, keep in mind that *the wrist should not be broken too strongly,* or too much. *A slight amount will suffice.* Too much of a break in the wrist can put too much pressure on the thumb, and could result in an early release.

A third method of altering the wrist position, one that is not normally used, is the *cocked* wrist. (This position is also illustrated on Exhibit 5-3). Our purpose for discussing this wrist position is to make you aware of the full range of wrist positions, and the implications of each type. You may be *breaking* your wrist, or *cocking* it too much, and creating problems for yourself. Only a person with a strong wrist and arm would be able to use the cocked wrist position effectively, and then only after a lot of practice. (Of course, practice is needed to make any of the delivery changes a natural and effective part of your

EXHIBIT 5-3

(RHB) Three Wrist Positions That Affect Lift

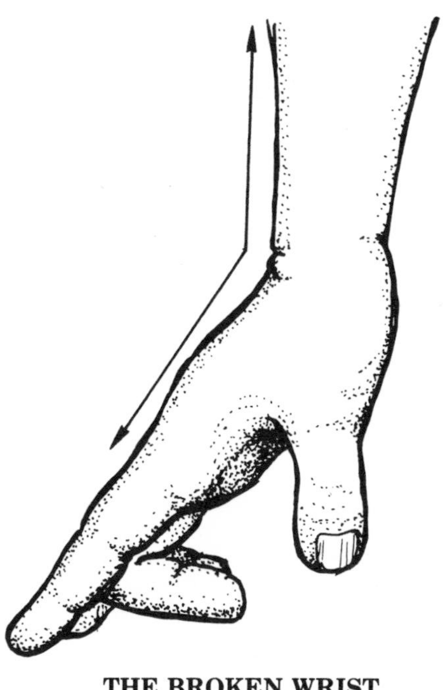

THE BROKEN WRIST

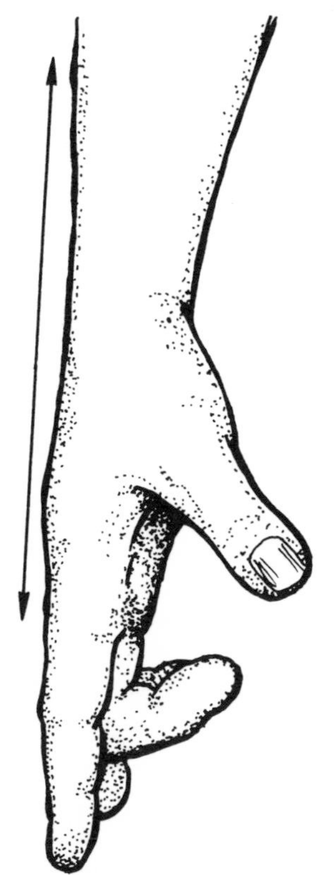

THE STRAIGHT WRIST

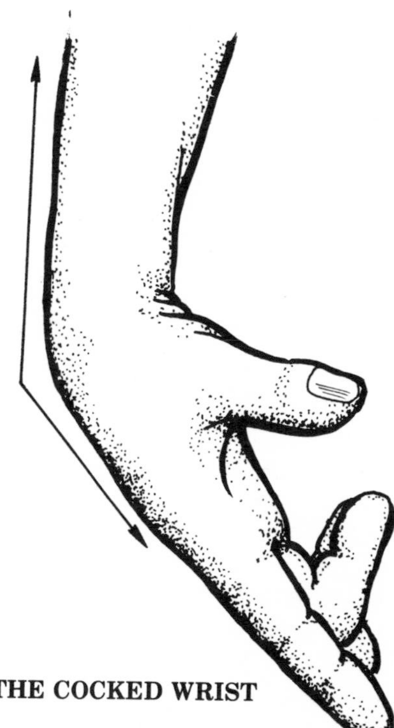

THE COCKED WRIST

game.)

If you are bowling on a hooking lane, and you wish to delay the break point until further down the lane, you might use the cocked wrist position. The ball will skid more than in the straight wrist position, because you can get your hand firmly under the ball.

As with all delivery adjustments, broken and cocked wrist positions should *only* be incorporated into your adjustment arsenal after you have fully explored the advantages and disadvantages of each one. You should, however, become aware of the impact of the position of your wrist on the action or lack of action that can be put on the ball at the release point. You may not decide to use any position other than the straight wrist, but you should be aware of a possible fault in your delivery so that you can correct it.

SECTION 6
ANGLE ADJUSTMENTS
(Left Handed Bowlers)

"There is one strike angle that will let you play the lane well. Find it; use it; and you will score well," Ellenburg.

CONTENTS PAGE

OVERVIEW

The most common adjustments made by all bowlers are line or angle adjustments. Such adjustments call for a movement to the left or the right on the approach. However, as you will see shortly, the proper way to play any angle requires more than a simple movement on the approach. Some changes occur naturally as you move from one strike angle to another. Other changes must be made deliberately.

This section presents a complete description of the proper methods for playing all strike lines and angles. We begin with a definition of the terms *line* and *angle*. Then we discuss the methods of finding *the correct angle* to play any lane at a given point in time. Our material includes *a personal formula* that will allow you to play any angle, and to *calculate the new stance location* when you change angles.

This section concludes with illustrations of the five strike lines and guidelines for properly playing any angle within any line.

The terms *line* and *angle* are frequently used interchangeably. They are, however, different but related types of angle adjustments. Since there may be some confusion as to the meaning of these two terms, we will begin by defining each term as it is used in this book.

DEFINITION OF LINE: There are five commonly accepted strike lines that a bowler might use at one time or another, largely depending upon lane conditions and the type of equipment (ball) being used. These five strike lines are called: the deep inside line; the inside line; the second arrow line; the outside line; and the deep outside line. All of these strike lines are illustrated on Exhibit 6-1.

Each strike line describes a general path from the foul line to the pins through a specific set of boards at the foul line and the arrows. For example, the deep inside strike line is one that starts from the center of the lane (approximately boards 20-27 at the foul line) and travels through boards 18-22 at the arrows. Exhibit 6-1 shows the path going through the fourth arrow, which is the 20th board at the arrows.

Similarly, each strike line is described by an area of the foul line (in specific boards) and an area of the lane at the arrows (also stated in specific boards).

There is general agreement upon the existence of these five strike lines. However, disagreements exist as to the *specific names* given to each line and to the *exact board numbers* at the foul line and arrows contained in each line. These two areas of disagreement do not in any way restrict the usefulness of the material in this section. The disagreement is usually within a single board one way or the other. And, whether the 12th board (for example) is considered to be in the second arrow line or the inside line makes no difference in playing any angle over that board.

DEFINITION OF ANGLE: Within each strike line there are a *set of foul line angles* that make up the entire strike line. For example, foul line angle 12-to-10 refers to the 12th board at the foul line and the 10th board at the arrows. The 11-to-10 foul line angle refers to the 11th board at the foul line and the 10th board at the arrows. However, both of these angles are within the second arrow strike line. (Foul Line Angle is explained in SECTION 2, FROM FOUL LINE TO ARROWS.) Therefore, *any angle is defined as the path a ball takes from the foul line to*

EXHIBIT 6-1
The Five Strike Lines for Left Handed Bowlers

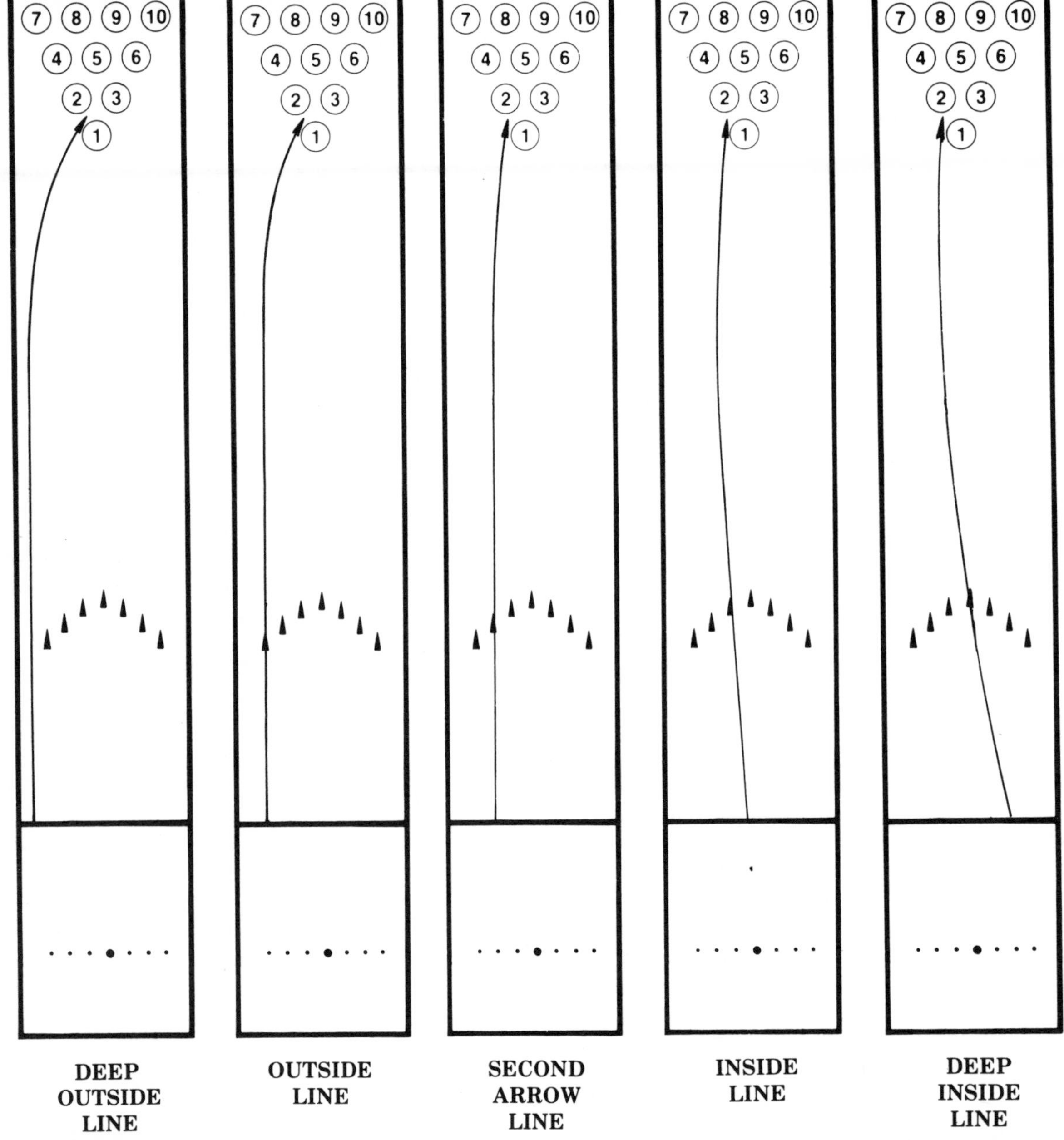

DEEP OUTSIDE LINE	Approximately Boards 1–3 at the Arrows
OUTSIDE LINE (1ST ARROW)	Approximately Boards 4–7 at the Arrows
2ND ARROW LINE	Approximately Boards 8–12 at the Arrows
INSIDE LINE (3RD ARROW)	Approximately Boards 13–17 at the Arrows
DEEP INSIDE LINE	*Approximately Boards 18–22 at the Arrows

*Boards are numbered from the left side of the lane. Although there may be differences of opinion as to the exact boards contained in any given line, there is general agreement upon these five strike lines.

the arrows, and is described by giving the board number at both locations. Notice that the *first number* in the foul line angle refers to the board at the *foul line,* and the *second number* refers to the board at the *arrows.* Since every ball has to pass over some specific board at the foul line (even if it does not hit the lane until it is 18 or more inches beyond the foul line) and it must also pass over a specific board at the arrows, the path taken by any ball can be described by two numbers that define the angle the ball takes down the lanes. Any foul line angle can be classified within one of the five strike lines previously described.

Now I think you can see why the two terms (line and angle) are used as though they were the same thing. On closer examination it becomes clear that the term *ANGLE is more specific,* whereas the term *LINE is more general.* When you make an *angle* change you are normally making a *small* adjustment. When you make a *line* change you are normally making a *larger* adjustment, moving from one strike line to another. In both cases you are changing your approach position. However, in the line change you are generally also making a change in your target boards at the arrows. In an angle change you are normally keeping the same target board at the arrows but changing the board you cross over at the foul line. (However, you could change from a 10-to-10 foul line angle to the 11-to-11 angle and still be within the same second arrow strike line, yet you have changed both your target board and the board your ball crosses at the foul line!)

FINDING THE ANGLE TO THE POCKET: Your objective, each time you bowl on a given lane, is to find the correct strike line and angle that will get the ball into the 1-2 pocket. And, you want to find that angle as quickly as possible, with a minimum of mistakes (splits, low counts, or very difficult spares).

Before you ever roll your first ball, you can gather a great deal of information about the lane. You may even be able to determine what strike line is most likely to be the correct one to use on this lane *at this point in time.* Many clues are available to help you *pre-read the lanes.*

What strike line and angle are some of the *high average bowlers using,* especially those who bowl with a style similar to yours, and who use equipment similar to yours? Are they using the deep inside line, the deep outside line, etc.? Are they scoring well with the line they are using? If so, then you may be able to use the same line or angle. If they are not scoring well, this might tell you not to use the line they are using. Any indication, before you bowl your first ball, that a line *may* or *may not* be the best one to use is a valuable piece of information.

Next, consider the *time of day* and the *amount of play* the lane has received prior to your session. If you are in a league that begins, for example, at 6:30 in the evening, and the lanes have just been conditioned for play, you can assume the *oil pattern* is unaltered by play. That is, the track has not been developed by play, the lanes have not been *broken down,* the oil has not been spread around by others, etc. Since you will get a few practice rolls, you will be able to determine for yourself what the lanes are doing. You can begin with the normal strike line and angle you use, and adjust from there. (Later on we will give you a personal formula for finding the correct line and angle into the pocket.)

But, if you are bowling in a later league, and a previous league has just completed their session, you know the lane track may have broken down. The pattern of conditioning has also been changed, and there may be wet or dry (spotty) conditions on the lane. You have to take previous lane play into consideration in determining the best line and angle to use.

If you are bowling in a tournament, watching other high average bowlers who have a style similar to yours is a good way to get a pre-reading of the lanes. What you are trying to do is find the best way to play the lane without wasting precious frames of your games. Some centers have a reputation as an *inside house,* a *track house,* an *outside house,* etc. Knowing this tendency for centers to favor or disfavor one strike line or another may also give you clues as to how you can determine the proper strike line and angle *before you begin* your game.

Often, if a tournament lasts for several days or a few weeks, the lanes *may* be conditioned differently at different times during the tournament. Keep this in mind when it is your time to bowl. In the early part of the tournament, scoring conditions *may* be difficult. This occurs, infrequently, when the tournament director does not wish to have large scores posted early in the tournament. (This might cause other bowlers to stay out of the tournament when they see scores already posted that they feel they cannot match.) Such a deliberate pattern of difficult scoring conditions during the early part of a tournament is seldom found, since most directors try to keep the same scoring conditions throughout the entire tournament. But, you should be aware of both situations, since each may occur. So no matter what conditions exist, watch what strike line and angle others are using successfully. This may help you align yourself quickly.

Ask other bowlers about the type of condition that exists. This is another way to determine the condition of the lanes and what line or angle might be best for you. As with all of the previous methods for pre-reading the lanes, this one is not guaranteed. But, each clue you get can be assessed when you get on the lanes. At least you will not be starting from zero information.

At this point you should be ready to step on the approach with an idea of the best strike line to play, although the actual angle within that strike line may be less certain. You will have to find the correct angle and approach position that is best for you at this time. To assist you in this search, one you must face each time you bowl, we have developed a *personal formula* that can help you find the correct angle and line into the pocket.

A PERSONAL FORMULA FOR PLAYING ANY ANGLE: It is possible to develop a personal mathematical formula for playing any angle. This formula will help you determine the exact stance location on the approach for every foul line angle. You may recall that *a foul line angle is the path taken by the ball from the foul line to the arrows.* Each foul line angle is described by two numbers, such as a 12-to-10 foul line angle. The *first number* always identifies the board at the *foul line* and the *second number* describes the number of the board at the *arrows.* A 10-to-10 foul line angle describes a ball that travels straight down the 10th board from the foul line to the arrows.

To properly play any foul line angle, it is necessary to determine the precise board on the approach where you take your stance. It is also necessary that you *align yourself* properly, *facing your target* on the lanes, and have the ball *swing along the intended angle.* The personal formula which we will present at this time will give you the exact board on the approach for your stance location. In every case we will assume that you align yourself properly once you have calculated the location for your stance.

This formula, which we call your *personal formula,* takes into account your walk pattern (drift) and the distance (in number of boards) by which you miss your ankle with the center of the ball when you deliver the ball. SECTION 2, THE APPROACH, explained how to determine both of these numbers for yourself. Since these two numbers are directly related to your personal game, the formula is tailored for you. Hence the title *personal* formula.

Your personal formula can be combined with other adjustment formulas to assist you in playing the various strike lines and all angles within these lines. However, before we discuss methods of adjusting from one foul line angle to another, we will explain *the formula for determining the exact stance location for any given foul line angle.*

It is necessary to use four numbers to determine the board to which you align yourself for your stance location. Later, we will reduce the requirement to only 3 numbers as we combine drift and the number of boards by which the center of the ball misses your ankle, into one personal number.

Two of the four numbers describe the foul line angle, giving the number of the board at the foul line and the number of the board at the arrows, or targeting zone. The third number relates to your drift pattern, and the fourth number describes the distance (in boards) by which the center of the ball misses your ankle when you deliver the ball onto the lane.

For purposes of illustrating the formula, we will select a specific foul line angle and show the method for determining the number of the board you use to take your stance. Keep in mind that after you have that board number, you must align yourself properly, face your target on the lane, and swing the ball through the intended foul line angle (path of the ball from the foul line to the arrows). Once we work our way through a specific angle, we will expand the discussion so that you can calculate the stance location for any foul line angle.

For illustrating the concept, we will select foul line angle 10-to-10, or the 10th board at the foul line (first number) and the 10th board at the arrows (second number). This is a straight line angle, and is perhaps the easiest to use to explain the concept of a personal formula.

The four numbers needed to determine the stance location for the 10-to-10 angle are as follows:

> #1 Select a *board at the arrows* that you wish to use as your target. (For our example, we have chosen board *10 at the arrows.)*
> #2 Select *the angle* you wish to play over that board. (For our example, we have chosen board *10* at *the foul line.)*
> #3 Consider your normal *drift* pattern. (Assume that you normally drift *1* board to the left when you deliver the ball.)
> #4 Consider the number of boards by which you *miss your ankle* with the *center of the ball* when you deliver it. (Assume that the center of the ball normally misses your ankle by 7 boards. Most bowlers will miss the ankle with the center of the ball by 6, 7 or 8 boards.)

The four numbers stated above can be used to determine exactly where you stand on the approach to play the 10-to-10 foul line angle. Later, we will show you how to combine #3 and #4 into a single personal number, and how to decide *if* this foul line angle is the correct one to use for getting the ball into the pocket. *For now, we are only trying to determine where you should stand on the approach to play this particular foul line angle.*

To recap, these are the four numbers needed to locate the proper stance location:

- #1 The 10th board at the arrows (your target board),
- #2 The 10th board at the foul line (the angle over that board),
- #3 The 1 board drift to the left (we assumed for you),
- #4 The 7 boards by which the center of the ball missed your ankle (we assumed for you).

If you wish to roll the ball down the 10th board at the foul line, and the center of the ball misses your ankle by 7 boards when you release the ball, then you have to slide at the 17th board at the foul line. If you slide at the 17th board, and miss your ankle by 7 boards, the ball will roll down the 10th board. BUT, we assumed that you drifted 1 board to the left in your approach. Therefore, to end up at the 17th board at the foul line for your slide, you have to start 1 board further *to the right* to compensate for this 1 board drift *to the left.*

Now to the formula. To determine the stance location on the approach for playing our selected 10-to-10 angle, follow this procedure. Subtract the number of the board at the arrows from the number of the board at the foul line. In this case; 10 minus 10, for a difference of zero. Add the difference (zero) to the number of the board at the foul line, (10 plus zero = 10). To this you must add the number of boards by which you miss your ankle, (10 plus 7 = 17). Finally, add to this number the number of boards you drift to the left, (17 plus 1 = 18). This gives you the number of the board on the approach with which you should align yourself for your stance location, board number 18.

Take your stance on board number 18; align yourself so you face your target on the lane and the ball will swing along your intended line; walk toward the foul line in your normal manner; you should drift to the left by 1 board and slide on the 17th board; miss your ankle by the 7 boards we assumed for our example; and roll the ball down the selected 10th board at the foul line. It should head straight down the 10th board, and roll over the 10th board at the arrows. You have now played the 10-to-10 foul line angle.

If you had *drifted to the right,* you would have to *subtract* one board from your starting position to end up at the foul line on the correct board. To compensate for drift, you always move in the opposite direction on the approach. This suggests that there must be some way to incorporate drift patterns and the number of boards by which the center of the ball misses your ankle, into a single number to simplify the formula. This is true, and the method for doing this is shown on Exhibit 6-2.

Exhibit 6-2 provides three charts which give you a way to determine your *personal number.* Each chart combines both a drift pattern and a specific number of boards by which the center of the ball misses your ankle. The result is a single number, your personal number, reflecting these two critical elements of your delivery. With this number you can make a very quick calculation to locate the exact board for your stance location for any angle you wish to use.

Locate your personal number by consulting one of the three charts on Exhibit 6-2. You may have to review the material in SECTION 2, THE APPROACH, to determine your drift pattern and the number of boards by which the center of the ball misses your ankle when you release it. But, once you have these two numbers, locate your personal number and mark it in the place indicated on the exhibit.

For purposes of illustration only, we will assume that you drift one board to the left and you miss your ankle by 7 boards as in our previous illustration. Chart #2 gives your personal number as 8. Now we can return to our previous example and use the personal number of 8 instead of concerning ourselves with drift and the number of boards by which you miss your ankle with the center of the ball. Both of these two items are taken into account with your personal number.

To play the same 10-to-10 foul line angle, subtract one number from the other (10 minus 10 = zero) and *add* the difference to the number of the board at the foul line (10 plus zero = 10). Then add your personal number (8) to get the number of the board to which you align yourself for your stance. (10 plus 8 = 18). Notice we still get board number 18 as the location for the stance for playing the 10-to-10 angle. This proves that the personal number is the same as taking into consideration both drift and the number of boards by which you missed your ankle with the center of the ball.

Any time you are playing a straight angle, when the board at the foul line and the board at the arrows are the same (12-to-12, 9-to-9, 8-to-8, etc.), your stance location is calculated by adding your personal number to the number of the board at the foul line. (Since both numbers are the same, it does not matter which one you add to your personal number; you will get the same result. But, for later calculations you will find it easier to *always add to the number of the board at the foul line.* This pattern will work for any

EXHIBIT 6-2
(LHB) Determining Your Personal Number

Your personal number is determined by two factors: the number of boards you *drift*, and the number of boards by which you *miss your ankle with the center of the ball when you release it*. The following charts allow you to determine your personal number by referring to the chart which corresponds with the second factor indicated above. For most bowlers this will be 6, 7 or 8 boards. Also, although zero drift is ideal, you can incorporate a drift of from 1 to 5 boards into an effective delivery. SECTION 2, THE APPROACH, illustrates how to calculate these two numbers for yourself. After calculating them, use the two numbers to find your personal number in one of these three charts. Then place it in the box that follows.

YOUR PERSONAL NUMBER IS: ☐

If you miss your ankle with the center of the ball by 6 boards, then use this CHART #1

Personal Number is	If your drift is:	Personal number is:
6	0	6
7 LEFT	1	RIGHT 5
8 LEFT	2	RIGHT 4
9 LEFT	3	RIGHT 3
10 LEFT	4	RIGHT 2
11 LEFT	5	RIGHT 1

If you miss your ankle with the center of the ball by 7 boards, then use this CHART #2.

Personal number is	If your drift is:	Personal number is:
7	0	7
8 LEFT	1	RIGHT 6
9 LEFT	2	RIGHT 5
10 LEFT	3	RIGHT 4
11 LEFT	4	RIGHT 3
12 LEFT	5	RIGHT 2

If you miss your ankle with the center of the ball by 8 boards, then use this CHART #3

Personal number is:	If your drift is:	Personal number is:
8	0	8
9 LEFT	1	RIGHT 7
10 LEFT	2	RIGHT 6
11 LEFT	3	RIGHT 5
12 LEFT	4	RIGHT 4
13 LEFT	5	RIGHT 3

EXAMPLES: If you miss your ankle by 7 boards, and drift 3 boards to the left, your personal number is 10.

If you miss your ankle by 6 boards, and drift 2 boards to the right, your personal number is 4.

If you miss your ankle by 8 boards, and drift 0 boards, then your personal number is 8.

If you drift more than 5 boards, either to the left or the right, you should make an effort to eliminate the drift, or reduce it to 3 boards or less. The less you drift, the more accurate you can be.

angle.)

What happens when the number of the board at the foul line is not the same as the number of the board at the arrows? This occurs when you play anything but a straight angle. It happens when you roll the ball across the boards on an angle to the left (called opening the angle) or when you roll the ball directly toward the pocket (called closing the angle). The formula can be used, with only *one minor modification.* But, you must know the relationship that exists for various strike angles, in reference to boards at the foul line and boards toward the back end of the approach where you take your stance.

Exhibit 6-3 illustrates the relationship that exists between boards at the foul line and boards on the approach, using the 10th board at the arrows as the target board. *A chart similar to this could be prepared for each target board at the arrows, and the relationship would remain the same.*

Notice that *for each 1 board angle change at the foul line, there is a 2 board change on the back of the approach.* The 11-to-10 foul line angle leads directly to the 12th board on the back end of the approach. The 12-to-10 foul line angle leads toward the 14th board. The 13-to-10 angle points toward the 16th board on the back end of the approach. NOTE: *The difference between the number of the board at the foul line and the number of the board at the arrows, when added to the board at the foul line, gives the board on the end of the approach.* The 13-to-10 angle (a 3 board difference) leads to the 16th board on the end of the approach. The 12-to-10 angle (a 2 board difference) leads to the 14th board on the end of the approach, etc. This relationship always exists when the angle is open, when the board at the foul line is higher in number than the board at the arrows.

When the angle is *closed,* the board number at the foul line is *lower* than the number of the board at the arrows. The same 2 board relationship exists, but you have to *subtract the difference* between the two numbers to locate the number of the board on the back end of the approach. The 9-to-10 angle leads to board number 8 on the end of the approach. The 8-to-10 angle leads to board number 6. The 6-to-10 angle leads to board number 2, etc. For all angles such as these (that point toward the pocket) you must take the difference between the two numbers describing the foul line angle, and *subtract* this from the number of the board at the foul line. This will give you the initial stance location board, to which you must still add your personal number. This *subtraction,* rather than addition, *is the minor change in the formula* which allows you to precisely calculate the stance location for any foul line angle.

Now we will summarize the use of the personal number, for both closed and open angles, and pull together all of the material related to our formula for calculating the stance location for any angle you might have to play. Perhaps a few specific examples will clarify all aspects of the formula.

Example #1 The 10-to-10 angle (a *straight* angle). The difference between the two numbers is zero.
Assume your personal number is 8.
A) Add the difference to the foul line number (10 + 0 = 10)
B) Add your personal number (10 + 8 = 18)
C) Align yourself with board 18 to play the 10-to-10 angle.

Example #2 The 12-to-10 angle (an *open* angle). The difference between the two numbers is 2.
Assume your personal number is 8.
A) Add the difference to the foul line number (12 + 2 = 14)
B) Add your personal number (14 + 8 = 22)
C) Align yourself with board 22 to play the 12-to-10 angle.

Example #3 The 20-to-15 angle (an *open* angle). The difference between the two numbers is 5.
Assume your personal number is 6.
A) Add the difference to the foul line number (20 + 5 = 25)
B) Add your personal number (25 + 6 = 31)
C) Align yourself with board 31 to play the 20-to-15 angle.

Example #4 The 8-to-10 angle (a *closed* angle). The difference between the two numbers is 2.
Assume your personal number is 6.
A) *Subtract* the difference from the foul line number (8 minus 2 = 6). NOTE: For a closed angle, we subtract.
B) Add your personal number (6 + 6 = 12)
C) Align yourself with board number 12 to play the 8-to-10 angle.

Example #5 The 6-to-10 angle (a *closed* angle). The difference between the two numbers is 4.
Assume your personal number is 7.
A) *Subtract* the difference from the foul line number (6 minus 4 = 2)

EXHIBIT 6-3
(LHB) Calculating The Stance Location on the Approach

There is a direct relationship between the number of the boards at the foul line, arrows, and back end of the approach. *For a 1 board angle change at the foul line, there is a 2 board change on the back of the approach.* This is shown by the sample foul line angles off board number 10 at the arrow zone. A chart similar to this could be prepared for each board number at the arrows, and the 2 board relationship would still be true. This relationship, combined with your personal number, allows you to calculate the stance location for playing any foul line angle. For example, *if your personal number is 6,* you would play foul line angle 12-to-10 from the 20th board on the approach. The 12-to-10 angle shows board 14 on the approach, to which you add your personal number of 6 to get stance location of board 20.

CLOSING THE FOUL LINE ANGLE

Take the difference between the board at the arrows and the board at the foul line, and *subtract* this from the number of the board at the foul line. This gives the *initial* stance location, to which your personal number must be added.

OPENING THE FOUL LINE ANGLE

Take the difference between the board at the arrows and the board at the foul line, and *add* it to the number of the board at the foul line. This gives the *initial* stance location, to which your personal number must be *added.*

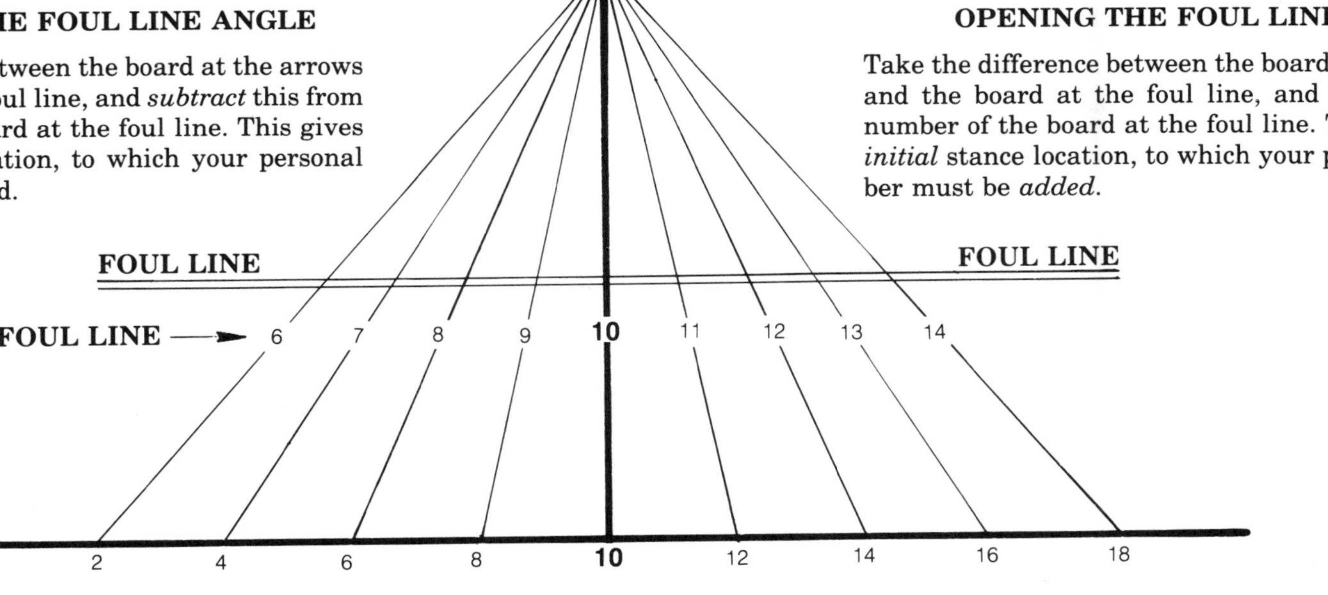

The *initial* stance location at the back of the approach, to which you must *add* your personal number. This gives you the board number on the approach which will allow you to play the appropriate foul line angle.

B) Add your personal number (2 plus 7 = 9)

C) Align yourself with board 9 to play the 6-to-10 angle.

These 5 examples cover the three types of angles you might have to play: straight, open, and closed. For *straight* angles, simply *add your personal number* to the foul line number to get the number of the board you use for your stance location. For open or closed angles, use this procedure: Calculate the difference between the number of the board at the foul line and the number of the board at the arrows. For *open* angles, *add this difference* to the foul line number and then *add your personal number.* For *closed* angles, *subtract this difference* from the foul line number, and then *add your personal number.*

To reinforce the formula into your thinking, the following table provides additional examples of foul line angles and the corresponding location to take your stance, assuming different personal numbers. *Keep in mind that the sole purpose of the calculation is to find your stance location on the approach.*

Foul Line Board		Arrows Board	Difference	Personal Number	Stance Location
17	-to-	15	+2 open	7	*17* plus 2 plus 7 equals 26.
16	-to-	14	+2 open	6	*16* plus 2 plus 6 equals 24.
12	-to-	8	+4 open	8	*12* plus 4 plus 8 equals 24.
10	-to-	10	straight	7	*10* plus 0 plus 7 equals 17.
8	-to-	8	straight	8	*8* plus 0 plus 8 equals 16.
8	-to-	9	−1 closed	7	*8* minus 1 plus 7 equals 14.
3	-to-	5	−2 closed	8	*3* minus 2 plus 8 equals 9.

As the preceding examples indicate, *the personal number is always added* in the formula. The *difference* between the two board numbers identifying the foul line angles is *added for open angles,* and *subtracted for closed angles.* If you keep these few rules in mind, and you properly determine your personal number, you can calculate the precise location for playing any angle.

SPECIAL NOTE TO BACKUP BOWLERS: If you roll a backup ball, and use the opposite side 1-3 pocket, you can still use the formula explained above. The only change you make in your calculations is to subtract your personal number at all times instead of adding it. You will, of course, be using boards and angles numbered from the right side of the lane. For example, to use the 10-to-10 angle into the 1-3 pocket (a straight angle), subtract your personal number (assume it is 7) from 10 and you end up on the 3rd board on the approach. Once you understand the principle of the formula, you should be able to adjust it to your backup delivery with little difficulty.

During our discussion of how to play the various strike angles, we assumed the angle was the correct one to get the ball into the pocket. But, suppose you did not hit the 1-2 pocket? Instead, you hit the head pin head-on and left a split. If you delivered the ball exactly as you had planned, then it is obvious this angle is not the one to use at this time.

Here is where you need another mathematical formula to help you find the correct angle to the pocket. Of course, you could simply *guess* how many boards to move your approach position, your target, and/or your angle. But that may take several frames of trial and error to find the correct angle, and you may run into splits or difficult spare leaves in the meantime. A mathematical formula can help you make angle adjustments and simplify the process of finding the correct angle to the pocket.

THE 3-1-2 MATHEMATICAL FORMULA: This is a mathematical formula that can help you make adjustments to find the correct angle or line into the pocket. The three numbers in the formula refer to three reference points.

a) The 3 refers to 3 boards at the *pin deck.*

b) The 1 refers to 1 board at the *foul line.*

c) The 2 refers to 2 boards at the *approach.*

The formula states: *For every 3 boards you wish to adjust the impact point of your ball at the pin deck, move your angle 1 board at the foul line, and move your approach position 2 boards.* The angle and approach moves will be in the *opposite direction* from the direction you want to adjust the contact point of the ball. In our example, to move the ball contact point back to the *left by* 3 boards (explained below) your angle move of 1 board and approach position move of 2 boards would be to the right, the opposite direction. If you wish to adjust to get the ball to hit more to the right, the angle and approach moves would be to the left.

In our illustration above, you hit the 1-pin head-on and left a split. From your knowledge of the pin deck (SECTION 2, THE PIN DECK) you know the center of the 1-pin is on the 20th board. The 1-2 pocket is the 17th board at the pin deck, you have missed the pocket by 3 boards to the right. You need to move your contact point back to the pocket, to the left by 3 boards. The 3-1-2 system can help you make this adjustment.

On our illustration you started the approach from the 18th board at the end of the approach. We assumed a 1 board drift to the left and missing the ankle by 7 boards. The angle was the 10-to-10 foul line angle, and we missed the pocket by 3 boards to the right.

To bring the ball back to the pocket (3 boards) using the 3-1-2 adjustment system, move the target at the foul line by 1 board to the right, and move 2 boards to the right in the approach position. The target and approach moves were in the same direction as the contact point on the pins. This is in accordance with the 3-1-2 formula, and follows a long standing statement in adjusting . . . *follow the ball.* If the ball is hitting to the left, move to the left in your target and approach. If the ball is hitting to the right, move your target or approach to the right.

Our new starting position on the approach is the 20th board. Our new board to hit at the foul line is the 11th board. Therefore, we are now using the 11-10 foul line angle. The angle has been opened slightly, since the new angle sends the ball slightly away from the 1-2 pocket to the left.

Now, face the target by slightly turning the feet to the left, square your shoulders to the intended line or path of the ball, and walk toward the foul line in your normal walk pattern. This slight angle change will cause you to walk back approximately ½ of the amount of movement in your approach position (½ of the 2 boards we moved) and you should drift to the left the same 1 board that we previously assumed for our example. You will therefore slide on the 18th board, miss your ankle by 7 boards, and the ball should be released on the 11th board (our 1 board foul line change that we used based upon the 3-1-2 system). Theoretically, you should hit the pocket after this adjustment, unless you made some change in your delivery (such as a speed change, loft, lift, etc.).

If, in our previous example, you had missed the pocket completely to the right, and had crossed over into the brooklyn side, you could still have used the 3-1-2 adjustment formula. The brooklyn side is board 23 from the left side of the lane. This represents a 6 board miss of the 1-2 pocket (the 17th board). The foul line target would then have been moved to the right by 2 boards, and the approach position would have been moved by 4 boards to the right.

The formula calls for a 1 board angle change at the foul line for *each* 3 boards you miss at the pin deck. And it calls for a 2 board shift of the approach position for each 1 board angle shift at the foul line. If the miss is by 6 boards *to the right,* then our foul line adjustment would be 2 boards to the right, with a 4 board change in the approach position (also to the right).

In summary of the 3-1-2 adjustment system, if you miss to the right, move your foul line angle and approach positions to the right. If you miss to the left, move both to the left. And, move your foul line angle 1 board for each 3 boards you miss at the pin deck. You move your approach position 2 boards for each 1 board change in foul line angle. Stated another way, if you want the ball to hit more to the left, move your target and approach positions to the right. If you want the ball to hit more to the right, then move your target and approach positions to the left.

This adjustment system will work consistently for you, if you deliver the ball in a well-timed and consistent manner. With practice, you can modify the formula slightly to suit your style of bowling, and to make adjustments that are not exactly in 3 board units.

THE FIVE STRIKE LINES: With this brief introduction to a system for finding the pocket, and a personal formula for adjusting your angle, we can now start to discuss the five strike lines that contain any angle you will ever have to play. *The ability to use each of these strike lines is a talent that should be in the adjustment arsenal of every serious bowler.*

The pattern for discussion is as follows: First there will be an exhibit illustrating the general nature of the strike line. This chart will indicate the specific boundaries of the line, including the boards at the foul line, and the boards at the arrows which comprise the line. The chart will also contain general information about the strike line, such as the two boundary foul line angles which separate one line from another. Keep in mind that these are somewhat arbitrary boundaries for analysis only. Whether a specific angle is within one strike line or the immediately adjacent one is not a material factor in the discussion. There is agreement on the existence of these five general areas for playing various types of lane conditions, even though there are minor differences in names for the lines, and the exact boundary from one line to another.

Following the illustration, the line is discussed from the point of view that more than a movement on the approach is needed to properly play any given strike line. You must face your target on the lane, which means that sometimes you are walking parallel to the boards on the approach, and at other times you are walking at an angle to these boards. You may have an unintentional change in your walk pattern (drift) as you go from one line to another. Your method of targeting or aiming may change. As you move to the inside lines, you might make a small change in your targeting or aiming, looking a little further out on the lane. As you move to the outside strike lines, you might bring your aiming in a little closer to the foul line. How much you alter your aiming is a matter of personal preference.

Try to maintain the same walk pattern as you move from one strike line to another. One way to help you achieve this, is to *let the ball guide you or pull you through the line.* Don't pull the ball! *Let it pull you to and through the foul line angle you have selected to play.* By starting the ball in the direction of the line you are playing, the ball can help you walk in a straight pattern. This action will help you overcome the tendency to drift which is often associated with the inside and outside lines.

Still other factors have to be taken into consideration when you move from one strike line to another. You may move to the extreme outside line and find that the ball return or a wall interferes with your approach and delivery. For some bowlers these items are a problem, but for others they are no cause for concern.

Lane conditions are the major reason for changing from one strike line to another. As lanes break down, as they begin to hook, you will find yourself moving to the inside strike lines. If you find that the lanes are not hooking very much, you may go to the outside lines. If the lane track is a benefit to you, the second arrow strike line might be the one to select. If the lane track presents a problem, you may have to go either to the inside or outside strike lines to avoid the problem. If you find an erratic lane condition, (high or low board, dry spot, spotty condition, wet spot, etc.) you will have to move from one strike line to another to get around the situation. *You should practice every one of the five strike lines,* and many foul line angles within each line, so you can use any line or angle to adjust to any lane condition you find.

A complete knowledge and understanding of each strike line is essential if you are to take full advantage of the adjustment opportunities each one offers. One strike line will be best to use on a given lane at a particular time. If you can find that strike line, and play it properly, you will significantly increase your chances for making strikes.

We will begin our discussion with the deep inside strike line, and proceed through the other lines to the deep outside line. Remember, all five general strike lines were summarized on Exhibit 6-1.

DEEP INSIDE ANGLES (Left Handed Bowlers)

This strike line is the only one in which you cannot roll straight down the boards, or from the left side of the approach. The 18th board (the left-most board at the arrows) is already to the right of the 1-2 pocket, board 17.

All angles within this line are right-to-left open angles: the 20-to-18 angle; 21-to-18; 25-to-22; etc. The two boundary angles of this line are the 20-to-18 and 27-to-22 angles.

Although this strike line does not include boards beyond 22 at the arrows, you may have to go to the right of board 22 to get the ball into the pocket. Some lanes will require you to go as deep as the 5th arrow from the left side of the lane, or the 25th board. This extreme inside line is used on lanes that are very dry and are hooking a great deal.

If you are playing the 25-to-22 line and the ball is still high in the pocket, don't hesitate to move further to the right side of the approach and use a deeper angle. The need to go much deeper than a 27-to-22 foul line angle is a condition that the league bowler will not normally have to play.

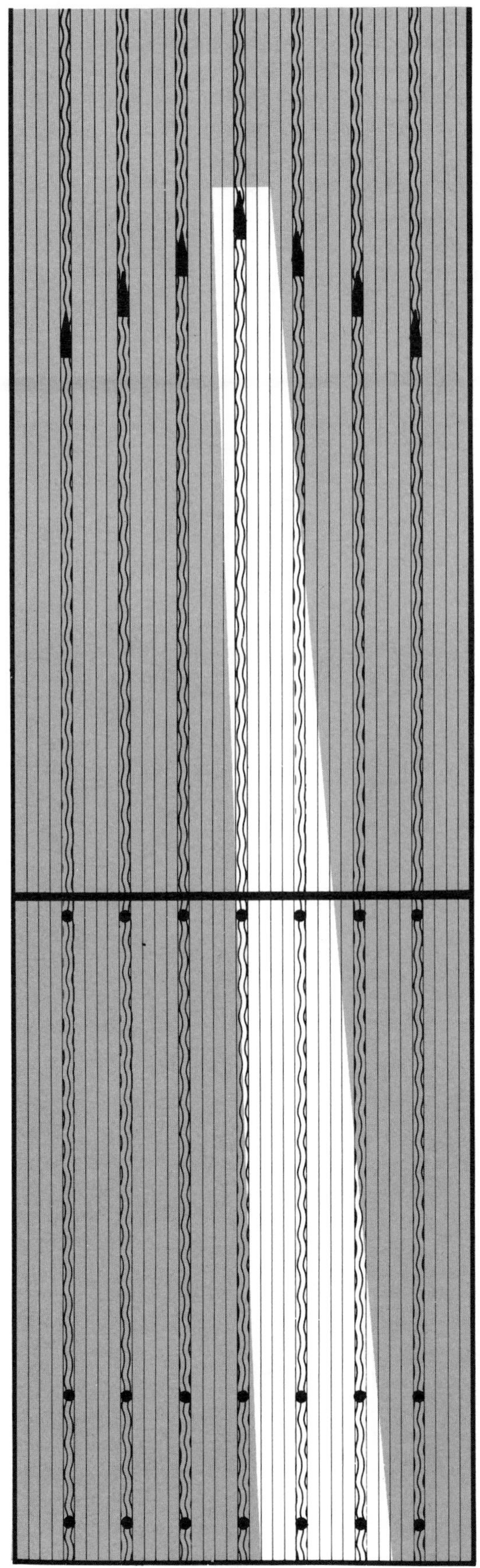

EXHIBIT 6-4
The Deep Inside Line for Left Handed Bowlers

BOARDS 18-22 AT THE ARROWS

BOARDS 20-27 AT THE FOUL LINE

PLAYING THE DEEP INSIDE LINE: In the next few paragraphs we will describe the conditions under which you might elect to use the deep inside strike line. First we will look at lane conditions that suggest the use of this line. Then we will cover aiming, alignment/walk patterns, and other factors related to the use of this strike line.

Lane Conditions: The deep inside line is used when the lanes are very dry and hooking a great deal. Under such lane conditions it is desirable to get the ball further down the lane before it begins its break to the pocket, and it is often necessary to cut down on the amount of the hook. Both of these objectives can be achieved by moving to the inside of the approach and using this strike line.

Another possible lane condition that could dictate using the deep inside line is when the lane track (if one exists) is so strong that it takes the ball into the pocket too quickly. Moving to the inside of the approach and using this line will get the ball further down the lane before it gets into the lane track. This late entrance into the track has two influences which will cut down on the hook. First, the ball will be angling away from the pocket, making it more difficult for the ball to hook strongly back to the right. And, secondly, the ball is in the track portion of the lane for a shorter time, giving the track less time to allow the ball to grip the lane. Thus, the existence of a strong lane track might be overcome by moving to this deep inside strike line. (LHB using a backup ball and the 1-3 pocket have to contend with the lane track of the RHB.)

Still another lane condition that might be played best from the deep inside line is when the lane has been conditioned with more oil (dressing, conditioning) to the right side of the second arrow zone. This additional conditioning can be used to get the ball through the heads with enough skid to delay the hook for a proper pocket angle for strikes. Perhaps the outside of the lane (toward the left hand gutter) is so dry that it is impossible to get enough skid (delay the break point) to prevent the ball from breaking too soon. Therefore, whenever you want to get the ball further down the lane before it breaks to the pocket, or whenever you wish to reduce the strength and intensity of the hook, this deep inside angle adjustment may work well for you. This assumes, of course, that you wish to reach these objectives by an angle adjustment instead of an equipment or delivery change.

Aiming: A general rule concerning the strike line you are using and the distance beyond the foul line that you aim states: As you move toward the inside of the lane (toward the center of the approach) you should move your target further down the lane; as you move to the outside of the lane (toward the left gutter) you should move your target closer to the foul line. Therefore, the point of aim for this deep inside line should be further down the lane than any other strike line, since this line is more *inside* than any other.

The reason for moving the target further down the lane for this deep inside line is that you will be better able to *extend* yourself and get the ball further down the lane before it breaks for the pocket. Since the target is further down the lane, you may automatically loft the ball slightly further out on the lane, a delivery adjustment that goes hand-in-hand with the use of the deep inside line.

Alignment/Walk Pattern: As you open the angle of your strike ball delivery, which you do when you use this deep inside line, you must align your feet toward your target on the lane. Your shoulders should be square to your target and not to the foul line. Then you walk in a straight line toward your target, which means you will be walking at a slight angle to the foul line and the boards on the approach. *It is this angled path to the foul line which causes some bowlers to drift, or to slightly alter their walk pattern.* Let's take each of the three conditions regarding drift and analyze them separately as they relate to this deep inside strike line: (1) you have no drift in your approach, (2) you drift to the left, or (3) you drift to the right.

If *you have no drift* in your normal walk pattern to the foul line, using this deep inside line might cause you to drift a little either to the left or the right. A left drift is possible since you are walking slightly to the left toward the foul line and you might walk a little too much to the left, creating a slight drift. You might, on the other hand, drift right by trying to walk in a straight line parallel to the boards on the approach, rather than the slight angle required to properly play this strike line. In either case, you need to be aware of what is happening, since this drift may make it difficult for you to hit your target on the lane. If any change in your drift pattern occurs because you are now approaching the foul line from an angle (and you can't correct it) you will have to incorporate this drift pattern in your calculation of where to stand on the approach to begin your shot.

If you have *a slight drift to the right* in your natural delivery, the use of the deep inside line may cause you to drift slightly less than normal. This reduced amount of drift is caused by the fact that you are angling toward the left when you play this line properly, and it is more difficult to drift right while angling to the left. Keep in mind, however, you may *not* drift any less while using this line, but the tendency is that you will.

If you have *a drift to the left* in your normal

delivery, the use of the deep inside strike line *may* cause you to drift slightly more to the left. This additional drift is created because you are angling to the left and drifting to the left. It is easier to increase the amount of your normal drift under these circumstances. Again, you *may not* drift more to the left, but the tendency will be to do so. And if you do drift a little more, you will need to make some correction in lining up for the shot, or work to eliminate the additional drift from your approach and delivery. *Letting your swing bring or guide you through the line can help insure a straight walk pattern, even when you are angling to the left.*

Whether your drift pattern is altered by the use of this strike line, or any other strike line, is not the important point. What *is* important is that you are aware of what *might* happen to your normal walk pattern as you use the various strike lines. Then you can decide whether you will try to eliminate the extra drift (through practice sessions), or to make some other correction in your game to use the drift properly. It is important that you end up at the foul line on the correct board at the moment of release, and that you place the ball on the correct board at the foul line. Therefore, observe your drift and walk pattern in this deep inside line (and all other strike lines) so you will be able to adjust accordingly.

Try to let the ball guide you to and through the foul line angle you have selected. When you start the swing properly, directly in line with the angle, the ball can help keep you in a straight-line walk pattern.

Other Factors Related to the Deep Inside Line: Changing your angle or strike line is more than a simple move to the left or right on the approach. We indicated that your drift pattern may change, and your method of aiming may be altered. There are even more factors you should keep in mind as you use the deep inside line.

Sometimes the use of a deep inside angle will put you nearer to obstacles that might not affect you from another line. If you are on the side of the lane where the ball return is located, or you are near a wall, these obstacles might cause you to deliver the ball in other than a normal manner. Some bowlers are afraid of hitting the ball return or wall with the free foot during the delivery. Others consciously or unconsciously walk away from the obstacles during the delivery, causing a change in their natural drift pattern and/or putting them at the foul line in a sideways position. This could cause a number of problems with the delivery or release of the ball. If such obstacles concern you, then you should either practice where such conditions exist, or make some other adjustment in your game to eliminate the possible problem. You might increase the speed of your delivery, therefore giving you the opportunity to reduce the angle slightly, and keep you away from the obstacles. (Delivery adjustments will be covered in a later section.) Or, you might make a change in your equipment to require less of an angle. However, it may be best to just practice until the problem is eliminated, so you can take full advantage of this strike line when conditions dictate its use.

Still another factor to consider when using the deep inside line is that you may be using a portion of the approach that has not been used much. This means you may either stick or slip at the foul line. Test this portion of the approach before you use it and there should be no problem. And if you are using the same deep inside line on both lanes you will have to test the condition on both approaches, since there is no way you can assume that the condition on one approach is the same on the other.

You may also wish to change your equipment or delivery (or both) in conjunction with the use of the deep inside strike line. Some of these possible adjustments will *complement* your move to the inside line, and others will *counteract* the move. Although these two major classifications of adjustments were fully discussed in SECTION 1, here are examples of additional adjustments you might wish to make. You could *increase your speed,* which goes along with the move to the inside line. Both are designed to get the ball further down the lane before the break to the pocket. Or, you could *reduce the amount of lift* you put on the ball, also delaying the break point. And, of course, you could change your equipment to a *different ball surface* or *balance*. All of these adjustments could be made in conjunction with the change to the deep inside line. Now you can see how many variables are at work as you try to find the proper strike line, equipment, and delivery technique to get the ball and lane working together for you.

The deep inside angle is designed to get the ball further down the lane before it heads toward the pocket. It is an adjustment to get the ball back to the pocket after it has passed by on the right side of the head pin. For those who use the hook ball, such an angle will get the ball further down the lane before the break begins to the pocket. This will delay the timing and intensity of the hook. These changes in the *timing* and the *intensity* of the hook are obvious methods for playing dry and hooking lanes.

INSIDE ANGLES (Left Handed Bowlers)

This strike line gives you the possibility of open, closed, and straight angle shots into the 1-2 pocket. The two boundary angles are the 21-to-17 and 11-to-13 angles. Between these two angles are a variety of other shots which are all part of the inside line.

Notice the wide area of the approach covered by this strike line. This provides a great deal of options for getting the ball into the pocket correctly. Most of the angles within this line are options for lanes that are hooking too much. On such lane conditions it is necessary to get the ball out to the left so the hook will be delayed until the ball is well down the lane.

As with all strike lines, this one may extend one or more boards to the left or right at the arrows or foul line. The purpose for illustrating all five strike lines, including this one, is to give you a more precise method for adjusting to lane conditions by changing your angle of entry into the pocket. Changing your angle from the foul line to the arrows (the foul line angle) will alter your pocket angle.

A general rule states that you should not play more than a 5 board angle across any board at the arrows. But, if you are playing the 21-to-17 angle and still hitting high in the pocket, don't hesitate moving in further and playing a 22 or 23-to-17 angle.

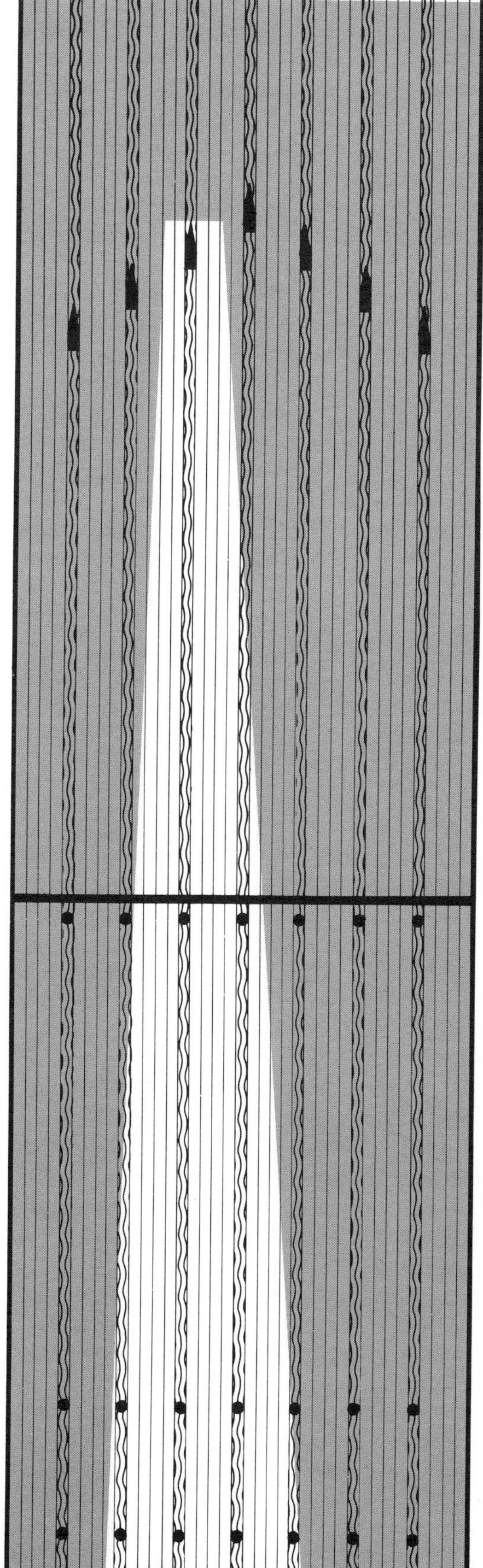

EXHIBIT 6-5

The Inside Line for Left Handed Bowlers

BOARDS 13-17 AT THE ARROWS

BOARDS 11-21 AT THE FOUL LINE

PLAYING THE INSIDE LINE: In the next few paragraphs we will describe the conditions under which you might elect to use the inside strike line, and the various foul line angles within that line. First we will look at the types of lane conditions suggesting the use of this line. Then we will follow the same pattern as used for the previous strike line (the deep inside line), by covering such topics as aiming, alignment/walk pattern, and other factors related to the use of the inside strike line.

Lane Conditions: The inside line is often used when the lane is a *little* dry and the ball is hooking a *little* more than you would like. Under such a condition it is desirable to get the ball a little further down the lane before it breaks to the pocket. High pocket hits suggest you might move in to this strike line, if you were using the second arrow strike line.

The lane track (if one exists) might also cause you to move to this inside strike line. The track might be *grabbing* the ball too soon, and taking it high into the pocket. Moving in slightly on the approach and using this inside strike line may be just enough to get the ball back to the pocket.

You may also be able to find more oil on this portion of the lane, thereby giving you more opportunity to get the ball *through the heads* and delay the hook or break point until the ball is further down the lane.

In summary, lane conditions suggesting the inside line are somewhere between conditions suggesting the deep inside strike line and those conditions which make the second arrow strike line the best to play. Therefore, we will not dwell too much on lane conditions for this strike line. The topic is covered fairly well in the discussions of those other two strike lines.

Aiming: The general rule regarding aiming and strike lines is used in deciding how far out on the lane you will target for this inside strike line. (This rule was explained under the deep inside strike line. Basically, it states that you might move your target out on the lane as you move to the inside lines, and target closer to the foul line as you move to outside lines.)

The exact distance for aiming while using the inside line will, of course, depend upon personal preferences. But the distance should be slightly closer than you would use for the deep inside line, and slightly further out on the lane than you would use for the second arrow strike line (discussed next).

Since you are still on the inside lines, you want to get yourself to extend properly, to perhaps loft the ball slightly further out on the lane than you would with the second arrow line (yet a little closer than you might for the deep inside line). By moving your point of aim, your target, these delivery adjustments should occur naturally, with no conscious effort on your part.

Alignment/Walk Pattern: The inside strike line contains straight, open and closed foul line angles. Therefore, depending upon which portion of the line you are using, you will have to be sure you are properly aligned to your target on the lane. At times you will be parallel to the boards on the approach (straight angles); at times you will be angling to the left (open angles); and at other times you will be aligned toward the pocket (closed angles).

In each case you must *square yourself to your target, walk in your normal pattern* to the foul line, and *let your swing pull you through the line.* The ball should be in line with the foul line angle you are playing.

Your drift pattern should not be affected by playing this inside line. When you are playing a closed angle within the line, you will be angling slightly to the right, and this may cause you to drift a little to the right when you have no normal drift. It may, however, cause you to drift less if you have a normal left drift, or to drift slightly more to the right when you already have a right drift in your approach.

On the other hand, playing open angles within the line might cause you to: (A) drift slightly to the left; (B) drift more to the left if you have a left drift; or (C) drift less to the right if you already have a drift to the right.

These changes in drift are *tendencies only.* Watch for these possible changes in your walk pattern so you can correct them, or incorporate *small* walk pattern changes in your adjustment calculations.

Other Factors Related to the Inside Strike Line: The inside line is used to get the ball back to the pocket after you have been using the second arrow strike line and hitting high or crossing over in front of the pocket. This strike line will often come into play when you notice the lanes are beginning to *break down* slightly as a result of play on them.

Of course, you could have been using the deep inside line, and not be getting up to the pocket. In that case, moving to the left on the approach, and using this inside strike line would give you a better angle into the pocket, bringing the ball up to the pocket.

You should encounter no obstacles (ball return, wall, etc.) when you use this strike line. Moreover, you might wish to use other adjustment techniques with this strike line. Less lift, a harder ball surface, and more speed are also adjustments designed to get the ball further down the lane before breaking for the pocket, which this strike line is designed to do.

We suggest that you only make one adjustment at a time, and preferably only the angle change. That way you will be in a better position to understand the result of the adjustment you have made.

SECOND ARROW ANGLES (Left Handed Bowlers)

This is the most commonly used strike line for right handed bowlers, but not so for the left handers. There are, however, many reasons why it might be a good angle to use as you begin your bowling career. The line is located in the center of the left half of the lane. This lets you make your delivery down the center of the approach, and deliver the ball to the left of your walk pattern. This might represent a comfortable feeling for many left handed bowlers.

This strike line provides a wide area on the approach and lane to adjust to various lane conditions. When lanes are neither very wet nor very dry, the second arrow angle can be effective.

This line is also consistent with the normal desire to avoid extremes, that is, not to play too near the gutter nor too near the center of the lane. Also, many high average bowlers develop a 6 to 7 board hook. This strike line is about that number of boards to the left of the 1-2 pocket, the 17th board at the pin deck.

If you are using this line, and many other left handers are using it at the same time, watch for a lane track to develop. The oil will be moved around, or removed from the lane. A high friction zone might be created, a lane track similar to that faced on a fairly regular basis by right handed bowlers.

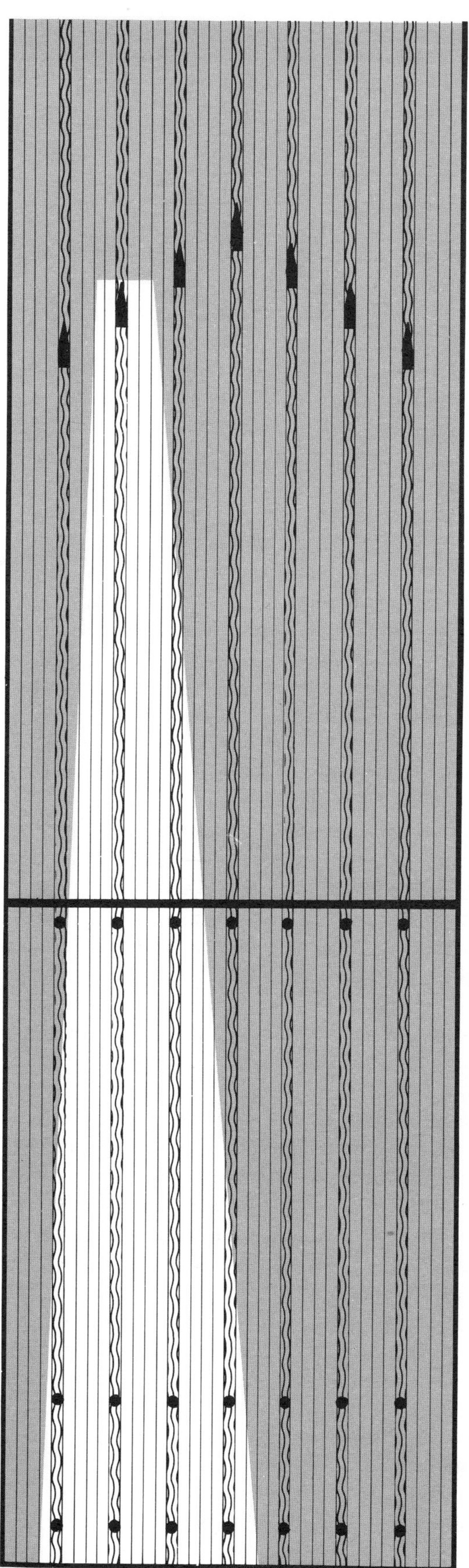

EXHIBIT 6-6
The Second Arrow Line for Left Handed Bowlers

BOARDS 8-12 AT THE ARROWS

BOARDS 6-17 AT THE FOUL LINE

PLAYING THE SECOND ARROW LINE: On the following page we state why this strike line is so popular and frequently used. In the paragraphs that follow we will take into consideration other factors you must also think about when you play this line, including: lane conditions; aiming; alignment/walk pattern; and other factors. It should be obvious at this point that an angle change is more than simply a movement to the left or right on the approach. Each time you change your angle you have to be aware of other needed changes, or accidental changes that may occur.

Lane Conditions: The second arrow strike line is used when the lanes are what most bowlers consider *normal,* that is, the lanes are not too dry and hooking nor are they too wet and not hooking. They are just right for you. Someone else bowling with you at the same time might conclude that the lanes are hooking too little or too much for them, but that is not important. They may be using a different delivery, different equipment, etc. Or they could just prefer another strike line and have made some other adjustment to allow them to use that line.

A second reason why the second arrow strike line might be recommended, or work well for you, is that the lane track (if one exists) is helping to guide the ball into the pocket. In that case it is best to get the lane and the ball working together for you. Rather than make a move to the inside of the lane and enter the track further down the lane, or move outside and enter the track on a more direct angle into the pocket, it may be best (under some lane conditions) to get the ball in the lane track immediately, and let them both work for you.

Still another reason why lane conditions might favor this second arrow strike line is when the pattern of oil or conditioning is erratic on both the inside and outside of the lane. Playing on either of these parts of the lane might cause an unpredictable reaction of the ball. Or it could be that the pattern of conditioning on either side of the lane is too dry, making it difficult to get the ball through the heads from those strike lines. When the lane is too dry from the foul line to the arrows the ball will tend to break too soon. You may be forced to increase your speed (a delivery adjustment) to prevent this early break. However, anything that gets the ball to skid further down the lane before the break begins, without requiring any change in your approach, release or delivery, will give you an advantage in hitting the pocket correctly. Finding the proper amount of oil on the heads is the easiest way to achieve this delay in the break point. And when this is found in the second arrow strike line (around boards 6-17 at the foul line and boards 8-12 at the arrows) then you should try to use this line. It is more difficult to bowl consistently when you are forced to make a change in your delivery.

In summary, the two types of lane conditions suggesting the second arrow strike line are either a good lane track condition, or an improper lane condition on either the inside or outside of the lane.

Aiming: Your aiming pattern for this second arrow strike line should be the normal one you use, since this is the most commonly used strike line. Any movement in your aiming, toward or away from the foul line, should be made with reference to your point of aim for this strike line.

The general rule regarding the strike line and aiming distance applies to this line, as it does to all others. As you use the inside portion of this second arrow line you might move your point of aim slightly further out on the lane. As you use the middle portion of this strike line (for example, the 10-to-10 angle) you might aim your normal distance. But when you use the outside portion of this strike line (for example, the 6-to-8 angle) you would move your point of aim closer to the foul line.

These adjustments in aiming are all designed to get you to use the proper amount of extension or reach in your delivery. The differences in aiming points are also related to the amount of loft you use. You are more likely to use more loft when you aim at a point further down the lane than if you aim at a point closer to the foul line. Additional extension and loft are helpful in getting the ball further down the lane before it begins its break to the pocket. Thus, the purpose of moving your point of aim is, in effect, to cause you to make a small change in your delivery without any conscious effort on your part. (In a later section we discuss delivery adjustments in more detail.)

Alignment/Walk Pattern: Your alignment and walk pattern is probably least affected by this second arrow line than any other. The alignment and walk pattern you normally use is what you should have when you use this line, the normal strike line for many beginning left handed bowlers. (High average bowlers usually move to the outside angles, to be covered next.)

There are several open angles within this strike line (those in which the ball is headed away from the pocket) as well as closed angles (where the ball is headed on a more direct line toward the 1-2 pocket). You will have a slight change in your feet alignment, and you might tend to have a small change in your walk pattern, as you use the boundary angles *within* this strike line.

The alignment of your feet should be straight toward your target. This is true in every case, with every strike line, but is worthy of repeating. *Face your target squarely, align your feet and shoulders toward the target and you are ready for your approach.* In the center of this line you will align your feet parallel to the boards on the approach, but for the outside angles within this line, your feet will be parallel to your intended path of the ball. *Then, let your swing guide you or pull you to and through your line.*

As before, let's take each possible walk pattern and look at how each might be affected as you use different strike angles in this second arrow line. We will begin with a zero drift walk pattern.

If *you have no drift* associated with your walk pattern to the foul line, you will have little if any tendency to drift by using this strike line, especially the middle portion of the line. As long as you are walking in a relatively straight line toward the foul line (such as when you are using a 10-to-10 or 11-to-11 angle), you will be walking parallel to the boards on the approach. No drift tendency should occur, other than any normal drift you might have in your walk pattern. When you elect to use an angle to the inside or outside portion of this strike line, you might develop a slight tendency to drift one way or the other. Using the inside portion of the line (toward the center of the approach) might cause you to drift slightly to the left (because your walk pattern is angled slightly to the left). Using the outside of this strike line (toward the left side of the lane) might cause you to develop a slight drift to the right (because you are angling slightly toward the right). In either case, you should be aware of the *possibility* that a drift *might* develop in your walk pattern, or your normal drift *could* be altered. If any change should occur in your drift pattern, you can either take this drift into consideration when you align yourself on the approach, or practice to eliminate the *drift tendency* when you use this strike line.

If your normal walk pattern includes *a drift tendency toward the right,* using the inside portion of this line might decrease your drift pattern, and using the outside portion of this line might increase your drift. Both of these possible changes in drift pattern are consistent with this thought: When you angle to the right in your approach you may *tend to* increase any normal drift to the right, and decrease any normal drift to the left. When you walk on an angle to the left in your approach, any left drift might be increased while a right drift in the walk pattern might be reduced. It is possible to develop or increase a drift pattern that is in line with the way you walk from your stance position to the foul line. Any drift opposite of the line you take to the foul line may tend to be lessened. Therefore, if you normally have *a drift to the left* in your walk pattern, the effect of using this second arrow line is as follows: It may increase when you use the inside of this strike line, or decrease when you use the outside. Using the center portion of the strike line (a 10-to-10 angle) should have little or no effect on your normal walk or drift pattern.

As previously stated, a small amount of drift is neither good nor bad. It is just something you have to be aware of and make whatever change is needed to use it effectively. As long as the drift pattern is constant for you, you can incorporate the drift into your natural game. *(However, you are much more likely to improve your bowling skills by eliminating drift completely.)*

Other Factors Related to the Second Arrow Line: The second arrow strike line may be used to either get back to the pocket after missing it to the right, or to get up to the pocket when you miss to the left. The inside portion of this line is an adjustment to get back to the pocket, whereas, the outside portion of the line is designed to get up to the pocket after having failed to do so.

Of course, this strike line can be used in conjunction with other delivery or equipment adjustments to get the ball into the pocket properly. You could combine the outside portion of this line with: less speed, a softer ball surface, more positive weights, less loft, or more lift on the ball. The inside portion of the line is similar to these types of adjustments: more speed, a harder surface on the ball, negative weights, more loft, and less turn on the ball. Later sections will look at each of these other adjustments independently, and in conjunction with each other.

OUTSIDE ANGLES (Left Handed Bowlers)

This is the first of two strike lines toward the left side of the lane. Both lines contain angles that give the ball more opportunity to grab the lane and hook.

The range of angles in this line is much more narrow than the second arrow or inside lines. The boundaries for this line are the 8-to-7 angle on the inside and the 3-to-4 angle on the left side of the line. These are much tighter and straighter angles than the other lines since there is less area for the ball to go to the gutter side of the line. A more direct shot is needed.

As a general rule, when you move your strike line to the outside, you are forced to use a narrower range of angles. This occurs because you are using a relatively small portion of the lane. From the inside angles you are able to use the full width of the lane to execute the shot.

This narrow shot may cause you to feel constrained or tight in your approach and delivery. If you keep this potential problem in mind when you practice these outside angles, you should be able to develop the same free and relaxed swing that is normally a natural part of using wider angles. You may also feel obliged to pull the ball away from the gutter. This potential problem can also be minimized with practice.

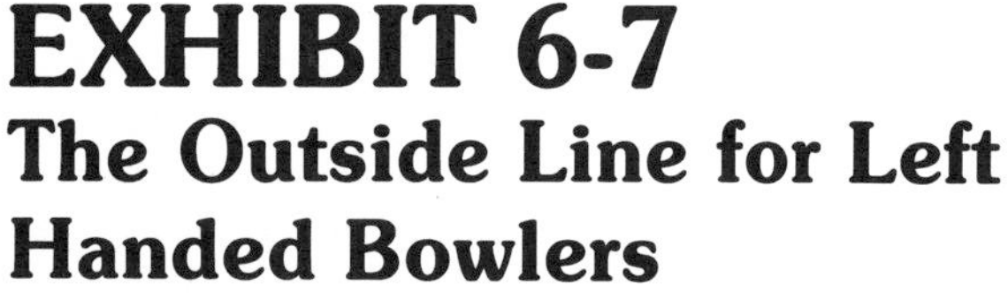

EXHIBIT 6-7
The Outside Line for Left Handed Bowlers

BOARDS 4-7 AT THE ARROWS

BOARDS 3-8 AT THE FOUL LINE

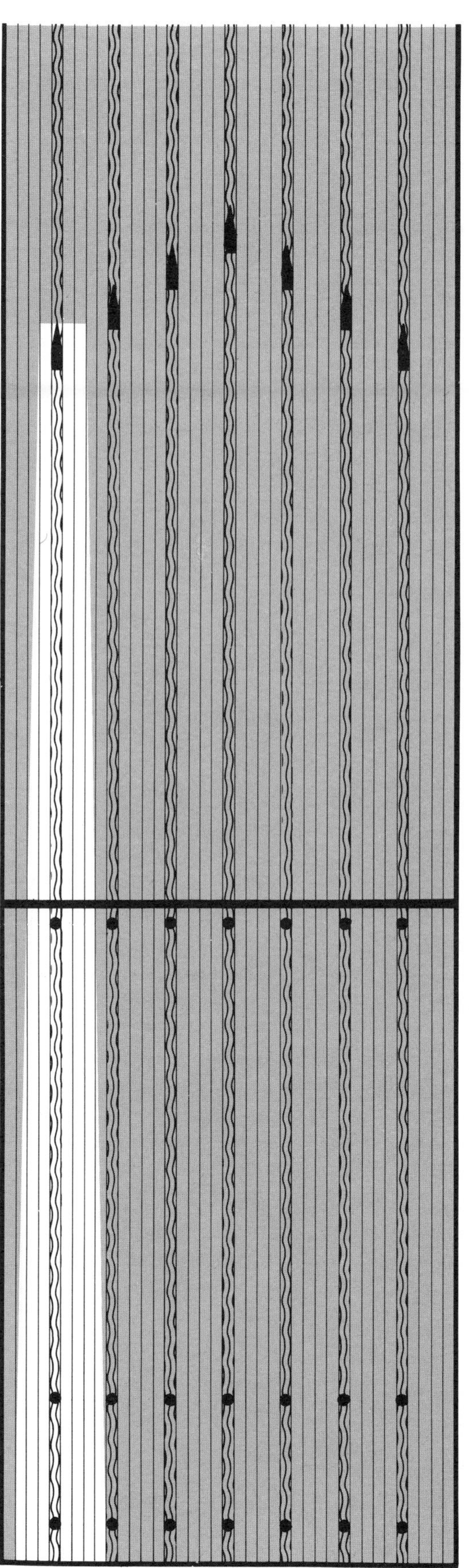

PLAYING THE OUTSIDE LINE: In the next few paragraphs we will describe the conditions under which you might decide to use the outside strike line, and the various foul line angles within that line. First we will look at the types of lane conditions suggesting use of this line. Then we will follow the pattern used for the other strike lines, covering such topics as: aiming; alignment/walk pattern; and other factors related to the use of the outside line.

Lane Conditions: The outside line is often used when the lanes are a little wet, and the ball is not hooking as much as you would like. Under such conditions it is desirable to get the ball rolling or hooking a little sooner, and this outside line will do that for you. Missing the pocket to the left is an indication that you might want to move to this outside strike line.

You may also find the oil on this portion of the lane is the proper amount to get the ball through the header portion of the lane and into a roll leading to the pocket.

The lane track (if one exists) might also cause you to consider using the outside strike line. Moving out on the lane may get the ball into the track at just the right time and angle to get a good pocket angle.

In summary, the type of lane conditions suggesting the use of the outside line are somewhere between those dictating either a second arrow or deep outside line. Therefore, we will not need to cover lane conditions too deeply here, since the topic is covered fairly well in the discussions of those two other strike lines.

Aiming: The general rule regarding aiming and strike lines is used for this line as well. The exact distance for aiming while using this outside line will depend upon personal preferences. But the distance should be slightly closer than you would use for the second arrow strike line, and slightly further out on the lane than you would use for the deep outside line (discussed next).

When you are using the outside line, you will probably loft the ball slightly less than you would for the second arrow line, and slightly more than you would if you were using the deep outside line. By moving your point of aim, this change in loft should occur naturally, with no conscious effort on your part.

Alignment/Walk Pattern: Most of the foul line angles contained in the outside line are relatively straight. There is not enough room in the line for very open or very closed shots. This situation is true of all outside shots. There is less room to open the angle since the gutter is so close to the left side of the line.

As with all strike lines, you must be certain that you square yourself to your target and walk in your normal pattern to the foul line. *Let the ball and your swing pull you through the strike line you are playing, keeping the straight pendulum swing, so essential to an effective delivery.* (More on this later.)

Your drift pattern should not be affected by playing this outside line. There may be a tendency to alter the drift pattern as you play the boundary angles in this line (either open or closed angle), but the shot is so straight that your walk pattern should not change. Be alert to the tendency for a walk pattern change, and take measures to eliminate the change. Or, if the change is small, you might be able to incorporate it into your walk pattern and adjustment calculations. However, a much better objective is to strive for no change.

Other Factors Related to the Outside Strike Line: The outside line is used to get the ball up to the pocket after missing to the left. Usually, these misses are not too far to the left, or else the deep outside line would be suggested. This strike line often comes into play when the lane is not hooking very well, usually the result of a heavy oil pattern around the second arrow.

Obstacles such as the ball return or a wall should not interfere with your approach when you use this strike line. This will occur, however, when you have to use the deep outside line, which we will discuss next.

Since you are usually not missing the pocket by much when you switch to the outside line, you might make other adjustments instead of using this line. For example, you could use more lift, a softer ball surface, or less speed to achieve the same objectives which the outside line allows you to reach. Or, you could combine one of these adjustments with a move to the outside line.

We suggest you make only one adjustment at a time, and preferably only the angle change, but you should be aware of other adjustments that have the same effect as the angle change to the outside strike line.

DEEP OUTSIDE ANGLES (Left Handed Bowlers)

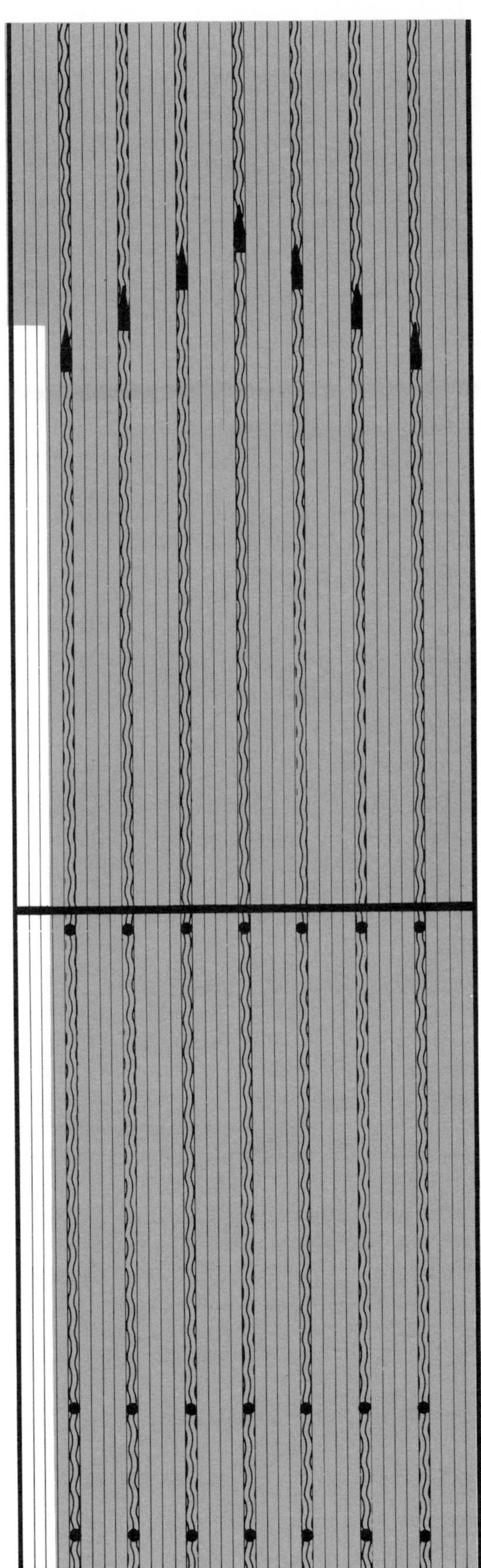

This is probably the most uncomfortable to play of the five strike lines. That is why it is not used by many bowlers, even though it may be the best line to use to get the ball into the pocket. Many LHB, however, prefer this line.

This is best when the lane will not hook at all and you must give the ball as much of the lane as possible for the ball to hook across into the pocket. Sometimes the inside portion of the lane is such that any shot to the left from that angle will not get back to the pocket. Or, this may be the line that will allow you to get the ball as far down the lane as possible before it begins to hook for the pocket. Sometimes this is called the *Gutter shot,* since it is right next to the gutter. This can be an extremely good angle into the pocket, but you can leave some very unusual and rare spares on occasion.

Notice how straight the shot has to be to use this strike line. There is almost no opportunity to open or close the angle of the shot. There are only 3 boards to use. As you move to the outside lines, this will happen. You are forced to play a much straighter shot down the lane. There is little margin for error on this line, and often you will see some of the best bowlers in the world roll a gutter ball while using this strike line.

Although this strike line is perhaps the most difficult to master, you should practice and develop it to give yourself that added flexibility to change the angle as the lane dictates.

EXHIBIT 6-8
The Deep Outside Line for Left Handed Bowlers

BOARDS 1-3 AT THE ARROWS

BOARDS 1-3 AT THE FOUL LINE

PLAYING THE DEEP OUTSIDE LINE: In the next few paragraphs we will describe the conditions or situations under which you might decide to use this deep outside line. First we will describe lane conditions which suggest using this strike line; then we will cover aiming, alignment/walk pattern, and other factors to consider.

Lane Conditions: The primary lane condition suggesting the use of the deep outside line is when the lane is heavily dressed (having a lot of oil) and not hooking very much at all. Moving to the deep outside strike line will allow you to get the ball into the pocket at a more favorable angle than any of the inside lines. Not having the lane track to contend with suggests that this is an excellent line for left handers to use.

The inside portion of the lane may also be spotty, with intermittent wet (oily) and dry spots. Such an inconsistent lane condition creates a very difficult condition in which to create a consistent and reliable shot to the pocket. Such an erratic path to the pins makes it difficult to read the lane well. Therefore, under such lane conditions it is usually best to move to the outside angles and strike lines.

The inside area of the lane may also have received heavy use or play. Perhaps the lane has broken down too much, making it difficult to use this portion of the lane. There may be no consistent lane surface upon which you can find a good angle to the pocket. You may have to roll the ball across oil, through dry spots, into oil, and back into the drier areas as the ball follows a path to the pins. Under such varying lane conditions it is also difficult to produce a consistent shot to the pocket.

Finally, many times the only smooth lane condition can be found in this deep outside portion of the lane. This situation could arise because of the lack of play on this area, or it could be a result of a rougher lane surface created by constant use elsewhere on the lane. A smooth lane surface will permit you to find the best and most consistent shot to the pocket, with no unusual or unplanned reactions between the ball and the lane. Since the LHB usually has no lane track on his or her side of the lane, a very smooth surface is normal on this part of the lane.

Aiming: The proper distance for targeting or aiming while using this deep outside line may only be 5 feet in front of the foul line, depending upon personal preferences. This distance represents the closest method of targeting of all five strike lines, since this is the most extreme outside line. You will recall that the targeting rule states to bring the target closer to the foul line as you move to the outside lines.

This closer aiming distance may be uncomfortable to those who are not used to using it, and there is little room for error when you are laying the ball down so close to the gutter. However, as with all of our general rules, you must modify it to suit your style of bowling. Select the targeting distance which allows you to play this deep outside line comfortably. If it works well, and consistently, then it is right for you.

Other Factors Related to the Deep Outside Line: This strike line gives you a stronger angle to the pocket. You can get a great deal of action on the ball even if you give it only a little bit of lift at the release point. Therefore it is very useful to practice this strike line so you will be prepared when some of the following situations arise.

If the pins are on the heavy side, above 3 pounds 6 ounces (3-6's), you may need the additional strength of this deep outside strike line to prevent the ball from deflecting too much to the left and into the 2-pin. Heavy pins cause more deflection than light ones. It is easier to compensate for heavy pins by a line or angle change than to make an equipment or delivery change.

On occasion you will need more action on the ball, and do not wish to change your delivery or equipment. In that case, you can get more action on the ball by simply moving to the left on the approach and using the deep outside line. Even a little lift on the ball will be sufficient to create a lot of action if it is combined with the use of this strike line.

There are some difficulties in using this particular strike line, as there are special problems associated with each strike line. The ball may hook too much because of the deep angle created by this line. As we mentioned previously, a small amount of lift or turn on the ball will often result in a strong hook. Just a little mistake in your release could result in a big error in the path of the ball. Some very difficult leaves are often the result of using this deep outside line.

The ball return, or a wall, may interfere with the use of this line. You may feel uncomfortable and constrained in the use of this area of the approach. The gutter is close, and there is often a tendency to pull the ball in front of the body instead of releasing it naturally in a straight line down the intended path of the ball. Therefore, it is important that you practice the use of this deep outside strike line in order to develop your natural delivery from this portion of the approach. Get used to laying the ball down on the 1st through 3rd boards, and doing it without any concern for the nearness of the gutter, the ball return (if it is located on this side of the approach), or a wall, if you are on a lane next to one.

You may also wish to make other changes in your game when you play this strike line. You may slow down your speed slightly, since this strike line is used when the lane is not hooking, and a slower ball speed facilitates the development of a hooking action. You may also loft the ball slightly less, which is another adjustment to counteract a non-hooking lane. Or, you may make any one of a number of adjustments which assist in the use of this deep outside line.

The deep outside line can be used to get the ball further down the lane before it breaks toward the pocket. This line will get the ball into a pocket angle that will either give you a lot of strikes or some of the most difficult spare leaves you will ever face. Sometimes this line is used to get the ball back to the pocket, and at other times it is used to get the ball up to the pocket, depending upon the condition of the lane. On occasion, two bowlers on the same lane will use both the deep inside and deep outside line at the same time. Equipment or delivery changes might have to be made to accommodate the two strike lines. Some bowlers favor this line, and will use it whenever lane conditions permit them to do so. Used properly, this can be an extremely effective strike line, particularly for left handed bowlers.

SECTION 7 EQUIPMENT ADJUSTMENTS (Left Handed Bowlers)

"Proper equipment is essential for high scoring."

CONTENTS — PAGE

OVERVIEW

This section addresses the three major types of equipment adjustments for left handed bowlers: ball *balance* adjustments, ball *surface* adjustments, and ball *fit* adjustments.

Prior to a discussion of these techniques for adjusting to various lane conditions, it is necessary to explore several topics directly related to equipment adjustments.

The first topic will be *total ball weight.* Since a bowling ball may be as light as 8 pounds or as heavy as 16 pounds, selecting the proper ball weight is a very important part of any equipment adjustment strategy. A choice of ball weight is generally no problem for most adult males, since they normally select the maximum weight of 16 pounds. *This is often a mistake,* since a ball of less weight may often be a better choice.

For young boys and girls, senior bowlers, and often for adult females, the decision regarding total ball weight is significant. Moreover, the decision is *not* a lifetime decision. You may wish to change to a ball of more or less weight at various times during your bowling career, and in fact you should do so in most cases.

Next we will begin our discussion of how weight imbalances are created when a bowling ball is drilled. We start with a look at several types of weight blocks, which permit drilling the ball so that the *center of gravity* is *not* located in the center of the ball.

An imbalance is created by drilling the thumb and finger holes closer to or further away from the weight block. Imbalance is *not* created by adding weight to a portion of the ball. Thus, it is necessary to understand the concept of a weight block, and the part it plays in creating ball imbalances.

Guidelines have been established regarding the *maximum imbalance* that can be created when a ball is drilled for use. These maximums will be reviewed from time to time by accrediting agencies. It is important that you understand the relative advantages and disadvantages of each type of weight imbalance that can be created.

Then we will discuss and illustrate the five typical types of *ball tracks* (the portion of the ball surface which contacts the lane as the ball skids, rolls, and hooks to the pocket). Any discussion of weights and imbalances as an adjustment technique must consider the ball track. The effect of a given amount of ball imbalance is directly related to the location of this imbalance relative to the ball track.

As part of the discussion of ball tracks, we will briefly explore the concept of *axis weight* as a ball imbalance adjustment technique. This is one of two common methods for changing the center of gravity of the ball, thus creating imbalances which can be useful for influencing the action of the ball. The other technique for creating imbalances is called *top weight* or *label weight,* in which the top half of the ball weighs more than the bottom half after drilling is completed. Top weight usually refers to creating an imbalance in the ball by positioning the thumb and finger holes relative to the weight block. Axis weight, on the other hand, usually means changing the balance situation after the thumb and finger holes are already drilled in the ball. (Of course, you can take into consideration the positioning of the holes prior to creating axis weight imbalances).

Label weights will be discussed extensively under the section titled BALL BALANCE ADJUSTMENTS. Axis weights will only be discussed in this introductory section following the coverage of ball tracks.

Equipment selection and adjustment is both an

art and a science. Selecting or creating proper weights and imbalances, the correct fit, and differing ball surfaces cover a complex subject. For example, any discussion of ball weights and imbalances must also cover such topics as total ball weight, ball tracks, and both label and axis weights. All of these factors have some influence on the roll of the ball and its ability to create proper pin and ball deflection patterns. To compound the subject of equipment selection and adjustment even further, we must consider lane conditions, the five strike lines and related angles, and the different types of ball releases and deliveries.

We cannot make you an expert on all aspects of equipment selection and adjustment in this section. We can, however, help you understand some of the fundamentals of equipment adjustments, and make it easier for you to *communicate with an expert ball driller.* Armed with this information, you should be able to get the best equipment, properly fitted and matched to your style of bowling. You should be able to avoid many errors associated with bowling equipment.

Most of the material in this section assumes that you roll a curve or hook ball. If you roll a straight ball you can still benefit from much of the material, especially on ball fit, ball surfaces, etc. You may decide to convert to a hook or curve delivery at a later time. In fact, the availability of so many equipment adjustment techniques to those who roll a curve or hook ball should be a further incentive to convert to one of those styles of bowling.

If you roll a backup, then you should refer to the equipment section for the right handed bowler, SECTION 4. As previously mentioned and discussed in more detail in (SECTION 8, DELIVERY ADJUSTMENTS), we suggest that you use the 1-3 pocket for strikes and roll the ball as a right hander would roll it. Therefore, you should read the material on equipment adjustments as though you were right handed. All translations of the material will have been made for you, and it should be possible for you to take advantage of these equipment adjustment techniques.

Lists of ball *surface,* ball *balance,* and ball *fit* terms have been prepared for each appropriate section. These terms are part of an extensive strike-related glossary of terms appearing in this book. Appendix A includes additional terms to assist you in learning the vocabulary related to making strikes. You might wish to review these three special lists of terms prior to reading the detailed material in this equipment adjustment section. They serve as good reference points for some of the terminology and discussion which follow. (Each list appears at the end of the related section.)

This OVERVIEW section will now continue with our discussion of *total ball weight.* Following this topic we will cover *the weight block, ball tracks,* and *axis weight,* in that order.

TOTAL BALL WEIGHT: A bowling ball will weigh from about 8 pounds to a maximum of 16 pounds after it is drilled. Most bowling balls will weight 10 pounds or more, with a majority of adult bowlers using the maximum 16 pound ball.

What weight is best for you? In general, the answer to that question is: "A ball that is as heavy as you can comfortably control during the swing and delivery stage of bowling." The two problems associated with total ball weight relate to your normal strength, and pin and ball deflection at the pin deck.

As you develop your overall strength you will be able to handle a ball of increasing total weight. Thus, young bowlers should start out with a ball that feels comfortable to them, one they can control instead of a ball that controls them. Adults should favor a ball of 15 or 16 pounds, since this weight can normally be handled by them. As you increase in age, your strength and ability to control a heavy ball begin to diminish, and you should consider using a ball of less total weight. There are no benefits, and many disadvantages to using the maximum ball weight when you are no longer able to control it properly. Change to a lower ball weight, one that you can still control.

Too many adults continue to use the maximum ball weight because they do not want others to know that their ball is less than a full 16 pounds. How foolish; scoring is bound to suffer. If you need a lighter ball, then by all means get one. You will still be able to bowl well (perhaps better) and can make other adjustments to compensate for the lighter ball. For the average bowler who must normally convert 7 spares per game, the lighter ball is almost certain to help maintain or improve his or her average. And, as for strikes, the lighter ball can be more effective since it will be rolled with more control. Let's look at some of the adjustments you can make to overcome some of the minor disadvantages of the lighter ball.

Pin deflection and ball deflection are the two major areas for consideration when you change to a lighter ball. Actually, ball deflection is of more concern, since the difference between pin deflection with a heavier or lighter ball will normally not cause you any problems. (In fact, the velocitation could be better with the lighter ball.) Ball deflection is another matter altogether.

A lighter ball will deflect more when it hits the pins, and may be deflected out of the ideal path through the pins. Therefore, as you reduce the total weight of the ball you can make a number of adjustments to keep the ball in the correct path of deflection.

Increased speed will keep the ball in the proper path of deflection. *More lift,* turn, action, etc. on the ball will keep it driving into the pocket. And it may be easier for you to put more action on a ball that you can control well. *A deeper angle* ino the pocket will also overcome the deflection problem. The use of *top or axis weight* can also give the ball more drive and reduce deflection. Any one or more of these adjustment techniques can overcome any problems with the lighter ball, and will probably cause your average to increase.

With so many adjustment techniques available to you, it makes no sense to continue using a ball that is too heavy for you to control. You will probably develop problems in your delivery, release, timing, etc. There is no merit in using a ball too heavy to control properly.

If you are *not* using a fingertip or semi-fingertip grip, then you might consider changing your span when you change to a lighter ball. You could go from a conventional grip to the semi or full fingertip. The added span will permit you to get more action on the ball, therefore giving the ball more of a chance to hold its line in the path through the pins.

In summary, the total weight of the ball is an important factor in determining how well you bowl. There is an ideal weight for you, depending upon your ability to control the ball. Find the ideal weight for you. Do not be afraid to drop to a lighter ball (or increase to a heavier ball) if that is called for. *Many people should be using a ball that weighs less than the maximum 16 pound limit.* Still others, but a lesser number, are using a ball that is too light for them, which can also cause control and deflection problems.

Take care in relying upon the stated weight found on most bowling balls. Often the ball will weigh as much as one pound *more or less* than the weight appearing on the ball. This is particularly true when you purchase a ball from any place other than a bowling center or pro shop. Have your bowling ball accurately weighed by an expert ball driller who has the correct equipment for doing this.

Increased control and comfort in delivery by having the proper ball weight could mean a significant increase in scoring ability. This is particularly important on spare leaves, where accuracy and not action (pin or ball deflection) is the key to success. Continue to assess the total weight of your bowling ball to determine if it is a factor contributing to your success or lack of success. Be ready to change to a heavier or lighter weight when the change is needed. Your scores should improve, and you will have added another valuable technique to your adjustment arsenal.

THE WEIGHT BLOCK: Thumb and finger holes must be drilled into the top half of the ball. It is illegal to drill holes into the bottom of the ball, opposite the manufacturer's mark. Such a ball could not be used in sanctioned competition. Since holes represent weight taken out of the top half of the ball, the manufacturing process has to make the top half of the ball initially weigh more than the bottom half. To do this, a weight block of some type is used.

Exhibit 7-1 illustrates the form or shape that a weight block might take. Other forms and shapes are used, but these illustrate some of the more common types of weight blocks. In each case, *the purpose of the block is to add weight to the top half of the ball during the manufacturing operation in preparation for weight removal caused by drilling the thumb and finger holes.*

To get this additional top weight, the ball is manufactured with an added portion of material which weighs more than the normal substance from which the core of the ball is made. The size, shape, location, etc. of the weight block will vary from manufacturer to manufacturer. There will be more research into the impact of weight blocks of various sizes, shapes, and locations (multiple weight blocks) within the top half of the ball. However, the purpose of the additional weight provided by the block or blocks will remain essentially the same, to make the top half of the ball weigh more than the bottom half in preparation for drilling, and to stabilize the roll of the ball.

If the top and bottom halves weighed exactly the same prior to drilling, then after drilling the bottom half would always weigh more than the top.

Ball drilling experts agree that top weight may be desirable to cause the ball to react differently (and beneficially) on the lane. Bottom weight, on the other hand, is considered an undesirable situation. Therefore, weight blocks will continue to provide sufficient additional top weight to more than compensate for the weight loss due to drilling the thumb and finger holes. The result will be excess top weight after drilling.

Drilling the holes with reference to this excess top weight is what causes ball balance (or imbalance, if you prefer) situations. Holes that are drilled close to the excess top weight have the least imbalance. Holes that are drilled away from the excess weight have the most imbalance. Imbalance is created by removing weight from the ball, not by adding weight anywhere. *Weight blocks give you the opportunity to create ball imbalances.*

BALL TRACKS: As the ball rolls down the lane, only a small portion of the surface of the ball actually comes into contact with the lane. That portion of the ball which touches the lane will, over

EXHIBIT 7-1
Four Examples of Weight Blocks

Weight blocks provide excess top weight. When the thumb and finger holes are drilled (removing some top weight) the top portion of the ball will still weigh as much as or more than the bottom half. Excess top weight may be very desirable, but excess bottom weight is rarely used.

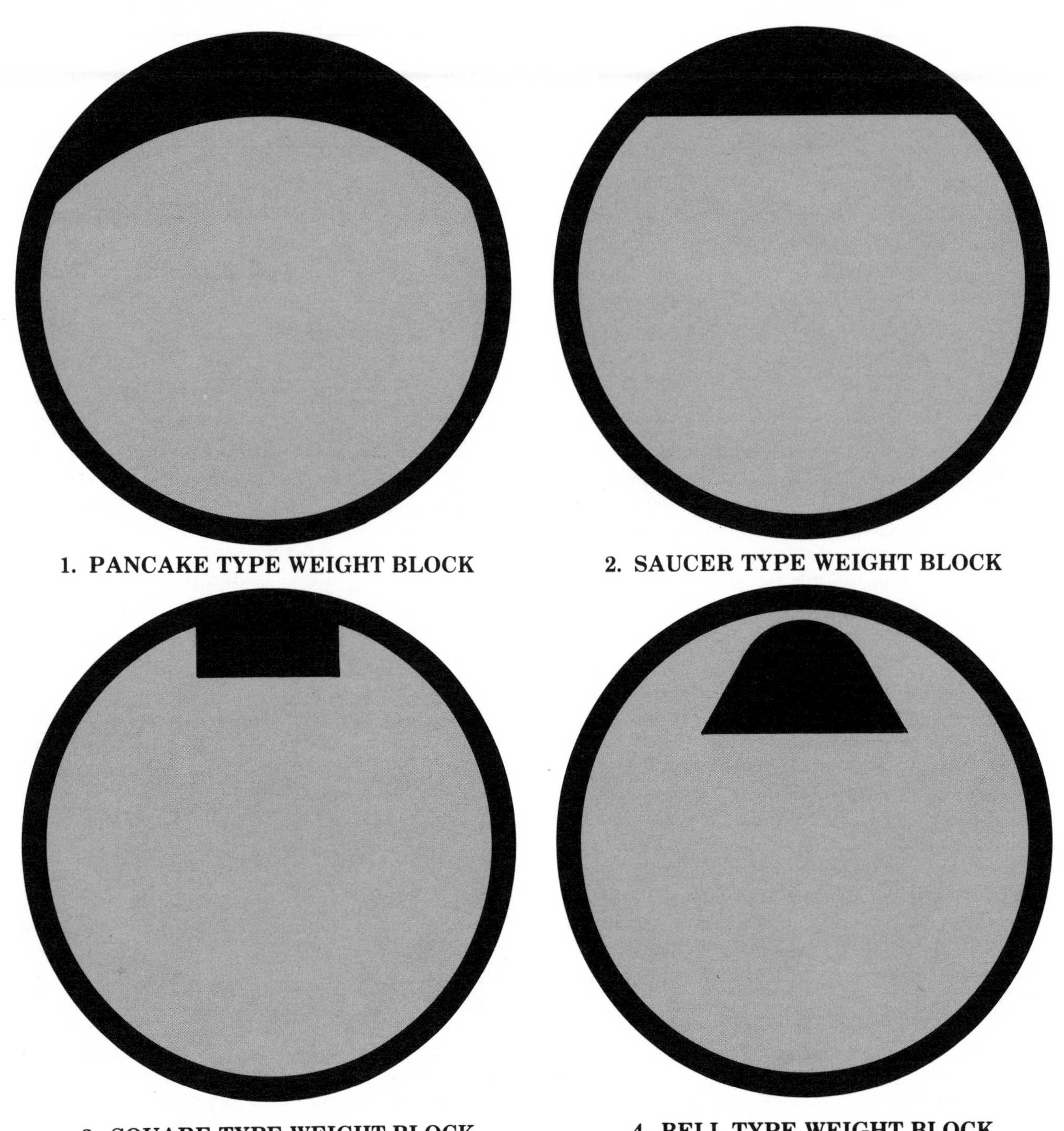

time, scratch a ring or circle around the entire ball, or some smaller portion of the circumference. *This circle or ring of wear is called a ball track.*

You can readily see the ball track by looking closely at the surface of the ball. A narrow ball track indicates a steady consistent ball release. A wide ball track indicates just the opposite situation.

Each pattern of scratch marks or tracking identifies a certain type of ball roll. With some ball tracks the ball rolls around the entire circumference of the ball. With other ball tracks, only a very small circle is created.

What is the significance of the ball track? Each type of ball track indicates how the ball might react on the way to the pins, and what impact the ball may have in terms of pin carry, ball deflection, etc. The ball track is also related to the utility of ball weights and imbalances. A given amount of ball imbalance will have more or less impact on ball roll, depending upon where the imbalance is located relative to the ball track.

Some ball tracks are more effective than others. Therefore, a knowledge of ball tracks will give you some idea of the potential scoring effectiveness of the ball. We will review the impact of each ball track on the action of the ball.

Over the years ball tracks have been called by various names, such as the full roller, high roller, 3/4 roller, spinner, etc. Very little standardization exists in the names and means for distinguishing one ball track from another.

Bill Taylor, author of many bowling publications, has attempted to develop a set of standards for determining the measurements which define the most common types of ball tracks. His purpose is "to attempt to standardize the definitions for efficiency and accuracy in the exchange of information regarding bowling ball tracks." (From *Balance,* by Bill Taylor, referenced in Appendix C. This is an excellent book containing enormous detail on ball balance, ball tracks, and many other concepts for the serious bowler.)

Exhibit 7-2 contains the chart for standardization of ball tracks by name, size, description, and other characteristics separating one ball track from another. This chart was developed by Bill Taylor, and represents the best attempt at standardization of ball track terminology that the authors have seen.

In the following material, we will describe the characteristics of the five types of ball tracks, and identify the scoring effectiveness of each one. We will also relate the use of top weight (sometimes called label weight) to the tracks, in addition to discussing lane conditions related to ball tracks. *In SECTION 8 we will outline types of releases which produce each type of ball track.*

The five ball tracks are, by name: *full roller, high roller, low roller, high spinner,* and *low spinner.* Each name is descriptive, indicating in descending order the percentage of the circumference of the ball covered by the track, as indicated in Exhibit 7-2. The *spherical diameter* of the full roller is 13½ inches, or a ball track that covers the entire circumference of the ball. On the other hand, the spherical diameter of the low spinner is the smallest of the five ball tracks, only 7½ inches. (Spherical diameter is measured by a tape measure across the full diameter of the track, and is curved by the shape of the ball. See Exhibit 7-2.)

The total distance between the ball track and the thumb and finger holes is another identifying characteristic separating the five tracks. These two dimensions, spherical diameter and distance from the thumb and finger holes, are the most important elements in separating one type of ball track from another.

Before discussing each type of track separately, it is important to keep in mind one essential element of ball balance (or imbalance) as it relates to ball tracks. The closer the ball imbalance is to the ball track the LESS effect it has on ball action. The further away from the ball track the imbalance is, the MORE effect on ball performance you can get. This relationship will become clearer after you read the material regarding BALL BALANCE ADJUSTMENTS. The usefulness of weights and balances is dependent upon the type of ball track.

The following paragraphs will only summarize the essential features and potential scoring effectiveness of the five types of ball tracks. If you wish to read a great deal more about each one, we refer you to *Balance* by Bill Taylor as referenced in Appendix C.

The Full Roller (Spherical Diameter of 13½ inches). This ball track has the largest spherical diameter of the five types of tracks. It travels between the thumb and fingers, and covers the full circumference of the ball. Traction is good on the full roller, but it is not possible to get any real benefit from the use of top or label weight with this ball track. The full roller normally does not get many ball revolutions and is inferior to some of the other ball tracks in this respect.

The High Roller (Spherical Diameter of 12 inches). This is the second largest of the ball tracks, and has been called by various other names in different parts of the country. Semi-roller, three quarter-roller, and high three-quarter-roller are some of the more common names. They suggest that the ball track covers approximately three fourths of the circumference of the ball. Because the track of the high roller does not intersect the top of the ball, and

EXHIBIT 7-2
Standardization of Ball Tracks (Left Handed Bowlers)

This chart represents an attempt to standardize the terminology of bowling ball tracks for left handed bowlers. It provides illustrations and descriptions of the five major types of ball tracks. It also characterizes each one by name, spherical diameter, angle of the ball track to the lane, distance between ball track and thumb and finger holes, and other pertinent features of each type of ball track.

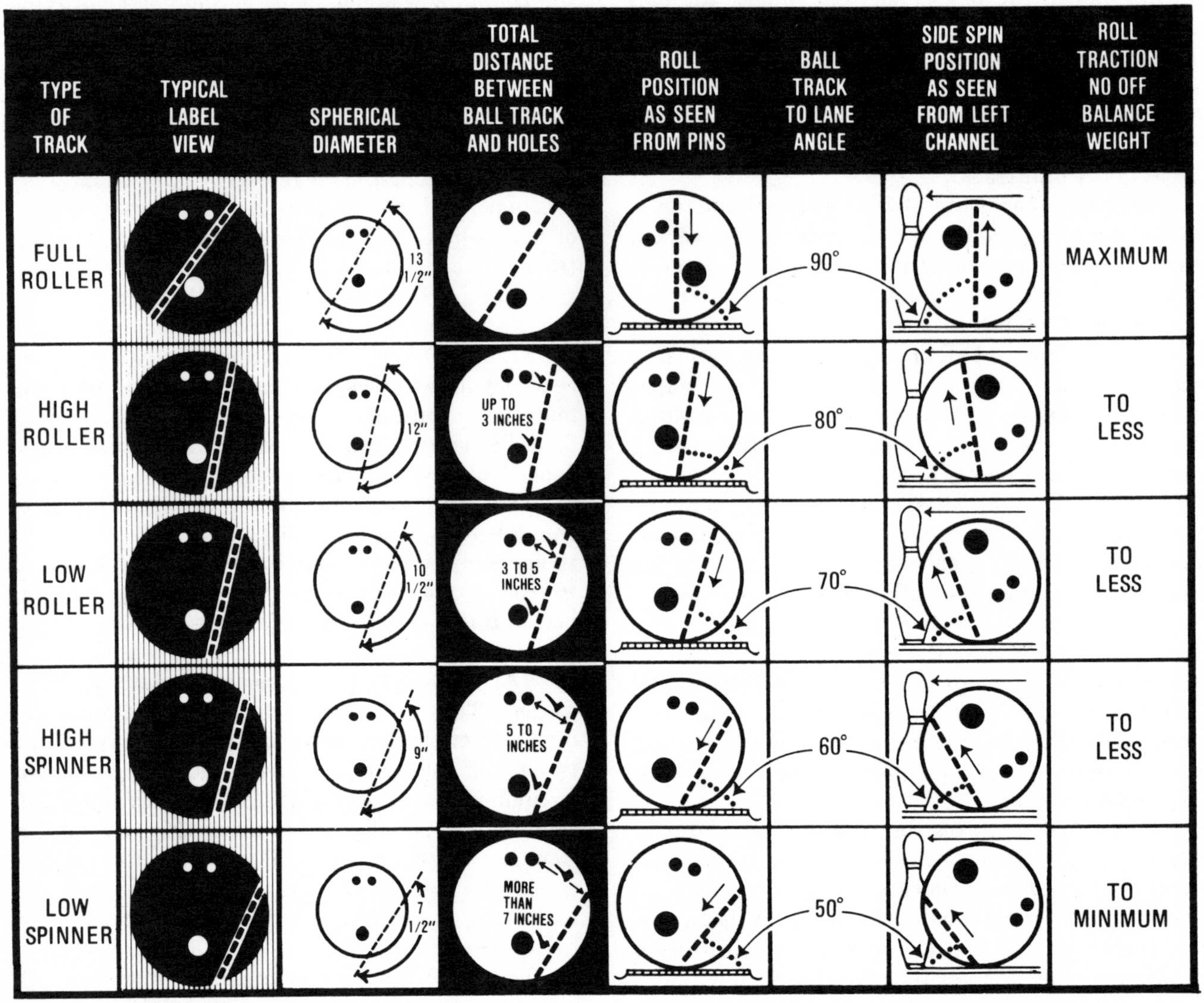

TYPE OF TRACK	TYPICAL LABEL VIEW	SPHERICAL DIAMETER	TOTAL DISTANCE BETWEEN BALL TRACK AND HOLES	ROLL POSITION AS SEEN FROM PINS	BALL TRACK TO LANE ANGLE	SIDE SPIN POSITION AS SEEN FROM LEFT CHANNEL	ROLL TRACTION NO OFF BALANCE WEIGHT
FULL ROLLER		13 1/2"			90°		MAXIMUM
HIGH ROLLER		12"	UP TO 3 INCHES		80°		TO LESS
LOW ROLLER		10 1/2"	3 TO 5 INCHES		70°		TO LESS
HIGH SPINNER		9"	5 TO 7 INCHES		60°		TO LESS
LOW SPINNER		7 1/2"	MORE THAN 7 INCHES		50°		TO MINIMUM

SOURCE: from *Balance,* by Bill Taylor. (Reproduced by permission.) For more details on this very useful book, consult the material in Appendix C.

misses the weight block area by more than an inch, it is possible to use top weight to affect the hooking of the ball. Since the track is relatively close to the fingers, top weight can be used to provide a relatively stable or steady path into the pins. Many top average bowlers effectively use the high roller ball track.

The Low Roller (Spherical Diameter of 10 to 11 inches). The next smallest ball track is the low roller, which tracks closer to the thumb but further away from the fingers. It is also called by names similar to the ball track we have labeled the High Roller, such as: the semi-roller and the three-quarter roller. Since the ball track is still further away from the top center portion of the ball, weight imbalances can be used with the low roller even more effectively than either the full or high rollers. However, the effect of the weight imbalance is less steady, and creates more of a *wobble and loping action,* as the imbalance revolves around the ball. As top weight gets further away from the ball track, the impact is greater as we have indicated, but the roll is less steady. The low roller can be used very effectively for many types of lane conditions, but is perhaps best from these three strike lines: inside line, second arrow line, and outside line.

The High Spinner (Spherical Diameter of 9 inches). The next smallest ball track, next to last of the five, is the high spinner. This ball track has also been called the semi-spinner, meaning it is near to the low spinner, but not quite there. Top weight can be used to advantage with the high spinner, and this type of ball track can be used effectively on most strike lines, but particularly on the deep inside and deep outside strike lines. Many high average bowlers use the high spinner ball track.

The Low Spinner (Spherical Diameter of 7 to 8 inches). This ball track is located farther away from the center of the ball than any of the other four tracks. It is not a very effective track to roll because of the poor traction it has with the lane. Negative weight imbalances might help the low spinner go into an effective roll. However, on normally conditioned lanes the pocket effectiveness of this ball track is not very good. The low spinner could be useful on very dry lanes where it can get good traction.

In summary, the most prevalent ball tracks are the high roller, the low roller, and the high spinner. These ball tracks allow you to use top weight (or axis weight) to increase the effectiveness of the ball. Yet the traction with the lane is still good. With the full roller, traction is better than with any other ball track, but you cannot use top weight or axis weight effectively to affect the roll and hooking power of the ball. With the low spinner, traction is greatly reduced as the ball spins down the lane.

Your ball track indicates your normal, natural release of the ball. Check your ball track. What kind is it? Is it the best for the conditions upon which you normally play? Perhaps your local ball driller or instructor can tell you whether your *ball track* and *ball balance* are helping or hindering your scoring potential. (SECTION 8 will show the release changes which create the various ball tracks.)

Speaking of ball balance, we will now discuss one of the two methods for creating ball imbalances to assist you in scoring: *axis* weight. Following this discussion of axis weight we will begin a lengthy discussion of the second way to create ball imbalances: *top* weight. But now let us look at axis weight.

AXIS WEIGHT: A bowling ball will rotate around an axis line roughly perpendicular to the ball track (at a 90 degree angle, and passing through the center of the ball). By drilling a hole somewhere along this axis line, you can create an imbalance in the ball on the side opposite the hole. This imbalance can influence the roll of the ball, the timing of the curve or hook, and the deflection pattern after it hits the pocket. Exhibit 7-3 gives three illustrations of axis weight, and shows the 90 degree relationship between the ball track and the axis line.

Axis weight is one of the two most common forms of creating ball imbalances. The other method is top (label) weight, which will be discussed later in this section on equipment adjustments. Both methods are designed to affect the timing and amount of curve and to have the proper strength when entering the pocket to maintain an ideal path of deflection through the pins.

The major advantage claimed by advocates of axis weight is that you can get the imbalance as far away from the track as possible, and therefore you can get the maximum influence from a given imbalance condition. As you will recall in our previous discussion on ball tracks, the influence of any imbalance is increased as the imbalance gets further away from the ball track. In label or top weight imbalancing, it is not possible to get the imbalance very far away from the ball track when that track is close to the label weight (weight block). This situation is particularly evident in the full roller and high roller, which run across the weight block (full roller) and very close to it (high roller).

Another advantage to axis weight is that you can create it *after* the thumb and finger holes have been drilled. With label weight, you create the imbalance by positioning the thumb and finger holes relative to the weight block. Of course, you can take into consideration placement of the thumb and finger holes in preparation for creating axis weight. For example, you can create 2 ounces of right side weight by drilling the holes to the left of the weight

EXHIBIT 7-3
(LHB) Illustrations of Axis Weight

A bowling ball rotates around an axis line roughly perpendicular to the ball track, and passing through the center of the ball. By drilling a hole along this line, you can create an imbalance on the side of the ball that is opposite of that hole. This imbalance can influence the roll of the ball and the pattern of deflection after it hits the pins.

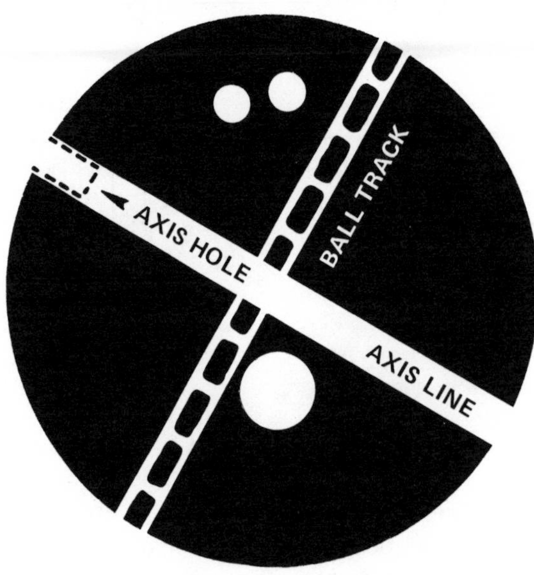

A. FULL ROLLER

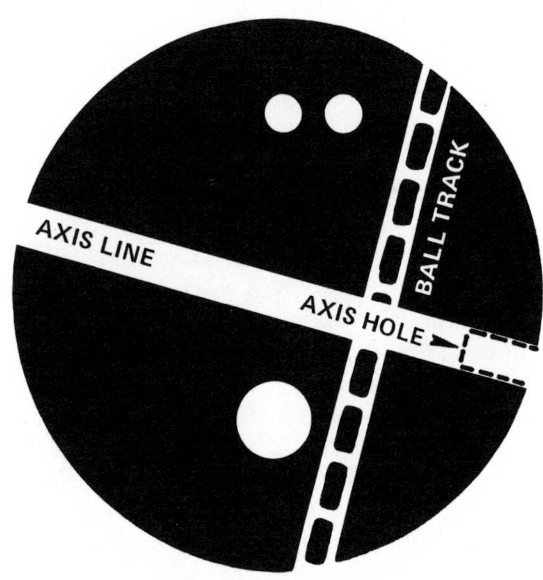

B. HIGH ROLLER

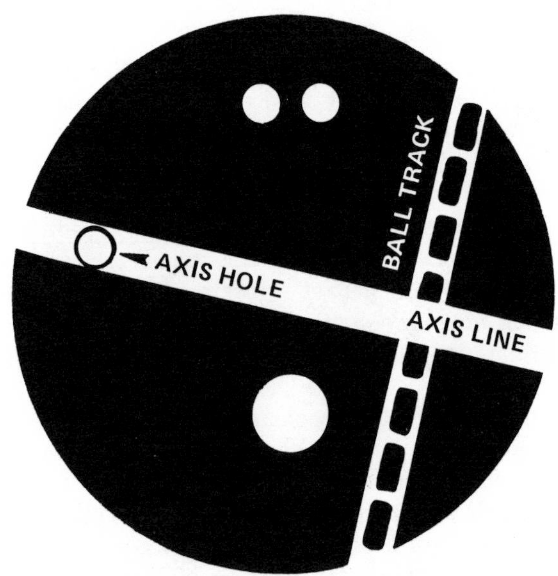

C. HIGH SPINNER

block, and then take 1½ ounces out of the right side to leave only ½ ounce of right side weight completely away from the ball track.

There are an enormous number of ways to create axis weight. Placement of the thumb and finger holes relative to the ball's weight block, combined with holes of various sizes along the axis line, make for limitless possibilities for creating axis weight. Of course, only one axis line hole would be legal in a ball, but through experimentation you could find the best axis weight for your style and ball track. Simply drill one axis hole; try it; and if it is not right plug it and drill another one. Eventually you will find what is best for you. Notice that you are not changing the thumb and finger holes, although you could do so.

Both label (top) weight and axis weight techniques have their advocates. Both methods for creating ball imbalances, to influence curve and deflection patterns, have their advantages. And both methods can be used in conjunction with one another to get the benefits of each.

This concludes the OVERVIEW section of equipment adjustments for the left handed bowler. We have discussed total ball weight, the weight block, ball tracks, and axis weight in preparation for the discussion of the three major types of equipment adjustment techniques. We begin that discussion with BALL BALANCE ADJUSTMENTS.

BALL BALANCE ADJUSTMENTS
(*Left Handed Bowlers*)

"Ball weights and balances will only work for you if you are a consistent shooter," Larry Lichstein, PBA Player Services Director.

After a bowling ball has been drilled, it must be subjected to a set of tests to determine if it falls within acceptable limits of ball imbalance. These tolerance limits determine what equipment can and cannot be used in sanctioned league and professional competition.

Two sets of weight or imbalance tolerance levels have been established: one set applies to bowling balls weighing 10 pounds or more, and the other applies to those weighing less than 10 pounds. Maximum ball weight is, of course, limited to 16 pounds.

Exhibit 7-4 illustrates maximum ball weights and imbalances for both the lighter (under 10 pounds) and heavier bowling balls. Briefly, limits for a ball weighing 10 to 16 pounds are:

A) The top half of the bowling ball cannot weigh more than 3 ounces heavier than the bottom half. Or conversely, the bottom half of the ball cannot be more than 3 ounces heavier than the top portion.
B) The weight of the left side of the ball cannot exceed the weight of the right side by more than 1 ounce, or vice versa.
C) The front half of the ball (the finger hole portion) cannot exceed the back half of the ball (thumb hole portion) by more than 1 ounce, or vice versa.

If the ball weighs less than 10 pounds, then the side portions (item B) and the front and back portions (item C) cannot differ by more than ¾ ounce, instead of the 1 ounce tolerance permitted for the heavier ball. The top and bottom imbalances are still the same 3 ounces.

A ball that exceeds these imbalance limitations would be declared illegal for use in sanctioned competition. Within these established maximums, or ranges, a multitude of imbalance situations could be created by positioning the thumb and finger holes at various locations on top of the ball.

You could, for example, have 2 ounces of top weight, ¼ ounce of finger weight, and ½ ounce of left side weight. Or, you could drill the ball to create this imbalance situation: 3 ounces of top weight, ¾ ounce of thumb weight, and 1 full ounce of right side weight. The variations are enormous, since normal imbalances are created by *fractions of an ounce*.

How do you get these imbalance situations? Why would you decide to have a particular imbalanced ball situation after drilling? To answer these very important questions, we will have to study top weight, look at ways to create various types of ball imbalances, and determine what each type means in terms of the action or reaction of the ball on the lane. First we will discuss top weight.

Top Weight: If the top half of the ball weighs more than the bottom half, the ball is said to contain top weight. For a ball to have top weight *after* drilling, excess weight must be in the top half of the ball which is greater than the weight removed by drilling the thumb and finger holes. Maximum allowable top weight *after drilling* is 3 ounces.

The impact of top weight, as with all other imbalance conditions, is largely dependent upon the type of ball track you use. The closer the imbalance is to the ball track, the less influence it has on the ball. The further away from the track it is located, the more impact it has.

For the full roller, with a ball track around the circumference of the ball, top weight will have very little effect on ball roll. The track goes directly across the weight block. The ball may tend to pulsate or oscillate (wobble) as the top half of the ball rotates on its roll down the lanes.

As the track moves away from the full roller type, toward high roller and then spinner, the impact of top weight is increased. Top weight will cause the ball to hook slightly more than will the absence of such an imbalance condition. This may cause the ball to break sooner, getting up to the pocket more than another ball without top weight. Such an imbalance would be favorable under lane conditions where the ball was breaking too far down the lane.

EXHIBIT 7-4
(LHB) Maximum Ball Weight and Balance Tolerances

After a ball is drilled, it must meet certain weight and balance standards, or it will be declared illegal for sanctioned competition. The indicated weights are for bowling balls weighing 10 or more pounds. Those weighing less than 10 pounds permit only ¾ ounce tolerance each place the chart shows 1 ounce.

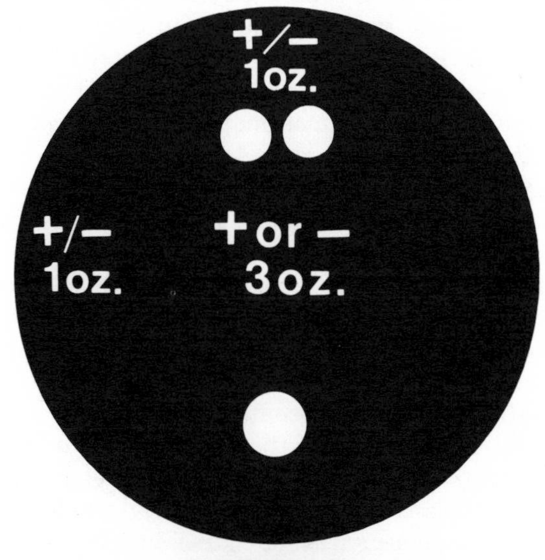

TOP weight can be plus or minus 3 ounces.

LEFT or RIGHT SIDE weight can be plus or minus 1 ounce.

FINGER or THUMB weight can be plus or minus 1 ounce.

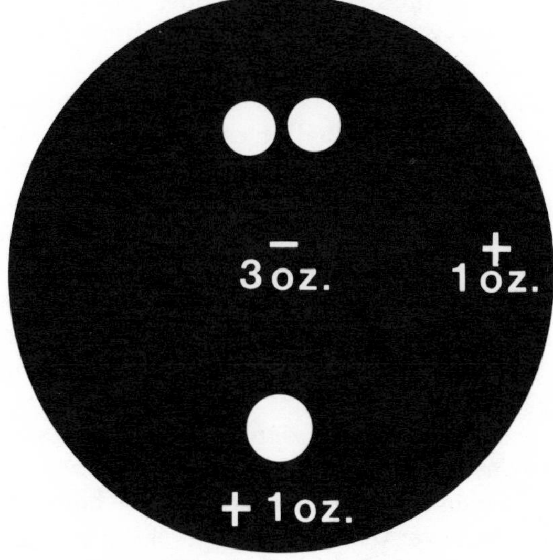

NEGATIVE WEIGHTS

The maximum imbalance permitted to cause the ball to begin the roll sooner and to curve less are:

3 ounces of bottom weight
1 ounce of thumb weight
1 ounce of right side weight

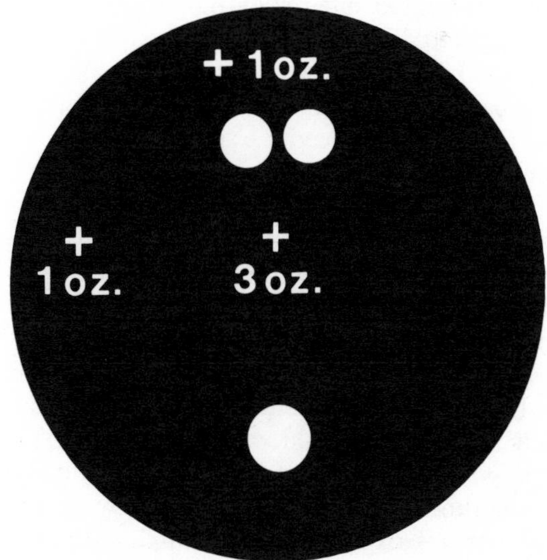

POSITIVE WEIGHTS

The maximum imbalance permitted to cause the ball to curve more and to deflect less are:

3 ounces of top weight
1 ounce of finger weight
1 ounce of left side weight

Of course, excess top weight might cause the ball to begin its break too soon, therefore losing some of its power upon impact with the pins, or causing the ball to cross over to the brooklyn side if the hook is too strong.

Top weight is a *source* of the other types of weight imbalances we will be discussing, such as finger or thumb weight, left or right side weight, etc. Many people are under the impression that there are three kinds of weight imbalances: side weight, finger weight, and thumb weight. But, top weight is a *source* of all three of these imbalance conditions. Without top weight there would be no side, finger, or thumb weight imbalances. This concept should become clearer as the section on weights and balances progresses, but let us digress for a minute to cover this idea in more specific terms. Later discussions might be more understandable after this explanation of how weight imbalances are created.

Imagine that the ball could be weighed in various segments: the top half versus the bottom half; the left side and the right side; the front half (where the finger holes are drilled) and the back half (where the thumb hole is located). In fact, *the ball can be weighed in such a manner.*

Now, if you remove any portion of the ball (as you do when you drill into it), an imbalance is created. Those portions of the ball where the holes are drilled will weigh less than the side of the ball opposite from the holes. This is how imbalance conditions are created: by removing weight from one section of the ball, you cause the opposite section to be heavier *by comparison.*

If a ball is perfectly balanced prior to drilling, that is, the center of gravity of the ball is exactly in the center of the ball, then all portions of the ball would weigh equally. The top and bottom half would weigh the same. The left and right side would weigh equally, and the finger and thumb portions of the ball (front and back) would also weigh equally.

After drilling our perfectly balanced ball, the ball's center of gravity would be located somewhere other than the absolute center of the ball. And, the portions of the ball would weigh unequally. Those portions with holes drilled into them would weigh less than those still undrilled. The new center of gravity of the ball could then be defined with reference to the previous center of the ball.

Three measurements or directions are needed to locate the *new center of gravity* of the ball. From the center of the ball you would measure: either up or down (top or bottom); left or right (the two sides of the ball) and front or back (finger or thumb portion). These three dimensions, these three directions, describe where the new center of gravity of the ball is located. Up or down, front or back, and left or right side. This is why many people think there are three types of imbalance conditions: *to locate the center of gravity of a drilled ball requires three measurements or directions.*

A ball that has a center of gravity at the absolute center of the ball will roll relatively true, in a straight direction. One that is imbalanced will not roll in such a manner, but will tend to roll in the direction of the imbalance. A bowling ball that is rolling will tend to favor the portion of the ball that has the center of gravity, the imbalance. Knowing this reaction pattern of an unbalanced ball, we are able to create such conditions and use them in our adjustments to various lane conditions. (For more details on this concept of center of gravity, and for the concept of the bowling ball as a functioning gyroscope when it is in motion, please see *Balance,* by Bill Taylor, as indicated in Appendix C.

Top weight alone would mean that the center of gravity of the ball is straight up from the exact center of the ball, and not toward either side or front or back. *Finger weight* means the center of gravity is up toward the top half of the ball and then forward toward the portion of the ball in which the finger holes are drilled. *Thumb weight* is the opposite of finger weight, with the center of gravity toward the top and back portion of the ball. *Right side weight* is an imbalance condition where the center of gravity of the ball is toward the top and right side of the ball. *Left side weight* is, of course, just the opposite condition, up and to the left side. *Bottom weight* means the center of gravity is down from the exact center of the ball.

Another way to look at these imbalance situations is to look at the ball in sections, comparing the relative weight of each section. *Top weight* means the top half of the ball weighs more than the bottom half. *Finger weight* means the half of the ball containing the finger holes weighs more than the half containing the thumb hole. *Left side weight* means the left half of the ball weighs more than the right half. *Right side weight* means the right side weighs more than the left side.

Placement of the thumb and finger holes determines the weight imbalance of a drilled ball. Since there is wide latitude as to where these holes can be drilled, and over the *initial weight* of the ball, a wide range of imbalance conditions can be created. Some imbalances will be favorable or unfavorable, depending upon the ball track, lane conditions, type of delivery, etc. This section looks at the various types of imbalances and the effect each has on the action of the ball.

Bottom Weight: Any discussion of top weight is by its very nature a discussion of bottom weight. A change to either the top or bottom half of the ball affects the other half. Taking weight out of the top half will change the *relative* difference between the two halves. If, after drilling the thumb and finger holes, the bottom half of the ball weighs more than the top half, then bottom weight exists.

Such a condition will only occur when the *initial* excess weight of the top half of the ball does *not* exceed the weight of the material removed in the drilling operation. For example, if the top half weighs 2 ounces more than the bottom half of the ball, and 2½ ounces are drilled out for the thumb and fingers, then the bottom half will be ½ ounce heavier than the top half. Bottom weight, excess bottom weight, will exist.

The maximum allowable bottom weight is 3 ounces, just as the top half cannot weigh over 3 ounces more than the bottom. And what is the value of bottom weight? There are no known advantages to having excess bottom weight, although this situation could change in the future as ball drilling and weights and balances are explored further. Bottom weight is rarely drilled intentionally; it usually happens by mistake. This occurs when the top and bottom halves of the ball *initially* are about equal in weight, prior to drilling.

It is currently illegal to drill into the bottom half of the ball. And virtually all bowling balls contain excess top weight (the weight block) when they are manufactured. Therefore, when the thumb and finger holes are drilled, excess top weight will exist, and not excess bottom weight.

Finger Weight: This weight imbalance is created when that portion of the ball into which the finger holes are drilled (often called the *front* of the ball) weighs more than the portion containing the thumb hole (often called the *back* of the ball). To create this type of ball imbalance, it is necessary to drill the finger holes close to the weight block. Or, stated differently, the thumb hole is drilled further away from the weight block.

As you may recall, to create excess weight in one portion of the ball it is necessary to remove weight from the opposite portion. Since thumb weight is opposite of finger weight, drilling the finger holes closer to the weight block places these holes closer to the thumb or back side of the ball. Therefore, excess weight is created in the finger portion.

This concept is illustrated on Exhibit 7-5. It shows that excess weight is created by the positioning of the thumb and finger holes relative to the center of gravity of the ball, which is somewhere near the weight block. All weight imbalances, in reality, are only changes in the center of gravity. In a perfectly balanced bowling ball, the center of gravity would be the exact center of the ball.

The maximum amount of allowable finger weight is 1 ounce for 10 to 16 pound bowling balls, and ¾ ounce for those weighing less than 10 pounds. But, what is the impact or utility of having a ball with excess finger weight? It causes the ball to hook or curve slightly more than if the weight were perfectly centered. This means that the ball may start to roll and break to the pocket later, but it will drive stronger into the pocket. The ball is less likely to be deflected out of its path through the pins. If, however, the roll or break begins too soon, then the ball may lose some of its drive upon reaching the pin deck. It will have *rolled out.*

Of course, the impact of a given amount of finger weight (for example, ½ or ¾ ounce) is dependent upon the ball track you use. As the ball track moves further away from the full roller (to the low spinner), the impact of finger weight increases. With the full roller, finger weight has little or no significant impact on ball roll.

Thumb Weight: Thumb weight is just the opposite in impact of finger weight. It is created by drilling the thumb hole close to or into the weight block, near the manufacturer's label.

The maximum legal thumb weight is 1 ounce for bowling balls weighing 10 to 16 pounds, and only ¾ ounce for those weighing less than 10 pounds. The impact of this imbalance is still dependent upon its position relative to the ball track.

As a general rule, thumb weight will cause the ball to curve sooner, to hook less, and deflect more. Such an equipment adjustment would be helpful when the lane is dry and hooking strongly. It is the type of adjustment to get the ball back to the pocket when the lane is taking the ball too strongly to the left.

Often thumb weight will be combined with other types of negative weight imbalances, such as right side and bottom weight. *The ultimate influence on ball action would be the sum of the combined negative weights.*

Left Side Weight: You can create another ball imbalance, left side weight, by drilling the thumb and finger holes in a certain location relative to the weight block.

By drilling the holes more toward the right side of the ball, excess weight will result in the opposite or left side. The maximum allowable left side weight is 1 ounce for 10 to 16 pound bowling balls, and ¾ ounce for those weighing under 10 pounds.

The effect of this aspect of positive weight is to cause the ball to skid more before it starts to break for the pocket. Also, the hook will be stronger than if no left side weight imbalance existed. The overall result is a ball that will bring you up to the pocket after left side hits.

The effect of left side weight is still dependent

EXHIBIT 7-5

(LHB) Creating Finger, Thumb, Left and Right Side Weight

The location of the thumb and finger holes relative to the weight block determines what ball imbalance is created. Removing weight by drilling into one portion of the ball shifts the center of gravity of the ball toward the opposite portion. The impact or utility of a given amount of ball imbalance is largely determined by the location of the imbalance relative to the ball track. One ounce of imbalance near the ball track has less impact on ball roll and deflection than an ounce further away.

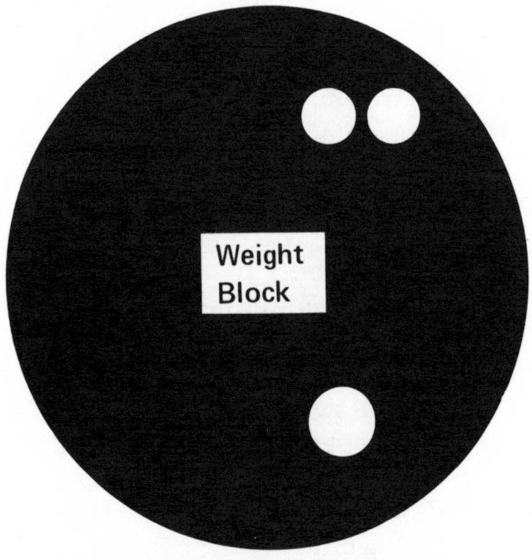

1. LEFT SIDE WEIGHT IMBALANCE

2. RIGHT SIDE WEIGHT IMBALANCE

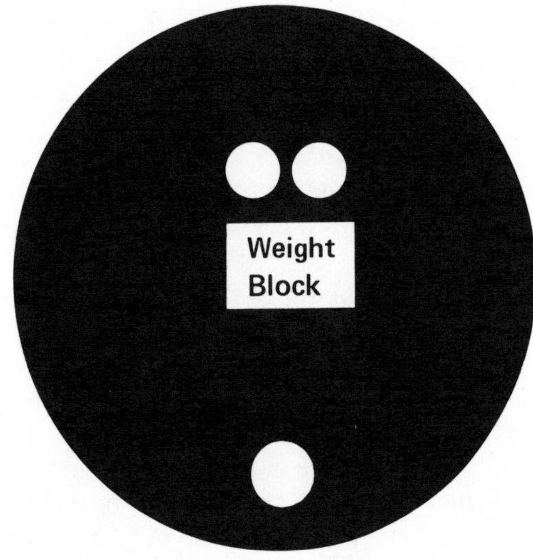

3. FINGER WEIGHT IMBALANCE

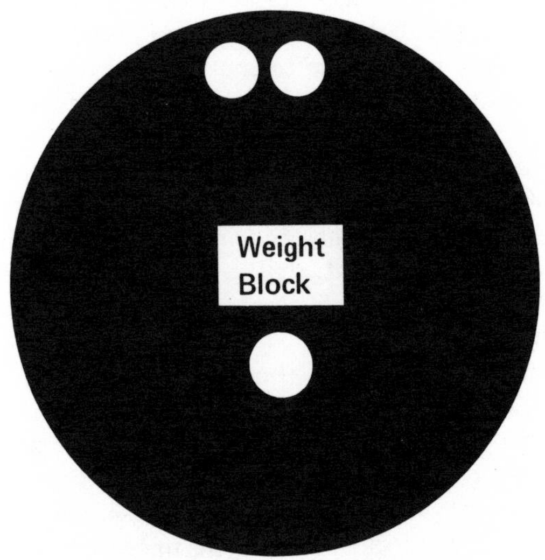

4. THUMB WEIGHT IMBALANCE

upon the nature of the ball track you use. The further away from the ball track the imbalance is located, the more impact left side weight will have.

Positive weight is a term associated with excess left side weight. The term actually refers to three types of ball imbalances: *top* weight, *left* side weight, and *finger* weight. These imbalances are grouped together since the impact of each is similar. All cause the ball to skid more and to delay the point at which the ball starts to roll. The ball curves more and deflects less at the pocket.

Right Side Weight: The last of our six ball imbalance situations is right side weight. Obviously the utility of this imbalance is just the opposite of left side weight. By drilling the holes more toward the left side of the ball, right side weight is created.

The maximum legally allowable right side weight is 1 ounce for bowling balls weighing 10 to 16 pounds, and ¾ ounce for those weighing less than 10 pounds.

The effect of this type of *negative weight* is to cause the ball to skid less, begin its break to the pocket sooner, and break less strongly toward the pocket. All of these adjustments are designed to get the ball back to the pocket after high or crossover hits. The effect of right side imbalance is lessened as the ball track moves from a full roller to a spinner.

Negative Weight is a term associated with excess right side weight. The term actually refers to three types of ball imbalances: *right* side weight, *thumb* weight, and *bottom* weight. These imbalances are grouped together since the impact of each one is similar. All cause the ball to skid less, begin to roll sooner, curve less and deflect more. This group of imbalances is, quite obviously, just the opposite from the positive imbalances previously discussed under left side weight.

This concludes our discussion of weight and balance adjustments. Exhibit 7-6 summarizes many of the concepts relating to this type of equipment adjustment technique.

EXHIBIT 7-6
(LHB) Ball Balance Terms

Ball weight: Refers to the total weight of the ball. The range of ball weight is from about 8 pounds to 16 pounds. Most high average bowlers use a 16 pound ball, but many also use one slightly more than 15 pounds.

Bottom weight: A ball that weighs more on the bottom half than on the top half where the thumb and finger holes are drilled.

Center of gravity: The point within the ball around which the total weight of the ball is distributed. If an undrilled ball had no weight block, then the center of gravity would be in the exact center of the ball.

Finger weight: A ball that has been drilled in such a manner that the top half of the ball weighs more than the bottom half, and the portion of the ball toward the finger holes weighs more than the portion toward the thumb hole.

Imbalance: A situation created in drilling the ball in which the center of gravity of the ball is *not* located exactly in the center of the ball.

Left side weight: A ball drilled so that the top half of the ball weighs more than the bottom half, and the side to the left of the holes (as you look at the ball) weighs more than the side to the right of the holes.

Maximum weights: The maximum imbalance allowed in a legally drilled ball. (See Exhibit 7-4 for complete details.)

Maximum weight tolerances: The outer limits (maximums) allowed in a legally drilled bowling ball. (See Exhibit 7-4 for details.)

Negative weights: Weight imbalance in these three areas: right side, thumb, and bottom (for the left handed bowler). These are defined in a different way for the right handed bowler.

Positive weights: Weight imbalances in these three areas for the left handed bowler: left side, finger, and top. The right handers' definition of positive weights are different, as explained in the appropriate section for RHB.

Right side weight: A ball drilled in such a manner that the top half of the ball weighs more than the bottom half, and the side to the right of the holes (as you look down on the ball) weighs more than the side to the left of the holes.

Side weight: A ball in which either the right side or left side contains the extra weight, in other words, the center of gravity is not in the center of the ball, but is off to the right or left.

Thumb weight: A ball that has been drilled in such a manner that the vertical half of the ball which contains the thumb hole weighs more than the half of the ball into which the finger holes are drilled.

Top weight: A ball that weighs more on the top half (where the thumb and finger holes are drilled) than the half which is opposite the holes. The top half of the ball is indicated by the label of the manufacturer.

Weight block: A segment or substance found within the ball and located in the top half of the ball which causes the top half to weigh more than the bottom half prior to drilling. This situation is created to compensate for the weight loss that occurs when the thumb and finger holes are drilled in the top half of the ball. (See Exhibit 7-1 for sample weight blocks.)

BALL SURFACE ADJUSTMENTS
(Left Handed Bowlers)

"The ball and the lane will always interact. You must select the proper ball surface to match the lane surface and conditioning."

The surface of the ball and the surface of the lane will always interact. There is nothing you can do about this interaction, except that you have some choices as to the surface hardness or softness of the ball you use. *There is a best ball surface for a given lane surface and condition, and the way you roll your ball.* Some lane conditions dictate a ball with a hard surface. Other conditions call for a softer ball surface. Reading the lanes properly will tell you which degree of hardness or softness to select. Once you have made your selection, the lane and the ball are going to interact in some manner. Your objective is to get both lane and ball surfaces working for you to get the ball into the pocket at the correct speed, angle and action to produce strikes.

Ball surfaces can generally be classified into two different but related categories: Hard Surfaces and Soft Surfaces. Of course, within each category there are varying degrees of hardness or softness. To measure the precise degree of hardness, a DUROMETER is used. This device measures the amount of pressure required to penetrate the outer shell of the ball. The more pressure required, the harder the ball; the less pressure needed, the softer the ball shell.

Legal standards have been developed for the degrees of hardness or softness that are acceptable for organized, sanctioned competition. In effect, the standard really refers to the degree of softness, since only a soft ball might be declared illegal for competition. (Of course, other factors such as weights and balances could cause the ball to be declared illegal for play.)

Ball surface standards for ABC, WIBC, WPBA, PBA, and AJBC may differ slightly, and these standards may change over time. But for sake of clarity in the subject of ball surfaces, the following exhibit gives the *general range* of relative hardness or softness of bowling ball surfaces, as indicated by the use of a durometer.

EXHIBIT 7-7
Ball Surface Hardness Classifications

Durometer Reading	Classification
Under 72	Illegal by some standards*
72-75	Very Soft
76-80	Soft
81-85	Medium
86-90	Hard
90-Above	Very Hard

*Standards of illegality differ among the organizations listed above. Check your appropriate organization to find out what lower limit is currently considered illegal!

To repeat a very important point, the above table is a *general* classification of the relative degree of hardness or softness of bowling ball surfaces. *Current rules and policies of each organization sanctioning bowling competitions should be consulted for current requirements needed to conform to legal and acceptable standards.*

Before we get into a discussion about what degree of hardness or softness is best under given lane surfaces and conditions, let's look at another way in which bowling ball surfaces are classified: (1) Rubber shell or surface, and (2) Plastic shell or surface.

It is possible to manufacture a ball of not only different material (basically plastic or rubber) but of widely varying surface characteristics, such as hardness and porosity. (More on porosity a little later.) You could, for example, have both hard and soft surfaced rubber bowling balls, and both types of surfaces in a plastic ball as well. So to compare a rubber versus a plastic ball, you must also take into consideration the surface hardness of each type. A rubber ball could be either softer or harder than a plastic ball, or vice versa. To simplify our analysis, we will discuss soft rubber and plastic surfaces first, then hard rubber and plastic.

A *soft rubber* bowling ball will, generally speaking, grip the lane more than a similar plastic ball. Therefore, when you need a ball surface that will grip the lane (when lanes are heavily oiled and more hook or roll is desired) a soft rubber ball would be the choice. Since rubber is generally softer than plastic (or is more porous) a greater portion of the ball track will contact the lane and the added friction will permit the ball to grip the lane for more hook.

A *soft plastic* bowling ball will, generally speaking, be more apt to skid further down the lane than a soft rubber ball under similar lane conditions. Therefore the hook will be delayed until the ball is closer to the pins. When the ball begins to hook it will hook less than a comparable rubber ball. The soft plastic ball should be used when lane surfaces and conditions are medium to heavily oiled.

A *hard rubber* ball will skid more and hook less than a plastic ball of similar hardness. When the lane is very lightly oiled, you might select a hard rubber ball and use a relatively straight angle down the lane.

A *hard plastic* ball, on the other hand, will skid less and hook more than a rubber ball of similar hardness. When the lane is lightly oiled, you might use a hard plastic ball and a relatively straight angle down the lane. Or, if the lane is very dry, very lightly oiled, you could use the hard plastic ball but a more open foul line angle.

Exhibit 7-8 illustrates, in general terms, the relationships that exist among hard and soft rubber and plastic ball surfaces, and the angles most likely to get the ball into the pocket under certain lane conditions.

The type of *lane surface,* in addition to the amount and pattern of *lane conditioning,* must also be taken into account when trying to select the proper ball surface to fit the playing condition. The lane surface might be of lacquer, urethane, or other artificial surface. This is the permanent aspect of the lane. *Conditioning* refers to the oil or conditioner used to prepare the lane for play. As a general rule, plastic ball surfaces react best on plastic coated lanes, and rubber ball surfaces are better for lacquer coated lanes. These are only generalizations. The hardness or softness of the surface of the ball is more important than the plastic or rubber content. And your style of bowling (as related to the ball track you generate, and other release factors) combined with the kind of lane conditions you normally find in the centers where you regularly bowl will also be determining factors. Consult a knowledgeable professional or ball driller where you bowl for more specific help on this subject. He or she can give you guidance to aid you in selecting the best ball surface to use.

The initial degree of hardness of your ball is subject to change. It is *not* a fixed, permanent condition. Of course, you could soak your ball in a variety of solutions to change the surface hardness, but such a process is both *illegal* for most competition and *extremely dangerous* to your health! What we are talking about is the effect of *temperature* and *use* on the surface hardness of the ball.

Ball *use* creates surface heat. This heat can drop the surface reading on a bowling ball. If your ball registers close to the lower end of the durometer scale (such as a 72 or 73 reading), the added heat from normal use of the ball could drop the hardness level. This might drop your ball into the illegal range if a measurement is required both before and *after* competition.

Temperature can also affect the surface hardness of the ball. Cold temperatures cause the ball hardness to rise to harder readings. Warm temperatures melt the surface of the ball and produce softer readings. This temperature effect is an important point to consider when storing your ball. Try to keep the ball stored in the same temperature range that will occur when you bowl. Keeping the ball stored in the trunk of your car for extended periods of time can affect the surface readings, and affect the interaction of the ball and lane during use. Taking the ball out of a storage place with a temperature higher or lower than you will encounter when you bowl, could cause the ball to act irregularly until the surface warms or cools to the normal bowling temperature. Keep

EXHIBIT 7-8
(LHB) Ball Surfaces and Lane Conditioning Relationships

The amount of oil suggests a given ball surface hardness or softness. Solid lines on the charts indicate the most desirable ball surface (plastic or rubber) and the degree of hardness. Dotted lines give alternative types of surfaces and hardnesses. *These are general patterns and guidelines only.*

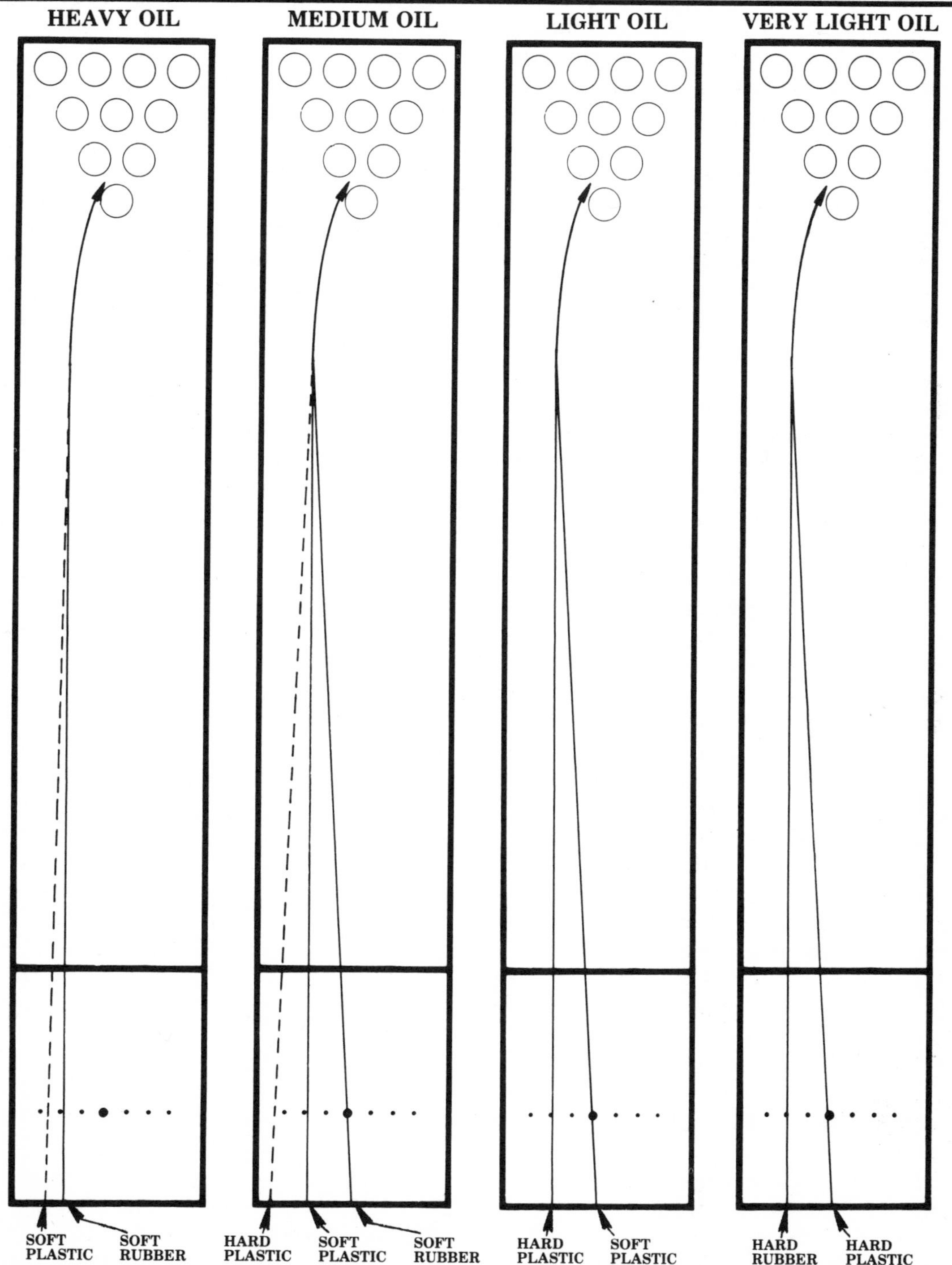

The conditions on which you normally bowl will dictate the exact type of ball surface you need. For full adjustment potential, you should have one soft and one hard surface bowling ball.

this temperature effect on the ball surface in mind at all times.

Now we can return to the concept of ball porosity mentioned before. *Porosity refers to the ability or tendency of the ball surface to absorb the oil found on the lanes.* A very porous surface will absorb more oil than a less porous surface. You will often see better bowlers cleaning the ball surface between each shot. This is one way to keep the surface of the ball as near to the same on each shot as possible. If the ball picks up oil from the lane, as it will with varying degrees of porosity, then the ball surface will be changing as you bowl. Keep the ball surface clean so you will know what the ball should do on each delivery. With a very porous surface, the ball will absorb oil in the ball track and cause the ball to act as if the lane surface were harder than it is. You should wipe the oil off the ball after each delivery. It is better and more consistent to bowl with the same surface on the ball than to have a constantly changing condition occurring as oil builds-up on the ball track.

In SUMMARY, to change the ball surface as an adjustment to certain types of lane surfaces and conditions can be very effective and beneficial. When you want the ball to hook sooner, to grab the lane sooner, to come up to the pocket, then a softer surface on the ball is the correct type of adjustment. On the other hand, when you want the ball to hook later, to grab the lane further down, to come back to the pocket, then a harder ball surface can help you.

It should be obvious at this point that, if you intend to include ball surface changes as part of your adjustment strategy and arsenal, you would be well advised to have two different bowling balls, with varying surface hardnesses—one toward the soft end of the durometer scale, and the other toward the hard end of the scale. It is not unusual for touring professional bowlers to have several types of ball surfaces from which to choose in a given tournament. The center in which they are to bowl, the surface of the lanes, plus the playing condition that has been created, all dictate which ball surface they will select for that competition.

For the once-a-week bowler, having such a large selection of equipment is not very practical. But having two bowling balls is a very good idea if you wish to have the full range of equipment adjustment options open to you. Having this additional degree of adjustment flexibility may well mean the difference between scoring that is average, or well above average. Ball surface adjustments can influence the number of strikes you get.

This concludes the discussion of Ball Surface Adjustments. Exhibit 7-9 summarizes many of the concepts relating to this type of equipment adjustment technique.

EXHIBIT 7-9
(LHB) Ball Surface Terms

Ball track: The portion of the ball surface that contacts the lane as the ball rolls toward the pin setup. The ball track is usually marked by slight scratches on the ball surface, and forms the figure of a ring around some portion of the ball surface.

Breaking-in period: Usually refers to the time required to create a ball track on the ball. The term might also refer to the time needed to get used to a newly drilled ball, especially if some change has been made in the fit, grip, pitches, etc.

Durometer: An instrument for measuring the surface hardness of a bowling ball, or other item. A durometer measures the amount of pressure needed to break the surface of the item being tested. The more pressure required, the harder the surface; the less pressure, the softer the surface.

Hard ball: A ball whose surface hardness reading registers high on the hardness scale, approaching 100. (See Rock, below.)

Hardness scale: A means of classifying ball surfaces in terms of surface hardness. A low number on the scale (such as a reading of 72) indicates a relatively soft surface. A high number on the scale (such as 90) is an indication of a harder surface. (See Illegal Ball.)

Illegal ball: A ball whose surface hardness has been declared below the level of acceptable hardness, as determined by the appropriate sanctioning organization. Such a reading is now near 72 on the hardness scale.

Plastic ball: A bowling ball constructed of a plastic type material, as opposed to one made predominantly of a rubber substance.

Porosity: The degree to which a bowling ball surface will absorb or not absorb the lane conditioner. A very porous ball will absorb the oil on the lane more readily than one with a less porous surface.

Rock: A term for a bowling ball whose surface hardness is 90 or more, indicating a very hard surface.

Rubber ball: A bowling ball constructed of a rubber type material, as opposed to one made predominantly of a plastic substance.

Soft ball: A ball whose surface hardness reading registers low on the hardness scale, generally less than 80 on the scale.

BALL FIT ADJUSTMENTS
(*Left Handed Bowlers*)

"A correctly fitted ball will feel very comfortable and allow you to release it properly."

Drilling a bowling ball is both an art and a science. The size and placement of the holes drilled into the bowling ball should feel comfortable during the swing and should permit good execution of the delivery. How the ball feels in your hand from the stance to the delivery is critical to the effectiveness of your game.

The two key terms related to ball fit are: Comfort and Release. A ball that has been measured and fitted correctly will be able to achieve both of these objectives well. If the ball is comfortable to the feel and can be held securely during the approach, it is possible to develop a natural, consistent, and well-timed delivery.

Some of the hand measurements needed to drill the ball are more related to one of these terms than to the other. That is, some aspects of ball fit are primarily designed to get the ball to feel comfortable, and to fit the structure of your hand, thumb, and fingers. Other measurements are more closely related to the type of release you wish to have, your style of bowling. This suggests still another way to look at ball fit: measurements that are *requirements* imposed by the structure of your hand, as opposed to *options* available to adapt the ball fit to your style of bowling. For example, the flexibility of the thumb (or lack of flexibility) requires you to do certain things in drilling the thumb hole. (More specifics will be given later in this section.) Yet, you can alter the forward pitch (an option) to affect the nature of your release. Another more obvious example relates to the span, the distance between the thumb and finger holes. If you choose to use a conventional grip, then the structure of the hand will determine the proper length of the span. Should you elect another type of grip, the fingertip, then the structure of the hand will again determine the length of span required. You could select either type of grip, but once you make your choice the structure of the hand determines the other measurements and adjustments needed to get the correct ball fit.

Exhibit 7-10 illustrates a sample Ball Measurement Chart giving guidelines to drill bowling balls. All of the normal measurements are indicated. Exhibit 7-16 at the end of this section on BALL FIT, gives definitions of each type of measurement. This set of definitions also covers other terms that will be used throughout this discussion of ball fit. It might be helpful to review these terms so the following material will be more meaningful to you.

The Ball Measurement Chart indicates five (5) measurement categories related to ball fit: (1) *width* of the thumb and finger holes; (2) *depth* of the holes; (3) *pitch,* or angle at which the holes are drilled into the ball; (4) *span,* or distance between the thumb and finger holes; and (5) *alignment,* or location of the holes. These five items define *ball fit.* Each one will be discussed in this section. But before that discussion, two questions need to be answered: Why is it important to understand how to fit the ball? And, what are the characteristics of a properly and improperly fitted ball?

Why is it important to understand how to fit the ball? A fundamental knowledge of ball drilling principles can be beneficial to you in many ways, and can greatly improve your overall adjustment strategy.

First, your current ball fit might *not* be correct for your hand and for your style of bowling. You can determine this by learning some of the principles of measuring the hand for the ball, and by knowing what options are open to you in the way your ball fits your hand and game. You need not be an expert at ball drilling, and this book will *not* qualify you to drill bowling balls. But the information concerning ball fit will be of assistance to you in evaluating how well your ball has been drilled.

Second, you will be able to communicate much better with a knowledgeable ball driller. This will help you explain to him or her your problems and desires in a ball fit. You should also understand more fully any comments or suggestions the ball driller has to make concerning ball fit. In this way a much greater chance exists to get the most comfortable fit for you, and to incorporate the best fit-options into your specific game.

EXHIBIT 7-10
Ball Measurement Chart

This chart is used to record your individual hand measurements in preparation for properly drilling the ball.

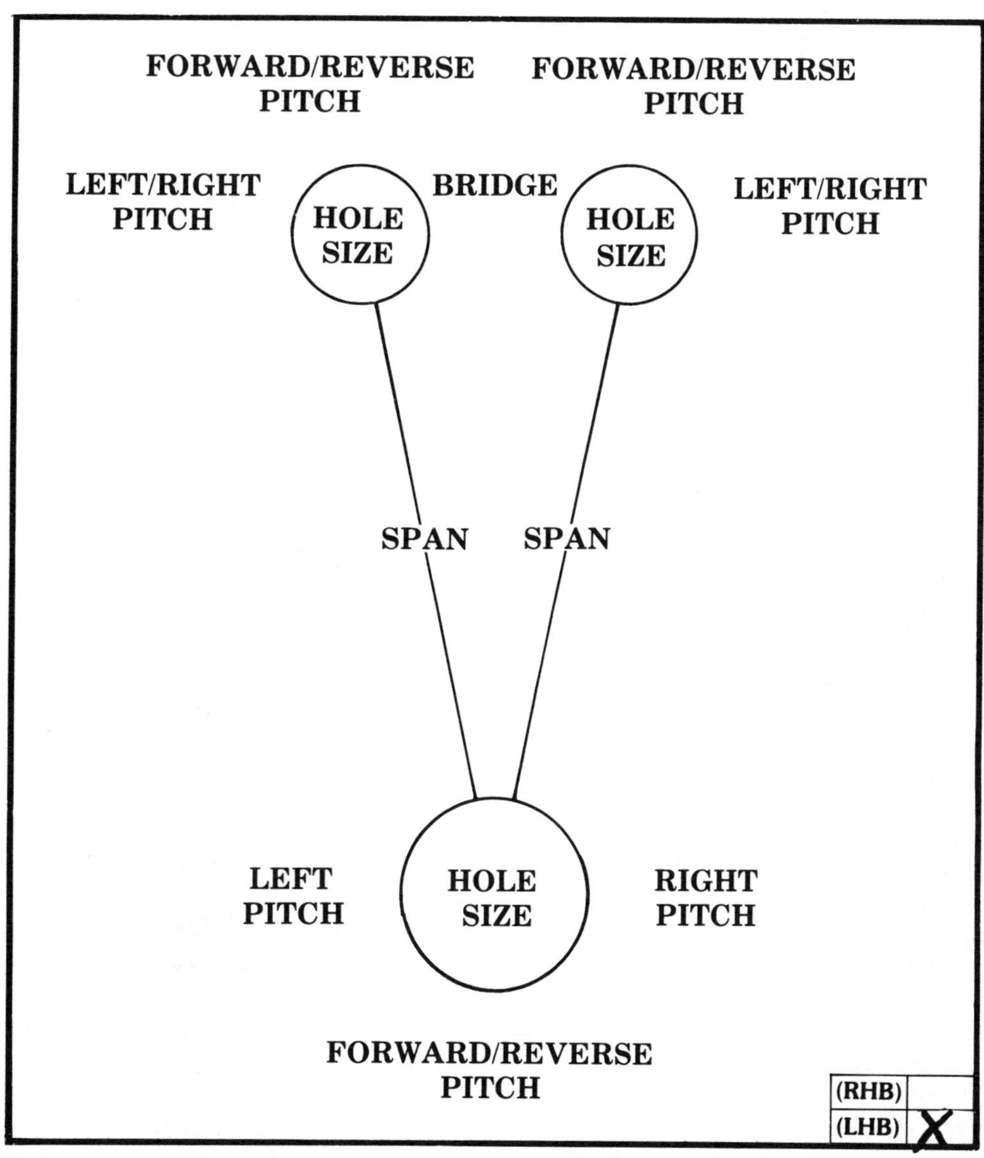

Several of these measurements are dictated by the structure of the hand. Others are the result of decisions you make: the way you elect to bowl; the bowling style you use; the skill level you have reached; and a number of other factors. Are you using a ball that fits properly? Do you know the correct measurements for your hand and bowling style? Why not get these measurements tested to see if they are correct for your ball?

Third, and closely related to the second item, is the knowledge of the full range of options in ball fit available to assist you in your game. If you wish to make a small change in ball fit, for example, to avoid making a change in your basic delivery, you will be aware of both the techniques for doing so and the expected results of the change. Two such ball fit adjustments will be discussed later in this section.

What are the characteristics of a correctly and incorrectly fitted ball? In general, a *correctly fitted* ball will be comfortable and will permit you to release it naturally for your game. More specifically, a correctly drilled ball will have, among other things: thumb and finger holes that are neither too small nor too large, and neither too deep nor too shallow; a span that is neither too short nor too long; proper pitches to fit your hand structure and the type of game you choose to play; bevels on the holes that are neither too sharp nor too rounded; an alignment of thumb and finger holes that fits the style of bowling you use and the structure of your hand and fingers; and holes located in the position to give you maximum advantage of weights and balances in the ball.

On the other hand, an *incorrectly drilled* ball will not meet the criteria stated above. Without a correct fit, here are a few problems you may have:

1. The hand, fingers or thumb may be strained, resulting in inconsistent deliveries, forced deliveries, poor timing, or sore portions of the hand.
2. You may be unable to achieve a natural rhythm to your steps and your swing, making it difficult to read the action of the ball on the lane.
3. You may be forced to squeeze the ball excessively during the delivery, resulting in improper and ill-timed releases. This situation often arises when the span is too short or the holes are too large (especially the thumb hole).
4. You may drop the ball during the swing or backswing, or just prior to the correct moment for releasing it. Dropping the ball is usually caused by (A) too short a span, (B) too large a thumb hole, (C) an incorrectly pitched thumb hole, or (D) the finger holes are too large.
5. You may not be taking advantage of the weight block, and in fact the weight may be working against you. (this area was discussed under BALL BALANCE ADJUSTMENTS.)
6. You may have to use a ball that is not the ideal weight for you, causing you to lose pin count and marks.

Of course, you might encounter many other problems with a poorly fitted ball. But, with a correctly fitted bowling ball most or all of these problems can be eliminated entirely. Therefore, it is important for you to know what measurements and techniques are available to correctly fit *your ball* to *your hand* and to *your game*. Like fingerprints, handprints are unique and require skill in measuring and interpreting the results.

A skilled ball driller can do this. And, since ball grip is one aspect of your game that can be completely controlled by you, it is not necessary to use any ball unless it fits your hand and your game. Your present ball can be plugged and redrilled so it will fit properly.

Now we will discuss the five categories of measurements related to ball fit. First we will begin by discussing the *width* of the thumb and finger holes. This will be followed by analyses of *depth, pitch, span,* and finally, *hole alignment.*

Width of Thumb and Finger Holes: It is vital that the width of the thumb and finger holes be correct: not too snug, causing soreness or making release of the ball difficult; nor too loose, causing the ball to be lost in the swing or creating an ineffective ball.

Perhaps the most important width measurement is the thumb. The role of the thumb during the swing and delivery is to help carry the ball to the point of release. At the moment of release the thumb should leave the ball first, in a smooth and natural manner. This will give the fingers time to impart lift to the ball.

Timing of the thumb release is very important, and is directly related to the width of the thumb hole. If the thumb comes out of the ball too soon, the ball may be dropped and the correct lift cannot be imparted by the fingers. If the thumb hangs-up in the hole, or drags during the moment of release, it will exit the ball later than it should and will interfere with the fingers imparting their lift. Also, this late release may cause you to miss your target on the lane.

When the thumb hole is too wide, there may be a tendency to grip the ball firmly. This causes the release to vary considerably from time to time since the ball cannot be released by relaxing the *un*natural grip on the ball. This situation—too wide of a thumb hole—is the major potential problem with the thumb hole.

Most ball drillers initially make the thumb hole a little smaller than they think it eventually will have to be. It is easy to enlarge a hole, but a lot more difficult to re-plug and re-drill! Since the smaller hole can be easily enlarged, and since it is usually obvious to the bowler that the thumb hole is too small, this method of drilling the width of the thumb hole is advisable, and should result in a hole that will allow you to barely touch the sides of the hole with your thumb when you insert and remove it repeatedly.

The *width of the finger holes* is relatively simple to measure and drill properly. The width may vary slightly depending upon the type of ball fit or grip you use: the conventional grip; the fingertip grip; or the semi-fingertip grip. The conventional grip calls for the finger holes to accommodate up to the second joint; the semi-fingertip, up to the first joint and half the distance to the second joint; and the full fingertip must accommodate the finger only up to the first joint. The finger holes can be slightly snug, but should not be too loose, especially as you move to the longer span grips.

In short, the width of the finger and thumb holes should be measured and drilled carefully. The thumb hole is slightly more important since it has the most impact on the timing and relative ease of the release. Yet both types of holes should be comfortable and fit your hand structure.

Depth of Thumb and Finger Holes: Two points are important in regard to the depth of the thumb and finger holes: The depth should provide for a consistent grip on the ball; and the depth is directly related to the type of ball fit or grip you select from among the three most common ones. Of course, the depth of the holes must take into account the size of the thumb and fingers and the structure of the hand.

If the holes are not deep enough, the fingers or thumb will not be able to be inserted properly. This may cause problems in the swing and in the release. There might be a tendency to squeeze or grip the ball too tightly with the thumb or fingers.

On the other hand, if the holes are too deep, the thumb and fingers may be inserted to varying depths during different deliveries. This could affect the swing and release. It could also create a situation in which the lift imparted on the ball would differ, resulting in inconsistent deliveries and also making it more difficult to properly read the action of the ball and the lane.

Once you select the type of fit or grip you will use, and the span you wish to use, the depth of the finger holes is largely determined. For the conventional grip, the shortest span, the fingers are inserted up to the second joint. This influences both the width and the depth of the holes, as already indicated in the section on *width* of the holes. Should you select the semi-fingertip grip, the depth will have to accommodate the fingers up to the first joint and half way to the second joint. And, of course the fingertip grip will require a hole depth sufficient enough to insert the fingers to the first joint.

The fingers should barely touch the bottom of the hole when the holes are at their proper depth. This will create the correct feel when the thumb and fingers are inserted, and should insure that you are getting the same grip on the ball from delivery to delivery. This may not be possible if you need to take the top weight out of the ball by drilling the holes deeper.

Span: This term refers to the distance between the thumb hole and the finger holes. The span can be relatively short, commonly referred to as the conventional grip, or it could be relatively long as in the fingertip grip. Also, the span from the thumb and the middle finger need not be the same as the span (distance) between the thumb and the ring finger. When there is a difference between the two spans, the difference is often referred to as *offset.*

Each span length has certain advantages and disadvantages. Of course each is related to the *structure of your hand* and *your style of bowling.* But each is also related to the amount and type of lift you can impart on the ball, and the degree of security you feel in the grip during the delivery. After discussing the three types of spans, we will look at the relative merits of all three.

Exhibit 7-11 illustrates the three most common spans, or ball fits, or ball grips. (All three terms are used interchangeably, but can mean different things in different parts of the country! Consult the Glossary of terms in Appendix A for clarification.) We will begin our discussion with the conventional grip, the one most often suggested for the beginning to average bowler.

In the *conventional* span the fingers are inserted to the second joint, and the thumb is fully inserted. This relatively short span provides the most comfortable and secure grip and feel to the beginning bowler. The ball does not feel as if it is going to slip off the fingers (if the span is proper) and the full strength of the fingers and thumb can be used to carry the ball during the delivery. Since the fingers are not stretched as in the longer spans, the ball can be carried in a more relaxed, natural manner. This will allow you to use a ball of the maximum weight for you. The added weight will give better carry and keep the ball in the path of deflection through the pins. In addition, any mistake you make in your delivery with the conventional span will *not* be magnified, as it would be with longer spans. This is a very important point. Since the beginning or low average bowler *will* be making mistakes, it is best to keep the magnitude of these mistakes to the lowest possible level. This is one strong point in favor of beginning your bowling career with this span. (Arguments for and against the use of the conven-

EXHIBIT 7-11
(LHB) Conventional, Semi-Fingertip and Fingertip Fits

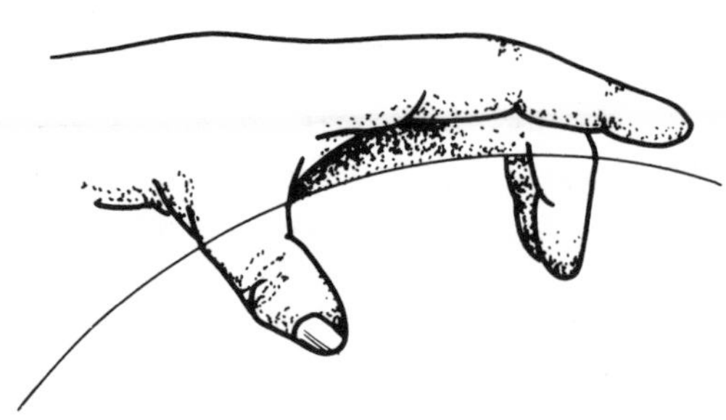

CONVENTIONAL FIT: FINGERS INSERTED TO SECOND JOINT.

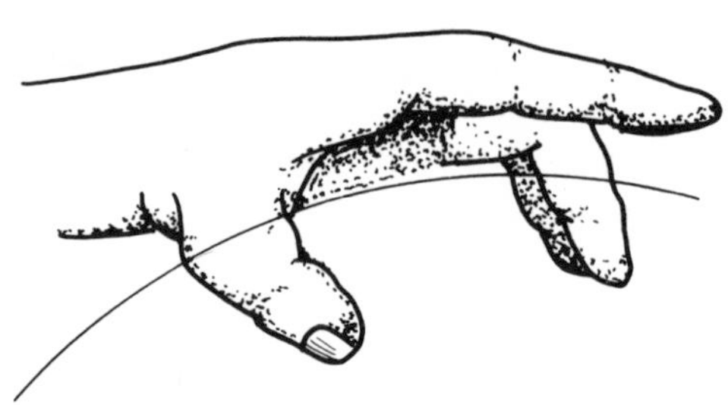

SEMI-FINGERTIP FIT: FINGERS INSERTED TO BETWEEN 1ST AND 2ND JOINT.

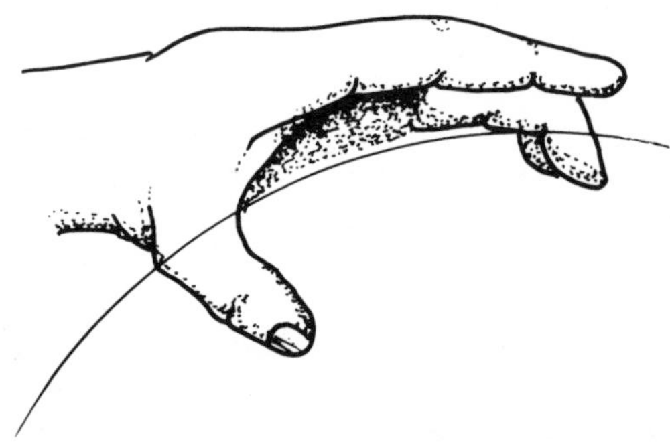

FINGERTIP FIT: FINGERS INSERTED TO FIRST JOINT.

tional span to begin your bowling career will be presented a little later in this discussion.) Moreover, it is not necessary for you to ever go beyond this conventional span. You could develop a very high average using the conventional grip, and many bowlers have done just that. However, the vast majority of top bowlers use a longer span. You should be familiar with the other spans, and decide if and when you might want to change to one of them.

Let's jump from the conventional grip to the *fingertip* span, skipping for the moment the intermediate span, the semi-fingertip. The fingertip grip or fit is the longest of the three normal spans. In it, the fingers are inserted only to the first joint. The thumb (as always) is fully inserted. Such a long span will cause you to feel you are stretching your fingers to get them into the holes, as indeed you may have to do. Also, some bowlers refer to a *relaxed fingertip* and a *stretched fingertip* grip, indicating the degree of stretching required to insert the thumb and fingers into the holes. Some people also use the term relaxed fingertip to refer to the *semi*-fingertip which we will describe next. Regardless of the name used, any grip beyond the conventional span will require some degree of stretching in the hand and fingers.

Unlike the shorter conventional grip, it takes a little time to get used to the fingertip fit. It feels uncomfortable at first because it is less natural than the conventional grip. The ball does not feel as secure in the hand since only the first joints of the fingers are holding the ball, rather than up to the second joint with the conventional grip. This means a certain amount of *strength* and *confidence* are needed to use this span. These two terms are critical to your decision as to *if* and *when* you might decide to use this longer span. A certain amount of strength is needed to handle wider spans with ease and comfort.

The major reason for selecting the longer fingertip span is the added amount of *action* you can get from the ball. It is easier to create a hook ball with the longer spans than with the shorter spans—to some degree. With more hook and action on the ball as it hits the pocket, it is easier to keep the ball in the path of deflection through the pins. You are able to play all 5 of the strike lines and the angles within these lines when you are able to hook the ball. (You can still play all of them with the shorter conventional grip, but some of the deep inside angles may be less effective with less action on the ball.) Since you are able to get more hook on the ball with the wider span, it is also true that a small error in your delivery will be magnified with the fingertip grip! Thus, you should be relatively consistent in your delivery when you are using it. Your mistakes will be more exaggerated, and this could have a detrimental impact on your scores.

Despite the disadvantages of the longer span, most top bowlers use this grip to give them the maximum potential for scoring. The added lift they can achieve is a benefit that far outweighs the possible problems associated with the fingertip grip. And once you get used to the fingertip fit, it feels just as natural as the conventional or semi-fingertip grips.

The *semi-fingertip* grip is between the smaller conventional span and the longer full fingertip grip. It is created by drilling the finger holes deep enough so the fingers can be inserted to a point between the first and second joint. The utility of this grip is similar to that of the fingertip: you can get more leverage at the moment of release and therefore get more action on the ball.

Some bowlers refer to the semi-fingertip as a relaxed fingertip. Still others see the relaxed fingertip as a span falling between the semi and the full fingertip. The difference in concepts is not important. The only important fact is that you can lengthen or shorten the span to accommodate a grip that feels comfortable to you, fits your hand structure, and gives you the amount of lift and resulting action you desire. What you call the grip does not matter.

These then, are the three most common types of span or grip: the Conventional grip; the Semi-fingertip grip; and the Fingertip grip. Which is best for you? Which should you start with? Should you lengthen your span as your skill level increases? These are personal questions, but general guidelines can be given to guide you to a correct choice for you.

One school of thought suggests that you start with the conventional grip first. Then, move to the semi or full fingertip grip after your skill level has developed to a point where you have a fundamentally sound delivery, and can consistently and confidently roll the ball. The reasons for using the conventional grip first are sound and include: The conventional grip is the most comfortable, most secure, easiest to use, can be used for your entire career, does not magnify the inevitable mistakes a low to average bowler will make, allows you to concentrate on the development of a sound delivery without undue concern for losing the ball in the delivery, permits you to develop your strength in rolling a ball at the maximum weight for you, will not put a strain on your hand or fingers, and has no major disadvantages for the beginning or average bowler. Given the many stated advantages, and few, if any, disadvantages, it is easy to see why many bowlers feel it is best *to start with* the conventional grip.

However, there is another school of thought on the matter. Virtually all top bowlers use a span in the range of a semi or full fingertip. Therefore, if you plan to use such a span at some time in your bowling career, you might just as well learn how to use it when you start so you will have no adjustment period when you make the conversion. Many people are able to handle the full or semi fingertip grip from the start, or early in their bowling career. Since they are able to handle the longer span grip, why not learn this first? Thus, this argument in favor of the longer span is plausible, but not as persuasive as that which suggests using the conventional grip when you first learn to bowl.

The decision could be handled in this manner: *if* you think you will want to switch to the longer span grip at some time in your future, and *if* you are able to handle the longer span grip at the present time, and *if* the longer span presents no special problems for you, then perhaps you should start with the semi or fingertip. If you have difficulty handling the longer span after trying it, or you are not sure you will want to use it in the future, start with the conventional grip.

Since the decision is largely a personal one, why not discuss the matter with a local bowling instructor or knowledgeable ball driller?

Hole Alignment: Several issues are involved in the decision of the correct alignment of the thumb and finger holes. First, there is the obvious issue of the structure of the hand. The holes should be aligned to provide the correct bridge size (the gap between the two finger holes). And the distance or span between the thumb and middle finger and the thumb and ring finger must contain the correct amount of offset (the difference between these two measurements, dictated by hand structure). Still further, hole alignment is related to your ball track and the ball imbalance you wish to create. The term imbalance, (concerned with locating the thumb and finger holes with reference to the weight block) was discussed under BALL BALANCE ADJUSTMENTS earlier in this section.

Each of the issues related to hole alignment will be covered under the appropriate categories. For now, we will limit our discussion to the three standard ways in which the holes are aligned, as illustrated on Exhibit 7-12.

The standard way to align holes, if there is such a thing as a standard, is the one in which the thumb aligns with the bridge (gap, web) between the two finger holes (#2 on Exhibit 7-12). This is sometimes called the *standard offset.*

Still another method of alignment is to arrange the thumb and middle finger as illustrated in #3 on Exhibit 7-12. This type of alignment is often referred to as the two-by-one method.

And the third common method for alignment of the thumb and finger holes is to align the thumb with the ring finger. This is shown as Item #1 on Exhibit 7-12. This method is often called the middle finger offset, since the middle finger is off to the right side of the line between the thumb and ring finger.

Of course, there are other methods of alignment, such as using any one of the three we have mentioned but combining it with some slight angle between the two finger holes. This situation is largely dictated by the structure of the hand, specifically the length of the middle finger in relation to the ring finger. These measurements create the need for offset as explained above.

One item that could be varied in the hole alignment is the width of the gap or bridge between the finger holes. If the bridge is too narrow, it may break. If it is too wide it may be uncomfortable, and it may prevent the two fingers from working effectively together as a unit. Therefore, the span should be kept at a width that is comfortable, fits the hand structure, and allows the two fingers to work as a team to impart lift and turn at the moment of release. The exact measurement will largely be determined by the structure of the hand.

Many of the other items of ball fit are directly related to the alignment of the holes, including pitch, depth, width, and the type of ball track you have decided to use. In aligning the thumb and finger holes for your particular fit, try for comfort and fit that will give you a natural release.

Pitches: Each ball is manufactured with an emblem or manufacturer's label embossed on it. This area is referred to as the top of the ball, and the thumb and finger holes are drilled into this portion of the ball. It is illegal, from a sanctioning point of view, to drill holes into the bottom portion of the ball.

Imagine a bowling ball in front of you, with the label facing you. This will allow you to visualize the direction of the pitches which will be described below.

Pitch refers to the angle at which the holes are drilled into the ball, all with reference to the center of the ball. Three kinds of pitch exist: *zero* pitch; *lateral* or side pitch; and *vertical* or forward/reverse pitch. In zero pitch the holes are angled directly toward the center of the ball. Lateral pitch exists when the holes are angled toward either the left or right side of the center of the ball. And, vertical pitch exists when either (1) the hole(s) angle above the center of the ball (forward pitch), or (2) the hole(s) angle below the center of the ball (reverse pitch).

Exhibit 7-13 illustrates the various types of pitches, giving a top and side view of both thumb and finger pitches. Notice how all the pitches are shown in relationship to the center of the ball.

What is the purpose of pitch? Actually there are

EXHIBIT 7-12
(LHB) Three Types of Hole Alignment

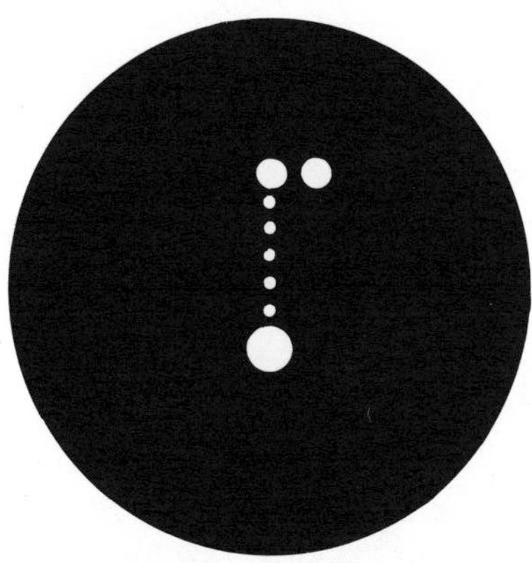

1) THE THUMB AND RING FINGER ARE IN ALIGNMENT

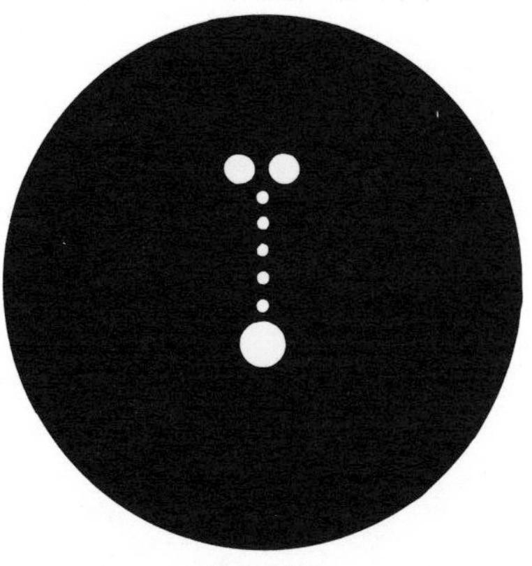

2) THE THUMB AND BRIDGE ARE IN ALIGNMENT

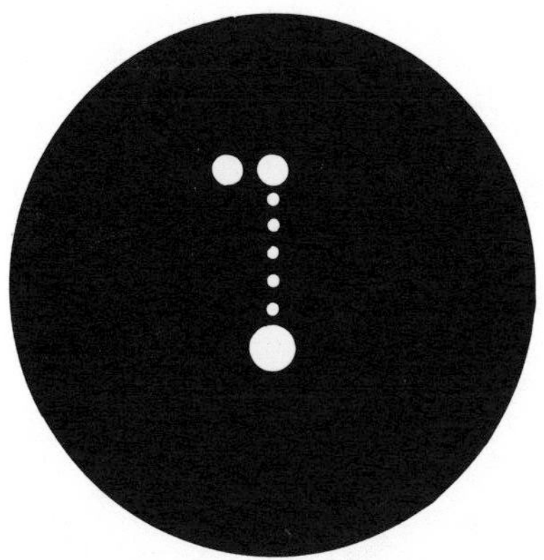

3) THE THUMB AND MIDDLE FINGER ARE IN ALIGNMENT

EXHIBIT 7-13
(LHB) Illustrations of Thumb and Finger Pitches

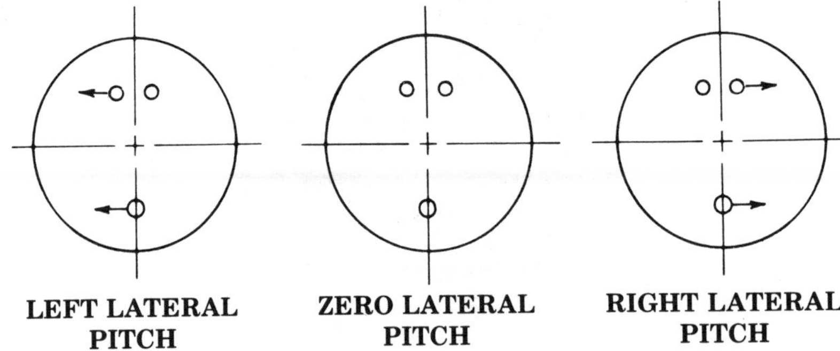

TOP VIEW: FINGERS AND THUMB

LEFT LATERAL PITCH | ZERO LATERAL PITCH | RIGHT LATERAL PITCH

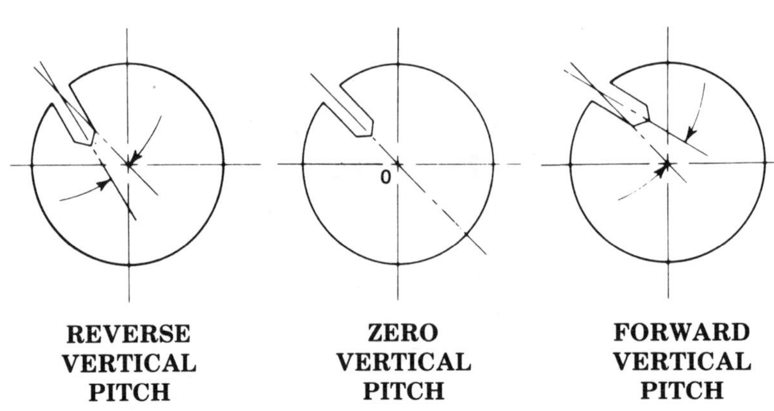

SIDE VIEW: THUMB

REVERSE VERTICAL PITCH | ZERO VERTICAL PITCH | FORWARD VERTICAL PITCH

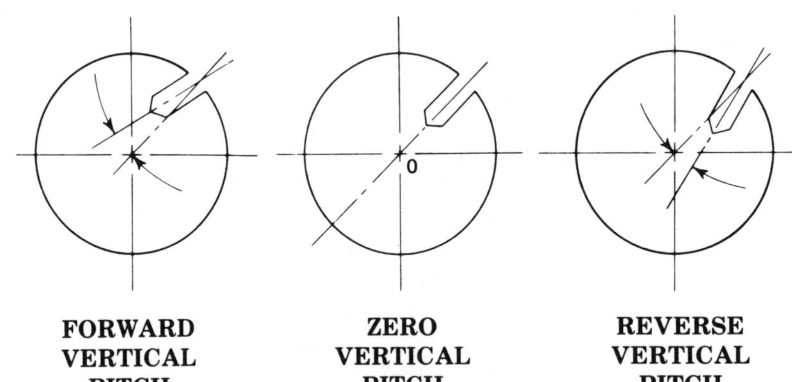

SIDE VIEW: FINGERS

FORWARD VERTICAL PITCH | ZERO VERTICAL PITCH | REVERSE VERTICAL PITCH

two objectives to be reached by drilling the correct pitch for the finger and thumb holes—*comfort* and *lift*. Some forms of pitch are designed to permit the ball to fit the structure of your hand so the ball will feel comfortable during the entire delivery. Still others are designed to give you more or less lift and turn at the moment of release.

Exhibit 7-14 indicates the major types of pitch that might be drilled into a bowling ball. This exhibit relates each type of pitch either to improving the comfort of the ball in the hand, or to affect the degree or amount of lift imparted at the moment of ball release.

Two general statements about pitch are in order at this time. (1) Those pitches that are related to providing a comfortable fit as their *primary* objective are (A) side pitch in the finger holes, and (B) vertical pitch in the thumb hole. (2) Those types of pitches more directly related to affecting the amount of lift or turn created by the release are (A) lateral or side pitch in the thumb hole and (B) vertical or forward/reverse pitch in the finger holes. These are generalizations only, since a pitch that is changed from uncomfortable to comfortable will probably improve the lift and bring about a more consistent release. One that gives you more lift may cause you to be slightly uncomfortable until the change has been incorporated into your game.

The relationship between vertical and lateral pitch in the thumb hole further illustrates this connection between comfort and lift. If you alter the side-ways pitch in the thumb hole (to raise or lower the ball track), the vertical pitch should be changed proportionately to keep the same degree of comfort in the fit. As a general rule, when you move the lateral (side pitch) of the thumb hole ⅛ inch, the vertical pitch should be changed by 50% of that amount, 1/16 inch. Left side thumb pitch should be accompanied by increased forward pitch or less reverse pitch. Right side pitch should be accompanied by reverse pitch or less forward pitch.This concept can be illustrated by the following exercise. (Exhibit 7-15.)

Hold your hand in front of you, with your palm facing away from you. Close your thumb and fingers until your thumb touches one of your fingers. (Which one it touches and where it touches will depend upon the degree of flexibility in your thumb!) Then, open and close your fingers and thumb several times, noticing the direction that your thumb moves. It will move at an angle, to the right and back at the same time. If there were no relationship, the thumb would move either straight back, or directly to the side. Since it moves both to the side and back at the same time, there is a relationship between these two pitches. So, when you increase the right lateral pitch in your thumb hole, you have to add some more reverse pitch to keep the same degree of comfort in your grip. When you move your pitch for the thumb to the left side, you have to take your current vertical pitch and move it more toward the front, increasing forward pitch.

This may be slightly confusing to you at first, but a closer examination of the movement of the thumb and fingers during the above exercise should help clarify this concept of thumb pitch. It should also suggest that as you lengthen or shorten the span in your grip, *there is a relationship between pitches and span*. Forward pitch on the thumb hole (like closing your hand) would create a shortening of the span. Reverse thumb pitch creates the need for a longer span. These complex interrelationships merely serve to illustrate that the art and science of ball drilling requires a great deal of knowledge about the structure of hands, and also about the influence of pitches on how you deliver the ball. (See Exhibit 7-15.)

EXHIBIT 7-14
(LHB) Relating the 12 Pitches to Comfort or Lift

Pitches may be used to (A) fit the structure of the hand in a comfortable manner, or (B) influence the amount of lift generated the moment the ball is released. This chart indicates the *primary* function of the 12 types of pitches that may be drilled into the holes of the ball.

TYPE OF PITCH	THUMB	FINGERS
Vertical-forward	Comfort-lift	Lift
Vertical-*zero* pitch	Either	Either
Vertical-reverse	Comfort-lift	Lift
Lateral-right side	Lift-comfort	Comfort
Lateral-*zero* pitch	Either	Either
Lateral-left side	Lift-comfort	Comfort

NOTES: Vertical and lateral thumb pitches are related, as indicated in later discussions. But vertical thumb pitch is primarily related to comfort, and lateral thumb pitch is primarily related to lift. Vertical finger pitches are primarily used to influence the amount of lift generated. Lateral finger pitches are more related to comfort and fitting the structure of the hand.

Changing from an incorrect (uncomfortable) to a correct (comfortable) pitch could also result in a change in the amount of lift you generate.

EXHIBIT 7-15
(LHB) Relationship Between Vertical and Lateral Thumb Pitches

A direct relationship exists between vertical and lateral pitches that are drilled for the thumb hole. Once a proper fit has been determined, any change to one should be accompanied by a change in the other. The dotted line indicates the approximate path of the thumb as the hand is opened and closed. It shows that the thumb moves on an angle, neither straight back nor from left to right. Any movement of the thumb is both a movement to the side and the front or back at the same time.

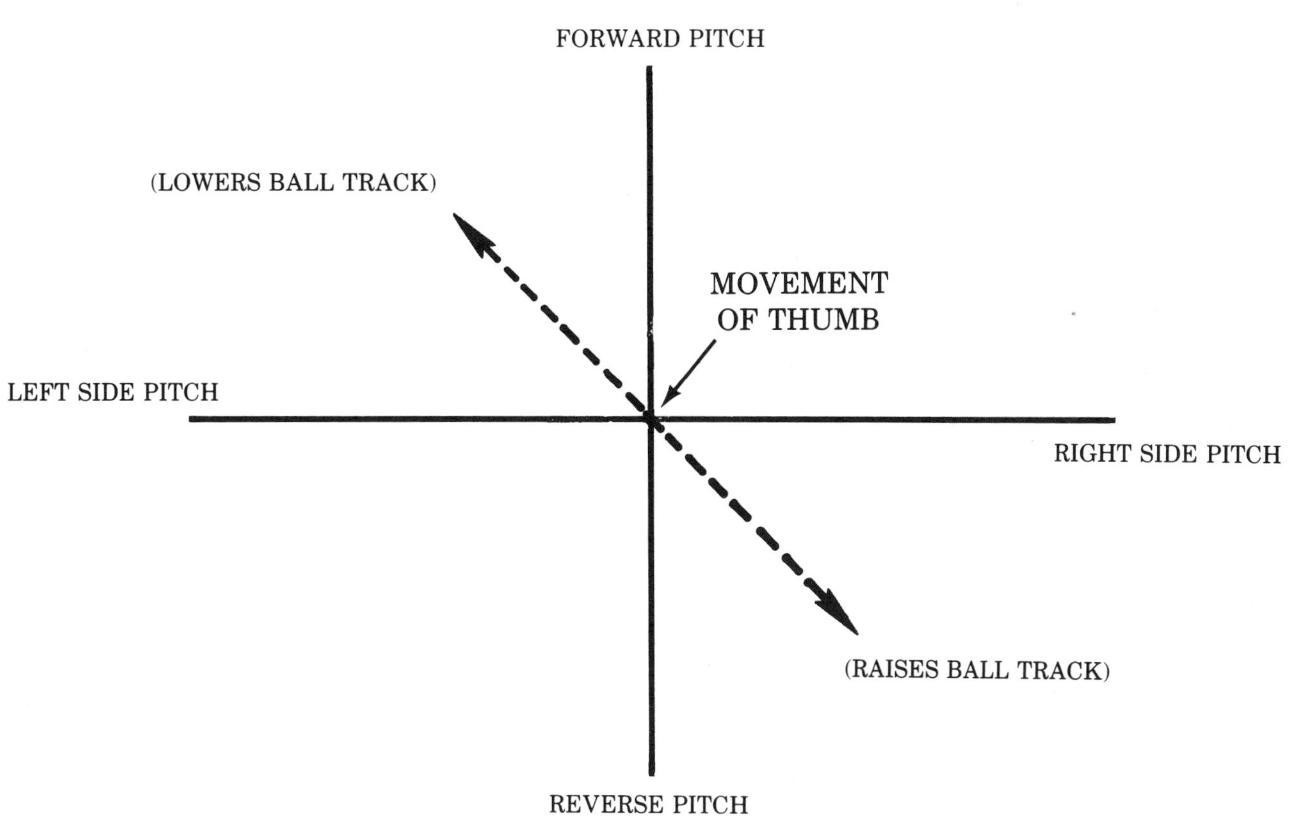

Notice that forward and left side thumb pitch will cause the ball track to go lower on the ball. Right side and reverse pitch will raise the ball track. Should you wish to move the ball track up or down on the ball, this is the type of ball drilling adjustment that could be used. Of course, the exact angle that would apply to a given bowler is related to the flexibility of the thumb and the structure of the hand. And the span may have to be changed to accommodate the change in thumb pitch.

EXHIBIT 7-16
(LHB) Ball Fit Terms

Bridge: The small area of the ball directly between the two finger holes.

Conventional fit: A method of gripping or fitting the ball so the finger holes are deep enough to insert the fingers to the second joint, and in which the finger and thumb holes are located relatively close to one another. This is a narrow span grip. The conventional fit is the easiest to learn to use and is the most common grip or fit among beginning or low average bowlers.

Fingertip fit: A method of gripping or fitting the ball so the finger holes are only deep enough for the fingers to be inserted to the first joint, and in which the thumb and finger holes are located far apart. This is a wide span fit or grip. The fingertip fit is very common among high average bowlers, since it provides the maximum opportunity to impart lift on the ball.

Forward pitch: Drilling the ball so the angle of the hole is above the center of the ball, instead of being angled below center, or toward the center.

Grip: A term which defines the total way the holes are drilled, including span, pitches, size of holes, location, alignment, etc. Sometimes the term grip is used to describe one of the three most common types of ball fit: conventional, semi-fingertip or fingertip.

Hole alignment: Describing the way in which the thumb and finger holes are aligned after drilling is completed. The thumb can be in line with the middle finger, the ring finger, or with the bridge or gap between the two finger holes. Other variations are also possible.

Left side pitch: Drilling a hole so it slants to the left side of the ball, instead of toward the center or right side.

Offset: The difference in span between the thumb and one finger and the thumb and the other finger.

Pitch: The angle at which a hole is drilled into the ball. There can be forward, reverse, side or zero pitch. These pitch angles are illustrated in Exhibit 7-13.

Reverse pitch: Drilling a hole into the ball so the hole angles below the center of the ball, instead of toward the center or above it.

Right side pitch: Drilling a hole so it slants to the right side of the ball, instead of toward the center or left side.

Semi-fingertip: A method of gripping or fitting the ball so the finger holes are drilled deep enough for the fingers to be inserted mid-way between the first and second joint. A medium span fit or grip. This fit is between the conventional and fingertip fit.

Span: The distance between the thumb hole and the finger holes. A wide span is considered a fingertip grip, and a narrow span is called a conventional fit or grip.

Stretch fingertip: A term implying that the span for the fingertip is rather long, causing the hand to be stretched for proper insertion. Often the regular fingertip is called a relaxed fingertip to separate it from the stretch fingertip.

Thumb-middle-finger alignment: Drilling the holes so the thumb hole and the middle finger hole are in alignment. (Sometimes called two-by-one.)

Thumb-ring-finger alignment: Drilling the holes so the thumb hole and the ring finger hole are in alignment.

Thumb-bridge alignment: Aligning the thumb with the bridge or gap between the two finger holes. (Sometimes called a standard offset.)

Zero pitch: Drilling the holes directly toward the center of the ball, as opposed to angling them to the top, bottom, left or right side.

SECTION 8 DELIVERY ADJUSTMENTS (Left Handed Bowlers)

"A consistent, natural, well-timed delivery is the foundation for high scoring."

CONTENTS PAGE

OVERVIEW

The purpose of this section is threefold: to discuss the essentials of an effective delivery; to describe the four most normal paths the ball takes to the pin deck; and to present the three most common delivery adjustments used by left handed bowlers.

Deliveries can be classified in a number of ways, including: (1) by the hand you use (left or right); (2) by the nature of the ball track; or (3) by the path the ball takes from the foul line to the pin deck (straight ball, curve ball, hook, or backup).

Other methods of classification exist, but we will limit our discussion of deliveries to the three types outlined above.

The first classification, left or right handed, has been addressed throughout this book. All material has been presented from both the left and right handed points of view. We have tried to make all translations of the material in each section.

In this way, each style is treated equally. (Volume 3, ***The Complete Guide to Bowling Spares,*** is also written in this manner, as are all volumes in this series.) *These may be the only books on bowling that treat left and right handed bowlers on an equal basis.*

The second classification of deliveries, by the path the ball takes from the foul line to the pin deck, will be covered extensively in this section. We will begin discussion of the straight ball, curve, backup and hook ball after covering the elements of an effective delivery.

Delivery adjustments are without a doubt the most difficult adjustments to make. *Most high average bowlers agree that delivery adjustments should not be made unless a change in angle or equipment cannot be found to meet lane conditions.* Yet there are times when you will have to make some change in the way you deliver the ball to capitalize on, or accommodate lane conditions. Therefore, you should add delivery adjustments to your adjustment arsenal.

A delivery change often upsets timing, rhythm or tempo. Those who have practiced making changes in the way they deliver the ball will make such adjustments very quickly and easily. As with all adjustments, the more you practice, the easier they are to make. Therefore, you should practice making at least three types of delivery adjustments: increasing or decreasing the ball *speed;* using more or less *loft* of the ball out over the foul line; and giving the ball more or less *lift* (turn, action, etc.)

Before we begin our discussion of these three delivery adjustments, it is necessary to review the fundamentals of a sound and effective delivery. *High scoring on any long term basis is dependent upon the development of a sound delivery.* Without an effective delivery of the ball it is not possible to take advantage of many of the scientific systems of adjusting that are covered in this and other volumes in the series. (Volume 1, ***The Complete Guide To Bowling Principles,*** concentrates almost exclusively upon the development of a consistent, natural and well-timed delivery.) For example, you cannot tell what your ball and lane are doing (how they are interacting) until you have control of your delivery.

ELEMENTS OF AN EFFECTIVE DELIVERY: What are the essential ingredients of a delivery upon which high scoring can be developed? Three elements stand out as most important, despite the particular type or style of delivery: Your delivery should be (1) consistent, (2) natural, and (3) well-timed.

Consistent: Your walk pattern from the stance

position to the foul line should be consistent. Your arm swing should be the same each time you deliver the ball. All elements of your delivery should be consistent. Inconsistency creates errors.

You can drift in your walk pattern, or walk in a perfectly straight line. You can take large or small steps, or shuffle to the foul line. You can do any number of things that may be considered poor form, so long as you do them with a high degree of regularity. You can be successful with any style of bowling, if it works well for you on a continuous basis, as attested to by the variety of styles displayed by the top bowlers in the world. But, whatever they do, they do in a consistent, predictable manner. It is part of their game.

Natural: Your delivery is influenced by your body build, your strength, and the way you learned to bowl. How you bowl feels comfortable to you since you have been doing it for some time. The things you do in your delivery may be similar to what others use, or they could be completely different. *There is no single perfect style of delivery that can be used by every bowler.* Any individual style, one that is natural to the person, can be developed into one that produces high scores on a regular basis. It may be easier or harder for you to overcome some natural tendencies you have, but with practice most delivery styles can be groomed into successful ones.

Observe the natural styles of some of the more successful bowlers. Notice the wide range of individual characteristics displayed. Yet we can say that their style of delivery feels natural to them. And, that is the important point. You do not need to become a carbon copy of anyone else. You should be you. *You should develop a game that is natural to you.*

It may be natural for you to take 3 steps, or 4, 5, or 6, or more. You may drift by 5 boards to the left or right in your walk pattern. You may bend your elbow during the swing. You may have a style that is unlike the classic styles often recommended. But, what you are doing may not be wrong *for you.* The result determines whether anything is wrong. If you can score well, on a regular basis, and you are able to adapt to changing lane conditions, then whatever you are doing is correct. You must determine what type of delivery will work for you, what feels natural to you, and develop your delivery along those lines.

Well-Timed: When you take your stance on the approach, there are two things you have to do to get the ball on its way to the pins. You have to (1) take a series of steps toward the foul line (although the number and size of these steps will differ from bowler to bowler); and you have to (2) swing the ball from its initial position in the stance until the moment it is released. These two factors, your steps and your swing, have to be well-timed.

Within this broad guideline of being well-timed, there is wide latitude as to how many steps you take, of what size, at what speed, and in what actual direction (with or without drift). Your ball could be held down at your side, waist level, higher or lower, and your swing could include a backswing of any height. As long as you are able to keep these elements of your delivery in the proper timing *for you,* in the right rhythm and tempo *for you,* you should be able to take advantage of all the adjustment techniques for getting the ball into the pocket correctly.

Your ball speed may be moderate, slow, fast, or very fast, as compared to other bowlers. But, as long as your timing in the delivery is such that you are able to score well, on a regular basis, then it must be that what you are doing is correct, and well-timed.

In summary, an effective delivery is consistent in every way, is natural for you, and is well-timed in steps and swing. Once you have such a fundamentally sound delivery, you are in a position to make small adjustments to accommodate various lane conditions.

Although there are a wide range of changes you could make in your delivery as you try to get the ball either up to the pocket, or back to it, three types of delivery adjustments are most frequently used: changes in ball speed; changes in lift imparted at the release point; and changes in the distance the ball is lofted out over the foul line. One or more of these delivery adjustment techniques may have to be made to properly play the lane. Following the discussion of the four common types of ball paths to the pins, we will explain how these three types of adjustments can be made. But, now, let's look at the straight ball, curve, backup, and hook deliveries.

FOUR PATTERNS OF BALL ROLL: All four paths to the pin deck are illustrated on Exhibit 8-1. Each type of ball can be effective under given circumstances. Each delivery has advantages and disadvantages, and it is possible to improve your average with any of them.

The path of the ball to the pocket is largely determined by the position of the thumb and fingers at the moment the ball is released onto the lane. Rotation of the ball *prior* to release, and altering the degree of firmness of the fingers at the time of release, will also affect the path to the pins.

The thumb is supposed to come out of the ball first, followed a split second later by the fingers. For this split second that the ball is held by the fingers, there is an opportunity to impart lift (turn, spin, fingers, action, etc.) on the ball. An early or late release of the thumb, rigid or limp fingers at the explosion point (the moment the ball is released by

EXHIBIT 8-1
(LHB) Four Common Paths to the Pocket

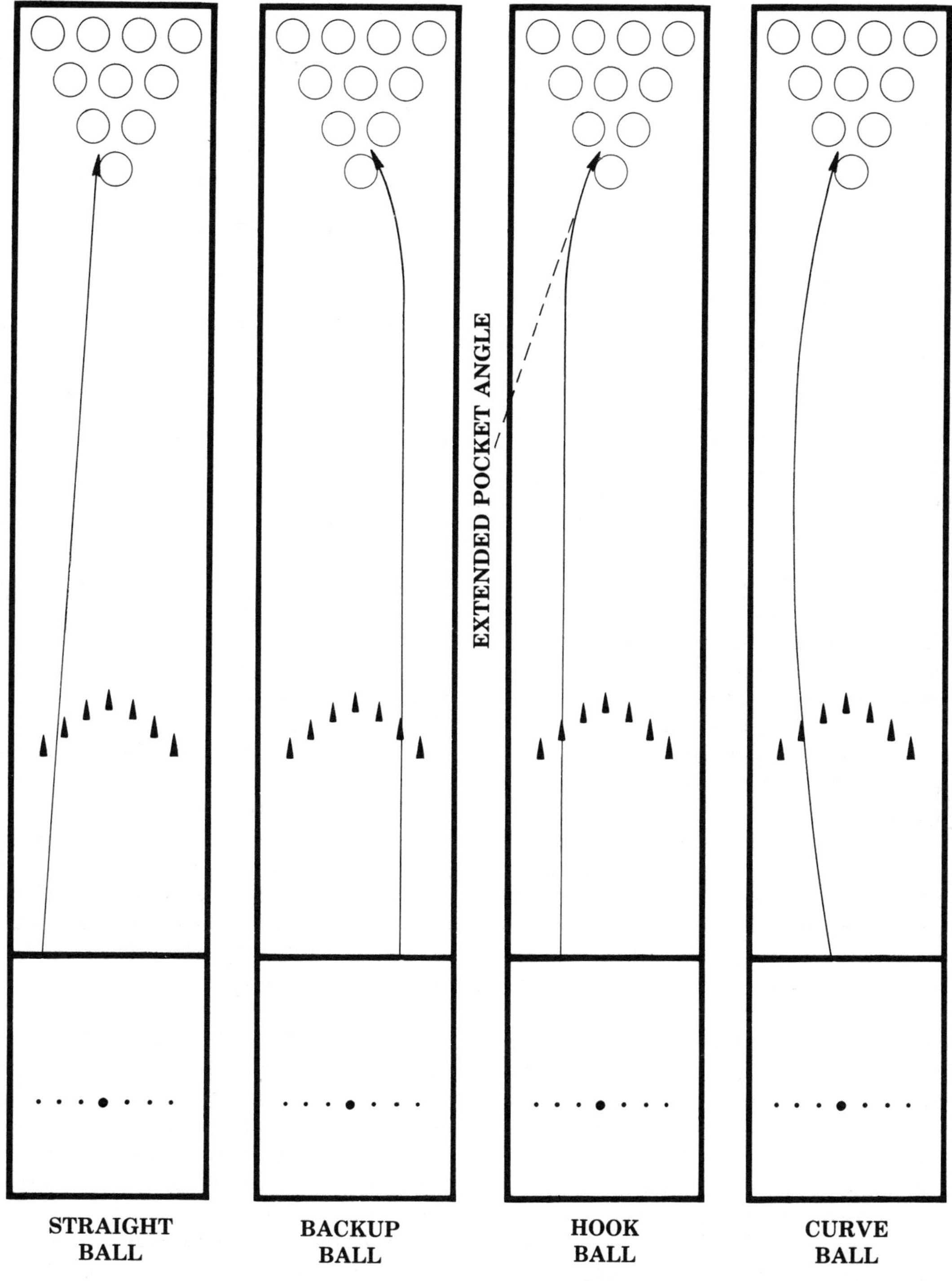

Most bowlers will roll the ball along a path similar to one of the four illustrated above. Notice that the backup ball pattern is similar to the hook ball rolled by right handed bowlers. Also, the pocket angle indicated for the hook ball would, if extended, go off the side of the lane about 20 or so feet in front of the pin deck. This correct pocket angle can only be achieved by rolling either a curve or hook ball, or a backup ball into the 1-3 pocket.

the fingers), or a strong or weak follow-through, are all factors that determine what path the ball will take. However, most bowlers will roll the ball along a path similar to one of the four general patterns shown on Exhibit 8-1.

Perhaps the best way to describe the position of the fingers at release time is with reference to an imaginary clock laid across the foul line on the left side of the lane. Imagine such a clock positioned with 12 o'clock facing straight down the lane, 6 o'clock to the rear, and 3 and 9 o'clock directly on the foul line.

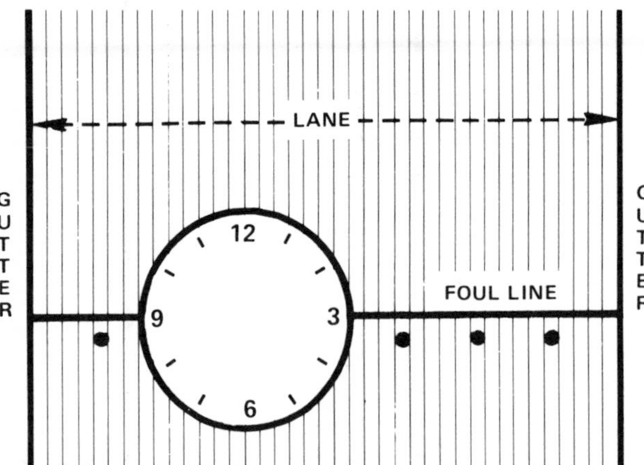

The four paths to the pin deck illustrated in Exhibit 8-1 are created by locating the fingers in these positions: the *straight* ball is created by having the fingers at a position at 6 o'clock; the *curve or hook* is rolled by having the fingers at a position somewhere between 7 and 8 o'clock; and the *backup* ball is rolled by having the fingers at about a 4 or 5 o'clock position as the ball is released.

Rotation of the fingers in a clockwise manner at release will tend to create a curve or hooking pattern. A rotation of the fingers in a counter clockwise manner at release tends to produce a full roller or a backup ball delivery, depending upon how far the fingers are rotated. Combining such rotations with other delivery changes will affect the eventual path of the ball to the pins. These generalizations should help you understand the relationship between finger positions at time of release and ball paths to the pins.

Since the fingers are naturally on the opposite side of the top of the ball (from the thumb) you could refer to the position of the thumb at the moment the ball is released to determine the eventual path taken by the ball. But, since the fingers are used to impart lift to the ball, attention should be focused upon their position at release time.

What are the relative merits of each of the four general paths to the pin deck? Which one is the most effective for making strikes, and why? To answer these and other related questions, we will review all four types of deliveries, starting with the straight ball.

The Straight Ball: The straight ball, as the name implies, follows a direct path from the foul line to the pins. Since the pocket is located on the 17th board at the pin deck, it is possible to roll a straight ball directly down the 17th board at the foul line. However, it is usually rolled from the extreme left side of the lane, from any one of a number of left-to-right foul line angles.

Pin and ball deflection represent the problem associated with using the straight ball for making strikes. A straight angle into the pocket is far less effective than the ideal angle created by the hook ball (to be discussed later). A ball rolled straight for the 1-2 pocket from the foul line is too easily deflected out of the pocket, causing the ball to hit the 2-pin too fully, and hitting the 5-pin either too lightly or not at all. Usually the ball will not hit the 5-pin because the ball is being deflected away from it, rather than driving into it, as is the case with either a curve or hook ball. The straight ball cannot penetrate into the 18½ board after contacting the pocket, unless the hit is slightly high or the speed of the ball will permit such penetration to take place.

The straight ball can, however, be effective in producing strikes. The key to successful bowling at the higher average levels is a consistently high percentage of strikes (50% or more). This is more difficult to achieve with the straight ball than it is with the curve or hook, because of less-than-ideal pin and ball deflection.

Three adjustments can be made that will allow you to use the straight ball and increase your percentage of strikes. First, use as much of an angle into the pocket as you possibly can. Roll the ball from the deep outside foul line angle position. This will permit the ball to penetrate the pocket more than one rolled from a straighter angle. Second, roll the ball with sufficient speed to keep the ball driving into the pocket after contact with the 1-pin. This will give the ball a chance to contact the 5-pin properly. And, third, hit the pocket slightly high on the head pin, so the ball is not deflected into the 2-pin too sharply. A slightly high pocket hit will permit the ball to maintain its path of deflection through the pins.

Of course, these suggestions mean you have to be a little more accurate with your strike hits, and you will run the risk of splits or high-pocket leaves. The result is a lower than 50% average in number of strike deliveries. But, using the above three adjustment suggestions should increase your number of strikes on the straight ball delivery.

There should be no overall disadvantage to you

if you use the straight ball for your spare conversions. Some spares will be easier for you, and others will be more difficult. But as a general rule, there will be no noticeable problems with your spares. In fact, many high average bowlers try to straighten out their shots for spares, since accuracy (not action) is the key ingredient in making spare conversions. (Just the opposite is true on all strike attempts!) Since these high average bowlers deliberately elect to use a straighter ball for their spares, to reduce the possibility for errors, it follows that the straight ball *may* even be more advantageous over the hook ball for spare conversions. This is definitely true in many instances (such as the 2-7 split).

If you converted almost all of your makeable spares, but were not able to produce a high percentage of strikes, your top average potential might be limited to about 175. This is a respectable average, and would place you very high in the standings in most leagues. But such an average is 25 pins below the 200 average level generally used to establish the cutoff point for separating the top bowlers from all others.

Therefore, if you are willing to accept a theoretical maximum attainable average around 175, then by all means continue using the straight ball. You can still roll some big games, enjoy the game more than if you held a much lower average, and *you could even go beyond this stated maximum.* But if you wish to move to higher plateaus, to as high as your skills will permit, then you should consider learning how to roll the hook ball. With the hook ball, there is no practical limit to how high you could increase your average. *To date the highest league average is a 240 season average by John Johns. The record for women stands at 227, set by Patty Ann of Arlington Heights, Illinois.*

The Backup Ball: The general path of the backup ball is similar to the path of a hook rolled by a right handed bowler. That is, the ball hooks or curves from right to left. This is an important fact, since it suggests that the backup ball delivery might be effective if it is rolled into the 1-3 pocket instead of the normal 1-2 pocket for the left handed bowler.

The backup ball is also known as a reverse hook, although there is a slight difference between these two deliveries. Both the backup and reverse hook follow a right-to-left path to the pins, but the reverse hook has a sharper turn to the left than the backup delivery.

To assess the effectiveness of the backup ball delivery, it is necessary to recall the pin and ball deflection required for a perfect strike hit. The ball should be driving *into* the pocket, contacting the 1-2-5-8 pins on its path through the pins. The ball should contact the 5-pin rather firmly and send it into the 9-pin.

A backup ball rolled toward the 1-2 pocket deflects *away* from the pocket, and particularly away from the 5-pin instead of toward it. The backup ball hits the head pin in a right-to-left manner, which causes the ball to deflect more toward the 4-pin than the 5-pin. A backup ball rolled for the 1-2 pocket by a left hander is exactly like a RHB rolling for a brooklyn strike! The hit and the angle of the ball are very similar.

It is easy to conclude that if you wish to continue rolling a backup ball, and you want to increase your percentage of strikes, then you should roll for the 1-3 pocket. Pin and ball deflection will be working for you when you use this opposite pocket. *In effect, you should roll your strike delivery similar to a right handed bowler.* You may not be able to get as much drive on the ball as a right hander would, but your possibilities for making strikes will definitely be greater than if you use the 1-2 pocket.

There is no major disadvantage associated with the backup ball delivery for spare conversions. Some spares will be easier for you, but others will be more difficult. On any spare in which the RHB has an advantage (because of favorable pin or ball deflection) you have the same advantage with the backup ball. Where the LHB has the advantage, your backup delivery would put you at a disadvantage. For example, the 7-pin is a most difficult non-split spare for the LHB, but the 10-pin is relatively easy to make. Just the opposite would be true with your backup delivery; the 7-pin should be very easy since you are rolling *into the pin.* The 10-pin might be difficult since the backup ball is moving *away from the pin.*

Since accuracy (not action) is the most important factor in making spares, the backup ball can be very effective. You can be just as accurate with the backup ball (with the correct amount of practice) as you can with a hook, curve, or straight ball delivery. Pin and ball deflection are *not always critical on spare* leaves, but they are *always critical on every strike try.*

Therefore, if you wish to improve your average significantly, and you want to continue rolling a backup ball, you can and should do so. Simply use the 1-3 pocket for your strike ball, and bowl the entire game as if you were right-handed. Do not use the 1-2 pocket for strikes, since a backup ball will produce fewer strikes using that pocket.

Don't be ashamed, concerned or embarrassed by using the so-called opposite pocket. You are increasing your percentage for strikes and bowling intelligently by doing so. If you wish to achieve the highest average possible for your potential skill level, then you should try to develop a hook ball. Your local bowling instructor can help you develop this type of delivery. Also, Volume 1 in this series ***(The Complete Guide to Bowling Principles)*** goes into great detail on that subject.

The Curve Ball: This type of delivery is rolled or created in much the same manner as the hook ball. The fingers are to the left of the 6 o'clock position at release time. The ball is rolled slowly with an exaggerated clockwise rotation of the hand at the moment of release.

The path of the curve ball is similar to that taken by the hook ball, but there are essential differences between the two paths to the pocket. The curve ball is rolled slowly and follows a gradual arc or curve to the pins, almost in the shape of an archer's bow. It goes out to the left in a gradual arc and then slowly makes a turn toward the pins. The curve ball crosses many boards on its path to the pins. On the other hand, the hook ball usually takes a more direct and straight path from the foul line until it reaches a breaking point, where it makes a sharp turn to the pocket. The hook ball crosses fewer boards than the curve ball. (More on the hook ball in the next part.)

Although the curve ball can be effective on occasion, it is difficult to be consistent with it. You *can* contact the pocket at the ideal pocket angle. But the ineffectiveness of the curve ball is a result of its gradual turn to the pocket and the excessive number of boards it crosses. As a general rule, the more boards a ball crosses on its path to the pins, the less accurate it is. There are too many chances of hitting erratic lane conditions over the wider surface of the lane. In addition, the gradualness or gentleness of the turn to the pocket may not leave the ball with enough action to drive into the pocket properly.

Still another disadvantage of the curve ball is that it is less useful for lane conditions suggesting strike lines other than the ones toward the inside of the lanes (the inside and deep inside strike lines). It can be used with the second arrow line, but this may call for entering the lane track twice on the way to the pocket. When lane conditions dictate the outside or deep outside strike lines, it may not be easy to get the curve ball to follow the proper or ideal path to the pocket. Thus, the curve ball presents a reasonable path to the pins under some types of lane conditions, but is less likely to provide a good shot at the pocket under all types.

Speed control is another disadvantage of the curve ball. It is difficult to maintain a consistent speed throughout the shot, and adjusting ball speed might be difficult. Although speed control could be developed with sufficient practice, altering ball speed is difficult to master with the curve ball without affecting the timing of the approach.

If you roll a curve ball, and wish to continue doing so, you can still develop a high average. Lane conditions may limit your ability to adapt, and you may only be able to score well when you hit your condition, but you can do fairly well with the curve ball. With a little practice, you could convert to rolling a hook ball, and that is what we suggest you do if you wish to raise your average to the highest possible level. So, let's look at the hook ball delivery.

The Hook Ball: Virtually all high average bowlers use some form of the hook ball. They roll the ball so that it takes a sharp break or turn toward the pocket, usually when it is within 10 to 15 feet of the pins. To create this hook ball, the fingers are situated between 7 and 8 o'clock at the moment the ball is released, although the fingers might have been rotated in a clockwise manner to get to this release point. Precise finger location determines to a large degree how much the ball will hook, as does any rotation of the ball during the swing. Lane conditions, the strike angle used, and ball weights and balances also play a part in the timing and intensity of the hook.

When and *where* the ball hooks are very important points to consider in reading the lanes. At times you will want the ball to hook sooner or later (timing of the hook) and at other times you will want the ball to hook more or less (strength or intensity of the hook). These are the major decisions which any hook ball bowler has to make: do I want the ball to break sooner or later, and more or less?

Our previous discussions about the perfect strike hit and the pocket angle give us an insight into why the hook ball is the most effective delivery for making strikes. Pin and ball deflection are best for carrying all ten pins when the ball enters the pocket from an angle that allows the ball to contact the 2 and 5-pins properly after hitting the 1-2 pocket. Too much of an angle will have the ball contacting the 2-pin too far on the right side, and hitting too much of the 5-pin. Not enough angle will cause the ball to hit the 2-pin too fully and hit the 5-pin too lightly on the left side. In both cases pin deflection will generally not result in a strike.

The correct pocket angle, extended back toward the bowler, would go off the left side of the lane less than 20 feet in front of the pin deck. Carried all the way back to the foul line, the extended line would be perhaps two lanes to the left! (See Exhibit 8-1 for an illustration of this point. Extend the hook portion of the hook ball pattern away from the pins in a straight line. It will go off the lane and cross over into the adjacent lane on the left side very quickly.)

The only way to get the ball into this ideal pocket angle is to delay the hook point (the breaking point) until the ball is well down the lane, perhaps to within 10-15 feet of the pocket. Breaking either too soon or too late will put the ball into the pocket at a less-than-ideal pocket angle.

A backup or straight ball cannot hit the 1-2 pocket from this ideal pocket angle. The curve ball could, as previously mentioned. Therefore, only a hook ball that begins its break toward the pocket after it is more than 45 feet beyond the foul line, can enter the pocket at the correct angle to produce strikes *consistently*. The backup ball, if rolled for the 1-3 pocket, could enter that pocket from the optimum angle to produce strikes consistently, as discussed in the previous section on the backup ball.

From this brief discussion of the ideal pocket angle, and the pin and ball deflection required for the perfect strike, it should be clear why almost every high average bowler uses some form of hook ball for strikes. This is the only type of ball pattern that has a consistent chance to keep its path of deflection through the pins, and which creates the proper pin and ball deflection to take out the six pins not taken out by the ball. Although there are many ways to strike, including the occasional strike which results when the head pin has been missed, the hook ball gives the best chance to strike *consistently*.

Consistency in striking is one of the two major ingredients in the game of top bowlers, making about 50% of their strike deliveries (averaging about 5 strikes per game). The second ingredient is making about 95% of their spare leaves. These two goals represent a standard to set for yourself if you wish to achieve the status of a 200 or better average bowler. Rolling the hook ball delivery would be the best way to help you achieve this objective.

Summary: To summarize the merits of the four types of deliveries, the major disadvantage to every type of ball roll except the hook ball and curve ball is the problem associated with pin and ball deflection on the pin deck. A backup, or straight ball can be effective on occasion, and you can raise your average and enjoyment of the game. But it will be difficult for you to approach the effectiveness of the hook ball and curve ball even under the best of circumstances. Only a hook ball or curve ball allows you to get the ball to hit the pocket from the correct pocket angle, with the right hit on the 1-2-5-8 pins, and with the correct amount of action on the ball to maintain its path of deflection through the pins.

Any one of the four types of deliveries may be effective for spare conversions, since accuracy and not action is the key to making spares. In fact, many high average bowlers try to straighten out their spare shots, indicating that the straight ball might be advantageous for many spares. But for making strikes consistently, the hook ball is far superior to the curve, backup or straight ball.

And now we will cover the three major types of delivery adjustments which should be a part of the adjustment arsenal of every bowler who wishes to increase his or her average to higher levels: speed adjustments, loft adjustments, and lift adjustments.

SPEED ADJUSTMENTS
(Left Handed Bowlers)

"Incorrect ball or foot speed is the biggest enemy of making strikes," Jeff Morin, Member, PBA.

The ability to adjust ball speed is an important skill to add to your adjustment arsenal. Very often you will have to increase or reduce ball speed to properly play the lane conditions you find.

A ball is supposed to skid, roll and then hook as it heads toward the pins. Too much speed increases the amount of skid and prevents the ball from getting the correct number of revolutions before it hits the pocket. (More on ball revolutions in a later section on LIFT ADJUSTMENTS.) The result is an ineffective ball, one that does not work for you by getting the pins to mix with the other pins for proper carry. Pins fly almost upright back into the pit and do not take out as many pins as they would if they were heading for the pit in a horizontal manner. Also, excessive speed drives the ball too deeply into the pocket and does not allow the ball to follow the ideal path of deflection through the pins.

Too little speed is equally ineffective, but of course in the opposite manner. A slow ball is too easily deflected out of the ideal path of deflection through the 1-2-5-8 pins. Pins do not velocitate sufficiently to give you good pin carry. It is difficult to take full advantage of the kickbacks when ball speed is insufficient.

Once you have established your normal and natural ball speed, you must develop the ability to increase or reduce ball speed to meet lane conditions. Since your ball speed will approximate 2.2 seconds, you should be able to roll the ball plus or minus 10% of this figure, or from 2.0 to 2.4 seconds. (Speeds far outside of these ranges are *not* common among high average bowlers.) Three very common methods are used for altering ball speed.

The first method for changing ball speed is to *change the height* at which you hold the ball in your stance. Holding the ball slightly higher will create a higher back swing and automatically raise ball speed. Holding the ball lower in the stance has the opposite effect, reducing the speed of the ball.

The second way to alter ball speed is to *apply slight pressure* in the pendulum swing to increase the height of the back swing. Or you could apply the pressure from the top of the back swing through the point at which the ball is released on the lane. Both methods will increase ball speed. The pressure should be from the elbow down, not from the shoulder, and should be gradual, not forced. Applying less pressure has the opposite effect, lessening ball speed. This ball speed adjustment is slightly more difficult to make than the one for increasing pressure. The ball should be applying all of the pressure during the swing, and therefore you should not be able to reduce this pressure, except by holding back slightly on the pull of the ball through the swing.

The third method for changing ball speed is to *alter the tempo or length of your steps.* A faster pace or longer steps will increase body speed to the foul line, thereby resulting in faster ball speed. A slower tempo or shorter steps will have the opposite effect, slowing down the speed of the ball.

A word of caution is in order at this time. Whenever you attempt to change a part of your delivery there is a chance you will affect your timing and rhythm. It is imperative that you keep your natural and proper timing when you attempt to change ball speed.

It is difficult to change your natural ball speed and to keep your timing. This ability will require long hours of practice to perfect. However, this skill can be very advantageous. In many instances speed control is the key element in making strikes. Other adjustments will just not do the trick.

Under what circumstances would you want to consider altering ball speed? If the lane is hooking too strongly, and you are hitting the pocket too fully, you may elect an increase in ball speed to overcome the situation. Increased ball speed is a delivery adjustment designed to bring the ball back to the pocket. If the ball is beginning its break too soon, or is breaking too strongly, then increased ball speed is an adjustment to correct either situation. Any one of the three methods of altering ball speed could be used to achieve the objective.

If the lane is not hooking as much as you would

like, and you wish to alter your ball speed to increase the amount of the hook, or to get the ball to start hooking sooner, reduced ball speed can achieve these corrections.

It would be helpful to have someone time your ball speed during league or practice sessions. Try to slow the ball down, or increase ball speed, by using any or all of the speed adjustment techniques mentioned above.

You should be able to vary ball speed to fit within the 2.0 to 2.4 second range. A speed slightly higher than 2.4 seconds could still be correct for you. Your normal speed might be 2.4 seconds, and your range could be from 2.2 to 2.6 seconds. A .2 of a second increase or decrease in ball speed is probably the most realistic speed adjustment to incorporate into an effective delivery.

Keep in mind that whether you roll the ball fast or slow is neither good nor bad, as long as it is near the general speed range given above. But the ability to change the speed of the ball as an adjustment technique for certain lane conditions is an ability you should develop if you wish to improve your percentage of strikes. It would be essential for you to develop such a skill should you decide you would like to become a high average bowler.

Develop a ball speed appropriate for your strength, your body build, your height and the particular style you have developed as natural for you. If your ball is always rolled the same way, with the same speed, you are in a very good position to control its path to the pins and to read lanes properly. Once you know what your ball will do on the lanes, and how to change the speed to suit changing lane conditions, you should be far more accurate on both your strike and spare deliveries. And you will have added a valuable adjustment method to your game.

LOFT ADJUSTMENTS
(Left Handed Bowlers)

"Proper lift and proper loft go hand-in-hand," Tom Baker, Member, Professional Bowlers Association.

There is a direct relationship between the timing of the release and the amount of loft you get on the ball. If you release the ball slightly sooner than you normally release it, you will place the ball on the lane much closer to the foul line than you usually do. If you release the ball slightly later than you normally do, you will loft the ball further out over the foul line than is true in your normal delivery. To properly play some lane conditions you may want to alter or change the amount of loft on the ball. This affects the timing of your release and the distance the ball travels out over the foul line before it contacts the lane surface.

A normal release of the ball is either just at the bottom of the pendulum swing, or just as the ball would be on the upturn if the swing were to be completed and the ball not released at all. It is at this moment of the release that you can get maximum lift (turn, action etc.) on the ball. But, there will be times when you want to give the ball more or less opportunity to grip the lane, hence altering the action on the ball. Adjusting the amount of loft can help you do this (as will other techniques which will be discussed under LIFT ADJUSTMENTS).

When the lane is hooking more than normal, and you wish to make a slight change in your delivery to correctly play the lane (instead of making an angle, equipment, or other delivery change), you might loft the ball slightly further out on the lane, perhaps to a distance of 36 to 48 inches, or more. Such an additional amount of loft will cause the ball to skid further, and will take the ball further down the lane before it makes its break toward the pocket. This type of delivery adjustment is designed to bring the ball back to the pocket after it has passed by, or hit high in the pocket.

When the lane is not hooking very much, or less than you consider normal for your delivery, you might reduce the amount of loft by placing the ball on the lane much closer to the foul line. (Remember, you cannot foul with the ball!) For a moderately conditioned lane you might loft the ball about 18 to 36 inches beyond the foul line. This amount of loft will give the ball more time to grab the lane and hook into the pocket. It is the type of delivery adjustment that will get the ball up to the pocket after it has failed to do so.

Loft adjustments can be combined with speed adjustments. Increased speed and increased loft are both delivery adjustments designed to get the ball to come back to the pocket. Reduced speed and reduced loft go hand in hand to get the ball to grip the lane and come up to the pocket. Therefore, you may have to combine these two adjustments for given lane conditions.

You should never loft the ball too far out on the lane, since this will alter or destroy the effectiveness of your ball. (Plus, it will not help the lane surface!) Also, you should not try to make any other changes in your delivery when you are making loft adjustments. Such changes will have an effect on the path of the ball to the pins.

When you are practicing loft adjustments, pretend there are three foul lines: the real one, and two others located 24 and 48 inches beyond the foul line. Then practice lofting the ball, in *a gradual arc,* out over the foul line to various distances.

If the center manager will permit you to do so, tape a towel on the lane at the foul line, and practice lofting the ball over the towel. Such practice will be beneficial to you when you decide a loft adjustment is the best way to make an adjustment to lane conditions.

In summary, more loft is used as an adjustment to get the ball back to the pocket after high pocket or crossover hits. Less loft is used to get the ball up to the pocket when it fails to do so. You may also use more speed with more loft, or less speed with less loft. These are complementary sets of adjustments, both working together to achieve the same objective.

LIFT ADJUSTMENTS
(Left Handed Bowlers)

"The location of the fingers at the moment of release determines the lift imparted on the ball."

Lift is an upward pressure applied by the fingers at the moment the ball is released. This release point should occur a split second after the thumb has cleared the ball. If the thumb is released too soon, the fingers will not have time to impart lift to the ball. If the thumb is released too late, the lift of the fingers will be minimized by the *drag* of the thumb in the ball. Therefore, to get the proper lift on the ball the release must be timed very precisely.

Although the fingers apply lift, other factors associated with the delivery also have an influence on the amount of lift the fingers can impart. If the ball is released in the downswing, the pressure of the ball will also act as force to increase the amount of lift. Raising up with the sliding foot at the moment the ball is released will pull the hand up and increase the amount of lift. A strong or weak follow through will determine how much lift is put on the ball. And a bending of the elbow will, of course, bring the hand up sharply, creating more lift. All of these factors, and the timing of the release of the thumb, determine the amount of lift.

More lift is needed when you want to get the ball up to the pocket after it has failed to do so. Less lift is an adjustment to bring the ball back to the pocket after a high pocket hit or a crossover to the brooklyn side. Since finger position is the most important factor influencing lift, let's review changes in finger location as they relate to lift.

Strong lift is created, or can be created, when the fingers are *under* the ball at the time it is released onto the lane. Very little lift can be imparted if the fingers are on the upper side of the ball. In between these two extremes are various locations for altering the amount of lift on the ball.

During your practice sessions you should alter the location of the thumb and fingers to see how lift is affected. Try to vary the amount of lift and turn on the ball. Try to alter the number of revolutions, either increasing or reducing the number of times the ball rotates around its ball track.

How many revolutions are needed to create an effective and working ball? The answer depends upon two factors: the type of ball track you are using and the condition of the lane. If a lane is non-hooking, you may only be able to get 5 to 7 revolutions. On a hooking lane, you may be able to increase this to more than 13 revolutions.

On a hooking lane you want the ball to skid further down the lane before it breaks for the pocket. A revolving ball will skid more than one making less revolutions. But, on non-hooking lanes you want to reduce the skid and get the ball rolling much sooner. Fewer revolutions are the result of non-hooking lanes. More revolutions are possible and desirable when the lanes are hooking.

The number of revolutions on the ball influences the action on it at the moment it hits the pocket. Ideally, the ball should still be gaining momentum in its revolutions (revs) when it hits the pocket. This gives the ball drive to keep it in the path of deflection and imparts a mixing action or velocity to the pins. The ideal number of revolutions should be in the 11 to 13 range, but on non-hooking lanes you may only be able to get 5 to 7 revolutions on the ball.

The ball track influences the number of revolutions. The smaller the ball track, the more revolutions you can get. The larger the ball track, the less revolutions you can get. For example, a full roller covers the entire 27 inch circumference around the ball, so you get fewer revolutions than with a high and low spinner, which have smaller ball tracks.

Rotating the fingers at the moment of release will determine what type of ball track is created. The amount and direction of the rotation will decide what kind of track the ball will have. The full roller is created by rotating the fingers in a counter clockwise manner, but all others are created by a clockwise rotation upon release.

Referring to our imaginary clock located at the foul line, here is the way ball tracks are created:

Full Roller—Rotate the fingers from 8 to 6 o'clock at release. This is a counter clockwise

EXHIBIT 8-2

(LHB) Rotating the Fingers to Alter Lift

Rotation of the fingers *at the moment the ball is released* will affect the lift imparted on the ball. Assuming a "normal" position for the fingers at 7 to 8 o'clock, rotating them in a clockwise manner will delay the break point and increase the sharpness of the break. Three methods of rotation are illustrated here, from 6 to 8 o'clock; from 5 to 8 o'clock; and from 4 to 8 o'clock. The more rotation, the later and sharper the break.

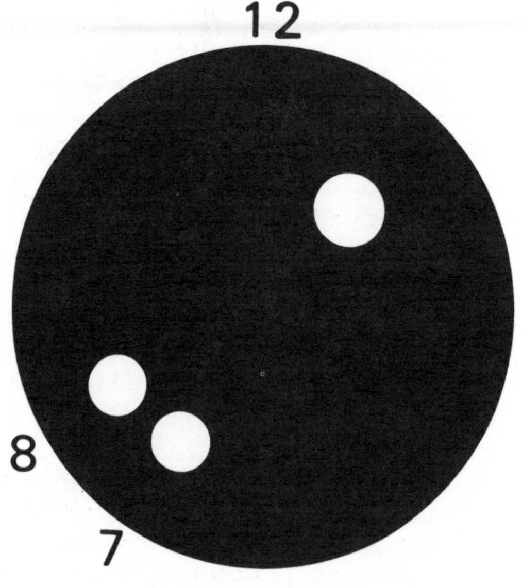

"NORMAL" 7-8 O'CLOCK POSITION

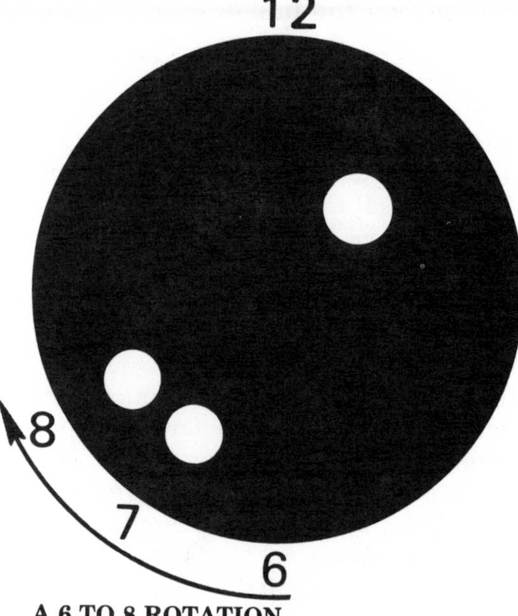

A 6 TO 8 ROTATION

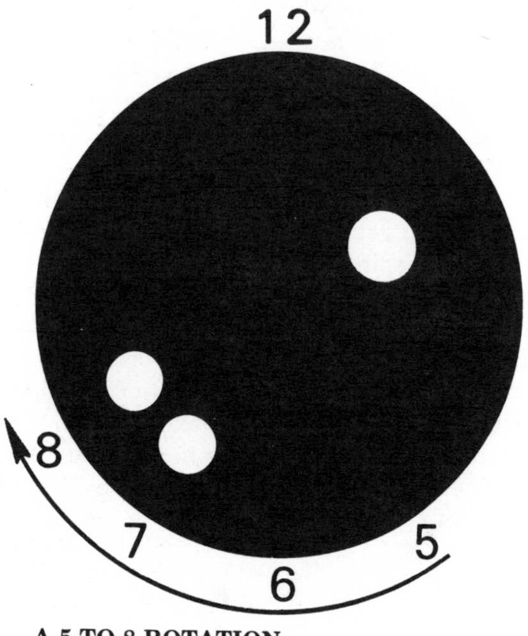

A 5 TO 8 ROTATION

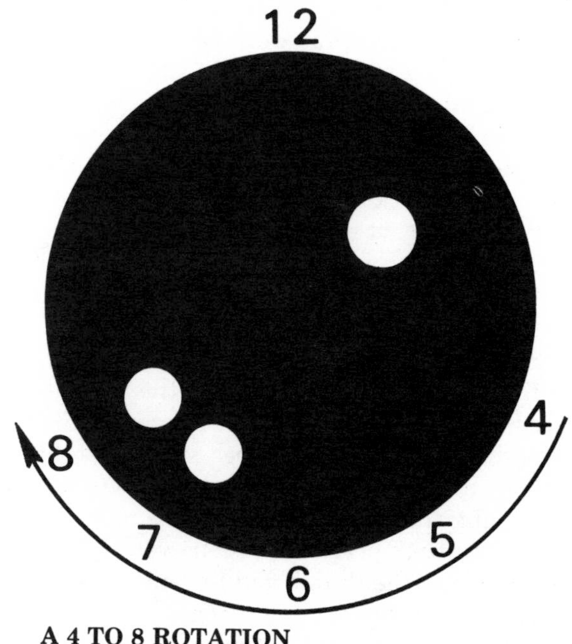

A 4 TO 8 ROTATION

rotation.

High Roller—Rotate the fingers to a 7 or 8 o'clock position, and then lift straight up to create this ball track. This is a clockwise rotation.

Low Roller—Rotate the fingers from 6 to 8 o'clock, but not beyond. This is a clockwise rotation, as in the high roller.

High Spinner—Rotate the fingers from 6 to 9 o'clock, clockwise. Here you are rotating around the ball, turning as well as lifting.

Low Spinner—Rotate the fingers from 6 to 10 or 11 o'clock to create this ball track. Here you are almost topping the ball, almost overturning it. This is generally an ineffective ball track.

The rotation of the fingers can start at 5 or 4 o'clock, instead of the 6 o'clock position indicated above. *Where you stop the rotation dictates what type of ball track is created.* Also, as you increase the amount of rotation beyond 8 o'clock, you lower the ball track, going from a high roller to a low spinner.

The two extremes, full roller and low spinner, are the least effective ball tracks. High roller, low roller and high spinner are the three types of ball tracks most frequently used by high average bowlers.

Other delivery adjustments, affecting the amount of lift imparted on the ball, relate to the timing and intensity of the hook. At times you will want to *advance the break point,* and at other times you will want to *delay the point at which the ball breaks for the pocket.* You may also want to cause the ball to *break stronger* into the pocket, or with *less strength.*

To delay the break point and to reduce the strength of the hook, either an angle or a speed change could be used. Moving to the inside strike lines will delay the break point until the ball is further down the lane. Also, the ball will be at a much straighter pocket angle, and will hit the pocket with less strength than a ball with the same amount of lift but coming from the outside strike lines. Similarly, increasing ball speed will delay the break point and will generally reduce the strength of the hook after the ball does break.

To delay the break point by making a release change, simply rotate the fingers at the moment the ball is released. This rotation should occur in a clockwise manner, as illustrated on Exhibit 8-2. Within the range indicated on this exhibit, increased rotation delays the break point and increases the strength of the hook. Such delivery adjustments will bring the ball back to the pocket after high or crossover hits, which frequently occur on hooking lanes.

Advancing the break point is simply a reversal of the above adjustments. Slower ball speed and the use of the outside strike lines will advance the point at which the ball breaks for the pocket. Reducing the amount of rotation of the fingers at the moment of release will also advance the break point. Such adjustments bring the ball up to the pocket after it has failed to do so, a frequent occurrence on a non-hooking lane.

At this point it should be obvious that delivery changes are difficult to make and require a great deal of practice to successfully incorporate into your adjustment arsenal. Each time you make a delivery change, you must be careful you do not create problems with your timing, rhythm or tempo. As a rule, make delivery changes only after you have tried angle and equipment changes first and have not been able to make a successful adjustment.

Wrist Positions: The position of the wrist is yet another factor to determine how much lift is put on the ball. *Minor* changes from a straight wrist can be an effective way to increase or reduce lift.

The most highly recommended and fundamentally sound position for the wrist is in a relatively *straight* line. (See Exhibit 8-3, for illustrations of *straight, broken,* and *cocked* wrist positions.) The straight wrist position is least prone to error, allows you to get the most natural feel and consistent lift on the ball, and creates less chance for developing an improper swing. This position is also the easiest of the three types to maintain in a natural manner. Also, many types of wrist aids are available to assist in maintaining the straight position.

If you wish to develop a little more roll on the ball, a little less skid, then the wrist can be *broken* ever so *slightly.* (See Exhibit 8-3.) This wrist position will place a small amount of weight on the thumb and the balance on the fingers, something that will give you a little less feel with the fingers. Because the fingers are now higher on the ball, and less underneath it (as with the straight wrist) there is less chance to impart as much lift. But, keep in mind that *the wrist should not be broken too strongly,* or too much. *A slight amount will suffice.* Too much of a break in the wrist can put too much pressure on the thumb, and could result in an early release.

A third method of altering the wrist position, one that is not normally used, is the *cocked* wrist. (This position is also illustrated on Exhibit 8-3). Our purpose for discussing this wrist position is to make you aware of the full range of wrist positions, and the implications of each type. You may be *breaking* your wrist, or *cocking* it too much, and creating problems for yourself. Only a person with a strong wrist and arm would be able to use the cocked wrist position effectively, and then only after a lot of practice. (Of course, practice is needed to make any of the

EXHIBIT 8-3
(LHB) Three Wrist Positions That Affect Lift

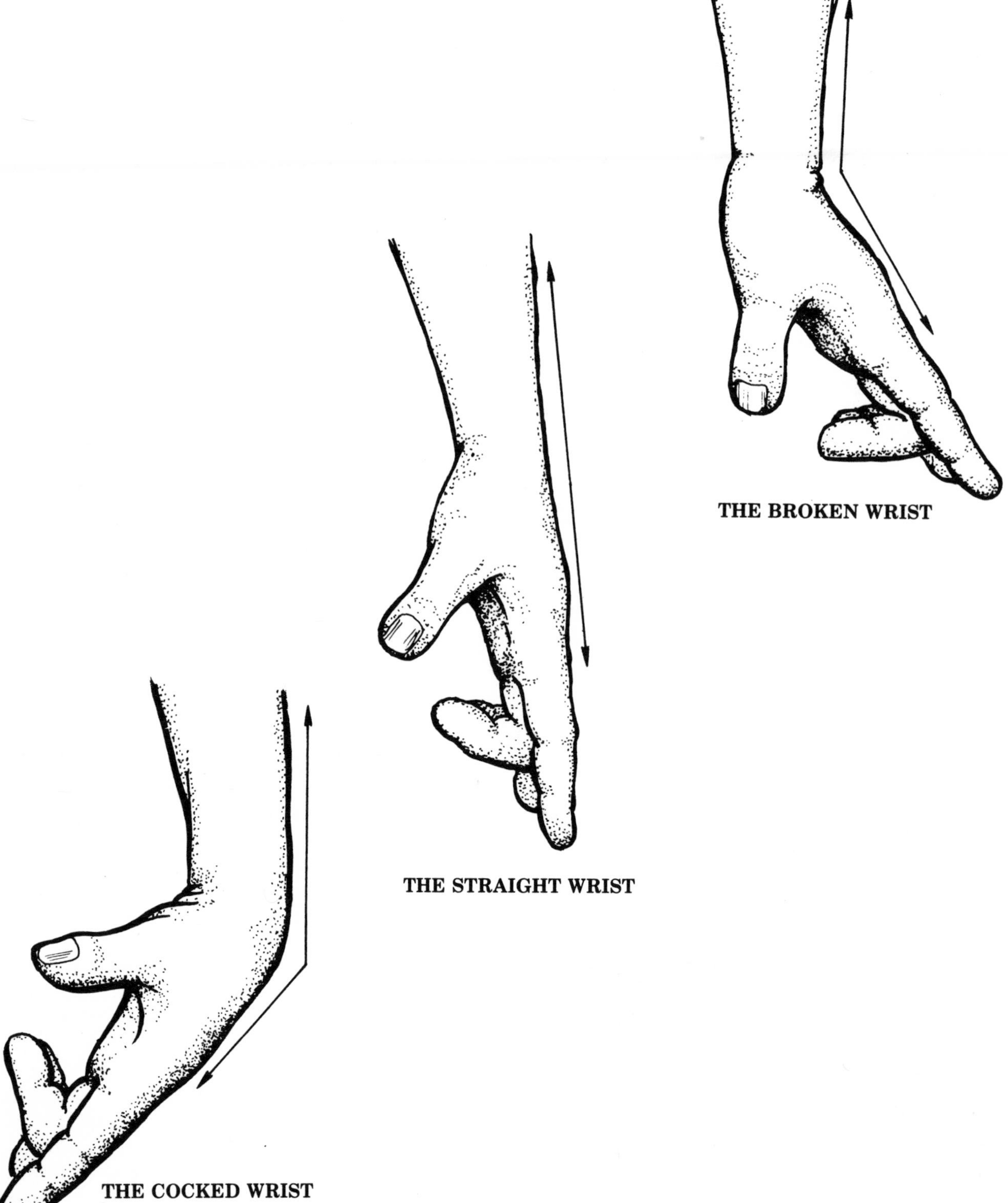

delivery changes a natural and effective part of your game.)

If you are bowling on a hooking lane, and you wish to delay the break point until further down the lane, you might use the cocked wrist position. The ball will skid more than in the straight wrist position, because you can get your hand firmly under the ball.

As with all delivery adjustments, broken and cocked wrist positions should *only* be incorporated into your adjustment arsenal after you have fully explored the advantages and disadvantages of each one. You should, however, become aware of the impact of the position of your wrist on the action or lack of action that can be put on the ball at the release point. You may not decide to use any position other than the straight wrist, but you should be aware of a possible fault in your delivery so that you can correct it.

APPENDIX A
DICTIONARY OF STRIKE-RELATED TERMS

Bowlers have a language all their own. The following list of strike-related terms should immediately upgrade your understanding of the principles and concepts discussed in this book. In addition to these terms, seven exhibits within the book contain words or phrases directly related to other topics on the subject of making strikes: Exhibit 2-8, Lane Related Terms; Exhibits 4-6 and 7-6, Ball Balance Terms; Exhibits 4-9 and 7-9, Ball Surface Terms; and Exhibits 4-16 and 7-16, Ball Fit Terms. A review of this appendix and these exhibits will greatly assist you in learning a wealth of material in a short period of time.

ABC: American Bowling Congress, world's largest sports participation organization, official rule-making body of tenpin bowling.
AJBC: American Junior Bowling Congress.
Alley: Playing surface, made of maple and pine boards, or an artificial surface material.
All the way: Means finishing a game from any point with nothing but strikes.
Apple: Bowling Ball. Also applied to bowler who fails to come through in a clutch situation.
Approach: Same as "Runway."
Baby the Ball: Too delicate, not enough emphasis on delivering the ball with accuracy.
Backup: A ball that falls away to the right for right handed bowlers, to the left for left handed bowlers.
Backup alley: A lane that holds or tends to stop a ball from rolling to the right.
Balk: An incomplete approach in which the bowler does not deliver the ball. To interfere or cause another bowler to stop his approach or not complete it in his normal fashion.
Ball track: Area of lane where most balls are rolled.
Bed: The alley bed, synonymous with a single lane.
Beer frame: In team play, when all but one of the players scores a strike, the one who doesn't must treat. Also any designated frame in which the bowler who scores the least must pick up a refreshment tab, usually liquid.
Belly the ball: Increase the width of a hook from an inside starting angle.
Big ball: A working hook that enables a bowler to carry strikes on something less than perfect pocket hits.
Blocked: A lane maintenance condition in which oil or some sort of lane finish is used to create a track.
Blow a rack: A solid strike hit.
Board: A lane consists of individual strips of lumber called boards. Pros call them by number, fifth board, fifteenth board, etc., for targeting purposes.
Bolsa: Same as "thin hit."
BPAA: Bowling Proprietors Association of America. Trade organization of the people who own bowling centers.
Break: A lucky shot. Also a stopper after a number of consecutive strikes.
Bridge: Distance separating finger holes.
Brooklyn: Left of headpin for a right-handed bowler. Right of headpin for a left-handed bowler.
Broom ball: A ball that hits the pocket in such a way that the pins scatter as though they were swept with a broom.
Channel: Depression to right and left of lane to guide ball to pit should it leave the playing surface on the way down.
Charge: Term used by pros to describe a sensational spurt of high scoring.
Cheese cakes: Lanes on which strikes come easy.
Clutch: Pressure situation.
Count: Number of pins knocked down on first ball of each frame.
Cranker: Bowler who uses cranking motion to roll wide hook ball.
Creeper: Slow ball.
Crooked arm: Hook ball bowler who bends his elbow.
Cross: Going to the left side for a righty. Same as "Brooklyn." Going to the right side for a lefty.
Crow hopper: Loose, clawlike grip on ball at release point.
Curve: Ball that breaks from right to left (for righty) in a huge arc. (Left to right for a LHB.)
Cushion: Padding at rear of pit to absorb shock of ball and pins.
Cutter: Sharp-breaking hook which seems to slice the pins down.
Dead apple, dead ball: Ineffective ball, usually

fades or deflects badly when it hits the pins.
Deflection: The movement of the ball or pins when both come into contact with each other.
Dive: The action of a ball that hooks greatly at the last second.
Division boards: Where the pine and maple meet on a lane.
Dodo: A bowling ball over the legal weight or out of proper balance.
Double: Two strikes in a row.
Dovetails: Area of lane where maple and pine boards join. Also called "splice."
Drive: Another name for alley or lane. Also the revolving action of a ball as it contacts the pins.
Emblem: The logo on a bowling ball, usually signifying the heaviest part of the ball.
Fast: In different sections of the country the meaning is exactly the opposite. In one area it means a lane that allows a ball to hook easily, while in another area it means a lane that holds down the hook.
Flat alley: A lane that despite perfect levelness doesn't run or hold with respect to the action of the ball.
Flat arc: The curved path of a ball in process of delivery when it is too low to the approach or off to either side and so not part of a perfect circle.
Flat ball: Ineffective ball, few revolutions, little action.
Floater: A ball that goes where the lane lets it. A ball released badly with no particular lift or turn.
Foul line: The marking that determines the beginning of the lane.
Foundation: A strike in the ninth frame.
Foundation, early: A strike in the eighth frame.
Frame: A tenth part of a game of bowling.
Frozen rope: A ball rolled with excessive speed almost straight into the pocket.
Fudge: Decrease revolutions on ball.
Full hit: A ball striking near the center of the headpin on a strike attempt or the middle of any pin you may be aiming at.
Full roller: A ball that rolls over its full circumference.
Grab: Means the friction between the lane and the ball is good, causing a sudden hook.
Grasshopper: An effective ball, particularly on light pocket hits.
Graveyards: Low-scoring lanes. In a high-scoring center applied to the lowest scoring pair of lanes.
Groove: Ball track or indentation in lane. Also applied to bowler who is performing well and has his approach and arm swing almost mechanically perfect.
Gutter: Same as "channel."
Gutter ball: A ball that goes into the gutter.
Half hit: Midway between a full hit and a light hit.
High board: Due to atmospheric conditions a board in a lane may expand or contract a tiny bit, but enough to change the course of a bowling ball should the ball roll in that area. Most boards contract leaving a low area or a low board, but it is still mistermed as a high board.
High hit: Ball contacting a pin near its center.
Higher: More to the left (RHB) or right (LHB).
Hold, holding alley: A lane that resists hook action of a ball.
Hole: The 1-3 pocket, 1-2 for lefties. Also another name for "split."
Home alley: Favorite lane or pair of lanes for individuals or teams.
Honey: A good ball.
Hook: A ball that breaks to the left (RHB) or to the right (LHB).
Hook alley: A lane on which the ball will hook easily.
Inside: A starting point near the center of the lane as opposed to the outside, near the edge of the lane.
In there: A good pocket hit.
Jam: Force the ball high into the pocket.
Jersey side: To the left of the headpin.
Kickback: Vertical division boards between lanes at the pit end. On many hits the pins bounce from the kickback knocking additional pins down.
Kick off: Smooth, effective ball delivery.
Kindling wood: Light pins.
Kingpin: The headpin or the number 5 pin, varying with local usage.
Lane: Playing surface. Same as "alley."
Late 10: When the 10 pin hesitates, and is the last to go down on a strike.
LHB: Left handed bowler.
Lift: Means giving the ball upward motion with the fingers at the point of release.
Light: Not full on the target pin, too much to the right or left.
Line: The path a bowling ball takes. Also one game of bowling.
Loafing: Not lifting or turning the ball properly, with the result that the ball lags and doesn't reach the target.
Lofting: Throwing the ball well out on the lane rather than rolling it.
Looper: An extra-wide hook ball, usually slow.
Loose hit: A light pocket hit which gives good pin action off the kickback.
Low: Light or thin hit on the headpin, as opposed to a high hit.
Maples: Pins.
Match play: Portion of tournament in which bowlers are pitted individually against each other.
Medal play: Strictly total pin scores.
Mixer: Ball with action causing the pins to bounce around.

Move in: To start from or near center of approach.
Move out: To start from or near corner position on approach.
Nose hit: A first ball full on the headpin.
Nothing ball: Ineffective ball.
NBC: National Bowling Council.
Out and in: A wide hook rolled from the center of the lane toward the gutter; the ball hooks back to the pocket—going out, then in.
Outside: Corner or near corner position of playing lanes.
Over: A professional bowling scoring a 200 average is used as par. The number of pins above the 200 average is the number of pins over or in the black.
Over turn: To apply too much spin to the ball and not enough finger lift.
Pack: A full count of ten.
Part of the building: Expression referring to 7, 8, 9 or 10 pin when it stands after what seems to be a perfec hit.
PBA: Professional Bowlers Association.
Pie alley: A lane that is easy to score on.
Pinching the ball: Gripping the ball too hard.
Pine: Softer wood used beyond division boards, takes over where maple ends.
Pit: Space at end of lane where ball and pins wind up.
Pitch: Angle at which holes in bowling ball are drilled.
Pocket: The 1-3 for righties, 1-2 for lefties.
Point: To aim more directly at the pocket, high and tight.
Powder puff, puff ball: Slow ball that fails to carry the pins.
Powerhouse: A hard, strong ball for a strike, carrying all ten pins into the pit.
Pumpkin: Bowling ball that hits soft.
Punch out: Strike out.
Quick eight: A good pocket hit which leaves the 4-7 for righties, 6-10 for lefties.
Rap: When a single pin remains standing on a good hit.
Reading the lanes: Discovering whether a lane hooks or holds, and where the best place is to roll the ball to score high.
Reverse: A backup ball.
Revolutions: The turns a ball takes to go from the foul line to the pins.
RHB: Right handed bowler.
Run, running lane: A lane on which the ball hooks easily.
Runway: Starting area. Also known as platform, approach. Ends at the foul line, where the lane starts.
Scenic route: Path taken by big curve ball.
Schleifer: Thin-hit strike where pins seem to fall one by one.
Set: Ball holding in the pocket.
Shotgun shot: Rolling the ball from the hip.
Sidearming: Allowing the arm to draw away from its proper position during back and forward swing.
Slick: Lane condition highly polished, tends to hold back hook.
Slot alley: Lane on which strikes come easy.
Small ball: Type of ball that doesn't mix the pins, must hit pocket perfectly for strikes.
Snow plow: A ball that clears all the pins for a strike.
Soft alley: A lane on which strikes come easy.
Span: Distance between thumb and finger holes.
Spiller: A light-hit strike in which the pins seem to melt away, taking a longer time than other type strikes.
Splasher: A strike where the pins are downed quickly.
Splice: Where maple and pine boards join on the lane.
Spot: Target on lane at which the bowler aims, could be a dot, a dark board or an arrow.
Stiff alley: A lane with a tendency to hold a hook ball back.
Strap the ball: Get maximum lift.
Strike: All ten pins down on the first ball.
Strike out: Finish the game with strikes.
Strike split: The 8-10. Ball looks like a good strike ball, but leaves the split. The 7-9 for left handed bowlers.
String: A number of continuous strikes. Also, in some areas, one game of bowling.
Sweeper: A wide-breaking hook which carries a strike as though the pins were pushed with a broom.
Tap: When a pin stands on an apparently perfect hit.
Telephone poles: Heavy pins.
Thin hit: A pocket hit when the ball barely touches the headpin.
Throwing rocks: Piling up strikes with a speed ball.
Topping the ball: At ball release when fingers are on top of the ball instead of behind or to the side. Causes a bad ball with little action.
Touch: Pin standing on a good hit.
Tripped 4: When the 2 pin takes out the 4 pin by bouncing off the kickback.
Turkey: Three strikes in a row.
Turn: Motion of hand toward pocket area at point of ball release.
Umbrella ball: A high hit on the nose resulting in a strike.
Under: In professional bowling scoring, a 200 average is used as par. The number of pins below the 200 average is the number of pins the bowler is un-

der or in the red.
Up the hill: Refers to coaxing a ball over a high board into the pocket.
Venting: Drilling a small hole (not a finger hole) to relieve suction in the thumb hole.
Water in the ball: A weak ball, one that leaves an 8-10, 5-7 or 5-10.
WIBC: Women's International Bowling Congress.
Winding them in: Refers to big-hook-ball bowlers who get their hooks around the pocket consistently.
Wooden bottles: Pins.
Working ball: A ball with enough action to mix the pins on an offpocket hit and have them scramble each other for a strike. The same ball will break up splits when it hits the nose.
X: Symbol for strike.
Yank the shot: When a bowler hangs on to the ball too long and pulls it across his body.
Zero in: Find the right strike spot on a lane.

APPENDIX B
INTERESTING FACTS ABOUT STRIKES

INTRODUCTION

All records are made to be broken, except in those rare instances in which perfection has been reached. In those cases, the record can only be tied. Most records in bowling will continue to be broken and those that are included in this appendix will surely be broken in the future or before this book comes off the press.

It is interesting to look back on the history of bowling to re-live those moments in which a new record was reached. Records stand as living recognition of scoring feats and as testimonials to the skills of those who have established them. Such records also stand as challenges for future bowlers.

Several certifying organizations exist, whose prime function with regard to scoring records is to insure that such feats are recognized, and that the effort was a legitimate or *acceptable* performance. The skill of the bowler, and the use of standardized equipment and conditions, should be the prime reasons for the record, not unauthorized assistance in the form of easy scoring conditions or improper equipment.

These organizations include: the American Bowling Congress, the Women's International Bowling Congress, the Professional Bowlers Association, and the Women's Professional Bowlers Association. The records and scores included here are derived from the archives and published records of these and other organizations. We wish to thank these organizations for the material provided to us.

For additional facts about strikes, "300" games, record scores, and other unusual and interesting statistics, we recommend the Annual American Bowling Congress Yearbook. This is published by the ABC, in Greendale, Wisconsin.

"300" GAME STATISTICS AND ODDITIES

Elvin Mesgner of Sullivan, Missouri has 27 perfect 300 games to his credit. He has also rolled 11 games of 299; 4 games of 298; for a total of 42 times that he has entered the 12th frame of a game with the possibility of a perfect game. He has recorded 8 perfect 300 games in one league season.

Fred Wolfe rolled a 300 game in 1931, and his next one came 44 years later, in 1975.

Back-to-back perfect 300 games have been achieved by at least a dozen bowlers.

Pete Weber (son of the great Dick Weber) rolled a 300 game as the 1st game of his sanctioned competition. (St. Louis, 1978, at the age of 15.)

Four *one-armed* bowlers have scored perfect 300 games.

The first 300 scored on automatic pinsetting equipment (no pin boy) was by Bob Phillips in Houston, Texas in 1953. The first 300 game scored on a synthetic lane surface occurred in 1977, by Jerry Edwards of Wood Dale, Ill.

Neal Bayes of St. Louis, Missouri recorded a 300 game at the age of 14, while bowling *left* handed. At the age of 21 he rolled a perfect game, but he was bowling *right* handed.

The youngest bowler to record a perfect game is Matt Throne, of Millbrae, California, who turned in the 300 at the age of 12 years, 7 months (AJBC). Six men, all age 74, share the honors for oldest bowlers rolling a perfect game.

Bowling a perfect game does not assure you a 600 or better series. Even a 550 series is not guaranteed. The lowest recorded three game series which contained a perfect game was a 530, rolled in 1941. The individual games in the series were 114-300-116, or an average of 115 surrounding the 300 game.

Harry Wilson recorded a perfect game, but his last ball did *not* hit the head pin. This happened in Bettendorf, Iowa in 1940. He also had a game of only 111 in his three game series, 111-125-300, for a 536 total.

Over 25 bowlers have recorded two 300 games in a three or four game series.

The first bowler in the United States to record a perfect game was George Wadleigh, in Jersey City, New Jersey on January 8, 1890.

Perfect 300 games have been scored by these combinations of relatives: husband and wife; father and son; father and daughter; father, mother and son; sister and brother; brothers and even by members of three generations!

The first 300 game bowled on *live* television was rolled by Jack Biondolillo in the TV finals of the Firestone Tournament of Champions, in 1967.

Pam Buckner, member of the Women's Professional Bowlers Association, bowled back-to-back 300 games in 1980; the only woman to achieve that feat.

Guppy Troup, member of the Professional Bowlers Association, rolled six (6) perfect games during the 1979 professional tour. There were 119 scores of 300 rolled during that PBA tour year.

Jimmy Mack and Paul "Pepsi" Petescola both rolled perfect 300 games in their doubles game at Q Lanes in Elmwood Park, New Jersey, in 1980. This is an unbeatable (but it can be tied) 600 doubles game. (Word of ABC approval of this record is not available at press time.)

Five (5) PBA members have rolled 3 perfect games in a single tournament. (One member rolled 3 perfect games, and 1 game in the 290's and did *not* make the top five for the television show. This was John Wilcox, in 1979.)

PBA members have rolled as many as 13 perfect games in a one week tournament. Wayne Zahn *opened* one tournament with a perfect game.

A sanctioned 300 game has been bowled on four lanes, instead of two. The lanes broke down after a three bagger, and the teams moved to another set of lanes. The bowler continued the string and made the perfect score.

Twelve (12) strikes have been rolled in a single game and the score was *not* 300! After a four bagger, a gutter ball was rolled, followed by a *strike* on the second ball (which, of course counted as a spare). After striking out, the score was *only* 270.

Bowling a perfect 300 game does *not* guarantee you a win in *match* play. Dave Chappel and Tim Honaker battled to a 300-300 tie in a 1980 event in Michigan. They split the 50 bonus points, and set an ABC match game record that can never be beaten, only tied. (The previous record? a 290-290 tie.)

STATISTICS AND ODDITIES ABOUT STRIKES

It is possible for a 5-man or woman team to score 15 strikes in the 10th frame. This *team strike out* has been achieved many times. In 1937, the Hermann Undertakers team recorded 35 strikes in the 10th frame of their 3-game series.

Lots of strikes can often result in *low* games. The lowest game with 9 strikes is 184; with 10 strikes is a 214; and with 11 strikes *from the first frame* is a 290, recorded by over 15 bowlers (a gutter ball or foul occurs on the 12th ball). The lowest game with 11 strikes (not consecutive) is a 252, scored by Robert Tkacz, in Connecticut, in 1974. He had a gutter ball and a 6 count second ball in the 3rd frame.

Brooklyn strikes occur with some regularity. Leon Kloeppner, of Milford, Connecticut rolled 16 brooklyn strikes in-a-row. Twelve of them occurred in a perfect 300 game.

The W-A-C-C team in Akron, Ohio rolled 50 strikes in their 1,320 game in 1947. For a team series, the Budweisers and Hermann Undertakers both recorded 138 strikes in a three game series. (More details on these records a little later.)

Three teams have scored zero (0) strikes in a 3-game series.

Nelson Burton, Jr. scored 34 strikes in a 3-game series, a record tied by 5 other bowlers. Burton scored 869 for his series.

Emil Joseph of Toledo, Ohio, struck out in 14 consecutive games in 1954.

John Pezzin, of Toledo, Ohio, rolled 33 consecutive strikes in a series of 259-300-300. He ended the first game with 9 in-a-row. Pam Buckner, a member of the WPBA, rolled 30 consecutive strikes in a tournament in 1980.

OTHER RECORDS

The highest sanctioned three game series is an 886 rolled by Allie Brandt, on October 25, 1939 in Lockport, New York. His frame-by-frame scores are shown below. Notice that he started each game with 10 in-a-row, and rolled 33 strikes.

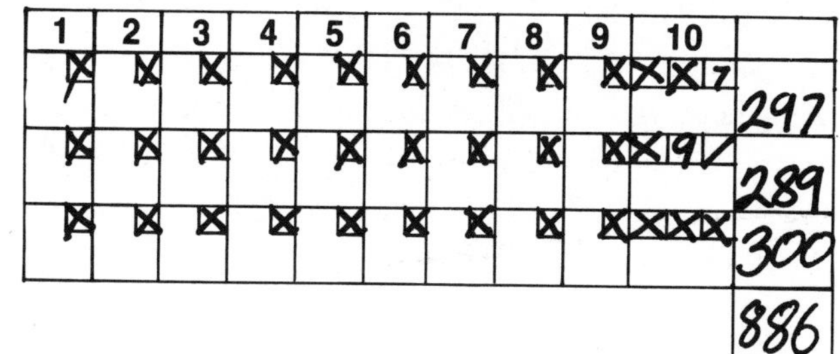

APPENDIX B

The Hermann Undertakers scored a team record of 3,797 in 1937 which stood for 21 years. The individual scores are summarized below:

	GAME #1	GAME #2	GAME #3	TOTALS
Buzz Wilson	246	217	246	709
Ray Holmes	256	236	300**	792
Fred Taff	277	246	243	766
Bob Wills	235	290	246	771
Sam Garofalo	247	222	290	759
TOTALS	1,261	1,211	1,325	3,797

The Budweisers topped the 3,797 total of the Hermann Undertakers, scoring a massive 3,858 on March 12, 1958 at Floriss Lanes in St. Louis, Missouri. The individual scores are summarized below, with a recap of some of the records they broke during this series.

	GAME #1	GAME #2	GAME #3	TOTALS
Don Carter	266	253	235	754
Ray Bluth	267	267	300**	834
Pat Patterson	246	222	268	736
Tom Hennessey	228	300**	231	759
Dick Weber	258	258	259	775
TOTALS	1,265	1,300	1,293	3,858

RECAP: The team rolled 138 strikes, and had 15 strikes in the tenth frame of the second game, tying both records. They had a team record of 24 consecutive strikes in the third game, still a record. Bluth was high man with 834 (Patterson was low with *only* 736) and his 33 strikes tied a record that was broken in 1970 by Nelson Burton, Jr. with 34.

APPENDIX C BOOKS FOR ADDITIONAL READING

Johnson, Don, "Inside Bowling," Contemporary Books, 1973, Chicago, Illinois.

Page 48 illustrates the targeting arrows imbedded in the lanes about 15 feet in front of the foul line. Page 26 gives an overview of the lanes, indicating the dimensions, the targeting arrows, the dots beyond the foul line, the approach markers, etc. Many other useful ideas to improve your game are found throughout the book.

Kouros, Thomas C., "Par Bowling," P.O. Box 181, Palatine, Illinois, 1976.

One of the most comprehensive books ever written on the subject of bowling. All major facets of the game are presented. It is difficult to read in parts, but that is largely because of the subject matter and not a fault of the author. A useful book for any serious student of bowling.

Pezzano, Chuck, "Professional Bowlers Association Guide to Better Bowling," Simon and Schuster, Inc., 1974, New York, New York.

Many of the top bowlers have contributed to this useful addition to the literature of bowling. It contains tips from a wide range of bowlers, most of whom have been successful on the professional bowlers tour. The book also contains a chapter related to the fundamentals of strikes, the subject of this "Encyclopedia of Strikes".

Taylor, Bill, "Balance," P.O. Box 42214, Los Angeles, California.

A detailed discussion of the weights and balances in a bowling ball. Taylor compares and contrasts the bowling ball to a functioning gyroscope. All ball tracks and balance techniques are covered. A difficult book to read, but well worth the time and effort to anyone interested in ball weights and balances. The material is well presented and clearly illustrated, but complex on occasion.

Taylor, Bill, "Fitting and Drilling a Bowling Ball," P.O. Box 42214, Los Angeles, California

A manual for pro shops and knowledgeable ball drillers. Contains a complete description of measuring and drilling a bowling ball. Many illustrations and examples are presented to clarify the concepts and principles he demonstrates.

Weiskopf, Herman, "The Perfect Game." Prentice-Hall, Inc. 1978. Englewood Cliffs, New Jersey.

This large and extensive book presents some of the best color photographs of *the perfect strike* hit that you will find anywhere. Page 198 contains a series of photographs to illustrate how improper deflection results in the 10-pin tap. The book is well researched and clearly written.

PERSONAL NOTES ON ANGLE ADJUSTMENTS